FOUNDATIONS OF
DEVELOPMENTAL GUIDANCE

HAROLD L. MUNSON

The University of Rochester

FOUNDATIONS OF
DEVELOPMENTAL GUIDANCE

ALLYN AND BACON, INC., BOSTON

Library of Congress Catalog Card Number: 75–145839

4-25-73

To three educators who have given freely of themselves that youth may find identity and commitment:

Frank Van Vleet
Bruce Shear
William Fullagar

To these men, I, too, am indebted and grateful, for as my employers they influenced my thinking in many, many ways; they not only allowed me to test my ideas, they encouraged me. They epitomize the innovative, generative educator that our times demand.

CONTENTS

vii

PREFACE

Guidance is not and never should be a fixed function in education. And it need not be approached in the same fashion in all schools. This book represents a developmental approach to guidance, expanding it from a base that considers the individual and the society in which he will learn and mature. It provides a rationale for the developmental approach, explaining its role and its dimensions. This conception charts a future replete with challenge and change. It poses a challenge for every school counselor either on the job or preparing for one. It seeks change, demanding the maximum use of all our human resources in obtaining it. It is ideal in that it establishes many goals, directions, and ultimates—all capable of achievement, but not easily or readily. It is real and practical in that it offers the means for tackling the challenges in the renewal of guidance and for fomenting change in the educative process. It has immediacy; it has a beginning but perhaps no end.

Some people will view this approach as too idealistic. Others may feel it is not sufficiently expansive or inclusive, since it has drawn largely from the past and only alludes to the potential for the future of some of the more promising developments such as systems analysis, cybernetics, simulation, and computerized instruction. That these will influence the theory and practice of the guidance role is beyond doubt. However, the impact of these newer developments will depend, first, on the ability of educators to reallocate and regenerate some of the more basic tenets of guidance.

In the developmental model of guidance as it has been established and characterized in these pages, the focus is on the adolescent and his learning-maturation. It is concerned with his growth and development and with his experiences in living and learning. It considers the conflicts and the ambiguities he faces in learning and maturing and the choices and decisions he must face as he attempts to resolve the conflicts to evolve his own self and his life style.

The work setting of the developmental counselor is the school—the center of the individual's planned learning experiences. The environment of the school and the conditions of learning are of immediate concern, as these impinge on the learning and maturation of the adolescent. Everyone in the school should be directing his efforts to make the individual adolescent's learning a more satisfying and meaningful experience. The counselor shares this responsibility with other school personnel and is in a position to assist in the creation of such learning experiences.

This book, written to be used in a basic course in guidance, attempts to provide a foundation for the further preparation of the developmental counselor. While I have focused on the work of the school counselor, I have hopefully challenged everyone associated with adolescent education—teachers, principals, pupil personnel specialists, parents, or any others who may be pursuing information about guidance in the secondary school.

In establishing the developmental model, I have drawn generously on an earlier publication, *Elementary School Guidance: Concepts, Dimensions and Practice.* This is not to equate elementary and secondary school guidance. Any similarities lie in the nature of human maturation and the teaching-learning process and the manner in which these converge on the adolescent as an individual and as a learner. The challenges to educators at all levels—elementary, secondary, and college—are in several ways based on similar understandings of man and his learning-maturation. Where I have found it necessary to the evolvement of developmental guidance in the secondary school, I have drawn on the earlier work.

In deference to a guidance stereotype, I have referred to the secondary school guidance position as that of school or developmental "counselor." I remain dissatisfied with this appellation and its restriction on the role. The developmental guidance role as it is developed in this book entails more than the counseling function. In the years ahead we may find it necessary to change the job title to one that more accurately accommodates and more clearly reflects the broader functions of secondary school guidance.

Once again I find myself grateful to a great many people. Most of all, of course, I appreciate my students, who have caused me to think more deeply about many aspects of the guidance role. When I am inclined to the ethereal, they return me to the realities of the educative process, thus enabling me to keep a realistic balance between theory and practice. I am indebted to Dorothy Simpson, who commented in detail on the entire manuscript, offering many suggestions that I have incorporated. To Clarence Karier and Glenn Immegart, colleagues, whose reviews of Chapters 3 and 6 have helped to sharpen the concepts and ideas presented there, I am especially thankful.

Every manuscript needs a critical and discerning eye and Evelyn, my wife, has been most helpful in bringing each chapter more clearly into focus. Her perspective on the educative process, as an elementary school teacher, has evoked a respect that I feel compelled to acknowledge here, and her thoughts permeate many sections of this book. Once again, for the preparation of the manuscript, I am indebted to Grace Weinstein and Carmel Adams, most efficient and loyal typists.

Harold L. Munson
Webster, New York

PART ONE

THE INTERDISCIPLINARY BASES
OF DEVELOPMENTAL GUIDANCE

Guidance is interdisciplinary, finding its foundation in a variety of disciplines and disciplinary branches. Part I seeks to draw from the various disciplines those beliefs and ideas that have meaning and purpose for school guidance. It endeavors to draw these ideas together, to relate and shape them in such a fashion that the practice of developmental guidance in the secondary school will have a firm, well established base. The continued support of guidance depends largely on the contribution it can make to the educative process. Guidance will thrive as a professional endeavor only insofar as it can benefit the growth and maturation of the individual. It can hardly survive as a kind of seat-of-the-pants operation whose functions and services are so diversified as to appear unfounded and disconnected.

The role of developmental guidance is an expansive one. It touches many people and is concerned with many facets of the school program; yet it is coherent and consistent. While the elements that constitute the basis for developmental guidance are assorted, they fit a planned work role that holds promise of being one of the most vital and most vigorous roles in all of education.

Chapter One, Historical Considerations and Influences, traces the evolvement of guidance since its founding over sixty years ago. It treats the beginnings of the movement, emphasizing the historical roots, the influence of the Parsonian model, and the stereotypes that have developed in its relatively short existence. The history of the movement is covered broadly with a view to the major trends, developments, and influences that have carried guidance into the seventies. Retrospectively, the chapter seeks to isolate the contributions and shortcomings of guidance as it has emerged and grown since World War II. Prospectively, it proposes some changes and some challenges with which guidance must deal in the years ahead.

Chapter Two, Sociological Concepts and Forces, draws heavily on the contributions of sociology, social psychology, and anthropology. Essentially three major sociological forces are considered: the changing nature of American society, the disadvantaged in American society, and the family as a changing social unit. The chapter further focuses on the changing and adaptive nature of developmental guidance as an outgrowth of social change.

Chapter Three, The Philosophical and Psychological Bases of Guidance, attempts to distill some of the more significant theories and theoretical threads that contribute directly, and most influentially, to the solidity of the developmental guidance base. As one would expect in a work role that is essentially oriented to human growth and maturation, the central support is dependent upon the contributions of psychology and philosophy. Culled from the wealth of resources available are those ideas that most clearly provide a base from which the various aspects of adolescent maturation can be understood.

Chapter Four, The Educative Process: Perspectives and Prospects, draws on the newer ideas and theories that are vital to the teaching-learning process. It considers some aspects of current educational practice with regard to the central purpose of education—human learning. More importantly, however, the chapter highlights the inner aspects of the learning process and the intimate relationship of human learning and human maturation. Developmental guidance is established as an integral, rather than a peripheral, part of the educative process. Its potential as a contributing force in the day-to-day maturation of the adolescent learner is firmly established.

Chapter Five, Developmental Guidance: An Initial Conception, distills and integrates many of the interdisciplinary theories and ideas in a series of beliefs about the adolescent and his learning-maturation. These beliefs are converted into statements that may be considered as a base from which programs of developmental guidance can emerge. The essence of the chapter is to solidify a rationale for developmental guidance: Chapter Five is initial and suggestive rather than final and prescriptive.

ONE

HISTORICAL CONSIDERATIONS

AND INFLUENCES

Practically all American secondary schools have made some provision for guidance, but there is a good deal of controversy as to its nature, scope, and purpose. Many view guidance as a program of services, others equate it with counseling, and some think of it in terms of college and job placement. This controversy is somewhat surprising to many people who have experienced or heard about guidance in one form or another and who expect a rather clear and definitive description of it. Those who inquire about guidance or take a basic guidance course are usually startled or perplexed by the number of conceptual variations they encounter. While this can be confusing initially, particularly to the person who seeks specificity and precision, the possibilities inherent in reacting to multiple views and in assessing the potential directions for guidance can be stimulating and challenging.

This is not to infer that guidance does not have any direction or any limitations in the educational scene. It very definitely does. Yet, it must be sufficiently flexible to respond to societal change and to the changing needs of the individuals in it. It must be adaptable to educational change, in fact it should be promoting and fostering needed modifications in the educative process. The verve of the guidance movement lies in its *responsiveness* to the ever-changing needs of the people it purports to help. Guidance that maintains the status quo, that fails to adapt to the times, and that remains blind to the vitality of people can never hope to be an institutional or societal force, nor can it achieve any lasting influence on the individuals it serves. Whatever we have learned about what guidance is or is not, we have learned that its essence lies in the interaction of people and that its uniqueness is expressed primarily by and through the people who represent it.

HISTORICAL PERSPECTIVES

Although guidance in the secondary school is essentially a post World War II phenomenon, its origins go back to developments early in the twentieth century. Frank Parsons is generally regarded as the "father" of guidance. Parsons founded the Vocational Bureau of Boston in 1908. It was primarily a placement center for youth who were in need of vocational guidance and job placement. The Parsons approach to vocational guidance was described in *Choosing A Vocation,* a publication which has become a classic. His description of the vocational guidance process has become the model for guidance in our secondary schools. His conception has been dubbed the "talent and task" approach. Referring to his approach in this way is obvious as one becomes familiar with it.

The Parsons Model

The Parsons approach is relatively simple to understand, yet the meaning and the significance of the model become rather complex in its implementation. At the time this approach to vocational guidance was promulgated, many of the tools that we take for granted today were unknown or unavailable.

Parsons proposed the following three-step method:

In the wise choice of a vocation there are three broad factors:

(1) a clear understanding of yourself, your aptitudes, abilities, interests, ambitions, resources, limitations, and their causes;
(2) a knowledge of the requirements and conditions of success, advantages and disadvantages, compensation, opportunities, and prospects in different lines of work;
(3) true reasoning on the relations of these two groups of facts.[1]

His first step, self-understanding, involves a most comprehensive self-analysis. In a form that he gave to his applicants, he listed 116 items to be considered, most of which were concerned with the individual's background and preferences. With the help of the counselor, the applicant also explored many facets of his physical and personal being such as his appearance, dress, voice, and personal characteristics.[2] It is important to note that Parsons obviously intended a very thorough and comprehensive self-investigation.

Parsons contended that the responsibility for this look at one's self

[1] Frank Parsons, *Choosing a Vocation* (New York: Agathon Press, 1967; reprint of original 1909 edition), p. 5.
[2] *Ibid.,* pp. 26–46.

rested primarily with the applicant. However, many of the illustrative case materials in his book indicated a considerable amount of counselor responsibility in the counseling conferences. Thus, one is left to presume that Parsons envisioned a process wherein the counselee was responsible for his own self-analysis and the decisions that emerged, while the counselor was an active participant in interpreting and reacting to the self of the counselee and in leading the counselee, through the power of persuasion and suggestion, to more appropriate goals.

Step two, essentially one of obtaining knowledge about the world of work, consisted in helping the applicants learn about and assess various work opportunities. The information-giving role of the counselor is well established through the documents that the Vocational Bureau developed or had available for applicants as well as Parsons's numerous references to the counselor's need for and use of information about work opportunities. In cases where the counselor could find "no basis . . . for a wise decision,"[3] the applicants were encouraged to read occupational materials, visit industries, talk to workers, and seek job exploratory opportunities. Although Parsons was concerned with vocational placement, he refers on several occasions to the counselor's need for and use of educational information in suggesting educational opportunities as they existed then in vocational schools, night courses, or apprenticeship programs. This, as we shall see, was a natural extension of the vocational guidance effort, particularly as educational opportunities expanded and as further higher education became mandatory for employment in growing numbers of occupations.

Step three, true reasoning or counseling, emphasized the rational, reasoning processes of man. In outlining the methods to be used in vocational counseling, Parsons offered the following advice in implementing this step: "This calls for clear thinking, logical reasoning, a careful, painstaking weighing of all the evidence, a broad-minded attitude toward the whole problem, tact, sympathy, wisdom."[4]

Parsons discussed his counseling approach in a chapter entitled "Counselors and Applicants." Many of his techniques were employed for their analytical usefulness. He did not emphasize the factors involved in human relating, nor did he deal with the dimensions of a counseling relationship in the modern vein. He described a very intellectual relationship in which the counselor appeared as the older, wiser, more knowing individual whose purpose it was to help a younger, less knowing one. The counselor clearly had a major responsibility for guiding the reasoning and the thinking of the counselee and for bringing out the significant elements of the problem so

[3] *Ibid.,* p. 19.
[4] *Ibid.,* p. 46.

that the counselee could examine them. In speaking of the preparation of the vocational counselor, Parsons claimed he "must be able to recognize the essential facts and principles involved in each case, group them according to their true relations, and draw the conclusions they justify."[5]

One has to marvel at the vision and the insight demonstrated in the Parsons formulations of guidance. One can readily identify many of his beliefs and ideas as they have been implemented and refined in the practice of guidance in the secondary school. In the years since Parsons introduced his model, expansions in our knowledge about human behavior, changes in our society, and refinements in our programs of public and private education have given his model further support and substance. Conversely, other developments that essentially challenge either the philosophical base of the model or the methods for its implementation have had less effect on the practice of guidance in our schools. The basic structure of today's guidance programs and the practices employed are fundamentally rooted to the three-step process of Frank Parsons.

The Beginnings of the Guidance Movement[6]

Parsons had made a strong pitch for the introduction of guidance in the public schools, encouraging other changes in the curriculum that would help to expand the knowledge of youth about work opportunities and to extend their practical on-the-job experience. Vocational guidance was first introduced in the public schools of Boston in 1909. Other school systems followed in the succeeding years, but the beginnings of guidance were slow and gradual. It was to take several decades for the movement to gain a national momentum.

In 1913, the National Vocational Guidance Association was formed to foster the development of vocational guidance in public schools and community agencies. It provided leadership for the guidance movement until 1952 when the American Personnel and Guidance Association was organized to serve a growing and diversified number of professional guidance and counseling workers.

In 1914 Jesse Davis, another pioneer in the evolvement of school guidance, described how teachers in a high school in Grand Rapids, Michigan, attempted to weld guidance and instruction by relating English to the tasks of self-analysis and occupational exploration.[7] The work of Davis rep-

---

[5] *Ibid.,* p. 95.

[6] For a complete history of the guidance movement prior to World War II, consult John M. Brewer, *History of Vocational Guidance* (New York: Harper and Bros., 1942).

[7] Jesse B. Davis, *Vocational and Moral Guidance* (Boston: Ginn and Co., 1914).

resented an effort to introduce guidance into the school, making it possible for *all* students to be exposed to guidance. Further, it attempted to integrate guidance and the educative process, making guidance an integral part of an individual's growth and development.

Also in 1914 Truman L. Kelley, at Teachers College, Columbia University, made use of the term "educational guidance" to describe the help given in choice of studies and in other school adjustments, thus extending the concept of guidance and ultimately the scope of guidance services.[8] Educational guidance was readily adaptable to the school. Selecting courses of study, school progress and achievement, and educational opportunities beyond high school were tailor-made topics for the secondary school guidance effort.

These beginnings, slow as they seem when we think of the modern opportunities for change, enabled the guidance movement to establish its many possibilities. From these pioneer programs the potential force of guidance in the school and community was recognized. The depression years of the early 1930s had both positive and negative effects on the guidance movement. The establishment of guidance programs was slowed by wholesale cutbacks in school personnel. Educational programs of all types were being curtailed rather than developed.

On the other hand the years of unemployment and the human deprivation experienced during these years highlighted the human condition. Getting the unemployed, both young and old, into the labor market spotlighted the need for vocational guidance. As the financial condition of the country became more stabilized and as this was reflected in the labor market, guidance appeared poised for a real period of expansion. Programs were beginning to sprout in even smaller communities, and education was ready to embrace this new concept in practice.

Once again, however, international conditions intervened. The nation became embroiled in World War II, and all efforts were concentrated on the mental and physical effort of winning the war. Thus, the emergence of guidance was delayed almost another decade following World War II and the period of recovery. In the meantime, however, the use of manpower in the armed forces and the need for vocational guidance in returning servicemen to civilian occupations again reinforced the guidance movement, leaving it in an even stronger position for implementation in the schools.

The Testing Movement

The standardized testing movement in the United States parallels that of guidance. Beginning with measures of intellectual capacity, such data was

[8] Brewer, *op. cit.,* p. 250.

deemed very helpful to self-analysis and self-understanding. By the middle of the 1930s, schools were beginning to employ standardized tests that purported to measure the intelligence of children. The intelligence quotient (IQ) became a common term among educators, and the use of the standardized test of mental ability expanded rapidly. While the results of these tests were seldom communicated to students or their parents in these early years, the restricted uses of these data were relaxed, and gradually, during the late 1940s and early 1950s, such information was interpreted to students and their parents. The public became enamored of the IQ, and parents clamored for data that would help them to understand their children.

By the time the lay public was beginning to understand the idea of an "intelligence quotient," research on the multiple factors of mental ability had progressed to a point where aptitude tests measuring a variety of mental abilities, such as verbal reasoning, numerical ability, perceptual speed, and spatial relationships, were being marketed. The decade following World War II had produced several such aptitude tests.

The marketing of these tests was concurrent with a tremendous surge in the employment of guidance counselors. There is little wonder that these new counselors, freshly prepared and eager and enthusiastic to do a good job, were very interested in the potential value and use of these tests in the programs they were developing. Many counselors, on the basis of promotional literature, proceeded to use these tests in their programs. The rapidity with which these tests appeared—a real bandwagon effect—caused considerable interest as well as concern!

The multifactor test batteries have been used, and perhaps overused, in educational and vocational guidance. They "fit" well into the Parsons model —even better than the earlier intelligence and achievement tests. While the predictive validity of many tests is questionable, they have been used by counselors as one major source of data for students and their parents in making decisions about courses of high school study or careers. The measure of influence that the development of so many standardized tests (intelligence, achievement, interest, aptitude, and personality) has had on the practice of guidance is difficult to assess. But assuredly their development has been timely and their use prominent. That they promulgated the Parsonian processes of vocational guidance is without doubt.

THE YEARS OF EMERGENCE—1945–1960

The immediate stimulus for guidance lay in the educational and vocational planning needed by the many thousands of servicemen who were being returned daily to civilian life between 1945 and 1947. Opportunity for a college education was available to all who had served their country. The ex-GI had but to formulate his plans. Many sought and received help. The Veterans Administration, through its counseling and testing service, aided many servicemen and women in reestablishing themselves as civilians. Those whose plans included higher education were assisted in locating institutions where appropriate programs could be obtained. Institutions of higher education were packed with returning servicemen. Suddenly guidance was afforded a significant role in the national educative process. It seemed very important to staff for it and to implement programs in the schools.

The Evolution of Guidance Programs

The first programs tended to be vocationally and educationally oriented. Much emphasis was placed on choosing an occupation and on planning the high school course of study. Most of the counselor's efforts were directed toward helping the individual with decisions and plans associated with these. Counseling was considered a part of the total guidance service. Equally important were several other activities such as the informational services, pupil appraisal (or analysis of the individual), and group guidance. Some of these activities were not too difficult to implement since many of the "new" guidance counselors were recruited from the ranks of the classroom teachers. In fact, teaching experience was a requisite for certification as a counselor in most states.

The courses required to practice guidance were very limited in the early years, necessitating only a few hours of graduate study to move from classroom teacher to counselor. Later, in the fifties, preparation requirements were extended in many states, but by then teacher-oriented counselors had already initiated a number of programs. Few counselors had had any real preparation for counseling. Courses in counseling consisted mainly of an intellectual exposure to counseling theory and techniques with very little, if any, actual supervised practice. Thus, in these early programs the teaching background of the counselor was obvious not only in the manner in which he attended to his job duties, the choices he made, and the priorities he established, but also in his work with individual students and groups of students. In short, the guidance counselor was a teacher with a new work role.

As we noted earlier, standardized tests were being marketed in increasing numbers. Here were data about the "talents" of an individual that could be used. Guidance counselors readily assumed (or were assigned) responsibility for involvement in the selection and administration of standardized testing instruments. Such involvement, in the days before machine scoring, left guidance workers with the chore of scoring the instruments or of coordinating the scoring and reporting process. This responsibility extended in many work situations to include the entire, systemwide program of intelligence, achievement, interest, and aptitude testing, ranging from selecting, ordering, administrating, and scoring the tests to interpreting the results to school administrators, teachers, students, and their parents. The testing program alone, as a part of the pupil appraisal service, constituted a large segment of the guidance counselor's responsibility and required a large block of his available time.

The guidance counselor had little in the way of occupational information. The available educational information consisted mainly of college catalogues designed to attract potential students. Very few reference sources or directories were available for identifying or screening sources of help, so the guidance counselor was moved to use his own resources and ingenuity. Files of occupational information, college catalogue libraries, and a host of affiliated plans and activities were identified with considerable haste. Guidance counselors moved swiftly to use all known informational resources and wailed loudly and clearly about the need for more and better informational resources.

Cumulative records were becoming more common to educational practice. Schools that maintained such records soon discovered that individual pupil records could be maintained and administered by the guidance counselor. Schools that did not maintain such individual pupil records were staffed by counselors who initiated efforts to inaugurate such records. The guidance counselor quickly discovered that while such information about the pupil could be most helpful to him and to teachers, the maintenance and supervision of records was another time-consuming activity. Yet, the value of records in pupil appraisal and diagnosis was uncontested for the most part.

By the late 1950s, the work of the guidance counselor was well established and the elements of what was generally considered a good guidance program had been identified. Six elements were considered basic to a well rounded guidance program: (1) articulation and orientation, (2) analysis of the individual, (3) informational service, (4) counseling, (5) placement, and (6) follow up activities. The nature and scope of the guidance service in the secondary school seemed rather clear. Certainly the assistance to be provided pupils and their parents, teachers, and school administrators had been detailed, and the guidance counselor was well immersed in the organizational and operational concerns of making these programs functional and effective.

Even though these six elements were considered essential to a well rounded guidance program, most programs emphasized the pupil appraisal and informational services. These activities, along with efforts to counsel each student, occupied the major portion of the counselor's time and energy. The continuation and maintenance of such programs cut heavily into the time commitments available. Counselors were trying to counsel, but there were too many students, too few counselors per school, and too much to do. Guidance in the secondary school, therefore, was primarily restricted to grades 9 through 12. Eighth grade students were perhaps afforded one individual conference to plan their high school course of study, and seventh graders were rarely seen except in those schools that were staffed with counselors whose specific assignment was to work with them.

The early counselors had to extend themselves widely from early adolescence to young adulthood, particularly in those schools where only one counselor was employed (a quite common situation in these years of emergence). One might say that these programs were "top heavy," since it was fairly standard practice to begin with the seniors and work downward as far as time would permit. This made some sense, since seniors needed to consider their post-high school plans in the fall and eighth or ninth graders needed to arrange for their high school course of study in the spring. This, then, depending on the size of the school and the number of counselors available, characterizes the general nature of guidance programs as they emerged.

In Retrospect—An Evaluative Commentary

These organizational years of program evolvement were the critical years when an image of guidance was being created. This was to be an enduring image, and counselors worked hard to prove the value of guidance in the educative process. Obviously they achieved this goal, for their efforts were followed by a decade of growth.

Starting with a Parsonian model, guidance had laboriously and assiduously augmented the opportunities to extend the potential inherent in the first two steps of the Parsonian process. It had capitalized on the available resources for obtaining information about the pupil—information that could contribute to the analysis of the individual. In keeping with the Parsonian beliefs, the counselor remained an active participant in these analytical activities. Yet contrary to the ideas of Parsons, most of this information remained unavailable to the pupil. The data in his individual record folder was rarely interpreted to him. Such data served instructional personnel far more often than it did the pupil. Test data was seldom interpreted to students, although counselors did a great deal to change the secretive nature of test data by working toward its utilization with students and their parents. The fact remains, however, that the little time left available for counseling did not permit more than a hurried interpretation of such data. Usually these interpretations were considered a part of the student's annual program-planning conference. More often than not such interpretations raised several more questions about his abilities and interests. Yet there never was enough time to deal with each. His own self-analysis was often left up in the air. Seldom was there time to seek, in any relaxed and analytical way, his reactions to these data, or, even more importantly, to solicit his perceptions of his own abilities and interests based on his own experiences. The contradictions and misunderstandings were often more confusing than helpful.

On the other hand, some programs—though far too few—were able to provide the kind of assistance that enhanced the pupil's understanding of himself. However, the unsatisfactory initial attempts to interpret the data for the students could be understood when we consider the "trial and error," exploratory nature of an emerging and expanding service to youth.

Thus while much of the practice had been developed from the Parsonian approach to vocational guidance, its application to the educative process resulted in a mixture of philosophical ideas that tended to dilute the Parsons practice beyond recognition. Guidance counselors (who were never fully trained in the Parsonian process) had become more absorbed in the guidance experience as it related to teaching, since they were more solidly prepared and extensively experienced as teachers. The distortions that evolved in transferring Parsonian theory to school guidance practice resulted in a conglomeration of program objectives and processes. While traces of the Parsonian model remain evident, its earlier focus had been lost. No other model more appropriate to the educative process was developed to replace it.

Programs very definitely were *guidance* programs. Counselors were guidance oriented. Counseling in almost any form was meager and insufficient. When it did occur, the situation was basically a crisis requiring immediate remediation of some problem. Counseling, as the third step in the Parsons process, was quite counselor-centered. In many instances it was more akin to interviewing. Guidance began to assume a distributive function. Getting students in appropriate programs of study and into the right institutions of higher education began to assume the highest time priorities.

During these years an image of guidance was created, but it was difficult to equate that image with the purposes and practices associated with its birth. Somehow, in the transition to the school setting, mechanistic routines and managerial-coordinative efforts became predominant to the process. The expectations for guidance had been firmly entrenched. Guidance had achieved a maturity and it had established an identity.

THE GROWTH OF GUIDANCE (1960–1970)

While dates and decades are sometimes useful guideposts to mark an era, they are at best mere indicators of time intervals when we talk about directions and trends. This period might be said to have begun with the passage of the National Defense Education Act of 1958 and the provisions for improving and extending school guidance programs under Title V-A and for preparing secondary school guidance personnel under Title V-B. Both had a decidedly positive impact on secondary school programs.

Under Title V-A, funds, administered by the appropriate state agency in accordance with a plan developed in cooperation with the federal government, were made available to secondary schools who applied for monies to improve their guidance services in accordance with the goals of the state plan. The achievements made possible through the use of these funds added significantly to the improvement of guidance. Previously unattainable materials were authorized. Professional positions were opened. Inservice activities were initiated and school counselors were encouraged, in some state plans, to attend professional meetings and workshops. In some states testing programs were expanded, and personnel were prepared to utilize more adequately the results of these tests.

Under Title V-B, institutes to prepare school counselors were approved. Proposal guidelines for the development of institute programs encouraged provisions for practice counseling under supervision as well as other important laboratory and didactic experiences. Counseling, the element of school guidance that had so long remained a less than vital program ingredient, became the focus of much attention. The counseling function began to achieve a "new look" in the totality of the guidance endeavor. This emphasis on the counseling function continued to grow throughout the sixties.

By 1970, the counseling role of the secondary school guidance worker had become the basis for his professional identity. The heretofore common job designation "guidance counselor" had become somewhat obsolete and the designation "school counselor" had replaced it. In just a few years the concept of school guidance had been markedly altered. Its identity had been changed! The American School Counselor Association's *Statement of Policy For Secondary School Counselors* stated,

> While secondary school counselors acknowledge the historical distinctions between educational, vocational, and personal counseling, they also recognize the limitations of such distinctions. School counselors see all counseling as concerned with the complete person and thus inevitably personal and psychological in nature.[9]

With this statement of policy, *counseling* rather than *guidance* became the major professional activity identifying the counselor in the secondary school.

[9] American School Counselor Association, *Statement of Policy For Secondary School Counselors* (Washington, D.C.: American Personnel and Guidance Association, 1964), p. 3.

Professional identity is important. It is interesting that the identity of secondary school guidance established in the years of its emergence—the identity that brought recognition and acceptance—is no longer the same professional role that is now being touted by the professional organizations and for which personnel are being prepared in their graduate studies. I believe we can account for this in a number of ways. First, and most importantly perhaps, guidance emerged so fast that a substantial rationale for its existence in secondary education was never developed. It was merely based on a model and a process that could hopefully be applied to the educative process. As guidance emerged and as it grew and flourished, it became increasingly apparent that guidance needed a *raison d'etre* from which purposes and goals could be formulated and operational procedures established. The awareness of this lack moved men and professional groups to fill this void. As this was accomplished, different aspects of the guidance function were highlighted, and new or modified roles emerged. These roles were often sufficiently different from previous role expectations to create a role paradox.

Secondly, the high school population by the late 1950s and early 1960s had increased by several millions, making it extremely difficult for guidance personnel to perform by any role standard. The addition of personnel, while yielding in some instances a lower counselor-to-pupil ratio, failed to meet the challenge of a changed work role. Counselors, bound by role stereotypes, were forced to assume even more mechanical and coordinative duties to keep abreast with growing school populations. Even in those situations where adequate pupil-counselor ratios were maintained, (or perhaps lowered), the threat of new role behaviors created too much anxiety and insecurity. Counselors, now established and often in leadership positions, resisted change, preferring to continue to meet the established (and accepted) role expectations of the past.

Complicating the professional resistance, and at the same time enhancing it, were the increased pressures of college admissions. Getting into college, and related educational guidance activities, consumed an even greater portion of the counselor's time. School counselors deemed it necessary to make "contacts" with college admissions officers. Attendance at professional conferences was often validated more on the basis of meeting and conferring with college representatives than on professional development. Counselors, many on their own time, visited college campuses. The school counselor became even more deeply enmeshed in the mechanical aspects of college admissions such as preparing transcripts, completing college recommendations, and arranging for applicant interviews and testing.

Such concerns were not restricted to work with graduating seniors but were extended downward to other class levels where preparation activities were highlighted. These changes in school guidance were not charted; they occurred in response to pressures. That assistance was necessary can be accepted. However, the nature of the counselor's involvement (particularly in the overwhelming clerical aspects of college admissions) and the degree of his participation (the responsibility the counselor assumed, his "need" to know admissions personnel, the necessity for his writing the college recommendation) can be seriously questioned.

At the same time that the counselor was becoming more involved in educational placement, evidence was beginning to appear which eventually could reconstitute his role in vocational guidance. Several investigations of the factors involved in choosing a vocation were suggesting a different approach to career choice. The process aspects were proposed by Super,[10] and the factors of decision-making were explored by Tiedeman.[11] Holland,[12] while proposing a model somewhat akin to that of Frank Parsons, emphasized personality orientations and work environments. (More detail about vocational development is found in Chapter 14.) Many other smaller, more particularized studies were also contributing new evidence to cause considerable reconsideration of the manner in which vocational choice was currently being approached. School counselors looked for help in determining how to work with these new ideas. In the meantime they continued to cling to older methodologies and to emphasize educational placement.

Perhaps one of the most important documents to be developed in the sixties was the *Statement of Policy For Secondary School Counselors,* which also included guidelines for the implementation of the statement. Over six thousand counselors contributed background data consisting of information about their positions as well as reactions to the preliminary versions and suggestions for revision. Other school personnel, including teachers and school administrators, also reacted and offered suggestions. Few professional statements have included so many voices. The statement, approved by the American School Counselor Association in 1964, represents the first complete attempt to specify the role and function of the secondary school counselor. It established a different professional identity of the school counselor and earmarked counseling "as the basic and most important help he offers to pupils."[13] With the publication of this statement, the work of the school

[10] Donald E. Super, *Vocational Development: A Framework for Research* (New York: Bureau of Publications, Teachers College, Columbia University, 1957).

[11] David V. Tiedeman, "Decision and Vocational Development: A Paradigm and Its Implications," *Personnel and Guidance Journal* 40:15–21, September 1961.

[12] John Holland, *The Psychology of Vocational Choice* (Waltham, Mass.: Blaisdell, 1966).

[13] American School Counselor Association, *op. cit.,* p. 5.

counselor, including his responsibilities, competencies, and preparation, was professionally formulated for the first time.

GUIDANCE STEREOTYPES AND THE SEVENTIES

The history of the guidance movement leaves us to deal with a number of stereotypes. We need to recognize these beliefs and examine their value and validity for guidance in the secondary school in the decade of the 1970s. (That they do in fact exist may be challenged.) The fact that I list them here is evidence that I believe they do. What school counselors do about any or all of these will be their challenge. What historians record about guidance in the seventies will attest to their concern for these stereotypes and to their behaviors in dealing with them.

The Stereotype of Responsibility

While guidance has long purported to enhance self-direction and to allow students to make their own decisions, the school counselor is viewed as the person who is responsible for student decisions or behavior. Parents, in particular, are prone to blame the school counselor for certain decisions, particularly those that are unpopular. It is the counselor's responsibility to ensure that students have enrolled in the "right" courses, have selected the appropriate college, or are achieving at the expected level in a subject. It is his responsibility to make certain that a student appears for and takes necessary examinations (scholarship exams, college boards), meets application deadlines, or dresses appropriately for a college admissions or job interview.

The list of responsibilities of a school counselor—assigned or assumed —has become continually longer with time. Its applicability to any particular counselor will vary, of course, according to his behaviors. What needs to be recognized is that a sufficient number of these responsibilities have been delegated to him. And the list will continue to expand until such time as counselors again raise the fundamental questions: Who is responsible for these choices and decisions? Who is responsible for the day-to-day behaviors of an individual? When these and related questions are answered, the counselors can assume appropriate role behaviors.

The Stereotype of Failure

A stereotype in which the counselor is seen as the person who keeps individuals from failing stems from a deeply embedded societal fear of failure. Whether it be the selection of a course or the establishment of a longer range goal, the counselor is increasingly the buffer between success and failure. The desirability of the risk in exploration is tempered by the opportunity for or chance of failure. It is the counselor's prediction of the outcome that often determines the direction of a decision. Some assume that he is there to prevent failure. He is there to assess risk. He is blamed for failure when and if it does occur.

Assuredly, the counselor is expected to provide judgments and predictions and to engage, actively if necessary, in assisting students and their parents in pursuing plans and decisions involving risk. Perhaps we are all so highly conditioned to doing the "right" thing, that, even as counselors, we fail to see the good that can occur from making a mistake or from failing. The school is a nurturer of the right (the *correct* answer, the *right* thing to do); the counselor is, or is perceived, as the one who prevents the wrong.

The Stereotype of Occupational Choice

Despite a great deal of counselor behavior to the contrary, he is still viewed as the person who can tell you what occupation you ought to enter. The counselor is the person with the interest and aptitude tests and the occupational files. For example, posters in the school have given him a good advance notice: "Don't take chances with your future! See your counselor now." "*You* are the genie! Consult your guidance counselor for verification of the qualities you possess for your chosen vocation." "Are you playing blind man's buff with your future? Don't blindfold yourself when planning your future. See your counselor!"

Of course the counselor is an excellent resource person to help adolescents explore and embark on a career. But these messages convey far more than assistance; they demonstrate very well the stereotype of the person who can tell you, who can verify for you. Implicit in this stereotype is the concept of *an* occupational choice—one decision to last a lifetime. It is no wonder that youth seek someone who will tell them what to be. What if they made a mistake? Better the counselor, than they. Though counselors, themselves, have tried to deal with this stereotype, it persists in the minds of men and it pervades the materials they use. Nothing short of an all-out attack— Madison Avenue style—can apparently lay to rest these underlying myths and their effect on the work of the counselor.

GUIDANCE: RETROSPECT AND PROSPECT

There is little doubt that the force of guidance was strengthened during the decade of the sixties. Despite the pervasive influence of the role paradox and some counselor resistance to a changing identity, a growing number of counselors entered the field in the many new positions that became available, and they made concerted efforts to shore up the breakdown in the guidance role that had begun to occur in the years of emergence. Programs of preparation had been strengthened considerably. The national and state professional organizations serving the school counselor were conducting outstanding conferences. The professional journals were reflecting the emphasis on the counseling function. Articles containing newer ideas and recent research findings pertaining to a variety of professional responsibilities provided a balance between theory, research, and practice. Yet even in the seventies the school counselor finds it difficult to become involved in the counseling function. The remnants of early role expectations bind him to responsibilities from which it is most difficult to detach himself. New counselors, prepared in accordance with the professional criteria contained in the ASCA *Statement of Policy,* have encountered some difficulty in establishing an identity consistent with the role for which they have been prepared. The dichotomy between the traditional and the newer approach to guidance is becoming more clear.

High school student reactions to their guidance and counseling experiences can no longer be ignored. While few schools have sought such data, a number of studies indicate a considerable amount of student dissatisfaction and discontent. The cry for more counseling time is a common and repeated report of our high school youth. Actual counseling time with students is still a major problem in secondary school guidance. While a part of this lack can be attributed to personnel shortages and heavy loads, the issue is more clearly a matter of time utilization and work priorities. Counseling per se is seldom a top priority in practice. Some would take the position that until school administrators remove mechanistic and clerical responsibilities, counseling will remain subordinate. There is also a growing recognition that in the performance of their role counselors will have to begin to deal more directly with this issue. Advocates of this counselors-must-help-themselves school believe it is time that school counselors accept full responsibility for their role behaviors. They contend it is time to meet this problem head-on. More discussion of this problem is contained in Chapter 6, dealing with role enactment.

The increasing tempo of the times has intensified the need for more individual counseling. The pressures and demands of a changing society are experienced very deeply by the youth across our land. While the home, like the school, has increasing responsibilities to deal with these matters, it cannot. Some of the pressures that young people face originate in the home, and it is unrealistic to assume that they can be handled adequately there, for while some homes can deal with these pressures, others cannot. When the home is unprepared to cope with pressures impinging on youth, then the school must be prepared to deal directly (and helpfully) with those individuals who need assistance that the home cannot offer.

Unfortunately, the school also contributes to the tensions and pressures that youth feel. Pressures for achievement (marks in particular) have increased, and the school has been unable to cope effectively with many of these within the teaching-learning process. Many of the anxieties and fears of adolescents can be attributed to methodologies employed in the educative process. The school has failed to adapt the teaching-learning process to the current demands of society while at the same time considering the needs and problems of a growing human being.

Criticism of the schools in the sixties was received by educators as the work of "cranks" and "dissenters." Early criticisms tended to be ignored or sloughed off. By the late sixties, however, the more astute school boards and school administrators had come to recognize that a rather thorough look at the educative process was needed.

Guidance finds itself involved heavily in the teaching and learning that occurs within the school and particularly with the *individual's* experiences in it and his responses to it. In many ways the school counselor is in an enviable position, albeit a difficult one. The active, alert, astute counselor who cares about individuals very quickly becomes attuned to the environment of the school and to the climate of each classroom in it. As the agent of the learner) and as an educator (one who knows about the teaching-learning process) he is aware of how the instructional program of the school affects the individual. He is in a position where he should be able to help the school staff accommodate the educative process to each learner. Much of the focus in the school in the past has been on fitting the individual to the instructional program. The responsibility for changes in these directions lies with the entire school staff.

The school counselor merely contributes to these changes, though his role can be extremely important if he chooses to become an active participant in the change process. His involvement suggests yet another function. Thus, at the turn of the decade, as the school counselor finds himself still deliberating on the dilemma that prevents his full involvement in the counseling activity, he can view his potential for innovation and change.

McCully was among the first to speak out on the responsibility of the counselor as an agent of change. He proposed a function for the school counselor which would cause him "to intervene in the lives of students and to intervene in the learning environment of the school toward the end of enabling students to learn through experience the meaning of freedom and.

responsibility so they may become free and responsible persons."[14] That McCully envisions a role in which the counselor gets closer to and more involved in the teaching-learning process is obvious. He says,

> The process of becoming free and responsible begins with awareness of self, with self-definition through the making of conscious choices within the limits of necessity. A primary though not exclusive method of generating this process would appear to be the counseling session. But more than this will be required for its nurturance. Conditions of the learning environment must be such as to require the student constantly to make choices within limits if he is to grow in self-definition and pursue the process of becoming a free and responsible person. With a particular kind and quality of preparation, not far afield from the best contemporary programs of counselor education, the counselor of the future could become an effective consultant to teachers with respect to these conditions in the learning environment—a human instrument of change.[15]

This new function (consulting), while inherent, has never been implemented in any important way. In fact in many secondary school guidance programs the communication between teachers and counselors has been minimal, and in some situations the communication barrier has resulted in a split between guidance and instruction. There is much promise in the consulting role of the secondary school counselor. The fact that we find ourselves in the early seventies with so far to move should not deter our movement in that direction. On the other hand, we cannot move blindly, remain ignorant of the issues and problems to be encountered. Nor can we. Rather, we must reassess our philosophical base, retool our manpower, and forge ahead.

Despite the gains that guidance has achieved in the last decade, its progress in changing its own practice has been far too slow. Too many programs remain mechanistic and clerically oriented. There is yet too little counseling. To move to the point where professional counselors could (and would) engage in guidance activities associated with the newer identity of the 1960s may seem remote and impossible. Difficult, yes. Impossible, no. Both the counseling and consulting functions are based in communication and interpersonal relations. Both can provide needed assistance for students, teachers, and parents. Counselors who are able to establish a relationship with another person or persons and who are able to communicate with these other people can readily engage in counseling and consulting functions. Such a person, in this *professional* role, can become that which he strives to be.

---

[14] C. Harold McCully, "The Counselor—Instrument of Change," *Teachers College Record* 66:410, February 1965.
[15] *Ibid.*

That this can occur with more rapidity than we can imagine is quite possible. It is only impossible when we allow it to be so.

SUGGESTED READING

BREWER, JOHN, *History of Vocational Guidance* (New York: Harper and Bros., 1942).

DAVIS, HOWARD V., *Frank Parsons: Prophet, Innovator, Counselor.* (Carbondale and Edwardsville, Ill.: Southern Illinois University Press, 1969).

PARSONS, FRANK, *Choosing a Vocation* (New York: Agathon Press, 1967). Reprint of original 1909 edition.

WILLIAMSON, E. G., *Vocational Counseling: Some Historical, Philosophical, and Theoretical Perspectives* (New York: McGraw-Hill, 1965).

TWO

SOCIOLOGICAL CONCEPTS

AND FORCES

Sociology is concerned with the environment of man—its society, its structure and organization, and the forces within it that shape its nature. Perhaps more than ever in the history of man it is necessary to consider all the facets and factors that contribute to our understanding of our environment and its influence on us. The ideas and the concepts presented in this chapter represent only a few of the sociological forces that are shaping and influencing our own lives. This chapter is by no means complete or thorough in its treatment of those sociological forces and influences that are important to the school counselor. Rather, it is selective in that it includes those that I feel have been significant to my own work and to those school counselors whom I have known. It is representative in that it touches on the home and the school—two very important forces in the life of an individual. But there are other forces that may be equally significant in other settings and in other lives. Thus, I consider this chapter one that will but introduce you to a few of the many constellations of ideas that will eventually shape your conception of your own world.

Our times have been characterized in many ways—as changing, as restless, as uncertain. The tempo has been fast and accelerating; the tenor has been moving and dynamic. And our youth in these times have been referred to as alienated and lost. Little about our modern way of life is directed toward stability and fixedness, yet we speak often of durability and the status quo. There is so much going on all about us that it is difficult to describe our society, except in generalities, with any degree of certainty. Our immediate life experience is like a series of kaleidoscopic vignettes that we understand momentarily. Before we are able to fit these understandings into a larger, more encompassing whole, they have slipped away to take another form. Such is the manner of our world and the changes in it. Our grasp of life—our understanding of society—is increasingly a matter of hindsight. We know too often when it is too late. Even though we are forewarned or alerted to events and trends in our life, we are accustomed to viewing change by a policy of wait and see. We must learn to assess our own ability to keep in touch with the times and to examine our own behaviors and reactions to the ongoing and upcoming.

Many philosophical questions concern education—questions that have been relegated in the past to philosophers and theoreticians. What is the role of education in such a society? How can education serve an amoebic peoples? What is its responsibility? Does it transmit knowledge? Does it interpret the culture? How does it transmit knowledge that soon goes out of date? How does it interpret a culture that may be all too soon out of style? How does a society change and what is the contribution of education to that change? Does education prepare one for changes in society? Is education responsible *to* society, or *for* society?

We can no longer just philosophize about these questions. We know that education is a responsible and responsive element in the growth of the individual and in the future of our society. Education must seek applications that will allow it to play the vital role of which it is capable. It must concern itself in more dynamic ways with the growth of the individual. It must contribute to the development of a person who can live in a volatile society. It must depend more on foresight and less on hindsight. It must risk more!

Several major aspects of American society are examined here in an attempt to highlight some of the sociological concepts and forces that can challenge the school to action. These are not comprehensive discussions; they are rather kaleidoscopic, serving to point to a few of the changes in our society though not necessarily to explain them. They are intended to alert you to the important things happening that have meaning for our work in human growth and learning. Hopefully they will challenge you to move more swiftly to understand those factors and forces that are vital to your work in education.

SOME CHANGING ASPECTS
OF AMERICAN SOCIETY

It has become a cliché to talk about our "rapidly changing society." It is one thing to talk about change; it is quite another to understand it. Each day our lives are being altered by political, social, and economic changes. New laws are drastically altering our behavior as citizens. Values are changing. Change is an integral and influential part in the life of every citizen.

Increasingly we interact with individuals who are confused and anxious, who seek aid in making sense of their environment, who do not understand the influences and the pressures in their lives. These are adolescents in the process of living and learning; teachers who work with youth every day in the classrooms; parents who care about their children and their country. The school counselor, in spite of obstacles that delimit his own understanding and regardless of his own values, can help these people to make some sense to their being and to understand better the world in which they live. To do this he must strive to gain an understanding of those influences and changes that he experiences. He, too, must *live*.

An Expanding Population

The population explosion about which we have talked for some years is a reality for an increasing number of Americans. Each year more and more people are affected in one way or another by the increase in our population. While population growth is one very tangible measure of our changing society, it is one that few people acknowledge. Some have become very concerned about our population growth and have expressed that our present and projected rate of growth is one of our most pressing societal problems.

Perhaps much of our complacency about the population growth rests in our inability to conceive of a world with so many people. In 1940, the population of the United States was approximately 131 million; in 1950, 150 million; in 1960, 178 million; and in 1968, 200 million. Projected estimates indicate that by 1980 the population will total around 250 million —an increase of about 25 percent from the 1968 figure. In the year 2000, it is projected, our 1960 population will almost double to around 350–360 million. Living with that many people is hard to imagine. Yet it appears that this will be the real world for the youth of our land. Furthermore, these young people are *now* in our schools.

The population increase accentuates problems in such areas as traffic management, highway construction, housing, and education. It highlights such societal issues as birth control and pollution.

The rapidity of our population increase could revolutionize our existence. More and more people will necessitate more and more control over the movement of man. To maintain standards of law and order more laws and more local regulations will be necessary. These will no doubt infringe on man's freedom. It is difficult to know now the extent or nature of these restrictions. While we shall continue to be concerned about the individual, the welfare of the nation will maintain its priority. Man may continue to achieve some benefits that will compensate for any loss of personal freedom. Mechanization and technology may provide man with other ways of coping with his needs and resolving his frustrations.

The strong ties of a community and the bonds of friendship that bring men together as we have known them are disappearing. The community is no longer the integrating unit in our society to the degree that it has been. The *esprit,* the pride that were kindled through community togetherness have been siphoned off by other groupings of people that demand the allegiance and energies that man at one time directed toward his community. While people still need people, as the popular song of a few years back reminds us, many aspects of human relating may undergo deep and abiding change.

Work and Leisure

Work has its historical, traditional meanings. Historically, work has been the means whereby man has been able to feed himself. From the very early days to the present he has had to forage for his own nourishment. But with increasing civilization man has formalized his work role, using it not only as a means of survival but as a means of establishing his own identity. He found satisfaction in his being through work that drew on his creativity, craftsmanship, skill, and reasoned judgment. Man became enamored with his own productivity, and his pride, contentment, and individuality in work performance assumed a highly significant aspect of his life. His vocation also was an expression of his service to his God and to his fellow man. His work was his "calling."

Our Puritan ancestry placed a high value on work (work is good and hard work is even better), leaving us with a value orientation to work that has survived until modern times. It is only recently, as technology has changed man's work routines, that we have come to question the traditional meanings of work in our heritage. Whereas leisure time was once considered wasteful or evil, man is now seduced from his work by the many enticing ways to pass his nonemployed time.

Mass production, the unionization of labor, work specialization, and advancing technology have all contributed in one way or another to the changing nature of work and leisure in man's life. Modern man finds himself working shorter hours and performing more highly specialized functions. In larger industries he is apt to find his identity in his association with the company or the organization rather than with a product or skill. His creativity, which once was a test of his own potency or a factor of his competitiveness, is now something that may be recognized through the company's suggestion award plan. Institutions and organizations, large and small, simple or complex, are seeking ways of motivating man and of helping him find a sense of identity at another need level—the psychological. In these ways the corporation can compete with man's search for fulfillment—a search that increasingly involves him in his nonemployed or leisure time.

Today man seeks to find many of the satisfactions in his life in activities that fill the ever increasing hours when he is not on the job. The growing number of ways whereby man seeks to find and satiate himself in his non-working hours is not only evidence of the changing nature of work and leisure but of the way they serve the needs of man in American life.

Recreation and travel, for example, consume a great amount of modern man's time and energy. He keeps the nation's parks filled to capacity with his trailers and tents. Whereas baseball was once the nation's leading pastime, it now shares its spectator thrills with many professional sports such as football, basketball, hockey, golf, and soccer. From participant to spectator, the American is busy finding ways to enjoy himself (suggesting perhaps that at the same time he may hope to find his "self") in his free time. From the years of denial, when pennies for leisure were literally not available, we have progressed to a time when recreation and travel have become a significant item in the average American household budget.

Affluence

By our older Puritanical standards, we are a wasteful and extravagant people. By almost any standard of thrift and economy we are lavish, excessive. From the times of great depression in the early thirties, when many folks wondered where and how the next meal would come, we have become a nation that ponders laboriously on where and when we will next "eat out." We have become a nation of gourmets and stylists. In food and clothing, we want the best and the most up-to-date. Our affluence has allowed us to move beyond the basic physiological needs of man and to concern ourselves with those psychological inner forces that allow man to become more fully aware of himself and others. It is cause for us to examine in more detail the very nature of our existence—our very humanness. Our affluence is testing the limits of our capacity to drug ourselves materially.

There are indications that some have found the satiation of materialism wanting. There are noticeable trends to indicate that people are searching for satisfactions of a psychological nature. Some of these movements suggest that man wants, above all else, to understand himself and to achieve an inner awareness and security.

Family income in the United States has risen sharply in the last decade. The war on poverty, which was initiated in the middle 1960s, is recognition of our concern for the less fortunate. It has already helped to make more Americans aware of the deprivation in our city ghettos and elsewhere in our land. It has sharpened our efforts to provide for all men in a number of ways. It has caused us to reexamine a number of our democratic principles and behaviors. These poverty conditions will continue to merit our attention for some years, and we cannot help but learn more about ourselves and our way of life as we try to rectify the situation.

Although we can look to the advantages of our affluence, we cannot ignore its problems. The "problems of affluence" weigh heavily on older values and attitudes inherited from eras of less abundance and less material extravagance. We find the influence of affluence in our drug and narcotics problem; in the rebellion and protest of youth; in crime and delinquency; and in family discord and tension. These are not problems with ready solutions nor are they problems that stem from affluence alone. They are, however, problems with which we all have to deal.

The Disappearing Generation Gap

When I first used this term people were confused. The protest, the "hippy movement," and the growing differences between the younger generation and the so-called establishment could hardly be viewed as diminishing or disappearing. In the past, many differences in beliefs and behaviors were explained by the "difference in generations." The younger generation has usually been characterized as the one that is "going to pot"—figuratively not (yet) literally. A generation has traditionally been viewed as approximately thirty-three years, so we're talking about differences between "teeners" and adults of forty-five years and over. As a traditional concept to characterize the differences between the old and the young in an evolving society undergoing gradual change, the term "generation gap" may serve an explanatory purpose. In the modern American society, if we continue to use the term, we may need to attune it to a more up-to-date idea of a generation. In the modern sense, a generation may constitute only a few years, perhaps five or less. To speak of the generation gap in this diminishing sense is to indicate several gaps between the adolescent and his parents. How do we get from the traditional generation gap of 33 years, to several shorter generation gaps, to none at all?

Change is so rapid and so frequent that a difference can exist within a very few years. The explanation here lies in technological advances that appear just too late for one group but just in time for the next. Take "the pill," for example. Think how it has influenced the beliefs and behaviors of those married five years before it was introduced as opposed to the beliefs and behaviors of those who follow five years after it was introduced. The effect of this one scientific discovery on the sexual behavior of these two groups of people in matters of birth control and premarital and marital sex experience serves to illustrate the possibilities for decided differences in values and attitudes between two closely allied age groups. Lifton, in referring to ideological change, noted the following:

> Until relatively recently, no more than one major ideological shift was likely to occur in a lifetime, and that one would be long remembered as a significant individual turning-point accompanied by profound soul-searching and conflict. But today it is not unusual to encounter several such shifts, accomplished relatively painlessly, within a year or even a month; and among many groups, the rarity is a man who has gone through life holding firmly to a single ideological vision.[1]

The limitless number of ideological changes and the rapidity with which ideas and values can be diffused among people will eliminate the traditional concept of a generation. All people will be subject to ideological shifts in accord with the tempo and tenor of the times. This portends the possibilities of ideological change for the established adult as well. Mass communication media may well influence people of all ages leaving us with but a few, if any, vestiges whereby we can label any age group with assurance.

The current establishment may well be the last to hold fixed, traditional ideologies. They may be the last in our society to undergo that "once a lifetime" ideological shift to which Lifton has referred. In but a few years, the current established generation will be replaced by many who have experienced several ideological changes, who are less fixed or set ideologically, and who are perhaps more flexible and adaptable than their predecessors. Hopefully they will also be less susceptible to viewing their younger counterparts with the critical and commanding eye that has characterized traditional appraisal of the younger generation. Continued acceleration and change may produce ideological diffusion, but such differences will be the product of man's reasoning and not of his age. Generations, as such, will disappear and men will challenge each other on another basis.

Geographic and Job Mobility

The recent statistics regarding geographic mobility indicate that people are moving in increasing numbers. About one out of every four or five families are moving each year. Employers, particularly the larger industrial and business firms, tend to move their employees with far greater frequency. This adds, of course, to the natural migration of people that has characterized

---

[1] Robert Jay Lifton, "Protean Man," *Partisan Review* 35:21, Winter 1968.

the development of the United States since early times. Now, with our lands fairly well occupied and settled, geographic mobility may tend to assume different dimensions.

According to the census figures of 1967, the greatest percent of population increase was in Arizona (3.1), California (2.7), and Alaska (2.6). California has replaced New York as the most populous state in the union. Other centers of mobility are in the urban areas, to which increasing numbers of people gravitate each year. As urban populations expand, rural populations decline, providing us with the statistical evidence to explain the many farms we find abandoned to hunting clubs and outlying suburban developers.

THE DISADVANTAGED IN AMERICAN SOCIETY

Deprived, underprivileged, impoverished, culturally deprived—all are terms that are used, often interchangeably, to describe a segment of people in our society that we have come to refer to most frequently as the disadvantaged. During the decade of the 1960s there was a growing concern for groups of people who, in one way or another, had been deprived of the advantages that are such an integral part of life for the average middle and upper class American. Essentially, there are five distinguishable groups of disadvantaged people:

(1) Negroes—both Northern and Southern as well as those in scattered urban and rural areas in all areas of the United States

(2) Spanish-Americans—including both the Puerto Rican immigrants, most of whom have settled primarily along the Eastern seaboard in both coastal and interior regions from New York to Florida, and the Mexican-Americans in population clusters essentially in the Southwest

(3) American Indians—now confined mainly to reservations, many of which are located in the Midwest and the Far West

(4) Appalachian peoples—consisting mainly of hill folk populating the mountainous interior of the Eastern coastal region

(5) Rural poor—an expanding group of people throughout the nation whose impoverishment has increased with the decline in the country's farm economy

The Meaning of Disadvantaged

Disadvantaged can have a variety of meanings, but essentially it is a human condition characterized by inequality, lack of opportunity, and social injustice. The concept of disadvantage finds its base in the cultural norms of the dominant group of American society—the middle class. Thus, the disadvantaged people are identified by the degree to which they suffer deficiencies in and denials of advantages that are regularly afforded the majority group. While we tend to assign this condition to groups of people, we must recognize that it is present in varying degrees within members of these groups. The degree of a person's disadvantage results from a combination of factors—economic, cultural, and psychological. Although we are often inclined to define disadvantage solely on one basis, we need to emphasize more that several considerations combine to give meaning to the condition and degree of disadvantage.

Pivotal to the problems of the disadvantaged in American society are concerns associated with education, employment (and income), and housing. It has been assumed that education is basic to the needs of the disadvantaged. It is the means by which upward mobility can be established. It leads to full employment, a regular income, self-sufficiency, and productivity. Steady employment leads to a home, responsible citizenship, and human dignity. There is little doubt that this is the path and the mark of upward social mobility for the average middle class person. In the following paragraphs we shall examine some of the factors associated with disadvantagedness and the extent to which these factors affect the upward mobility of the disadvantaged.

Economic. Much of our focus on the disadvantaged has been economic. The Economic Opportunity Act of 1964 was designed to eliminate poverty and to provide opportunity for everyone regardless of race or ethnic background. It became in a short time a symbol of this nation's "war on poverty." While being poor is not necessarily synonymous with being disadvantaged, it is one of the most frequent characteristics and a qualification for eligibility to participate in many of the government programs. In the past decade we have become increasingly aware of the many low income families that reside not only in our slum and ghetto areas but in the rural and mountainous regions where clusters of people reside.

Many contend that the goals and values of the disadvantaged do not differ from those of the typical middle class American. They believe that success and affluence are universally American and apply equally to all segments of our society. Thus, economic deprivation, according to this point of view, is basic to disadvantage. On the other hand there are those who emphasize the multicultural aspects of disadvantage (especially with regard to the disadvantaged black), indicating that cultural differences are sufficiently varied to produce a different value hierarchy. Those who accept this point of view stress the cultural and psychological factors of disadvantagedness as well as the economic.

Cultural. Cultural disadvantage can be represented in a variety of societal differences and deprivations. While some cultural differences may be caused by deprivation and denial, we must accept the reality of other cultural differences and learn to use them in a more productive fashion rather than attempting to change them. Rather than disregarding language and value differences among groups, we must accept them as a part of a multicultural society.

Deprivation and denial, on the other hand, must be squarely faced. Disadvantaged people who are the victims of racial or ethnic prejudice in the form of discrimination and injustice must be guaranteed human equality and opportunity. The facts of racism, educational inequality, and prejudicial employment practices are well known. These are being attacked in numerous ways through state and national legislation.

The Manpower Development and Training Act (1962) provided for the establishment or extension of facilities to train skilled workers in a variety of needed occupational endeavors. This and later legislation, such as the Elementary and Secondary Education Act of 1965 and the Higher Education Act of 1964, have emphasized the support of programs in areas having high concentrations of low-income families.

The Economic Opportunity Act of 1964 provided many programs focusing on services and activities for the children and youth of the disadvantaged. Head Start, Youth Opportunity Centers, and the Job Corps are illustrative of the core programs that were developed to provide education and opportunity for those who were suffering from discrimination and deprivation.

The Civil Rights Act of 1964 may someday be recorded as the most important single act of Congress in promoting human equality. Aimed primarily at the social injustices of racism and the denials of human dignity that these injustices perpetuated, this legislation prohibits segregated facilities, educational or other, for people on the basis of color and made it unlawful to prevent people from using public facilities because of color or ethnic background. Through this legislation we are directly challenging the hostility, the hatred, and the misunderstandings underlying the attitudes and intolerance that have been the very basis of these denials.

Psychological. Perhaps more a characteristic than a condition is the tendency of the disadvantaged to have inadequate feelings of self-worth. His position in a minority group has helped to create a less than positive view of self. These feelings of inadequacy contribute neither to personal motivation nor to the types of interpersonal relationships that can contribute to the promotion of attitudes more favorable to motivation. Failure in school or at work (that is, a general lack of achievement or success) only generates stronger feelings of resentment and hostility leading to the creation of attitudes that usually inhibit rather than enhance the individual's potential and his possible contributions to society. Before we can ever hope to help move the disadvantaged *toward* self-actualization, we must ensure that their basic physiological needs are being attended to. At the same time we need to provide the psychological support that can lead the individual to an acceptance of himself and generate conditions and attitudes that will help him to find himself in his society.

The self-concept, therefore, and all that it entails, becomes a necessary consideration in dealing with the disadvantaged. Interpersonal relationships are a necessary ingredient in the cultural mainstream, and it seems appropriate to consider the internal aspects of one's being as these are manifest in social and emotional behaviors. The implications of the psychological components of disadvantagedness have considerable importance for the type of work that the individual may find appropriate as well as the manner in which he relates to his peers and his superiors on the job.

The Disadvantaged and the Nation's Manpower

One of the most pervasive efforts undergirding all of the government programs has been the assistance provided to help each individual become an active, more productive member of the labor force. The efforts in this direction have encompassed three major groups of disadvantaged people: (1) the unemployed, (2) the "underemployed," and (3) the unemployable. Perhaps a word of clarification about each of these groups would help in distinguishing among the problems of the disadvantaged.

The Unemployed. Basically, these people are willing to work and are actively seeking employment, but for one reason or another they cannot find suitable employment. They simply do not have a job. Intensive efforts have been focused on helping them locate work. In many instances discriminatory employment practices have been stopped as a result of the combined efforts of a variety of community resources. Government agencies and community groups have cooperated in a number of programs throughout the country that have eliminated unfair employment policies or have caused businesses and industries to extend or expand employment opportunities to people they would not commonly consider.

The "Underemployed." These people have some kind of employment, but they are not utilizing their work capacities or skills fully or they are not employed full time. A direct attack has been made on this problem in several ways. Businesses and industries have established programs providing opportunities, usually within the plant, to gain additional skill training that would more fully utilize their work capacities. Many programs focusing on upgrading the work responsibilities of the underemployed have also been established through manpower programs, community service, and continuing education opportunities.

The Unemployable. Unemployable persons fall into two categories. First there are those who are unemployable because they lack needed work skills: there are simply no jobs available for which they can qualify. They may not be able to read or write or to perform up to the general standards of work prevalent within their community or region. While these people may have been employable at one time, technological advances and manpower requirements have changed sufficiently to result in job displacement.

The other category consists mainly of those who are unemployable as a result of poor attitudes toward work or who lack the motivation to work. These people, if they seek employment, are considered high risk candidates and usually do not obtain a job. Their problems are often deep-seated and the most difficult with which to deal.

For any number of reasons, the disadvantaged in both categories have suffered essentially as products of a cultural environment that has insufficiently inspired and prepared them to compete with most middle and upper class Americans, who have not experienced life in the crowded ghetto or in the isolation of a rural community. These unemployables represent a segment of society that tends to draw heavily on welfare programs and other sources of subsistence. They are a real challenge to the nation's manpower development since they represent a sizable and salvageable source of labor. Central to helping these people is a counseling function that would help them to assess some of the attitudes involved in their employability—their attitudes toward immediate and longer range gratifications, toward employers and paid employment, and toward achievement.

The Problems of the Disadvantaged

The problems of the disadvantaged are multiple and complex; one can only capture an overview of some that seem more relevant and crucial at any particular time. Certainly the problems of the disadvantaged are pervasive and deeply imbedded in the American society. There is no tailormade solution. There is but a continual confrontation with those causes that we are able to identify.

Family life deprivation. Family styles of togetherness, size, conditions, family rituals, and child-rearing practices are but a few of the elements that make the pattern of family life in the disadvantaged home different from its middle class counterpart. The female is often the head of the household, necessitating that she regularly assume a number of male roles (such as wage earner and disciplinarian). In the typical two-parent, low-income family, the husband is often emotionally, as well as physically, removed from a relationship with either his wife or the children. Raising the children is the job of the mother, and the father often spends a great deal of time outside the home. Since respectability is not assured, as is generally the case in the middle class home, it must be earned. Children are taught early to obey and to be polite. Youngsters are reared to a code that emphasizes more the social rather than the psychological components of human development. Discipline is strict and individuality is subservient to conformity. Thus, both mother and children suffer from a type of psychological deprivation that has implications for self-concept development as well as for socialization and valuing patterns. The ultimate behavorial outcomes can be observed in the motivational problems of disadvantaged youth.

Educational deprivation. Educational deprivation has been characterized by a number of conditions (such as inadequate school housing and facilities and less competent teachers) that have been the basis of current demands for "quality education." While it is a fact that some of the schools in the inner-city areas and rural areas are old and out-of-date, there is reason to emphasize more the changes needed in school programs to counteract deprived children's psychological and cultural deprivation. Not only have they had less opportunities to travel, to visit museums, to spend time in the country or in the city (in the case of deprived rural youth)—all frequently cited aspects of the limited experiential background upon which these children can draw—, but they are often unprepared to engage in the processes of thinking and learning that are commonly assumed for the middle class child. These children are often identified as perceptually handicapped, lacking in mental ability, and unmotivated. In short, by the usual school program standards, they simply are not ready for the usually assigned tasks of the school.

It is possible to attribute some of these deficiencies to the cultural background of these youngsters, so the school must begin to provide necessary program adjustments and enrichments for them. Head Start, one program initiated under the Economic Opportunity Act of 1964, represents a preschool action program that was designed to help the disadvantaged child catch up. In this program, activities are designed to help with the social and self-concept development of the child, to improve his language skills, and to aid in the development of his ability to process information. Children in these and similar programs throughout the country at both preschool and elementary school levels, have been greatly aided in developing more positive attitudes toward self and others and in creating attitudes that foster motivation and a desire for achievement.

Thus, while the present focus on the disadvantaged is directed at all types and facets of deprivation and at all age levels, we are beginning to make significant observations that determine what direction future efforts will take. The following are of vital importance to the development of school guidance services at both the elementary and secondary levels.

(1) The attitudinal and motivational problems of the unemployable can be reduced by early childhood programs of a preventive (or developmental) nature. Not only do preschool programs offer an effective and powerful means of helping the disadvantaged child early, but the continual provision of such curriculum and classroom activities throughout school life offers much possibility of enhancing his potential to achieve societal usefulness and personal gratification.

(2) Community cooperation is an integral part of the attack on poverty and human inequality. All of the resources must be involved, in one way or another, in effecting needed attitudinal as well as operational changes. The school can and must be an active agent in planning and implementing these changes. While changes within the school program are essential, the school must reach out to the community—to the businesses, industries, and homes in the areas or regions it serves. It must expend less effort in castigating the home and more in adjusting to it and in helping to effect needed societal changes that will improve the plight of the disadvantaged home.

(3) Communication and value barriers between the middle class and the disadvantaged community do, in fact, exist. That the standards of the middle class prevail (and will continue to do so) there is little doubt. The facts of American society are clear. One must be able to read, to write, and to speak, and one must be prepared to offer and adapt oneself to the society in which one lives. The barriers between groups and among people must be understood though they need not be destroyed. To work with the disadvantaged *at this time,* however, one must be alert to these differences in values and in the manner whereby they are communicated.

THE FAMILY AS A CHANGING SOCIAL UNIT

The family as a unit has quite a different character today than it had ten to twenty years ago. The factors responsible for a different approach to family living make it difficult to generalize about family life. The modernization of the home from the automatic clothes and dishwashers to the electric can opener, from packaged food mixes to garbage disposals, has very definitely changed the pattern of home operation and the roles to be performed in it.

The housewife who used to spend most of her time washing, ironing, cooking, and preserving food now finds that less time is necessary in the kitchen and laundry, giving her more time to work in the yard, to shop, and to engage in activities of her own choosing. She has more time to be a mother, although her role is quite different.

The family of the working mother and the traveling father is quite a contrast to the family of twenty years ago. Family togetherness is experienced much differently, tending to evolve in blocks of time rather than day-to-day existence together. Responsibilities in the home are of a different order and degree, not only for the parents but the children as well. The interdependence of household members has given way to an interdependence among several households or among groups of a secondary nature formed among individuals outside the home. While the nature of family life has changed, the societal expectations of the home and the family remain essentially unchanged.

The Working Mother

An increasing number of women are becoming working mothers. The pattern that typically has been followed by women since World War II goes something like this: Upon completion of her formal education the female enters the labor force, remaining there until marriage or her first pregnancy. At that time she becomes a full-time housewife and mother, remaining in this role until her youngest child is in school so that she can comfortably return to full- or part-time employment. This has resulted in the availability for employment of a number of women in the 30–40 age range. Some have prepared for their return to work by engaging in "refresher" studies; others have taken part-time work, gradually increasing to full-time work as their family responsibilities permit. According to *The Nation's Youth,* a publication of the Children's Bureau, "One-third of all mothers with children under 18 are working now, compared with only one-fifth in 1950."[2]

There is some reason to believe that the period of the full-time "mother" role is being decreased. Nursery schools and day care centers are allowing mothers of young children to reenter the labor force at an earlier time. Manpower figures show that the number of working mothers with children under six years of age has risen gradually over the past twenty years to a point where approximately one in five working wives have children under six years of age.

[2] Children's Bureau, *The Nation's Youth* (Washington, D.C.: U.S. Department of Health, Education and Welfare, 1968), text opposite Chart 17.

Affluence makes it possible for some women to remain in the home, if they choose to do so. On the other hand, rising costs make it necessary for many women to take a job as soon as possible. It is difficult to account for this contradiction solely on the basis of economic factors. Some women enjoy making clothes, preparing or preserving foods, or engaging in similar household occupations that provide some degree of self-satisfaction. Other women, of course, do not enjoy doing these things and may seek other forms of human fulfillment in work outside the home. Whatever the causes or factors, the working mother is an interesting phenomenon in modern society —one that will bear constant observation in the years ahead.

The Traveling Father

At one time in our history, mothers could threaten the hard-to-manage or disobedient child with "You wait until your father comes home and hears about this!" Today, father's arrival could be quite a wait. Air transportation has increased worker travel and men are sent on missions that range from a day or two to several weeks. It is ironical in many respects that we have focused so much attention on the "fatherless" home as it has been traditionally defined, when the life of the traveling father can result in some serious family discontinuties and disturbances.

Part-time fathers are not easy for sons to identify with, making it more difficult, perhaps, for sons than daughters. The "traveling father syndrome" includes more than just his frequent or periodic absences for trips. It encompasses the missed dinners while working late, the evenings out for business or civic affairs, and the other multitude of reasons that keep fathers on the go. The pressures and demands on the male breadwinner, particularly the junior executive on his way up, represent another force in the changing character of the family unit.

Both the working mother and the traveling father remind us of the suburban adolescent. Life in suburbia is a whole new mode of existence and one that we have neglected, for it has seemed safely middle class. The problems of the suburban home have been upstaged by the more obvious ones of the inner city and the ghetto. We have watched one housing development after another spring up all around the major population centers of every state in the union. Have we been lulled into complacency by the neat, green lawns, the freshly painted exteriors, and the two-car attached garages? Have we equated family life in suburbia with family life in any average American city or town? Have we assumed that the only difference for the suburban youngster lies in his need for a chauffeur to transport him from one organized activity to another?

Marriage and Family Ideals

Many of our ideals and beliefs about marriage and family life are being challenged. Within the partnership that marriage represents, tremendous changes are occurring. The role of the male as the family patriarch was never as pronounced in America as in European cultures. Tody, the male frequently shares his role with the female who seeks and assumes a far greater involvement in the decision-making processes of family existence. The female, as wife and mother, is as often the family accountant, chauffeur, painter, gardener, and disciplinarian. The male, as husband and father, is likewise as often the baby sitter, cook, house cleaner, family shopper, and dishwasher. Family roles are increasingly interchangeable.

The family ideal of "togetherness" is becoming more myth than fact. Many families eat in shifts, passing each other as they arrive from or leave for the next scheduled activity in a crowded daily agenda that includes Little League, Scouts, lessons of all varieties, school athletics, civic and social gatherings, and a host of other events. This situation is not necessarily bad; it merely challenges a long standing ideal of the family unit. It is possible that a great deal of positive benefits accrue from the wider, more active participation of all family members.

Perhaps one of the more difficult aspects of family living is related to the idea of shared responsibilities. Modern conveniences of all types have reduced the opportunities for the delegation of responsibility and the sharing of obligations in the operation of the home. Even the garbage is automatically disposed in some homes. Those tasks that do remain can be completed so quickly that youngsters hardly have the feeling of accomplishment. While this leaves more time for other activities, even these are so carefully planned by adults that there is little chance for the child to become involved in any responsible way—he just participates!

There is little opportunity for youth to test their own ideas and values in responsible ways—in ways in which they can fail as well as succeed, thus allowing them to modify and change their beliefs and their behaviors as they grow. This is an aspect of family life that needs our immediate attention. Since we cannot return to our ideals of the past, we must search for other ways to provide similar opportunities and experiences for the youth of the present.

Divorce

The divorce rate in the United States is steadily increasing. It is evidence that, for many couples anyway, marriage does not represent the "until death do us part" bond of the past. The very idea that a marriage is not "forever" is most threatening. It can shake the very foundation of our societal views of marriage and the family. Marriage is one of the most sacred institutions of our culture. Legislation in many states has made the dissolution of a marriage most difficult except on grounds of proven infidelity. Church dogma either forbade or frowned on divorce except in unusual circumstances. Only a few decades ago, to become divorced was ignominious; to be a "divorcee" was at once both a damning and a saucy appelation. Today, legislation has been eased considerably and many religious positions have been modified to accommodate the incompatible partnership. The unsuccessful marriage, while still viewed as a difficult and unfortunate circumstance, is more easily and readily acknowledged. Personal recrimination and ridicule has been replaced by more understanding and acceptance.

Divorce is always most difficult where children are involved. While the "broken home" constitutes one aspect of divorce having implications for the family, remarriage and the reconstitution of the family is another and more complex situation. Until most recently, few studies of this situation have been conducted and very little has been reported. Remarriage involving children from previous marriages establishes a very intricate, often delicate, network of family relationships. We know little about this increasing phenomenon and yet we must begin to familiarize ourselves with the problems of such family constellations. We must begin to recognize, rather than stigmatize, the legitimacy of such familial situations and to prepare to deal with the elements of such family relationships, for they are becoming more the rule than the exception.

Family Security

Ours is a nation that can be said to be buying its security (or a good part of it anyway) on credit. To offset the many possibilities of financial disaster, we have established for our families a number of protection programs. Our several medical insurance programs and our clinics are designed (ideally) to provide adequate medical attention for all. As a result of our improved health programs, both public and private, we are not only saving lives but extending them. More babies are living to become adults and more adults are living longer. The life span of man has increased by several years in just the past few decades.

We have moved to protect our longevity by providing income for our years after retirement. The Social Security Act of 1935, and its amendments and revisions over the years, has helped to contribute to the security and financial independence of older members of the family unit. Grandpa and grandma, when their health permits, can continue to live by themselves for a continued period of freedom and independence. In the past this was a period when the older folks have rejoined their families. Children, living with their grandparents or great-grandparents, were able to experience more fully and deeply both the gracious and the agonizing aspects of the older years. To be denied this experience, on whatever grounds, has both its positive and negative effects. The concept of the family as including the grandparents, aunts and uncles, and cousins has never been predominant in American society. And yet, their nearness to one another and their reunions on holidays and weekends has provided a measure of interpersonal affection that is disappearing as family members become more widely separated and remote from these possibilities.

THE SCHOOL COUNSELOR AND SOCIAL CHANGE

Changes in our society being as rapid as they are and as they will continue to be, necessitate first and foremost an examination of the processes whereby education can attune itself to the times. Education is reputedly slow to change and the old educational lag is well known.

But schools have become big business. To be successful in their bid for the tax dollar (from whatever source—local, state, national), educators will have to assume more aggressive positions. They must assume positions that deny resistance to change. They must encourage programs that not only meet the current needs of the society but also prepare young people to meet the presumed needs ten to fifteen years hence.

To hope that education can move from its lagging position to one of leadership may be too idealistic and overly optimistic, yet society cannot afford less! We shall have to find ways for education to accommodate to the changing times. Unlike business or industry, the new product cannot be wholly designed and the machinery to process it quickly installed. Educational change involves changing people as well as processes. This means that the school counselor must prepare himself as well as his program for the renewal and the transformations which are hopefully ahead.

The Counselor's Self in a Changing Society

The school counselor must be able to read with as much accuracy as possible the nature and trends of the society he serves. He must be aware of the movements within the structure of his society and the possible implications of these for the lives of those students he represents and serves.

The counselor is a member of society. He grew up in it; he was schooled by it; he learned what was deemed necessary at whatever time or period he engaged in the formal educative processes. He learned from all his experiences in school, at home, and elsewhere in his community. His values, his beliefs, his attitudes are the result of all that he has encountered.

Thus each counselor must first look at his own life and times. Beyond that, he needs to look at his own *self* in relation to these. And he needs to bridge the years between his growing toward maturity and the maturity he has achieved. Two counselors working side by side can represent quite different worlds. They can be very different in their views—one being influenced greatly by, say, his experiences in the depression years of the 1930s, the other with views that have been shaped mainly by mass communication and the growing affluence of the postwar society.

Both have their own individuality and both are very real to their publics. Neither needs to succumb to the other, neither needs to yield his own identity, neither can say that the other is wrong. Both can glory in their uniqueness and find hope in their differences. Yet neither is of any value to his students or to the adults with whom he works if he cannot associate himself with his own beliefs and values and at the same time disassociate them from the expressions and beliefs of others. If he uses his position to sell his view of the world, whether new, old, or whatever, he fails to serve in the most effective way. If he fails to examine the times, to search for new identities, to chart new courses, he cannot hope to be a part of any new creation. He cannot lead—in fact, he may even find it difficult to follow. While this may seem discouraging or personally demanding, I believe it is only as he is able to do this that he will be able to help others. And it is only as everyone in education is able to engage in this process that we can hope for a world in the school that will school young people to live in the world.

The School Counselor in the School Setting

The school counselor who can learn to apply the concepts of role and power, which we shall examine in Chapter Six, will find himself better prepared to cope with the challenge of changing his role image. In Chapter One we introduced the idea of the counselor as an agent of change within the school. Supporting this newer aspect of his role is the consulting function, an aspect of the guidance role that has seldom been implemented with the force that is presently implied. To accomplish the needed modifications in the role of developmental guidance as it is being developed, the school counselor will have to become more professionally alert in his interpersonal relating. In applying both the concepts of role and of power the school counselor will find himself attending to the inner and more personal aspects of his own role behavior. While role statements are useful guidelines to his practice, the individual nature of the choices and decisions he makes about the activities in which he will engage will determine to a large degree how others view him. His relationships with other members of the school staff will assume an added significance as he works toward extending the nature of his assistance to them.

School counselors have never had sufficient time to provide adequate counseling for all the students who could use their help. One might wonder then how he can conceivably undertake or expand his consulting responsibilities. Basic to assuming this function is, of course, the counselor's own understanding of the developmental needs of the adolescent and the ways of dealing more directly with them. In succeeding chapters a good deal of the focus will deal specifically with these matters. The school counselor and the classroom teacher have much in common in their mutual concern for the well being of the student. Their combined efforts may more adequately provide for youth and their growth and development than they could independently accomplish. These efforts will often revolve around changes in the teaching-learning process. While these changes may be more difficult to evolve, they may be most lasting and more beneficial to more young people. If this can occur then the educative process has been enhanced and those who participate in it have been truly aided.

The Counselor and the Family

The school has long been noted for pointing the finger of blame at the home as the source of many problems that both students and their teachers encounter. Surely the school cannot yield to every parental or family whim, nor can it ever hope to serve fully every family and every familial peculiarity. But it should be able to represent each child and to work as cooperatively as possible with each family.

Regardless of the school's claims that it does, this is not always the case! It very often rejects either the child or the home, or both. Nothing could be less helpful or fruitful. The school is *not* always right even though it seldom admits to being wrong. Yet it quickly communicates to parents (and to students) that they are wrong. This is a basic condition that every school needs to examine. The question of guilt is irrelevant. The issue at stake is the point at which both the school and the home can work cooperatively for the benefit of the student. In the light of these changing times, can so many homes be wrong? Or has the school failed to assess these trends and to account for them in its own policies and technologies?

With the American home undergoing drastic and dynamic change, certain basic assumptions that undergird the structure of familial relationships must be examined. One of the most urgent of these involves the interrelationship of human needs as these are evidenced in modern living and human values and as these have been inherited and acted upon in the home. One basic value that creates some difficulty, for example, is the belief that to be a "good" person one must be able to put the needs of others ahead of one's own. This form of self-denial poses a dilemma for parents, who increasingly find it necessary to attend to their own needs and feelings, as well as for their children, who are searching for their own identity. The working mother, leaving the home in an attempt to provide for her own individuality, experiences feelings of guilt whenever she encounters situations that suggest she might not be attending adequately to her children. Yet her means of attaining self-fulfillment in modern society often necessitate her leaving the home. To deny this "self" may not, for many people at least, be the most effective vehicle, for unless a person can learn to accept and care for himself, it may be very difficult to care for and accept others. This can lead to a form of self-alienation that keeps an individual out of touch with himself and his real feelings.

Parents often deny their own intrinsic needs. They support their children in all their efforts, feeling that their position in life is to meet the needs of their children even if this requires suppressing their own. This reliance on their children is often expressed in subtle demands and expectations of what they think their children should be. Young people then have to cope with these demands and expectations in the form of the pressures and tensions they create. These, added to those which are routinely a part of seeking one's identity, can be overwhelming.

It is becoming increasingly obvious that the home may no longer be able to fulfill all its previous responsibilities. It is today a quite different place. Although it is still the central source of affection and care, of control and regulation, of communication and inclusion, the manner of attending to these and the time available has changed considerably. Perhaps in the years ahead we will come to know better how to cope with the changing nature of home and family structures. In the meantime, even though the home will be reluctant to relinquish (or to admit that it has in fact relinquished) some of the responsibilities it once had, the school may need to provide some of these experiences for young people.

Individual counseling needs increase when adolescents find it less easy to communicate with their parents. In the school, counselors—and more likely teachers—are apt to serve as role models. The demands for interpersonal relationships may assume dimensions that far exceed the ordinary teacher-student relationship that one currently observes. That these and the many other types of interactive changes occur does not necessarily mean that the school must step in to fill these voids. It must recognize them, however, and prepare to face them more frequently.

School personnel need to understand these changes and the dilemmas (societal as well as personal) they create. Perhaps the one contribution that education can offer lies in the way in which it can adapt its procedures and practices, allowing it to work more effectively with the home rather than in opposition to it. One approach, which is already being explored by some secondary school counselors, involves a type of group counseling called *family counseling*. Aimed at opening up communication among members of a family, this activity appears to have some merit in helping individuals reassess home responsibilities and obligations and patterns of interpersonal communication in the home. Family counseling, then, may afford an opportunity for the school and the home to work cooperatively on problems of all types but particularly on those which emerge as a product of the times.

Student exposures and experiences are of a wider variety than ever and families are often faced with dilemmas, the source of which is unfamiliar to them. Student experimentation with drugs is a prime example of this. Most parents simply know little about drugs and their use and few have had any experience with them. The likelihood of these situations multiplying over the next decade is high. Family consultation may thus become an integral part of the consulting function.

Though the American home appears to be engaged in an all-out effort, albeit a frantic and frustrating one, to cling to all its traditional responsibilities, it is becoming more clear that it will be unable to maintain its historical position in all these if the present trends continue. The next few years may help to clarify the presently vague direction of the family as a social unit.

SUGGESTED READINGS

GOSLIN, DAVID A., *The School in Contemporary Society* (Chicago: Scott Foresman, 1965).

HEISS, JEROLD (Ed.), *Family Roles and Interaction* (Chicago: Rand McNally, 1968).

LLOYD-JONES, ESTHER M., and ROSENAU, NORAH (Eds.), *Social and Cultural Foundations of Guidance* (New York: Holt, Rinehart and Winston, 1968).

STEWART, LAWRENCE H., and WARNATH, CHARLES F., *The Counselor and Society* (Boston: Houghton Mifflin, 1965). Chapters 1–5.

WEINBERG, CARL, *Social Foundations of Educational Guidance* (New York: The Free Press, 1969).

THREE

THE PHILOSOPHICAL AND

PSYCHOLOGICAL BASES OF GUIDANCE

As the guidance movement gained momentum in the years of its emergence, more attention was directed toward firming its philosophical and psychological foundations. Several authorities, such as Beck[1] and Wrenn,[2] have explored in detail many of the philosophical and psychological ideas that are basic to establishing a sound foundation for the practice of guidance in the schools. Yet guidance has never been pinioned to the educative process. It remains on the fringe of education—peripheral rather than integral. Part of its position as an adjunct to education is related to the fact that its base has never been firmly established in the process of education. It has been conceived as an important service but not an indispensable one. As is so often the case in all aspects of education, practice has tended to precede theory rather than stem from it. Guidance is no exception and many of the programs have emerged as a collection of practices and techniques with little consideration of their philosophical or psychological underpinnings. Now, however, with a quarter century of experience in secondary schools, it is time to attend to this lack and to firm the bases for guidance thus bridging the gaps between theory and practice.

This chapter points to some of the more significant areas of knowledge that can be used. It portrays in a series of brief sketches some of the more

[1] Carlton E. Beck, *Philosophical Foundations of Guidance* (Englewood Cliffs, N.J.: Prentice-Hall, 1965).

[2] C. Gilbert Wrenn, "Philosophical and Psychological Bases of Personnel Services in Education." In *Personnel Services in Education,* Nelson B. Henry (Ed.), The Fifty-eighth Yearbook of the National Society for the Study of Education (Chicago: The University of Chicago Press, 1959).

important philosophical or theoretical positions from which a point of view about, and an approach to, guidance in the secondary school can be drawn. Its purpose is to point to the potential wellspring in each of these areas and to suggest a number of ideas that students of guidance should pursue further in developing their own ideas about guidance. In this way the chapter is an attempt to alert the potential secondary school counselor to the many concepts and understandings of a philosophical and psychological nature which, when analyzed and synthesized, can provide a base for the guidance effort and a direction for the professional performance of the school counselor role. The chapter is necessarily panoramic and in no way provides the depth of information essential to the completion of this task. It suggests many avenues for exploration but leaves the investigation of these to other courses and other books.

PHILOSOPHY AND GUIDANCE

In the 1959 Yearbook of the National Society for the Study of Education, C. G. Wrenn wrote of the contributions of philosophy and psychology to personnel service in education.[3] In that discussion Wrenn distinguished between philosophy and psychology, saying

Philosophy and psychology may be thought of as complementary in that one contributes to an understanding of truth, meaning, and purpose and the other to an understanding of human behavior within the larger setting of total existence. *Psychology is, first of all, a science, a systematic ordering of observations of human behavior.* As in all sciences, it describes rather than explains. Where inferences are drawn from observations in the development of a law, principle, or explanation of behavior, this is an explanation within the strict boundaries of the man as an organism. The meaning of this behavior within the cosmos, the nature of the knowledge possessed, *the nature of behavior and of existence itself is the province of philosophy.* Psychology is thus seen as more exact but also more limited than philosophy—philosophy as more inclusive in subject matter but less exact in that it cannot be limited to empiric observations.[4]

In that publication Wrenn proceeded to define the dimensions of philosophy and to briefly detail some of the philosophies he felt were relevant to personnel services in education. His treatment of the philosophical bases of personnel services is one of the very few available. Some have criticized his analysis as too narrow, indicating that it is based on a very limited view of science.

[3] *Ibid.*, pp. 41–81.
[4] *Ibid.*, p. 49.

As I mentioned earlier, guidance has been primarily concerned with "how-to-do-it." Yet, philosophy has much to offer for the meaning and purpose of guidance and the school counselor who has not reached out to philosophize about man and his existence may have missed the significance of meaning and purpose in the routine application of practices. Guidance without any philosophical base is a ritualistic attending to the external features of living. Mechanistically viewed, guidance would have little to offer the individual with regard to his own life style. Developmental guidance in our schools portends more than the mechanistic and the ritualistic. It offers hope in helping the individual to examine his own way of life as it takes on meaning and purpose for him. D. B. Gowin,[5] in discussing the prospects for philosophic inquiry in guidance, has suggested that counselors engage in the "processes of philosophizing" as opposed to the comparative study of "philosophic systems." He concludes,

> To the extent that philosophizing illuminates the ordinary experience of individuals, it is providing a service in the guidance of man toward manhood. To the extent that philosophizing elicits a vision of what man's experience could become, it is providing a service in the guidance of man toward rational control. And to the extent that philosophizing recalls man to a closer scrutiny of actual outcomes and consequences, it is providing a service in the guidance of man toward tested meanings and verified truths. These concludings seem more important than a set of fixed conclusions or a forced eclecticism because they encourage continued inquiry and philosophizing.[6]
>
> Eclecticism violates the philosophic criteria of coherence and consistency; it enables a person to accept his current beliefs without testing and revising them since he can find reasons for them somewhere in a variety of philosophies.[7]

While this latter is a valid caution, it does not preclude the welding of ideas into an appropriate, workable base. I, too, would encourage the process of philosophizing, but unlike Gowin, I would not reject the eclecticism that results when one picks and chooses from among the many ideas and beliefs available those which best represent the synthesized conclusions of his own investigation. Obviously one's synthesized conclusions must be consistent and coherent. Ideas and beliefs have to synchronize in the integrated whole. Philosophizing about guidance raises the question of unanimity. Must all philosophies of guidance agree? This seems hardly feasible and perhaps less desirable. Since guidance serves human growth and development, it must be as broad as man. What does seem essential is that each counselor clarify,

[5] D. B. Gowin, "Prospects for Philosophic Inquiry in Guidance," *School Review* 69:191–205, Summer 1961.
[6] *Ibid.*, p. 204.
[7] *Ibid.*, p. 194.

insofar as he is able, his own philosophy of guidance and, particularly, his own philosophy of life. He must bring these into juxtaposition as a school counselor.

Four Philosophic Conceptions

Since the school counselor is responsible for building his own modus operandi, it seems fitting to present a representative grouping of philosophical systems, sufficiently varied, about which he should be knowledgeable and from which he is most apt to draw his own conclusions. Four philosophic conceptions could be considered to encompass the realm of philosophic inquiry for the school counselor: rationalism, empiricism, romanticism, and mysticism. We might think of our philosophizing as two intersecting continua, one representing the polar positions of the rationalist-empiricist, the other the romanticist-mystic.

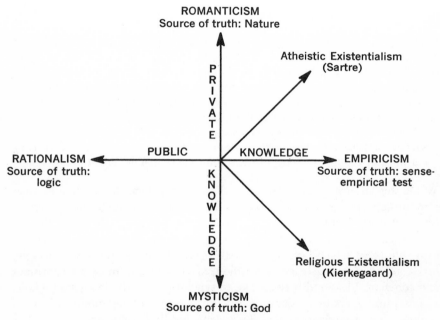

Figure 3.1.   Four Poles of Philosophic Thought

Mysticism. Mysticism finds its roots in the supernatural. The spiritual realm transcends the physical, thus the body and the mind are subservient to a supreme or supernatural power. In ancient times men were guided by superstition, the mythical, or the occult. Christianity converted this earlier supernatural paganism to a belief in God as the Supreme Being, supplanting earlier rituals with religious worship and ceremony. Mysticism is rooted in the fact that God is the source of light and truth, and intuition is the guide. It is not dependent on a depraved man—a man who is basically evil or sinful—but rather on love and understanding. In an omnipotent, forgiving God, man can find salvation and freedom provided he is willing to abide by the rules God has established. In our culture the Puritanical beliefs of work (preferably hard work), penitence, compassion, and frugality are illustrative of the values and beliefs whereby man could save his soul from the fires of Hell. Mysticism relies on the intuitive and the esoteric, although it accepts as secondary man's ability to reason. Thus man's rationality, while recognized, is conditional upon his acceptance of the spiritual and his submission to the supernatural. The inner religious aspects of mysticism and the private nature of one's own experience make it very subjective and individual. On the other hand, the regimen of organized religion has counter tendencies leaving it to the individual to balance the institutional (the church, the state) and the personal.

Romanticism. At the opposite extreme are other very private, very subjective, but different ideologies. The romantic finds his truth in the world, in nature. Romanticism embraces a positive view of man holding that man is good and capable of directing himself. Since man can discipline himself, he does not need the restraints of religion, though he is free to believe in the supernatural (to accept a religion) if he chooses to do so. One of the main differences with the Mystic philosophies is that Nature is God. The romantic tradition emphasizes the "heart," the inner feeling and experiencing of man. Thus while recognizing man's power to reason, romanticism does not yield solely to the sovereignty of reason, recognizing that man may act on intuition and feeling. Existentialism (associated with romanticism), with its origins in nineteenth-century continental Europe, is a philosophy of protest and despair. Then, as now, it was concerned with the individual— his being. The earlier European existentialists tended to be pessimistic and despairing. Existentialism comes in a number of varieties, from theistic to atheistic, depending on whether one reads Kierkegaard, Tillich, Buber, Sartre, May, or Maslow. Essentially the philosophy emphasizes one's existence ("existence precedes essence") and that a person in the course of extending out, creates his own being—his own essence. One *is*. His existence is what he makes it. Man is an individual who believes in his own being. Man assumes responsibility for those decisions and acts in which he believes. The "here and now" of life is most important; the past is remote and only influential in terms of its residue for the individual.

Empiricism. At one end of a more pragmatic continuum is empiricism, a philosophy where the search for truth is based on the rational processes but whose validation of truth is based on sensing and experiencing. Truth is in the individual experiencing, yet it is subject to public, rather than private, validation. It has a scientific orientation, though it does not rely on the application of the scientific processes. Empiricism stands in contrast to rationalism as the philosophy that emphasizes individualism yet subjects it to the test of scientific logic and consensus. In this sense, then, even though empiricism allows for individuality and stresses practicality, the individual is dominated by the sanctity of scientific purpose and social conformity.

Rationalism. Rationalism represents the superiority of the mind of man. It finds truth through logic and the sovereignty of man's reasoning. It is the scientific philosophy maintaining that the verification of truths can be obtained through the scientific method. Idealism, positivism, and other offshoots of rationalism account scientifically for the existence of natural law. Man is secondary to these natural phenomena; he is subject to their force, he cannot control them. While man can learn about his universe, he can, at best, only hope to control the social order of his environment. Only in this sense, then, can man control his own destiny. Rational philosophies use science to understand, control, and determine the future of man.

The sources of philosophic thought span the history of man. The questions concerning man's existence and his essence, of truth, and of goodness have been the subject of man's study for as long as he has existed. In all these years, hundreds of philosophic streams of thought have been introduced to represent the beliefs and the ideas that have guided man's conduct of himself and his world. Although the school counselor need not be a scholar of philosophy, he needs to engage in the philosophizing process so that he can, for himself at least, reflect more insightfully on the more basic question "What does it all mean?" And while this may not end his search for meaning and purpose, it does mark a significant point of departure for it.

SYSTEMS OF PSYCHOLOGY

Most school counselors lack an understanding of the psychological bases of guidance. This stems from two sources. First, to the degree that guidance has been conceived as essentially vocational and to the extent that the approach of Frank Parsons has been the model for secondary school guidance, an extensive background in psychology has not been necessary. Second, since most school counselors have been recruited from the ranks of classroom teaching their background in psychology has been, until recently, limited to those courses that were included in programs of teacher education, plus any that were required in the additional graduate study needed to qualify for guidance. Over the years, as counselor education programs have been inaugurated and expanded, more and more emphasis has been placed on providing exposures which will help the school counselor to better understand human growth and behavior. This is even more important in those guidance programs which will have a strong developmental emphasis.

Psychological Thought

Numerous experts have attempted to classify and to categorize the types of psychological thinking which have emerged over the years. Psychology is one of the newer of the behavioral science disciplines. It is only logical that man search for ways to envelop these ideas and to master their meaning. Thus he has involved himself in comparing and contrasting these ideas and in identifying similarities and distinguishing differences.

Paul Bruce discusses ". . . three forces or schools of influence in psychology. . . . These are associationism—particularly as represented by reinforcement (S-R) theory; Freudianism or classical psychoanalytic theory; and the third force which is relatively new and has no consistent label as yet, but goes under the names of humanistic psychology, perceptual psychology, existential psychology or neo-Freudianism"[8] Carl R. Rogers also speaks of these three forces in an associated vein. He says, "These resemble three ocean currents flowing side by side, mingling, with no clear line of demarcation, yet definitely different. Like the flotsam and jetsam which float on each ocean current, certain words and phrases identify, even though they do not define, these separate flowing trends."[9]

Each of these systems has its own identity. Each has its own conceptual strains and offshoots. It is easy to compound one's understanding of psychological thought by insisting on specific classifications to cover all the hybrid and eclectic structures. We can gain an understanding of the guidance movement and of the influence of psychological thought if we begin by examining the three major systems. Psychology has influenced the *process* or practice of guidance more than its nature or direction, as we shall see in the following characterizations.

[8] Paul Bruce, "Three Forces in Psychology and Their Ethical and Educational Implications," *The Educational Forum* 30:277, March 1966.

[9] Carl R. Rogers, "Toward a Science of the Person." In *Behaviorism and Phenomenology,* T. W. Wann (Ed.). (Chicago: The University of Chicago Press, 1964, Phoenix Edition, 1965), p. 109.

Scientific Psychology

The oldest, the classical system of psychology is represented by those systems whose explanations of human behavior rely heavily on scientific processes and experimentation.

This stream of psychological thinking is represented in education today in the application of the work of such eminent psychologists as Thorndike (connectionism), Watson (behaviorism), and Hull (reinforcement). These conceptions are essentially early twentieth century, evolving from objective, quantitative laboratory studies of experimental psychology. Many of the assumptions which undergird the scientific psychologies are related to a view that equates man with animal and subjects him to similar laws of learning. Man's responses can be conditioned. He is a creature of habit. Man adjusts to his environment. Learning is mechanistic, utilizing repetition and reward (or punishment). Building on the work of these early theorists, their modern day counterparts, who might be called neobehaviorists, such as B. F. Skinner, emphasize the concepts of conditioning and reinforcement. Human responses grow out of the primary needs or drives of man and these are essentially biological. Man develops his higher level thought processes in relation to his earlier conditioning and behaviors. Thus, for example, in the operant conditioning of Skinner, man can be conditioned to behave (that is, to respond) according to predetermined, fixed standards. The modern day efforts of the neobehaviorists have implications not only for counseling and the teaching-learning process but for social engineering and social melioration as well.

The highly scientific, objective, external orientation of behavioristic psychology, utilizing such concepts as stimulus-response theory and the ideas of reinforcement, association, and conditioning, have been readily applied to the educative process. Thus man, as a higher order animal with reasoning capacities, can be taught (and trained) to behave in certain ways. Much of the teaching-learning process in the schools today flows directly from these beliefs. The vocational guidance model of Frank Parsons, as we have seen, was rooted to a rational view of man and much of the Parsonian process was geared to the counselee's learning.

The scientific psychologies, while emphasizing the external or the behavioral, do not deny the internal of man. But the inner man, his feeling, his striving and desiring, and his perception of himself in his many life situations are considered less significant and, therefore, are rarely accounted for in the learning process. Most important are the behavioral manifestations of an individual's experiencing. These are controlled by the stimulus situations or by prior conditioning. Validation, therefore, depends on external means. If one purports to be jolly, then this can be verified by observing the appropriate behaviors. The behaviorist finds it difficult to deal with the subjective, inner world of the person primarily because this inner self cannot be readily described nor can it, therefore, be easily reinforced. Thus within the operating principles of the various behavioristic theories there is an acknowledgment of the internal—the inner self of man—but little attendance to it.

Psychoanalytic Psychology

Psychoanalytic psychology, founded and fathered by Sigmund Freud, originated in Europe in the latter part of the nineteenth century. Freud's ideas, as these were formulated in the psychoanalytic approach to human behavior, were introduced in the United States in the first quarter of the twentieth century where they have been applied to educational practice. Psychoanalytic psychology, consisting of Freudian and neoFreudian conceptualizations, became very popular in the 1920s and 1930s. Developing from a quite different base, it quickly challenged some of the existing notions about the development and behavior of man.

Freud's view of man was essentially classical or tragic. He believed that man has two basic instinctual drives—aggressive and libidinal. These often are in conflict with his environment, necessitating compromise. Maintaining the balance between one's basic desires and realities is essential to one's mental health. The psyche, consisting of the id, the ego, and the superego, represents the center of the compromising process. The id (the unconscious) is the source of the instinctual and irrational in man. The ego (the conscious) is the repository of learned experiences and the center of man's reasoning capabilities. The superego (the social conscious) is the mediator between the id and the ego. Man's behavior is often founded in his unconscious. Psychoanalytic psychology, therefore, utilizes the recall of early childhood experiences, emphasizing the cause of man's current behavioral problems in his past history. The process of "free association" which has been so pictorially popularized, showing the relaxed patient describing his childhood years while the psychoanalyst listens, serves as the vehicle of recall while the therapist, as the interpreter, helps the patient to recognize (consciously) the source of his mental problem (insight).

Some of the more contemporary interpretations of Freudian psychology have minimized or discounted the libidinal urges and have established social learnings or environmental experiencing as fundamental sources of human difficulty. Karen Horney, for example, has developed the concept of basic anxiety induced by social pressures which is manifested in "neurotic needs." Harry Stack Sullivan reorganized the psyche posing a more holistic construct of the self.

Freudian ideas and beliefs have become established in educational practice though their application has been quite different. Scientific psychology has influenced directly the methods and materials of the teaching-learning process, while the psychoanalytic psychologies have contributed more to the interpretation of teaching and learning behaviors. In this way they have helped to bring to the educative process an emphasis on the internal aspects of man and his learning which the classical psychologies failed to provide. Further, the therapeutic applications of psychoanalysis have been readily, but not easily, transferred to the identification, assessment and remediation of pupils with personality disorders or, to a lesser extent, with learning difficulties. We might generalize by indicating that classical psychologies have been applied mainly in the instructional areas of education, while psychoanalytic psychologies have contributed to the pupil personnel services. In another way, and one that we shall be examining in greater detail throughout the remaining chapters, the contribution or impact of psychoanalytic psychology on education is related to the nature of the communication between members of the instructional and pupil personnel staff of a school.

Phenomenological-Self-Existential Psychology

The "third force" psychology is the newest and the most difficult of the three to define. Yet it is not so difficult to characterize. It is represented by several newer psychologies that stress what man is, his *being* (in the present) and what he is *becoming* (in the future). This combination of forces, this conglomerate of self, existential, and phenomenological psychologies, emphasizes the individual and the inner world of his feelings and perceptions.

Borrowing from the ideas of other earlier psychologists, Snygg and Combs develop a phenomenological point of view in *Individual Behavior: A Perceptual Approach to Behavior.*[10] Phenomenology has grown side by side with self psychology, another elusive appellation covering a range of beliefs. Both systems focus on the individual. Both are concerned with the person and his experiencing—assigning these the highest priority. The reactive, deterministic aspects of scientific psychology have been transposed, giving man a very active role in the determination of his self and his behavior. It emphasizes the growth potential of the individual—the inner forces and resources which, when activated and used, can help man to achieve all that he is capable of (self-actualization). While other psychologies emphasize cause and effect behavior (capitalizing on the past), the third force psychologies utilize the self concept and self-perceptions in the here and now,

---

[10] Donald Snygg and Arthur W. Combs, *Individual Behavior: A Perceptual Approach to Behavior* (New York: Harper, 1949).

the present. Man's being and his becoming are the focus of his experience.

These psychologies affirm man. They are rooted in a positive view of man that subscribes to his essential goodness. They attest to the capacity of man to assume responsibility for his growing, his self-actualizing, and his so-cializing behaviors. The beliefs hinge on what man *is* and on his growth toward a maturity that utilizes, maximally, all his inner resources in realiz-ing his fullest potential. The third force conglomerates rely heavily on the inner facets of man's existence—his needs, attitudes, feelings, values, and the very subjective and complex nature of their internal interaction as they influence and determine individual behavior.

More recently, advocates of humanistic psychology have initiated ac-tivities that are designed to facilitate human awareness and interpersonal relationships. Encounter groups and sensitivity experiences are examples of the growing number of programs that are offered to enhance the self and in-crease self-awareness. In the last few years there has been a marked increase in the establishment of human growth centers to sponsor these programs.

In many ways, the views of the self-existential-phenomenological psy-chologies are in direct contrast to those of the more scientific variety. These newer psychologies, with their emphasis on the inner aspects of man, have been challenged by the older, more established beliefs. Despite the rather rapid adoption of these views, their position in the family of psychological thought is neither a firm nor wholly accepted one.

Its precarious position was noted by Matson in his Presidential Address in August 1969. At that time he reported the following to the membership of the American Association of Humanistic Psychology,

And because of our tolerance of the nonverbal and nonrational, because of our receptivity to sensory experience and our sponsorship of the affective world, I am sure the AAHP has seemed to many people to have become a haven for the *ir*rational and the *anti*-intellectual—for all that is exotic, erotic, and psy-chotic. . . .

But if this image of us is indeed illusory, we had better take a sharp look at, and get a firm grip on, our real and authentic self. We had better work to redress the balance; or, rather, to strike a new balance. It may be that we shall want to add some new repudiations and oppositions to the old list of things we can do without. It may be that we shall wish to draw the line on our total hos-pitality toward all the causes and characters that come knocking at our open door.[11]

The impact of these self psychologies on educational practice, includ-ing guidance, is just beginning to be felt. While its influence has been dif-

[11] Floyd W. Matson in his Presidential Address, "Whatever Became of the Third Force?" Delivered to the Membership Meeting, American Association for Humanis-tic Psychology, August 29, 1969.

fused among all levels of education, its immediate relevance to the practice and processes of guidance has resulted in many adaptations of these beliefs in programs of guidance and counseling. In many schools the initial exposure to third force psychology has stemmed from the efforts of the school counselor. Perhaps its most dynamic application has resulted from the theoretical views of Carl Rogers as he promulgated them in his client-centered therapy. Although many of his views were essentially incorporated in what inappropriately was termed "non-directive" counseling, recent applications have been more sophisticated and representative of his beliefs. Two very recent programs, *Self-Enhancing Education* (a program to motivate learners) and the *Human Development Program* (a program for promoting self-awareness, self-confidence, and social interaction in young children), are being promoted in the elementary schools. These programs draw extensively on the ideas, beliefs, and practice of humanistic psychology. They hold promise for influencing the teaching-learning process and for shaping new approaches to human awareness and communication.

While ways of believing can and do change, and while new ideas can be and are introduced, it is difficult to alter, even slightly sometimes, existing ways of doing things. In education, unfortunately, this is far too often the case. Thus we find people who really do not believe in what they are doing (very often because they do not understand its basis) engaged in a practice or activity neither theoretically suitable or practically sound. The school counselor who is well prepared will understand the premises of existing practice and thus be able to spot inconsistencies and discrepancies in translating theory to practice.

THE ADOLESCENT YEARS

In the following sections, I have attempted to highlight several aspects of human development that are crucial in a program of developmental guidance for the adolescent. These selections represent my own biases and oversights. On the other hand, it seems necessary to come to grips with each of these in establishing and augmenting a developmental guidance program. Certainly, every school counselor should have an understanding of the various prominent theories of adolescence and their contributions to guidance in the secondary schools.

Adolescence Defined

Adolescence is most often defined as the years of growth between childhood and adulthood. We can think of adolescence as extending from around age twelve or thirteen to twenty-one or twenty-two. Some authorities establish the beginning of the adolescent years with the onset of puberty; others have characterized the transitional years of adolescence more broadly including the years prior to puberty (early adolescence) as well as those extending into the twenties (young adult). Some look upon adolescence as a developmental process emphasizing the physiological-psychological aspects of human growth; others have chosen to emphasize the sociological. The conceptual differences that one encounters in various theories of adolescence are usually differences of degree and emphases concerning those factors that influence the growth of the adolescent toward maturity. Adolescence is the business of the developmental counselor, and his growing and learning is the core of the counselor's existence. It is because of our concern for his growth and development, coupled with our responsibility for his education, that we need to consider all possible factors that may influence the nature and the direction of his motivation.

Adolescence and Maturation

Using a developmental frame of reference, Arnold Gesell and his associates Ilg and Ames[12] have formulated a most comprehensive description of human growth and development. They describe the adolescent patterns and stages of growth in their book *Youth: The Years from Ten to Sixteen.*[13] While they believe that every child is unique and has his own individual pattern of growth, they describe the growth process in a series of year by year profiles and traits that can be anticipated at each stage and age of human development.

Central to Gesell's delineation of the pattern and processes of human development are his concepts of *maturation* and *acculturation*. Maturation is essentially an innate process based on the genetic endowment of the individual. In this sense, then, maturation is fixed and sequential with the maturation of the individual basically determined by his individual readiness to progress through a patterned cycle of growth. On the other hand, the development of the individual is influenced by his environment and the learning and experiencing that it provides. His sequencing of the growth patterns into the "gradients of growth" allows for the environmental and individual experience factors. He terms these influences *acculturation*.

[12] Much of Gesell's writing in his later years was co-authored with his two best-known associates, Frances L. Ilg and Louise B. Ames. While I shall refer to Gesell, whose ideas I am discussing, it is necessary to note the actual contributions of his colleagues who worked many years with him and who have been carrying on his work at the Institute since his death.

[13] Arnold Gesell, Frances Ilg, and Louise Ames, *Youth: The Years from Ten to Sixteen* (New York: Harper & Row, 1956).

Human maturation is characterized by Gesell as a gradual, sequential, on-going, orderly, patterned process. Yet, within this process, one must take into account the *environment* and *individuality* of each human being. The behavioral manifestations of one's growth toward maturity, while keyed to the developmental aspects of the process, are subject to gradation and variance. There is, even within the patterned sequence, some overlap, regression, and vacillation. Yet, the trends toward maturity and the "general ground plan" of each individual can be a useful guide to the characterization and assessment of individual maturation.

Adolescence and Self Identity

Erikson proposes a concept of human development that concentrates on the gradual emergence of an ego identity. Ego identity, according to Erikson, is a complex developmental process in which the individual deals both with *himself* and his *environment*. He speaks to this interaction as follows:

. . . in psychological terms, identity formation employs a process of simultaneous reflection and observation, a process taking place on all levels of mental functioning, by which the individual judges himself in the light of what he perceives to be the way in which others judge him in comparison to themselves and to a typology significant to them; while he judges their way of judging him in the light of how he perceives himself in comparison to them and to types that have become relevant to him.[14]

This interactive process, then, can be viewed in terms of the discoveries and differentiations that individuals experience in the process of forming their own identity. These psychological and social forces are in constant interaction throughout the life cycle.

Erikson's formulation of ego identity is not a theory of adolescence but more a conceptualization and characterization of the psychosexual development of man. Yet, it concentrates on the highly integrative and configurative aspects of these years of youth. His description of the eight stages of man represents what he considers to be the successive points of crisis in identity formation. The identity process begins at birth and extends well into the adult years.

The period of adolescence is critical and demanding and it is little wonder that we often refer to this period of human growth as "the turbulent years." Adolescence makes critical demands on the ego. Erikson speaks to the demands of this period:

[14] Erik H. Erikson, *Identity: Youth and Crisis* (New York: W. W. Norton and Company, Inc., 1968), pp. 22–23.

It is the ego's function to integrate the psychosexual and psychosocial aspects on a given level of development and at the same time to integrate the relation of newly added identity elements with those already in existence—that is, to bridge the inescapable discontinuities between different levels of personality development. For earlier crystallizations of identity can become subject to renewed conflict when changes in the quality and quantity of drive, expansions in mental equipment, and new and often conflicting social demands all make previous adjustments appear insufficient and, in fact, make previous opportunities and rewards suspect.[15]

The school cannot afford to overlook its vital and significant role in the psychosocial development of the individual. It is an important part of the adolescent's world and a significant source for helping the individual to cope with the conflicts and discontinuities of his life as these are so evident in the stress and strain of normal ego development. The developmental guidance program seeks to deal directly with these concerns of self-identity. It wants to provide the means whereby the adolescent can be assisted in the sifting and sorting of ideas and the weighing of experiences as he attempts to make the differentiations that help him to gain a better sense of who he is and where he is. Perhaps most of all, the psychosocial aspects of human development, as we are coming to understand these through the efforts of Erikson and others, provide us with a needed base for tapping more directly the inner resources of our students and for "tuning in" more frequently and more humanly on the state of their inner being. It may help us to achieve a more human balance, developmentally, between the "here and now" of identity formation and the "planning for the future" which has characterized so much of our guidance practice to date.

Adolescence and Mental Growth

I have chosen to incorporate the views of Piaget primarily because of his emphasis on the cognitive development of the child. Intellectual growth and development are at the core of Piaget's concepts. His theory, more than the others, concentrates on the growth of the mental processes in the human and their relation to other aspects of human growth. Piaget describes the development of the child in four periods: (1) the sensori-motor (from birth to approximately 2 years); (2) the preoperational period, including two phases which he calls the preconceptual and the intuitive (covering roughly the years from 2 until 7); (3) the concrete operations (from 7 to 11); and the formal operations (from 11 to 15 years and beyond). Students may

[15] *Ibid.*, p. 162.

wish to examine the characteristics of these periods in considerable detail. Briefly, these periods can be described as follows.

The sensori-motor period. During this period the child develops his basic reflexes and responses, some of which are innate, others acquired. His responses increasingly indicate discrimination and adaptation. Gradually he acquires responses that are gratifying, and these become regular, habitual responses. His movements become better coordinated, more variant, and experimental. His activity indicates an ability to relate and coordinate responses and reactions and form the basis for the other exploratory behaviors.

The preoperational period. In the preoperational period, as the sensori-motor skills are being further developed and adapted, the child begins to establish a mental repertoire consisting of perceptual and symbolic processes that constitute the beginning of conceptual thinking. While the child remains basically dependent on his perceptions of his world, relying mainly on his sensory experiences, he becomes less egocentric and more social. Although he can deal with only one object or idea at a time, he is able to establish concepts even though they are not necessarily coherent or consistent and are not integrated in any organized way.

Concrete operations. This period represents the growth and integration of the cognitive processes. The child begins to utilize a variety of mental processes involving classification, ordering, and seriation whereby the child can deal logically with concrete situations and experiences. While he cannot abstract, he is able to deal with several perceptions at a time and to relate and to manipulate these in a concrete way.

Formal operations. The period of formal operations represents the development of the higher thought processes such as hypothesizing, generalizing, and summarizing. In particular the individual develops the ability to engage in abstract thinking, allowing him to think symbolically. He is able to combine and to integrate ideas and to engage in thinking processes that engage both inductive and deductive reasoning. The child can now manipulate a variety of situational variables into combinations and permutations that allow him to engage in more complex problem solving or decision making ventures. This may be considered to culminate in intellectual maturity, leaving the individual to expand and to utilize his mental processes in ways that will enhance his own life and world.

The cognitive development of the child begins with what Piaget calls *adaptation*—the process whereby the individual seeks balance or equilibrium between himself and his environment. This involves *assimilation* and *ac-*

commodation, which are defined by Baldwin as follows: ". . . assimilation describes the capability of the organism to handle new situations and new problems with its present stock of mechanisms; accommodation describes the process of change through which the organism becomes able to manage situations that are at first too difficult for it."[16] This process is central to the development of the individual and focuses on a more encompassing process which Piaget calls *equilibration.* According to Baldwin,

> . . . Piaget assumes that the individual gradually acquires some of the elements of the operational system, perhaps through social learning or experience with the environment. At some point these unorganized ideas or beliefs produce a conflict, however. An unorganized system is not adaptive and leads to conflict and self-contradiction. . . .
>
> Because these unorganized belief systems do contain inherent self-contradictions and conflict, force is set up to harmonize the child's ideas one with another. This is process of equilibration. As a result of equilibration the child, independent of any further experience, tends to reorganize his beliefs into a coherent, harmonious, and equilibrated system."[17]

Piaget's theory recognizes both reason (the intellect) and emotion (feeling) even though his formulations seem to emphasize the mental process. While it may be more inferential than real, one must assume that the environment includes more than the physical, that is, the social, the philosophical, and the psychological. The self, which Piaget views in the holistic sense, includes man's inner resources and feelings as motivators of action. Thus the affective nature of man is a part of his striving, his desiring, his feeling and is, in his totality, a significant part of his behavior. One has to assume that the adaptation process (including both assimilation and accommodation) and the process of equilibration, draw heavily on the *affect* of man. While Piaget accepts the feeling part of man, he waits for man to operate cognitively on his feelings and in this sense he depends on the conscious and aware man to deal with his being in his environment.

Piaget helps us to understand better the facets of mental growth and the nature of thinking and learning in the maturation process. He leads us to think about the nature of developmental guidance as a contributing force in the day-to-day learning and experiencing of students. Piaget's conceptions suggest the involvement of the developmental counselor in the teaching-learning process. They demand that he consider more carefully than ever the combinational effect of human learning and human maturation.

[16] Alfred L. Baldwin, *Theories of Child Development* (New York: John Wiley, 1967), p. 176.
[17] *Ibid.,* p. 296.

THE CASE FOR A DEVELOPMENTAL
APPROACH TO GUIDANCE

Our knowledge of human development has expanded greatly in the last few decades. The many theories and conceptualizations of human growth, while at times causing confusion and controversy, do, in fact, contribute to consumer use and application of theory. It is when we assume a wait and see posture that we allow the times to pass us by and cause young people to suffer for our lack of courage in applying new ideas to educational practice. Education in particular, whether individuals in education choose to recognize it or not, has great need to use and apply this knowledge. Despite differences that do exist in the psychological and philosophical views undergirding the guidance function in education, certain considerations seem to have substantial basis to merit reflection and application.

The combination of affect and reason as these merge and emerge in the growing, developing human are important. Most theories of human development account for both man's thinking and feeling. Most views accept the influence of the cultural, the environmental. Thus man the organism and his environment have been welded in a manner that causes us to be concerned with both internal and external, with both the objective and subjective factors of his existence. The mutuality of reason and emotion need to be considered with reference to their composite combination as well as their interactional effect on the individual.

The whole idea of adjustment and the functions of the school that refer and cater to the adjustment of the individual have their roots largely in how educators view youth's struggle for maturity and stability. Inherent in most of the theories of human development is the notion of how man deals with himself and his environment and the compromising aspects of his behavior in striving toward maturity and adulthood. The philosophical questions concerning the nature of man—individuality, personal autonomy, freedom, responsibility, conformity—are all related to how one eventually constructs his own ideas and beliefs about human development.

For guidance in particular two very vital issues come to the fore. First, the traditional "adjustive" function must be reexamined with reference to its purpose and nature. We need to examine our ideas about student adjustment and the processes we are employing in helping young people to deal with the conflict and the ambiguity of their own existence. Current theories of human development emphasize the highly individual and complex nature of human maturation. Helping the adolescent maintain personal and social balance in the face of the conflict, ambiguity, and uncertainty surrounding him and his experiences is indeed a challenge to the educative process and to a program of developmental guidance. In recognizing some of these conceptions about the process of human maturation we are afforded a quite different approach to student adjustment—a developmental one. All students are served in such a program, and the program emphasizes efforts to accommodate the developing nature and needs of adolescent youth. Student adjustment in the form of remedial or corrective efforts remains essential in the school program, although the emphasis on (and the implementation of) these adjustive efforts may be quite different.

Adolescence is viewed by many as transitional years when many of the problems and concerns of adaptation and identification are most keenly felt and experienced. While theorists vary in their description of the stress which the adolescent experiences (normatively speaking), there is wide agreement that these are the crucial years in the maturation process. Thus the extent to which education, that is, learning, contributes to the development of the individual and his growth toward maturity becomes of prime importance. Professional incompetency, whether in teaching, administering, or pupil service, can only inhibit and hurt. Activities, programs, and services must be formulated and conducted to enhance this growth.

Individual growth and development can be characterized by the idiosyncratic nature of *differentiation*. Internalization, the process whereby one integrates something he has learned or experienced as his own, results in an individual uniqueness of differentiation. Any one internalized idea or percept can be in and of itself unique. When it is integrated with other internalized learnings, the chances of individual uniqueness are magnified. In some way the educative process will have to come to recognize and to provide for the uniqueness of the growing individual. To do less is to ignore the developmental character of human growth and to treat maturation on a mass production basis.

SUGGESTED READING

ALLPORT, GORDON W., "Psychological Models for Guidance," *Harvard Educational Review* 32:373–381, Fall 1962.

BALDWIN, ALFRED L., *Theories of Child Development* (New York: John Wiley, 1967).

ERIKSON, ERIK H., *Identity: Youth and Crisis* (New York: W. W. Norton and Company, Inc., 1968).

HITT, WILLIAM D., "Two Models of Man," *American Psychologist* 24:651–658, July 1969.

KARIER, CLARENCE J., *Man, Society and Education* (Glenview, Ill.: Scott Foresman, 1967).

MAIER, HENRY W., *Three Theories of Child Development* (New York: Harper & Row, 1965).

MUUSS, ROLF E., *Theories of Adolescence* (New York: Random House, 1962).

WRENN, C. GILBERT, "Philosophical and Psychological Bases of Personnel Services in Education." In *Personnel Services in Education*, Nelson B. Henry (Ed.), The Fifty-eighth Yearbook of the National Society for the Study of Education, Part II (Chicago: The University of Chicago Press, 1959).

FOUR

THE EDUCATIVE PROCESS:

PERSPECTIVES AND PROSPECTS

Education is the business of the school and learning is the core of education. It is, or should be, the hub of all that occurs within the school. The process of learning involves the tripartite considerations of (1) the behaviors to be learned; (2) the learner, in this case the secondary school student, and his ability to cope with the learning tasks established for him; and (3) the conditions of his learning, that is, the school and the personnel who will create the learning environment and establish the climate in which the learning process occurs.

Contributing to the establishment of the *behaviors to be learned* are the general objectives of education and the more specific educational goals as represented by the various desired or intended outcomes in the cognitive, affective, and psychomotor domains of human learning. These provide direction to the learning process. These directions are implemented through the establishment of an instructional program. There are distinguishing features and characteristics of instruction which can be used as guides in establishing the pattern and sequence of the learning sequence. The instructional program may be viewed as normative and prescriptive since it is developed to identify the most effective routes to learning. It is concerned with identification of basic concepts and principles in any area of learning that will lead the learner to discover other meanings and relationships.

The *learner,* the secondary school student, is the object of these planned learnings. His educational experiences must take into consideration the physical, intellectual, social, emotional, and vocational aspects of his growth and development. Some attention should be directed to the nature of his past experiences and achievements, his present plans and performance, and any future goals he may have established for himself. Consideration must be given to the types of experiences with which the normal child can deal effectively in the various stages of his development, and, of equal importance, to his own reaction to these experiences. The learner, then, must be viewed not only in terms of his uniqueness but in terms of his wholeness. Any phase of his development or any facet of his behavior must be considered in relation to his total pattern and life style as they affect his needs, his values, and his internal well-being, as well as his external behavior and progress in the various work settings of the school.

The *conditions of learning* reflect, essentially, the manner in which the behaviors to be learned (the instructional program) and the learner (the secondary school student), and all that these entail, are combined. In bringing these together, many things occur. The tenor of learning situations, the environment of the school, and the psychological atmosphere of the classroom should be considered vital elements of the learning process. The influence of teacher behavior and classroom social interaction are illustrative of other factors affecting the learning environment. The school, the setting of the educational experience, can be considered as a network of social relationships comprising a social system as intricate as any within society. The phenomenon of the school as an institution, as an organization of individuals, must be recognized and understood. Teaching-learning occurs within this social milieu. In viewing instruction, teaching, and learning, it is important to consider the effect of the system on the individual and on group role and function, and the net effect of these on the atmosphere of the school and classroom.

HUMAN LEARNING AS AN INNER PROCESS

Human learning is more than the accumulation of knowledge to be stored in the human mind and regurgitated. It is more than the mastery of a skill to be repeated. Human learning may be considered an inner process in which the individual assimilates his experiences, internalizing his learnings in a fashion which takes on meaning for him. Gradually, and over a period of time, each individual integrates these internalized learnings into a pattern significant to himself and useful to him in dealing with life situations. Through a combination of the cognitive, the affective, and the psychomotor components of learning, the individual establishes a self-identity and the ability to interrelate and regulate the self and the self-in-situation. This is human behavior—the result of human learning.

The Classification of Educational Objectives

Education is concerned with human behavior. It has established goals or objectives designed to influence and affect the direction and meaning of human existence. These are (1) self-realization, (2) human relationship, (3) economic efficiency, and (4) civic responsibility.[1] These are not necessarily discrete goals for education. There is some commonality in all of these objectives. One such commonality is the development of the individual's ability to think.

The Taxonomy of Educational Objectives, Handbook I: Cognitive Domain[2] and *Handbook II: Affective Domain*[3] offer assistance to educators at all levels in providing a classification of educational goals. With the help of the *Taxonomy,* they can clarify and refine specific instructional objectives. This is *not* an easy task, but it does make it possible to plan and organize learning experiences specifically designed to give direction to the learning process and to provide for the consequences of the learning experience through anticipated or expected behavioral outcomes.

The *cognitive* domain deals with educational objectives that are concerned with processes of assimilating and using knowledge and is concerned with the development of the intellect. The *affective* domain focuses on the development of objectives that are associated with the formation of values and attitudes and deals with the awareness and internalization aspects of beliefs and values. The third domain, the *psychomotor,* is concerned with the development of muscular, motor, and manipulative skills. At present, there is no publication to detail the elements of objectives in the psychomotor domain.

Figure 4.1 attempts to show the interrelationship between the objectives of education and those three basic considerations essential to the teaching-learning process. The instructional program as it deals with cognitive, affective, and psychomotor learnings serves as the connecting link, providing direction and focus to the learning process.

Instruction-Teaching-Learning

The implementation of educational objectives remains with that complex triumvirate—instruction, teaching, and learning. As a coalition they are

[1] Educational Policies Commission, *The Purposes of Education in American Democracy* (Washington, D.C.: National Education Association, 1938).

[2] Benjamin S. Bloom (Ed.), *Taxonomy of Educational Objectives, Handbook I: Cognitive Domain* (New York: David McKay, 1956).

[3] David R. Krathwohl, Benjamin S. Bloom, and Bertram B. Masia, *Taxonomy of Educational Objectives, Handbook II: Affective Domain* (New York: David McKay, 1964).

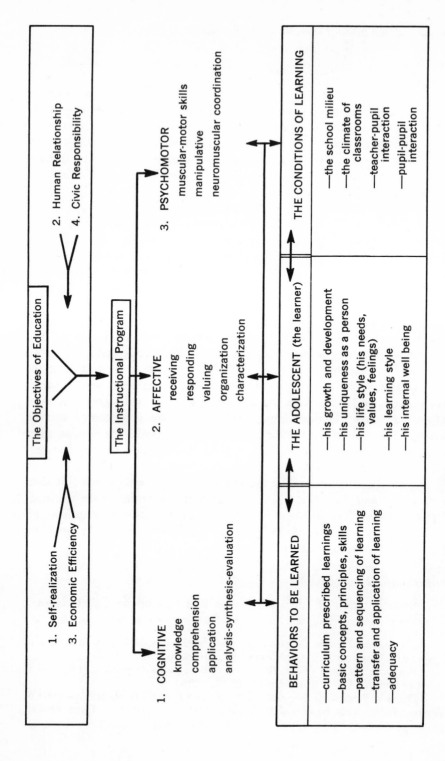

Figure 4.1. The teaching-learning process in the secondary school

difficult concepts with which to deal; their differentiation and their reciprocity have been debated for some time. It is not the intention here to identify minutely the distinguishing features of any one or all of these concepts; their relationship is obvious. In differentiating between instruction, teaching, and learning it would appear that one might distinguish them on the basis of their relationship to the *process* of education or human learning.

Instruction might be characterized as the systematic, planned, intended aspects of the process and, therefore, would be concerned mainly with the content, form, and order of learning experiences. Thus instruction would involve the selection of the educational objectives to be achieved and the direction, structure, arrangement, and sequencing of the instructional activities to attain the desired behavioral outcomes. Instruction may attempt to pass on the heritage but it should not impose it. It may encourage the spirit of tradition but it should not resist change. Insofar as it does not impose specific behaviors on the learner it cultivates individualism. Insofar as it does not resist change it encourages creativity and promotes curiosity. Insofar as it is concerned with the development of individuals it provides for both conformity and nonconformity. To the extent that it is able to provide for a variety of individual behaviors, it fosters change.

Teaching engages the learner in the process of education. It involves the execution of those activities that will produce the intended or desired behavioral outcomes. It is concerned primarily with the rate, transfer, and adequacy of the learning experiences. It involves providing the conditions, situations, and activities for the learner, adjusting the pacing and sequencing of the learning experiences, aiding the learner in transfer manipulations leading to the application of learning in new ways and in other forms, and assisting the learner to explore and test the adequacy of his learning. Teaching is not shaping, directing, or controlling, but rather leading, exploring, and discovering. Teaching, then, is an activity that should be dynamic and personalized, not rote and mechanized. Teaching not only encourages creativity and promotes curiosity; it actualizes these by providing opportunities for spontaneous pupil exploration, by creating challenging tasks, and by encouraging individuality. Teaching is that activity whereby the cognitive, affective, and psychomotor components of human learning can be developed and integrated so that the learner can piece together his self-identity and the meaning of his existence.

To the extent that learning is expressed in behavior, it is possible to define *learning* as the product of instruction and teaching. Yet not all learning is planned; learning may result from unplanned experiences both in and peripheral to the school and classroom. It may occur, as well, from the combination of planned and unplanned experiences, the resultant behaviors being neither intended nor anticipated. Human learning seems to be a personal and dynamic phenomenon in which the *process* rather than the product, or goal, is the essence of the experience. The continuing nature of learning, the increasing complexity of personal meanings, and the many and varied transfer manipulations are evidence of the highly individual, dynamic character of learning.

Learning, then, seems to be characterized by an ever-changing warehouse of personal perceptions and meanings that are constantly being restructured. As new relationships are established, shifts or changes in behavior are noted. The adequacy of any learning is constantly under individual surveillance and its longevity as a guidepost to human behavior is subject to its relative position and priority in the individual's inner learning hierarchy. Recent accelerated efforts to examine and separate these three concepts are causing those concerned with education to investigate their nature and characteristics and their relationship to the whole process of education. Learning theory has, to a large degree, dictated the direction of teaching and instruction. Much of this theory has not been concerned with human learning, and little investigation of or experimentation with the processes of human learning has been undertaken in the school. There is a growing interest in developing theories of instruction and teaching; there is an increasing awareness of human learning as an inner process.

Planning and developing the instructional program, the teaching process and the directions of pupil learning involve the understanding, efforts, and considerations of many different people. Very often the program is imposed upon the school through required courses of study, exacting syllabus materials, or by measuring instruments (standardized examinations) that tend to limit the diversity and creativity that might otherwise occur. That this does frequently happen is unfortunate; however, despite these restrictions and outside prescriptions, there are many possibilities for the application of new research and for educational innovation in the classrooms of our schools. The developmental counselor, with his knowledge and understanding of human learning as an inner process and the relationship of this process to instruction and teaching, can assist greatly in enhancing the school's ability to provide more dynamic and worthwhile learning experiences. He can assist school personnel in understanding, interpreting, and using the normal learning variants to improve and extend the learning activity of the school.

The Concept of Variant and Deviant Learning

Education is not a stable, static process: Although education is normatively based, the resultant learnings are not routinely normal. Education should be a dynamic, growing, changing process; resultant learnings should vary widely, should lead the learner in many directions, not just one, and should allow for individual rather than conforming behaviors.

The combination of broadly stated educational objectives and the classification of educational goals into the cognitive, affective, and psychomotor domains provide sufficient direction for the learning process. From these statements it is possible to deduce the desired or intended behaviors that will result from the learning experiences planned for boys and girls. It is neither possible nor desirable to control completely the inner manner in which the learner will assimilate, internalize, and integrate his learnings. It is not possible to foresee the inner meaning that various learning experiences will have for any learner. It is not possible to predict the combinations of manipulations the learner will employ in converting, interrelating, or transferring his learnings to other tasks and other situations. These individual internalizations, meanings, and combinations of transfer manipulations, the inner process of human learning, constitute the *learning variants* of the learning process. The learner can only be directed to those learning experiences which are felt to be most helpful to him as an individual and to the society in which he will live.

It is obvious that there are many opportunities to plan and provide for improved learning experiences for young people. It is equally evident that not all these learnings will unfold or develop consistently, uniformly, or regularly for all pupils. The school should be prepared to deal with a host of normal learning differences and with a variety of normal learning irregularities—the normal learning variants. These variants of learning are normal, everyday occurrences; they stem from the human aspects of learning, from the human aspects of teaching.

It is with these normal learning variants in the educative process that the developmental school counselor is concerned. He is concerned that these combinations of learner manipulations be directed toward helping the individual assimilate and internalize learnings that contribute to the fulfillment of the objectives or goals of education and enhance, rather than hinder, the individual's ability to deal with various elements of the instructional program. He is concerned that the act of teaching account for these individual learning variants and that it provide situations that will foster or create learning episodes necessary to the more effective individualization of instruction. He is concerned with the influence of the school and classroom environment on individual learning and with the interpretation of these environmental conditions. He is concerned with the learning of youth and the conditions in which the learning process occurs. He is concerned with the behavioral outcomes of learning, particularly as these contribute to the ability of the learner to gain self and social identity and to deal with self-in-situation. He is concerned with these variants of learning and their behavioral

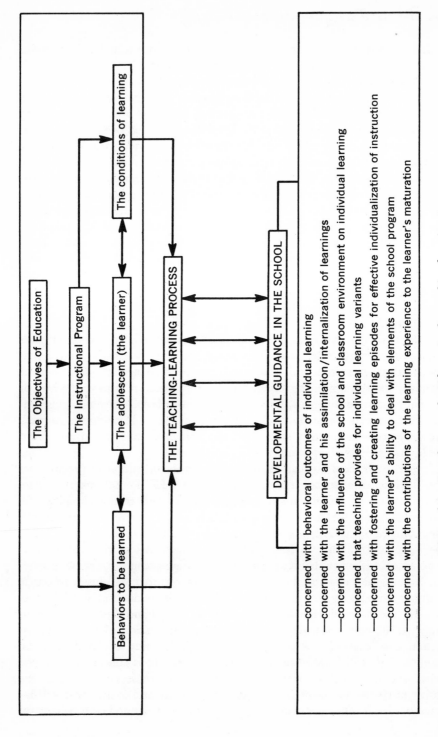

The Objectives of Education

The Instructional Program

The conditions of learning

The adolescent (the learner)

Behaviors to be learned

THE TEACHING-LEARNING PROCESS

DEVELOPMENTAL GUIDANCE IN THE SCHOOL

—concerned with behavioral outcomes of individual learning
—concerned with the learner and his assimilation/internalization of learnings
—concerned with the influence of the school and classroom environment on individual learning
—concerned that teaching provides for individual learning variants
—concerned with fostering and creating learning episodes for effective individualization of instruction
—concerned with the learner's ability to deal with elements of the school program
—concerned with the contributions of the learning experience to the learner's maturation

Figure 4.2. Developmental guidance in the teaching-learning process

manifestations, as well as their inner meaning for the individual. Figure 4.2 indicates the relationship of developmental guidance in the secondary school to the teaching-learning process.

The concept of normal learning variants has implications for many aspects of the total school milieu. It has meaning for the construction of the curriculum; the general learning environment of the school; the individual teacher's classroom climate; the instructional methods employed; the type and variety of teaching styles permitted; faculty understanding of the internalization process; and recognition of the interrelationships among cognitive, affective, and psychomotor objectives. These matters, as they are related to the individuality of the learner and the uniqueness of his learning style, form the basis for the facilitative-developmental aspects of the school guidance role.

At the opposite extreme are the *learning deviants*. These are the students with learning difficulties or learning disorders of a deviant nature. Such learning problems usually originate in the individual's physical, social, intellectual, emotional or vocational development or from environmental sources associated with the community, the home or the school. Very often, in fact with more frequency than educators care to admit, the sources of deviant learning can be attributed to such causes as poor teaching, an inadequate classroom climate, lack of student motivation, teacher domination, unrealistic instructional goals, pupil rejection, or teacher inability to provide for individual pupil needs. Most frequently, deviant learning results from a combination of individual and environmental factors. Ofttimes, learning difficulties are associated with the individual's physical or maturational development. Sometimes learning disruptions are due to emotional stresses such as anxiety, fear, or guilt. Whatever the causes or factors related to deviant learning, such disorders do exist. Difficulties in all subject areas are common—perhaps too common. Certainly, underachievement, inability to read, dislike of school, psychological disturbances, and social immaturity are typical of pupil attitudinal-behavioral malfunctions associated with ineffective learning.

The school, having recognized the growing numbers of such learning deviants and the need to provide some service for dealing with pupil learning deficiencies and difficulties, has employed a number of specialists to provide the necessary remedial assistance to help individual students cope with the regular learning tasks of his school situation. In short, when the individual deviates from the normal educational pattern, remediation is suggested in order that he or she may once again assume a normal student role. Such services, whether psychological, health, or personal, have been very successful in some cases, quite unsuccessful in others. Not all deviants have been salvaged; however, we have probably had sufficient success to continue

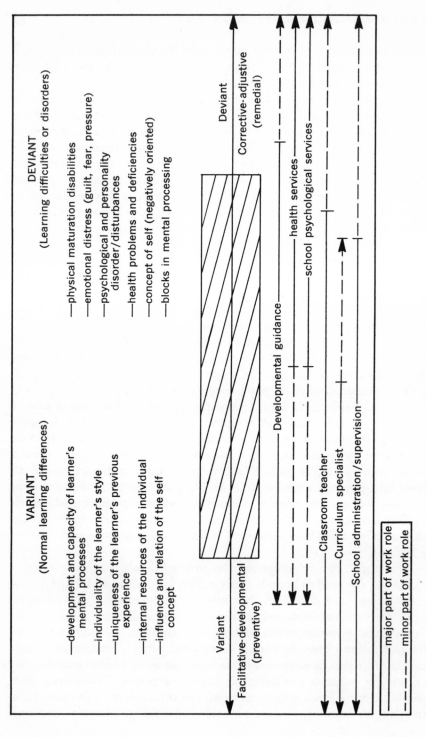

Figure 4.3. The concept of variant and deviant learning and education work roles

these services, and certainly we have sufficient knowledge about the educative process and about human growth and development to recognize and try other ways of helping the learner with learning problems. These efforts, with their emphasis on helping the student with learning difficulties and disorders, form the basis for the corrective-adjustive aspects of the school guidance role as well as for the other pupil personnel services.

The concept of variant and deviant learning is shown in Figure 4.3 in relation to the facilitative-developmental (preventive) and the corrective-adjustive (remedial) continuum of secondary school guidance. The shaded middle area represents efforts that are combinations of both the preventive or remedial—the "gray area" of operation. As the figure aptly portrays, these are well within the continuum of the secondary school guidance responsibility and to label them either one or the other is merely semantic. Yet the developmental school counselor will work with all members of the school staff—administration, instruction, and pupil personnel. Figure 4.3 shows the role emphasis of developmental guidance in relation to other selected roles in other areas, the solid line indicating where the major role efforts are most likely to be directed. This points clearly to the role relationships that may exist between guidance and the others portrayed. For example, the developmental school counselor is apt to have as many role relationships with administrative and instructional personnel as with pupil personnel.

THE EDUCATIONAL DILEMMA—
THE OLDER ISSUES

Probably no institution in American society receives as much criticism—pro and con—as the school. The school is perhaps the one universal experience of all members of the society. We reached a point in time a few decades back when, regardless of age, most everyone had experienced some facet of the educative process providing them with a basis for commenting on the school and its activities. The school has been praised, the school has been damned; some have chosen not to react to the school at all, and a few have remained complacent. The school is one of the very few institutions in American society that remains controlled essentially by the people it serves. The taxpayers in each community, in their control of school finances, can speak directly to the courses of action taken by their school administrators. It is in this manner, under these controls, that the school may be said to truly serve the desires—though not necessarily the needs—of its community. In this sense, considering varying community needs and desires and the uniformity inherent in the necessity for fiscal support and approval by regulatory state agencies, it is difficult to identify the universality, if indeed there is any, in

American education. True, there are commonalities and similarities, but the ingredients of almost every educational system contain their own uniqueness and individuality, depending upon the community in which the school exists.

It is perhaps due to this kind of community control that the traditional "lag" in educational progress and process is so common in our schools today. Our schools are controlled by powers that often perceive only what has been rather than by proponents of what will be. Schools, for the most part, have been directed and guided—and in many cases staffed—by people who assess the nature of the school's products in terms of the past rather than in terms of the future. The value of the educative process as well as the content focuses more on the promotion of the American heritage and ideals than on the recognition of change and the establishment of new directions. The claims of American education are rooted in the established values and facts of the past, and the realities of the present and the potentialities of the future are rarely considered in proposals for changing the conditions of American education.

This situation is saddening to say the least. The young kindergarten child of today will face a world far different than the one that the school of today is attuned to prepare him for. It is time that we examine most carefully the present claims of education and that we plan changes in the educative process—that we develop new directions in teaching and learning that will better prepare our young people to serve whatever kind of society they may find themselves living in. Let us now examine a few of the claims of present-day education and some of the new directions and dimensions it might take in the future.

The Doctrine of Individual Differences

Perhaps no idea in education has been more solidly or repeatedly sounded than the doctrine of individual differences. The interest in and concern for the individual as a fundamentally unique and different being has been repeatedly cited in statement after statement of educational philosophy in system after system throughout the United States. There are few school districts, if any, that do not recognize this doctrine. Yet it is the rare school system that has been able to actualize the doctrine: it is one belief in American education that has been consistently violated and mutilated. While school personnel continually attest to their belief in the doctrine, few have been able to deal effectively with it. Children in classrooms of 25 or 30 or more have been first to yield to the needs of the group or to the domination of the teacher. Classroom control and good discipline have prevailed. In fact, in many communities a good school is identified by its record of discipline. Some school personnel who seek promotion within the system are quick to sense the importance of student control and are even hastier in applying it. Many teachers who have tried to teach for individuality and to the individual differences of their students have found their positions in jeopardy where classroom noise and pupil activity were found to disturb the peaceful, eternal quiet of the school.

Somehow in the years ahead we must learn that education is an exciting and noisy process. We must learn that children need to utilize their own uniqueness and difference in the educative process. We must recognize that the continued health and vitality—the very strength—of our nation lies in helping our young people to express themselves and to learn how to utilize this expression of self in ways that will enhance not only their individual growth and development but the growth and development of our society and our ways of life.

Conformity vs. Individuality

This is not only one of the major issues facing education, it is one which is central to the future direction of the guidance movement. In our expanding population individuality pays a severe price, as we noted in an earlier chapter. Increasingly conformity is rewarded while punishment tends to accompany expressions of individuality. Education is no exception, for children are expected to conform to the demands of the school. This conformity often goes beyond obedience to rules and regulations which, of course, are necessary safeguards in the operation of any institution. At times these expectations exceed the bounds of rational reasoning. For example, students are often expected to write their names or head their papers in precise ways for no purpose whatsoever. Students are expected to perform certain tasks at certain times under very definite conditions, and failure to abide by these conditions or to perform these expected operations can result in punishment. Even creative ideas are often considered cataclysmic to the operation of the school. Thus it is little wonder that the exuberance and enthusiasm of the child when he enters school has been lost to weariness and boredom by the time he reaches the secondary school level. Now he knows the game and the rules; he is probably well aware of the personal sacrifice—the loss of self— that he has had to pay in order to function in the school according to its rules and demands. Many, probably most, survive. Yet far too many, if our high school dropout figures are accurate, do not. Many give up in disgust and go on to find a way of their own in the best possible manner. It is possible that the high school dropout is indicating that the price for his individuality is too high, that he cannot and will not succumb.

On the other hand, it is readily apparent that individuality and the conditions of individual expression must be tempered by the needs and processes of regulating a school with many adolescents in it. Chaos and bedlam are not desirable conditions for learning and they are not conducive to the physical safety of the students in the school. Restraining and regulatory measures are essential to the operation of a school. However, it does seem that our educative process should be sufficiently flexible to allow for some expression of individuality. It seems logical that the school can maintain order and control yet allow for a measure of student exploration.

Schools today are moving gradually in the direction of allowing for more individualized behavior and are seeking to involve students more actively in the determination of the social setting of the school. These directions are encouraging and promise to provide a fuller, richer learning experience. In such an atmosphere students can be encouraged to examine their own behaviors and to use their experiences as means of assessing their own maturational progress. Perhaps, above all, allowing for more expression of individuality will do more to foster the development of individual creativity and originality than we have heretofore been able to generate.

Responsibility—Whose? How?

The school has purported to contribute to the development of responsible and mature citizenry. If responsibility is equated with acceptance of the status quo, recitation of societal values, and complacency with social, political, and economic issues, then perhaps we can claim to be educating responsible citizenry. On the other hand, if responsibility is equated with an analysis and questioning of social, political, and economic issues, and with an ability to respond to these issues in an active and dynamic way, then perhaps we need to question the extent to which the school is developing responsible behaviors. It would seem that a responsible citizen is one who is enlightened, who is aware, who thinks. This seems to be more consistent with the central purposes of education. Above all, it would seem that a responsible citizen is one who is capable of acting, who relies on his own judgment, and who is capable of assessing a situation and acting in accordance with his judgment of it.

Responsibility is a learned activity. Learning to be responsible for one's behavior is more than learning information and facts. It is learning what to do with content in life situations. It requires practice and experience; it necessitates help in assessing or evaluating experiences. The school has tremendous potential for teaching responsibility, even though this may be a shared adventure with the home, the church, and the community. The school can provide the environment where opportunities to engage in responsible behaviors can be explored. It can enhance these exploratory experiences by providing situations where children are free, rather than fearful, to speak out and step forward. In light of the presumed lessened opportunities to deal with responsibility in the family, which were mentioned earlier, it may be even more vital that the school insist on fully activating the opportunities it can afford youth.

Motivation—An Old Saw

The whole idea of motivating students has been a complex educational problem for some years. School administrators and teachers often cite the motivation problem as one of their most perplexing and baffling concerns. It has been the subject of many workshops and in-service sessions for teachers. There is enough evidence to suggest that the perennial problem of motivation is a many faceted one and one that pervades the educative process. Easy answers and tailormade solutions simply are not, and probably will not be, available. Progress in tackling the questions of motivating students will be achieved as school personnel hammer away at improving the teaching-learning process on a day-to-day basis. We may need to begin by investigating some of the purposes of education and some of our expectations of students. "Motivation for what?" is a most appropriate start.

Is it realistic to expect that all students can be motivated toward *all* aspects of the learning experience at *all* times? The answer would probably be a resounding "no." Yet sometimes this is what the school demands of every student. He is expected to be enthusiastic about all four or five or six of his subjects, every day, throughout the day. He is never expected to be bored or to be less than enthusiastic about the material set before him. This is to say nothing of the manner in which the material is placed before him. Some students are correctly bored, for the material is presented to them in the most boring and dry fashion. While the question of motivation is related to all aspects of the school experience, we might make some gain by directing our attention to internal and external aspects of the teaching-learning process. If we could consider learning as a pleasant experience, if we could consider learning as a noisy and active experience, if we could consider learning as an *individual* experience, and if we could consider any human reaction to the learning experience as a valid one, then we might be better able to cope with the concerns and problems of motivation. Instead of being floored, we might be encouraged.

Relevancy or Faith

So many of the high school students of today tell me that much of the content to which they are exposed they have had to learn to take on faith. They tell me that they are told (and for a time they accept this) that much of the learning to which they are exposed is necessary for some part of their future life—be it college or work or some other aspect of their future living. By the time they reach the senior high school years they have become somewhat fed up with learning on faith. In recent years college students, and now students at the high school level, have begun to ask the question of relevancy. Undoubtedly there is legitimacy in both content that must be accepted on faith and in learnings that have relevancy for immediate application. Probably what is most important is the recognition of both content and purpose and the manner of their blend in the teaching-learning process. If we are able to shape our curriculum in a fashion that relates directly to our purposes and goals in education, then the old saw "motivation" and the issue of teaching for relevancy would further dissipate. The old adage about teaching mental discipline would also be laid to rest, since the purposes of education would lend themselves more appropriately to the newer concepts of teaching for thinking.

THE EDUCATIONAL DILEMMA: THE NEWER DIRECTIONS

The current literature in education speaks frequently and strongly to programs that provide a different kind of learning for the secondary school student. While the current literature is strong in its appeal for educational innovation and change, it does not appear that schools will make any dynamic or dramatic structural changes that will incorporate immediately some of the newer concepts or purposes. At best, it would appear that we can anticipate the long, slow, and gradual incorporation of these concepts into the educational process. While these newer directions are geared to preparing young people for the world of the future, they remain, for the most part, theoretical beliefs and professional ideals. This process of gradual and conservative change would be appropriate for a stable, static society.

But today's American society can hardly be characterized by stability and dormancy. It is a dynamic, changing society, which necessitates abrupt and radical changes in its educational structure. Education can no longer afford the traditional 20-year lag. It can no longer afford to ignore the changes that society will heap upon it. If its purposes and goals are to be accomplished, even in part, changes will have to be incorporated utilizing processes which are not gradual but abrupt. In other words, change will *of necessity* have to be forced. Some of the changes which appear to be immediate, rather than long range, are discussed in the following sections.

Flexibility—Adaptability

In the past the premium on education seemed to be developing the "knowing" man. Man's value and worth seemed to be measured in terms of the amount of information he had been able to store for use in various ways in his life. Also it was possible to train a man to occupy a work role in the society and, with a modicum of in-service work here and there over his professional or work life, he could maintain a level of competency that allowed him to contribute to the overall growth and development of our country. This type of occupational preparation and development was sufficient for the times, not only for professional endeavors, but for most of the skilled and semi-skilled occupations.

This idea hardly seems adequate for the modern world. Man is in constant process of achieving new information and of finding himself facing new experiences and situations with which he has not heretofore had to cope. It is doubtful if, in this society, one can ever truly become "experienced" in the traditional sense in which we have used the word. In all phases of his life—occupational, social, economic, political—man finds himself needing to reassess and adapt to new ideas and techniques. Man increasingly must become flexible and adaptable and the old ideas of stability no longer fit the self-actualizing, self-fulfilling individual.

While man is a creature easily addicted to habit and routine, he increasingly finds this is a handicap to his functioning rather than a help. He is rapidly becoming aware that he can no longer rely on the stability of his life nor on the enduring qualities that have characterized it. Like his automobile, his television, and his clothes, his style of life is being outmoded. Thus, not just in material ways but in very deep and personal ways, he is encountering obsolescence—a cultural obsolescence.

Learning Can Be Fun

Learning for learning's sake and learning as a rigorous form of mental discipline are but two of the outmoded concepts we find less frequently—yet all too often—in educational practice today. The emphasis on the learning of factual information has become an incredibly hopeless task for the student. Information is expanding at a rate which makes it almost impossible for anyone ever to hope to become master of even one small segment of data in any given field. Almost as much has been written about the "knowledge explosion" as about the population explosion. The recognition that students can never cope with all the knowledge available, combined with the fact that knowledge, too, can become obsolete rather quickly, is leading to changes in the structure of the curriculum and in the teaching-learning process.

We are coming to believe that learning need not be the dull, stultifying, tiring process that has been so universally experienced in our culture. We are coming to recognize that learning can indeed be an exciting and challenging task—one filled with the thrills of discovery and the surprises of accomplishment and satisfaction. Curricula designed to present concepts rather than facts and teaching methodologies which encourage children to "discover" are illustrative of the newer and promising innovations in helping children to learn and in making the learning process a more dynamic and challenging experience. Just imagine how exciting it would be if we were able to incorporate some of these newer ideas in *all* of the American classrooms at one specified time.

Obviously, such a move would be impractical, for the implementation of new ideas and approaches requires school personnel who believe in these changes and understand them. Further, there is merit in allowing a school system to select those innovations which it feels are best suited to its program and practices. Yet if we are to move away from the long and agonizing procedures we are conditioned to expect in the change process, we shall have to abandon some of our existing notions about change and experiment with other ways—ways which may seem radical and reckless.

We are well aware of the arguments against hasty and abrupt changes. We have been "schooled" to anticipate change on the basis of research evidence. In short, we have been trained to move slowly and cautiously. We have cause now to question the validity of this policy with regard to its effect on student learning. To fail to change *may* impose more deleterious effects on youth than even the most radical of some of the proposed innovations. Of one thing we can be fairly certain—we have failed miserably in changing the educative process even in the light of overwhelming research evidence indicating not only the desirability of change but the necessity for it.

If we believe that learning can be an exciting experience for students, then we need to explore these channels and to test these approaches. We have proved rather conclusively that learning is not much fun for too many young people. To reverse our direction we not only have to change some of our approaches but, more importantly, some of our ideas and attitudes about the conditions and sources of learning. We may find that the fun of learning is rooted in such factors as spontaneity, need, wonder, desire, anticipation, and surprise, and we need to begin to explore these concepts for application in the educational enterprise.

Learning To Think Rather Than To Repeat

While the school is concerned with all aspects of human maturation (social, physical, mental, psychological), it has always been more significantly involved in the intellectual development of the student. In this regard the school has long been concerned with the development of the mind and the reasoning powers of the individual. Our notions and conceptualizations about intelligence have contributed significantly to the act of teaching and to our knowledge about the processes of human learning. They have most definitely had their impact on the curriculum of the school as well as on the technologies employed in the classroom. However, today we are in the process of reexamining and reassessing some of these notions and conceptualizations. We are questioning, perhaps for the first time, some of our classroom technologies in light of newer findings. Considering all the changes which our society is currently experiencing, we are coming to realize that a good deal of the teaching-learning process involves helping children learn how to think. We are realizing that the development of the mental processes involved in thinking and learning are significant in the mental maturation of the individual. While the ability to memorize and to recall factual information is still considered an important mental process, we are coming to recognize that other mental processes are equally important in children's thinking. The ability to interpret, classify, generalize, hypothesize, and compare are illustrative of other important mental processes which are necessary to continued learning and productive living. It is becoming increasingly necessary to provide classroom experiences that develop the thinking processes of children. Therefore the old process of recall and regurgitation so common in American educational practice will, of necessity, need to be modified. The creative, productive person in tomorrow's society, if not in today's, will find that repetition and regurgitation of information are no longer sufficient to solving the problems of life.

The Three R's and the Development of Thinking Operations

It is not uncommon to find the parent today who indicates that the "three R's" are sufficient to the schooling of the modern generation. The idea of "what was good enough for Grandma is good enough for me" is hardly conducive to meeting the challenges of life in the modern world of the seventies and beyond. Even the parent, school board member, or taxpayer who exudes the old fashioned approach to education doesn't drive to work in a horse and buggy or catch the eleven o'clock news on earphones! Chances are he uses his earphones to listen to his stereo and watches the news on color TV.

The adult who justifies modern educational practice with the preface "When I was a boy . . ." represents the type of traditional thinking that deters educational progress and change. In spite of all the many changes which our society has undergone—the landing of a man on the moon while a nation of two hundred million watched it "live" on television, for example—and the technological advances that are represented hourly in our daily lives, there are many adults in our society who still believe that the three R's are sufficient to the educative process. While the skills of "readin', ritin', and 'rithmetic" are as essential as ever in daily life, they represent only a segment of the skills that are demanded of people every day.

To compete in the modern society, the effective citizen must be capable of engaging in a variety of mental operations such as judging, analyzing, generalizing, and evaluating. Facility with these skills is of equal importance. The housewife must not only read the labels on the many items she encounters in the supermarket but she must be able to use this information in analyzing and comparing products. In just one day the average citizen employs these thinking operations in an endless number of situations. While learning to think has always been important (selectively, depending on one's work), today, being able to think is essential.

Humanism in Education

While we have afforded self-realization a lofty position in our statement of educational purpose, it is only recently, through the challenges afforded by humanistic thinking, that we are beginning to question the extent to which we have developed practices in education which lead to the accomplishment of this important goal. Humanistic philosophy and psychology is, as we have seen in Chapter Three, one of the more recent strains of thinking to affect educational thought. Humanistic thinking is causing educators to focus more on the internal, the inner aspects of man's experiencing and the psychological dimensions of it. This is causing us to become more cognizant of the feelings of the student in the educative process, not only with regard to the content of his learning but with regard to himself.

In recent years we have become extremely conscious of the self-concept of the person and his perceptions of himself. While many of these internal considerations in the teaching-learning process are being considered, we have barely begun to cultivate those in educational practice which will take more adequately into account the self of the individual. Yet the contributions of humanistic thought to educational practice can no longer be avoided by the professional educator. The concept of man as an emerging being, ever in process of becoming, provides a base from which the ideas and contributions of humanism can be interwoven into the educational process. Humanism, too, will contribute to educational practice which emphasizes the facilitative, "self-actualizing" aspects of human development which hopefully can expand our human potential and utilize more fully our human resources.

The very positive nature of humanistic thinking (note the view of man upon which most humanistic thought has been developed) provides a new base for approaching the educative process that differs somewhat from the more objective and externally oriented psychologies that have heretofore permeated educational practice. Views of the male and the female and our ideas of masculinity and femininity may undergo some scrutiny as we emphasize more the human, rather than the role, aspects of living.

In Summary

To be effective the school counselor must be continually alert to the present claims of educational practice and to the new directions which may provide for the fulfillment of our educational goals. Certainly if developmental guidance in the secondary school is to contribute in any significant way to the process of human maturation and to educational practice, it is essential that the guidance worker be aware of these ideas and that he be prepared to function in ways that can help to shape the new directions for educational practice. The new directions in education promise to contribute significantly to the development of the individual and his capacities—a goal which has long been of vital concern to guidance. Guidance in the years ahead will not necessarily be accomplished on just the one-to-one basis utilizing the counseling experience. It will incorporate functions that can help the school counselor to contribute significantly to the changing educational process, to initiate practices, and to develop technologies that will affect *all* children.

Guidance has long maintained its concern and interest in the development of *all* children. It has been advertised as a service for all youth; it has been concerned with all children. While it is not difficult to find guidance programs which are remedial in their emphasis, it is expected that guidance programs in the future will continue to explore and develop those aspects which will facilitate human development and learning. In these ways guidance will foster change, and guidance personnel will act as leaders in the change process.

SUGGESTED READING

BLOOM, BENJAMIN S., (Ed.), *Taxonomy of Educational Objectives, Handbook I: Cognitive Domain* (New York: David McKay, 1956).

BRUNER, JEROME S., *The Process of Education* (New York: Vintage Books, 1960).

HILGARD, ERNEST H., (Ed.), *Theories of Learning and Instruction.* The Sixty-third Yearbook of the National Society for the Study of Education, Part I (Chicago: The University of Chicago Press, 1964).

HOLT, JOHN, *How Children Fail* (New York: Dell Publishing Company, 1965).

KRATHWOHL, DAVID R.; BLOOM, BENJAMIN S.; and MASIA, BERTRAM B., *Taxonomy of Educational Objectives, Handbook II: Affective Domain* (New York: David McKay, 1964).

LEONARD, GEORGE, *Education and Ecstasy* (New York: Delacorte Press, 1968).

SCHEFFLER, ISRAEL, "Philosophical Models of Teaching," *Harvard Educational Review* 35:131–143, Spring 1965.

SILBERMAN, CHARLES E., *Crisis in the Classroom* (New York: Random House, 1970).

D E V E L O P M E N T A L   G U I D A N C E :

A N   I N I T I A L   C O N C E P T I O N

I remain hopeful that guidance personnel will find the strength and the resources to move forward in establishing the kinds of programs that will more adequately meet the needs of youth and the educative process. While much has been written about developmental guidance, its basic conceptions have been somewhat vague and its practice tied closely to the traditional. This chapter is an attempt to clarify one approach to developmental guidance in the secondary school. It essentially incorporates many of the ideas about man, his society, and his education as these have been presented in the earlier chapters. It represents a synthesis of our knowledge about man and his development as it can be applied to the guidance effort. This is only a partial conception at this point and should be subject to further deliberation and development. It does, however, represent the basis for developmental guidance in the secondary school as it is conceived in this book. The remaining sections, Parts II and III, provide further delineations of theory and practice and suggestions for their implementation in the role and function of school guidance.

Only a short time ago, almost as a prelude for the renewal of guidance in the seventies, a joint ACES-ASCA policy statement concerning the school counselor, entitled *Expectations and Commitments,* was released.[1] This brief document was prepared for superintendents of schools and for school boards and succinctly delineates broad expectations for the work of the school counselor as it contributes to the purposes of education. It spells out

[1] Joint ACES-ASCA Committee, *Expectations and Commitments* (Washington, D.C.: American Personnel and Guidance Association, 1969).

the commitments these school leaders must make to the role and function of guidance in the school. This statement speaks directly to an important role expectation. It states *"The superintendent and the board have a right to expect the work of the counselor to be founded on sound rationale. This is one of the distinguishing characteristics of the work of the professional."*[2] Part I, with this chapter as its concluding one, has been directed toward establishing a rationale that gives purpose and meaning to guidance as an integral part of the educative process. The statements that follow attempt to provide a substantial basis for the practice of developmental guidance in the secondary school.

Some Basic Beliefs

Some of the following beliefs are neither new nor innovative. They are modifications of the guidance position representing the factors of individuality in human growth and behavior. Others are concepts and beliefs about human development as they can be applied to the developmental approach to guidance. Overall, these beliefs represent an effort to be more specific about the nature and function of the guidance position within the total educative process. School guidance is founded on some very fundamental beliefs about the worth and dignity of man and the uniqueness of the individual. The very essence of the guidance role is geared to that which motivates and activates man. Developmental guidance in the secondary school seeks to get at the heart of human development. Because of its alliance with the goals and purposes of education, it plumbs the depth and breadth of the finer aspects of the learning-maturational sequences as these are provided by the program of the school. It summons, for the benefit of the individual, all the resources that can converge on his day-to-day experiencing. It seeks to aid the individual in the difficult and complex process of integrating all his experiences into a meaningful pattern of understandings and identities that will foster his being and becoming.

About the Individual

(1) The dignity and uniqueness of the individual is basic to the educative process and is affirmed only as each student in the school is recognized and respected for his individuality and worth.

(2) The uniqueness of an individual is expressed in the self of the person as this is represented by both the external and internal dimensions of his feeling, thinking, and behaving.

[2] *Ibid.*

(3) The self of an individual is an evolving, changing dynamic of human maturation resulting from the interaction of an individual's experiencing and learning.

(4) An individual learns about himself through exposures and experiences concerning a variety of physiological, psychological, and sociological factors and forces—this combinational learning results in his growth and maturation.

(5) Human maturation has several aspects:
   a. The physical growth and development of the individual, his perceptions of his physical self and the manner in which he uses his physical being are represented in *physical maturation.*
   b. An individual's *self maturation* is represented by his identification with himself. This includes his feelings about himself and his ability to express these feelings, his acceptance of his uniqueness and the qualities that identify it, his awareness of the evolving and changing nature of his self and of the processes whereby he can plan and control these changes, his inner sense of well-being and his continual growth toward the realization and utilization of his self.
   c. The development of the individual's ability to receive, store, and retrieve information about himself and his world—that is, to process information in both concrete and symbolic ways in thinking and learning—is represented by *mental maturation.*
   d. The extent to which an individual can express his uniqueness, maintain his personal freedom and autonomy, and accept responsibility for his behavior by balancing these in accordance with the demands, needs, and restrictions of his society is represented by *social maturation.*
   e. The readiness of an individual to accept responsibility for his career planning, including the exploration of educational and occupational opportunities and requirements; and the readiness to deal with the choices and decisions that are attendant to planning and arranging for the future, are evidence of initial progress toward *vocational maturation.*

About the Learning-Maturation Process

(1) Learning-maturation stems primarily from the combinational effect of all learning in all aspects of human maturation. Its highly individual character rests in the variant nature of each person's learning and in the willingness of each individual to assume a measure of responsibility for his own maturational progress.

(2) Learning-maturation involves the manner of an individual's integration of his life exposures and experiences—physiological, psychological, sociological—separately and collectively. The uniqueness of the individual rests in the particular manner of this integration as it is evidenced in his beliefs, values, attitudes, and interests and expressed in his behavior.

(3) An individual's integration of his learnings involves the process of internalization in which an individual formulates his own beliefs, values, attitudes, interests, etc., as he deals with his exposures and experiences on a reactive continuum ranging from initial awareness and response through differentiation and choice to fitting, customizing, and owning.

(4) Central to the internalization process is the individual's need to maintain both personal and social balance.

    a. *Personal balance* is represented by the individual's ability to more clearly identify and establish his personal needs, values, beliefs, and attitudes which, as integrated in the totality of his being, identify him as a person and are used by him consistently as guidelines for his behavior. The individual in the process of achieving personal balance experiences, over the years of the learning-maturational process, many points or periods of confusion and ambiguity. These confusions are *normal* occurrences in self-identification; they are *temporary* pending individual clarification; they are *necessary* as the individual explores new and unknown domains of his experiencing. These periods may be characterized by increased tension and anxiety but are relieved as the individual achieves a condition of personal equilibrium.

    b. *Social balance* is represented by the extent to which the individual can achieve harmony between his own motivations, aspirations, and goals and the expectations and demands which his environment places upon him. The individual seeking social balance must cope with the incongruities and inconsistencies between himself and his environment (including the people in it), particularly as these are evidenced in the pressures and demands that impinge upon him. The individual experiences periods or points of societal demands and pressures. These, too, are normal, temporary, and necessary and are dealt with in the learning-maturation process as the individual seeks a condition of social equilibrium.

    c. The extent to which the individual is able to cope with matters of his personal and social balance is directly associated with his continual learning-maturation and the development of his own identity.

(5) The essence of human maturation lies in the extent to which an individual is able to achieve a measure of personal autonomy allowing him to move toward self-actualization, both ingredients leading to self-fulfillment.

(6) Learning-maturation is a life-long process. It is most intense in the adolescent years, extending well into young adulthood when the gradual unfolding of the individual's identity has achieved a sufficient stability to afford a picture of his uniqueness as an individual. Much of the learning-maturation process beyond this point is concerned with individual change and exploration necessitating alterations in his already internalized learnings. As these changes are accomplished, changes in the character of the individual will be observed.

(7) Education and guidance are intricately and inextricably involved in providing for the individual in the learning-maturation process, particularly during childhood, adolescence, and the young adult years. The mutuality of their purpose is obvious and the contributions of all school personnel should be directed at serving the development of the individual. To this end, a program of developmental guidance offers considerable promise and potential.

Some Notions About Developmental Guidance

Using these basic beliefs, we can establish some statements that can be considered as further guidelines for the delineation of developmental guidance. These statements, while broadly conceived, constitute the basis for the role of developmental guidance (as it is presented in Part II) and for its dimensions (as elaborated in Part III).

(1) Developmental guidance is basically facilitative in that it provides exposures for the individual which are designed to extend his experiencing by expanding the opportunities for him to test and explore further the nature of his learning-maturation. It extends opportunities for the individual to examine and to clarify how he feels and behaves. It helps to keep him in touch with his own being and becoming.

(2) In developmental guidance the focus is on the individual—on *his learning* and on *his maturing*. These are seldom disparate; they are associative and relative. To deal with one is to deal with the other. Human learning-maturation is the prime concern of education. The developmental counselor, like others in the school, finds his purpose in the phenomena of learning—in helping the individual (and those others who work with him) to encounter and to deal with himself and the situations in which he finds himself in the learning-maturation process.

(3) Developmental guidance occurs in the educational setting. It is oriented to the educative process. While the developmental counselor is ever in danger of becoming all things to all people, he is most importantly involved in the teaching-learning process as it contributes to the cognitive and affective experiencing of the individual. He not only helps the individual to view and to assess himself in these situations of learning and maturing, but he helps others (teachers and parents primarily) to help them. He helps these others establish worthwhile and meaningful experiences and conditions which can enhance the individual's learning-maturation.

(4) Developmental guidance, in seeking to focus more directly and with greater influence on the learning-maturation of the individual, deals primarily with all aspects of human maturation—physical, mental, social, vocational, and self.

(5) Developmental guidance is concerned with the total development of the individual and with his uniqueness. This necessitates attending to both *reason* and *affect* in the search for a balance that allows man to think and to feel, to trust both his mind and his emotions. The adolescent is not always rational (nor should he be expected to act thus) at all times. The very essence of learning-maturation during these years is dependent upon the exploration of behaviors which to another person may seem irrational, irresponsible, or out of character. As the individual's powers of reasoning are developed—that is, as he grows toward mental maturity— he is better able to accommodate his thinking and feeling in behaviors that are socially acceptable and individually satisfying. This search for individual freedom within the demands of societal conformity and the many alternative avenues of self-expression it affords, as well as those it does not afford, is one that must allow for permissive exploration within specified limits. Society, as represented by adults, must establish these limits yet insure that sufficient latitude is available for the individual's learning-maturation.

(6) Developmental guidance is concerned with with the growth and learning of *all* individuals. While he may not have sufficient time to work individually with every student and while every student may not need nor trust him sufficiently to necessitate a human (helping) relationship, the developmental counselor shares this concern with the teachers who influence these individuals every day. By working with teachers, the counselor through and with others helps the school to reach all the individuals in it. This is a shared and mutual concern that incorporates the facilitative and developmental aspects of learning-maturation. While the corrective-adjustive aspects of deviant learning are of concern to everyone in the school, the concern for all individuals necessitates the extension of the guidance effort to accommodate the needs of both variant and deviant learners.

(7) The five dimensions of developmental guidance—physical, mental, social, self, and vocational—grow out of the day-to-day demands on the individual in his living and learning. His interaction with others as well as the interactive aspects of his development constitute the dynamics of his learning-maturation. At any point or period in his growth any one of these dimensions, singly or in combination, can result in conflict or distress with which the individual must deal.

(8) Developmental guidance finds a purpose in helping the individual in his learning-maturation as he experiences personal confusion and social pressure. Such conflicts and demands (by whatever theory of human development one chooses to follow) are natural and normal occurrences associated with the process of human maturation. While theorists differ in their description of adolescent conflict or stress, most theories characterize the transitional years of adolescence as the crucial ones during which the individual strives to establish the basis for his social and self-identity.

These are the years, then, when the individual seems to have the greatest difficulty in developing and maintaining personal and social balance as he strives to establish and identify his own individuality. To deny this quest for individuality is to deny the essence of adolescence.

(9) Developmental guidance is integrally involved in providing for the process of internalization as it contributes to individual learning-maturation. The developmental counselor is concerned about the learning exposures and experiences of each individual as these contribute to his exploration of human beliefs, values, attitudes, interests, abilities, and needs. Developmental guidance offers assistance in helping to insure some breadth and depth to these exposures and experiences. As individuals seek to establish their own identity through the internalization process—that is, as they deal with their experiences on the reactive continuum of internalization—they often require further assistance with personal concerns having to do with selecting, clarifying, or integrating. The developmental counselor can be particularly helpful when these concerns affect personal and social equilibrium. The more continual and pervasive aspects of individual identity are achieved in the day-to-day exposures and experiences of youth. Obviously, in terms of the educative process, the classroom is the center, or the focal point, of the school experience. The developmental counselor can be of assistance to the classroom teacher in planning and implementing experiences which will help students in the internalization of values, beliefs and attitudes and in helping the teacher to interpret the impact of the classroom on the teaching-learning process and on individual learning-maturation.

(10) Developmental guidance seeks to serve a function for society as well as for the individual. A healthy, growing, democratic society is one that contains individuals who are creative, secure, and flexible. It produces people who are able to deal with the issues of the times, who are free to express their opinions, who are capable of assuming civic and social responsibilities. The developmental counselor, probably more than others in school, should be knowledgeable about trends and changes in society. To the extent that he is a man among men in the school, he should be sharing his interpretations of the changing times and the demands of them. The freedom of the individual and the expression of his individuality must be protected against forces of dehumanization and depersonalization as these exist in the school as well as in the society. Thus within the school he not only represents the individual but he stands for the continual creation of conditions which allow for the learning-maturation of the individual and for expressions of his uniqueness.

(11) Developmental guidance is concerned with helping the individual to initiate and to progress in the career planning process. Although there are many dimensions to career development, the individual's *readiness* to engage in career exploration, his ability to accept *responsibility* for the choices and decisions attendant to it, and his *understanding* of the life

long and decision making aspects of career evolvement are primary evidence of his growth toward vocational maturation. An individual's vocational maturation is dependent on his concomitant growth in other aspects of his learning-maturation and it is integrally associated with his total development. The developmental school counselor will plan a variety of activities and experiences designed to motivate and encourage students to engage in career planning, to provide informational and experiential exposures, and to develop insights into the meaning and process of career evolvement.

DEVELOPMENTAL GUIDANCE—
A PROCESS OF RENEWAL

The Process of Renewal

The translation of these beliefs into actual programs of developmental guidance is not a simple task. It will require the utmost in effort and attention, the ultimate in human interaction. It will involve a great deal of human understanding. Above all, it will take time and commitment! Some will undoubtedly reject developmental guidance as too ideal and a few, perhaps, will be either unable or unwilling to make the personal and program sacrifices essential to establishing such programs in the schools.

(1) The process of renewal as a means of establishing developmental guidance in the secondary school suggests an evolving change rather than an abrupt one. This *is* the process. Overnight renewals ignore the day-to-day battles of role evolvement which are essential in building a new image and in creating new relationships that will provide for the understandings essential to change. The process must be rooted in an unwaivering commitment to change and a desire to inaugurate action that will revitalize and renew the secondary school guidance role.

(2) The school counselor must initiate the renewal process for it will flow mainly from his behaviors. It will not resolve itself in formal statements of policy and role, nor through the most comprehensive in-service programs beamed to inform administrative and instructional personnel. While role and position statements (such as the Joint ACES–ASCA statement *Expectations and Commitments*) enhance the process of renewal and help in obtaining support, they are at best supplementary and complementary. The secondary school counselor's ability to apply concepts of role theory in the day-to-day enactment of his role in his own behavior constitutes the basis for the process. Therefore, guidance personnel assume prime responsibility for their performance. This in itself is not an easy task and involves a good deal of personal sacrifice and endurance, for it involves being able to deal with a host of interpersonal reactions and conditions of both a negative and a positive nature.

(3) Renewal constitutes energizing the forces of guidance *away* from activities which do not serve the purposes of education nor the goals of developmental guidance. Renewal necessitates dispensing with the nonprofessional aspects of guidance as these are currently evidenced in the mechanistic and clerical routines in which many school counselors are engaged. Renewal involves refraining from participation in any activities that do not clearly portray the role of guidance in education and its contributions to the learning-maturation process. In short, it involves saying "No" to those role expectations which are far removed from the real world of the adolescent.

Refusal to meet these role expectations assumes a number of responsibilities. It assumes that the developmental counselor can define and delineate the nature and direction of the activities in which he does engage and that he can support his position. It presumes a professional competence guided by one's understanding of his role and not by traditional stereotypes or individual idiosyncracies. It demands an inner strength that tests one's professional and personal priorities. It assumes that one is prepared to deal with the interpersonal dynamics involved in the renewal and revitalization of guidance as this is accomplished in the day-to-day enactment of the guidance role.

(4) The renewal process is basically one of interpersonal communication. Each individual encountered by the developmental counselor has his own conception of guidance and his feelings about it. These perceptions of the guidance role will vary widely, as will the feelings that accompany them. The counselor must respect these though he may not agree with them. He will have to deal with these within the context of his relationship with each individual. His skill and competency here, and the judgments and sensitivity he is able to employ, will determine the extent to which he is able to engage in the process of renewal as well as its pattern and pacing.

(5) Each school system will have to determine where to begin the process of renewal. It can begin any time with any person or any number of people. It can begin by eliminating irrelevant and unimportant activities or by assuming new responsibilities and functions. What is most important is that the counselor commit himself to the renewal of guidance and to the form that this renewal will take.

To those who would choose a developmental approach to guidance, this chapter and the remaining sections can serve as a program rationale.

PART TWO

THE ROLE AND FUNCTION
OF DEVELOPMENTAL GUIDANCE

That the nature of guidance will move to accommodate the tenor of these changing times has become obvious. The comments and reactions of students, teachers, parents, administrators, and even school counselors themselves are daily indications that new and fresh ideas must be pumped into the guidance process. The satisfactions and the dissatisfactions of these people must be carefully and thoughtfully considered as the work role of the school counselor is modified or altered to reflect needed changes and accommodations.

What is not so obvious—and hasn't been for quite some time—is the manner and the process whereby the renewal of guidance can be wrought. Pat answers and tailormade solutions are not readily available and the likelihood of decoding the riddle of change in the near future is small indeed. It appears that changes in the guidance role will be hammered out through the complex process of human communication, with the results reflecting the energies and skill that counselors themselves have put into the task.

Questions concerning the changing functions of guidance, possible directions, and promising procedures for revitalizing the guidance role are treated in this section. The essence of the developmental guidance role and the functions vital to its implementation are portrayed. Drawing on segments of the elementary school guidance role as I have developed it in a companion publication,[1] the functions of the developmental counselor have been divided among the big three C's—counseling, consulting, and coordinating. This is not to suggest that we equate the guidance effort in the elementary and secondary school. What this division means to suggest is that these three functions have a real purpose in the implementation of developmental guidance concepts and that these functions can be employed as a means to fulfilling the developmental guidance role. While I believe there are similarities between elementary and secondary school guidance, these lie mainly in the theory for approaching the learning-maturation process of the individual as both education and guidance provide for and help in this process. The applications and practice will differ insofar as educational practice differs between these two levels and with regard to the differences in the learning-maturation process among young children, adolescents, and young adults. Whatever the case, it remains the responsibility of each counselor to shape the developmental guidance role and its functions in a real and vital fashion. Its role cannot be prescribed; it must evolve. This section will help the school counselor to ascertain direction and will suggest sources of momentum to get him started.

Chapter Six, Concepts of Role and Power in Role Enactment, develops the concepts of role and social power as they can be employed in establishing the role of developmental guidance. Delineations and explications of role and power concepts are offered to enable the counselor to establish more firmly in his mind how changes in the guidance role can be effected. The day-to-day concerns of enacting the developmental guidance role and the interpersonal, interactive elements of it are described and discussed.

Chapter Seven, The Counseling Function, elaborates on the specific expectations and role behaviors that constitute the basis for the counseling function. The dimensions of the counseling process are elaborated and counseling practice is discussed in terms of its communicative, structural, and positional aspects. The need for each counselor to establish his own position and some of the elements that go into building this position are reviewed.

Chapter Eight, The Consulting Function, presents an older, less used function in a new light. The developmental counselor, in relation to his concern for the individual's learning-maturation and in view of his potential for promoting change in the school, is encouraged to engage in consulting activities with teachers and parents. The concept of the consulting function is expanded introducing three levels of effort. The theoretical base for this

[1] Harold L. Munson, *Elementary School Guidance: Concepts, Dimensions and Practice* (Boston: Allyn and Bacon, 1970).

function as it is developed in this chapter draws heavily on the contributions of medicine and social work though the application emphasizes how the developmental counselor can work primarily with teachers in providing for the learning-maturation of the individual and in promoting educational change that will enhance it.

Chapter Nine, The Coordinating Function, seeks to bring into focus much of the present guidance practice. Many of the procedures and activities that are presented in this chapter are associated with the more traditional view of the guidance role. Many are essential to the developmental guidance position though they are largely organizational and managerial in nature. These activities, as they are presented with a view to their coordinative aspects, allow the reader to place these functions in relative juxtaposition to those of a counseling or consulting nature. While a variety of current guidance activities are reviewed, it is anticipated that some will remain an integral part of the guidance effort while others may disappear. Some of these activities may be assumed by other role functionaries or by para-professionals as programs of guidance are modified toward the developmental model.

SIX

CONCEPTS OF ROLE AND POWER

IN ROLE ENACTMENT

The school is a social organization involving the interaction of many people. The network of communication among these people, both formal and informal, is an aspect of work performance that is often ignored. The social milieu in which the educative process occurs is seldom considered. It is as if we have considered all the parts—the plant, the program, the personnel—, but rarely do we concern ourselves with the whole—the *environment* of the school.

We have presumed far too long that given a building and teachers *learning* would occur. Of course learning does occur under these circumstances but it is the product of a very intricate and complex milieu, the social system of the school. Now we are beginning to recognize the phenomena of this social system; we are beginning to examine its influence on the educative process. The extent to which this learning is directed toward the goals of education involves a variety of institutional forces with two of the most important having to do with concepts of role theory and social power.

If the developmental school counselor is to be successful in establishing a more professional role for himself in the school, he is going to have to apply his understandings of role and power to the changing nature of his work. In the quarter-century of guidance covering the years of its emergence and growth, the secondary school counselor, like a good bird dog, has largely depended on his "nose" to guide him through the pitfalls and unknowns of role evolvement. That he successfully surmounted many of his difficulties is obvious as he approaches the threshhold of exciting new challenges in the professionalization of his field. That he yielded to a variety of pressures and forces, wisely as well as unwisely, is generally ceded. In much of his role behavior he depended on the support and understanding of others; he succumbed at times when he might better have fought. But the theoretical aspects of his role enactment were unclear and his task was an emerging one. He had little to guide his efforts. He had to depend on himself. The modern counselor can build on these earlier efforts but he need not continue to make the same mistakes.

Some understanding of the concepts of role and social power and their dynamics can enhance greatly the opportunities for effecting a truly developmental guidance program. This knowledge can help the developmental counselor to understand and interpret better what really is occurring in the process of role definition and mediation; it can help him to deal more effectively with the dynamics of enacting his role; it can help him to find ways for modifying or changing his traditional role behaviors so that his work efforts can reflect more consistently the theory and practice of developmental guidance. Developmental school counselors who understand and can employ the concepts of role and social power can help to shape and create their own roles. They can be effective in influencing the process of defining and mediating school guidance programs. They can be effective forces in initiating and implementing the process of renewal.

THE CONCEPT OF ROLE

Every individual in the school has a role that emanates from established expectations. Roles reflect the personalities of individuals. Work roles and their enactment provide the basis for the social dynamics of the school. Roles within the school are complementary. Generally speaking, we have emphasized the complementary nature of roles by attempting to establish definitive and detailed pronouncements about these various positions in the form of role definitions and descriptions. Within the institutional structure, role harmony has been valued and much energy has been expended in distinguishing among roles and in delineating operational relationships. The emphasis has been on clarifying roles and on specifying the activities of each position. This has led to considerable expenditures of effort in establishing work roles with which everyone could agree (role consensus).

Essentially, role consensus relies on the "normative" and the "patterned." The American School Counselor Association's *Statement of Policy for Secondary School Counselors* is an example of role consensus. Their statement was the product of much study and discussion involving guidance personnel on a nationwide basis. Consensus about a role leads to a rather specific set of prescribed or expected behaviors (role expectations). Since the notion of role consensus is so popularly accepted, it is easy to understand why there is so much interest and concern for specificity in formulating work roles.

While the postulate of role consensus has historical precedence, there has recently been a number of contemporary sociologists and psychologists who have moved away from the idea of role consensus and have suggested a concept of role that relies less on pattern and prescription. They have indicated that the idea of role consensus is somewhat outdated. Rather they suggest that roles are more the product of an individual's concept of his role and his relationship to other individuals within a social system. Roles, therefore, are a product of interaction with others with role definition emerging more as a product of the personality and the interpersonal relations of the individual than as an absolute or prescribed role definition to which one must conform. This view of role definition would emphasize more variability in role performance, such performance being dependent on one's understanding of his own work role, his understanding of the work expectations *as perceived by others,* and his own individual personality as it is utilized in his on-the-job role behaviors.

J. W. Getzels and E. G. Guba have developed a psychosociological conception of a social system that helps greatly in understanding the interactive aspects of role performance. They state,

We conceive of the social system as involving two major classes of phenomena, which are at once conceptually independent and phenomenally interactive. There are, first, the *institutions* with certain *roles* and *expectations* that will fulfil the goals of the system. Second, inhabiting the system there are the *individuals* with certain *personalities* and *need-dispositions,* whose interactions comprise what we generally call "social behavior." Social behavior may be apprehended as a function of the following major elements: institution, role, and expectation, which together constitute the *nomothetic,* or normative, dimension of activity in a social system; and individual, personality, and need-disposition, which together constitute the *idiographic,* or personal, dimension of activity in a social system.[1]

These two dimensions and their interaction are illustrated in Figure 6.1.

Let's apply this model to the secondary school guidance position (a role). First, let's look at the *nomothetic* dimension. The ASCA *Statement of Policy* established, nomothetically, a definition of the secondary school counselor role, and it delineates procedures for its implementation. The nomothetic nature of school guidance is rooted in such statements, which

---

[1] J. W. Getzels and E. G. Guba, "Social Behavior and the Administrative Process," *The School Review* 65:424, Winter 1957.

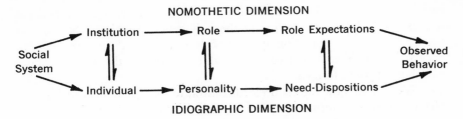

Figure 6.1. General model showing the nomothetic and idiographic dimensions of social behavior. (Reprinted from J. W. Getzels and E. G. Guba, "Social Behavior and the Administrative Process," The School Review 65:429, Winter 1957.)

suggest or prescribe a set of role behaviors. The ASCA *Statement of Policy,* therefore, contributes to defining the role and to delineating reasonable institutional role expectations. It provides the basis for legitimate practice and is used by the school counselor as a guide in determining his job performance (role behaviors).

On the other hand, the ASCA statement of role does not guarantee the universality of these given role expectations. The very fact that people have experienced guidance in many different ways, that they have heard about it from other people, or that they have read about it in a book could result in widely differing expectations of the guidance role. However different these may be from individual to individual, there are common features in these views that represent a stereotype of the school guidance role (he helps individuals choose a career, he helps individuals get into college). Role stereotypes that develop over the years represent another facet of the nomothetic dimension that influences the role behaviors of the school counselor.

Thus there are two major contributing forces that the school counselor must consider in enacting his role: first, formal role statements that help to prescribe the role and functions of the secondary school guidance job; second, the individual and stereotypic views of the people in the public he serves (the societal stereotypes of the school counselor).

Turning to the *idiographic* dimension, we must consider the personal or individual factors of role behavior. Each school counselor has his own individuality that finds expression in the way he performs his role. His own personality is directly reflected in his interactions with his public. Obviously, his feelings, his needs, his motivations, his values, his interests are all a part of the "person" that he brings to the role. He also displays his own conception of the school counselor position in his behavior and the particular activities in the role that he perceives to be primary. Both of these join to become a major force in the determination of the role as it will be enacted by a given counselor. These are all involved in his sensitivity to the position and its demands and are factors in the judgments he makes. Therefore, if we really consider the idiographic aspects of role performance, we can understand why there could be considerable variation in the way the school guidance role is performed.

We can see how the counselor is central to the evolvement of his role. His judgment in determining what he shall do and how he shall do it is of prime importance. Thus, his actual performance—his verbal and non-verbal communications, the activities in which he engages, and the manner in which he conducts these activities—represent his *role behavior.*

Despite all that we know about the development and enactment of the school counselor role we persist in the idealistic quest for *clarity* and *harmony* in role performance. Somehow or other we continue to depend on the magic of role definition. In this search for role clarity and harmony we fail to account for the changing needs and nature of role performance and, even more importantly, for the interactive, interpersonal aspects inherent in the idiographic dimensions of role enactment. Perhaps it is more realistic to recognize and deal with the *conflict* and *ambiguity* that steadfastly persist. Perhaps it is more timely to turn to the realities of working *with* rather than working *out* the secondary counselor role. It is time to learn how to face and cope with the turbulent forces and pressures of day-to-day functioning. The developmental counselor cannot close his eyes and dream of his ideal state. The tired ways of "telling and selling" in search for support of guidance have been tried and found wanting—helpful, but far short of the illusionary hopes for the perfect role condition. It is unlikely that he will ever achieve the serenity of complete role harmony. It is doubtful if he would want that, for the continual demands of a changing society will necessitate that he change course as his destiny at any given time may dictate. This is not to say that the school counselor in the secondary school vacillates with every wind of a passing fad. Not at all. But it does mean that he must be free to operate innovatively and creatively. And to do this he must have not only a degree of role flexibility but he must have the knowledge and the skills to create these possibilities. This means he must understand the dynamics of role enactment and be prepared to deal with innumerable situations and incidents to which his responding behaviors cannot be programmed.

All this is not to say that statements of role are not important. They have been and they will continue to be helpful. Surely school boards and school administrators, as well as teachers and parents and secondary school students, have every right to ask about the role of the school counselor. The professional school counselor has an obligation to respond. What I am saying is that he can no longer hide behind role statements hoping that his condition will improve. I am suggesting that he attend to the idiographic dimensions of his role, that he recognize the discrepancies in the expectations of his public, and that he proceed to attend to these in his day-to-day efforts.

THE CONCEPT OF POWER

Inherent in the human interaction of evolving the school counselor role is the concept of social power. Knowledge about power and its use in affecting the learning environment of the school is important in the armamentarium of the school counselor. If school counselors are going to be effective in modifying the role and function to accommodate a truly developmental approach to the guidance effort, they are going to have to effect these changes within the power structure of the school.

Ever since the emergence of guidance we have talked about the understanding and support deemed essential to guidance program evolvement. And school administrators have been the prime focus of these discussions. Administrative power has been recognized, and most efforts have been directed toward reeducating the perceived power structure of the school system. The approach has consisted mainly of attempts to inform the administrative hierarchy of school guidance objectives and to explain the role and function of the counselor. While undoubtedly this helped to "sell" guidance in earlier years, resulting in the inauguration of programs, it has not contributed greatly to establishing a work role or to the development of work role relationships that will allow the school counselor to achieve his greatest potential. Counselors have long been overburdened with mechanistic and clerical routines—one evidence of the failure of guidance to exact a working relationship within the power structure. In fact, the present work role dilemma of the school counselor in many situations is an example of how power has been used by others to his disadvantage.

Power as a function of interpersonal relationships serves to illustrate and emphasize the interrelationship of roles and the importance of communication in role enactment. Power is a broad, encompassing concept, and its sources and manifestations in the operation of any organization are often difficult to ascertain and assess. Understanding power is not projected as a panacea for the school counselor's dilemma. Nor does it carry a guarantee that in application role modifications will emerge. Rather, learning about power and understanding how it is used represent another area of the school counselor's competency, granting him insights upon which he can draw in determining the direction and intensity of selected role behaviors.

To many people the notion of power has a negative connotation. Power is something to be avoided. It implies coercion. It denotes control, authority, or influence. Yet, everyone agrees that someone has to have power. We accept power in its *intended* form and we see it as legitimate in the power hierarchy. Yet we often fail to understand it as a positive force. It is usually viewed in "totem pole" fashion with the top man wielding all the power while the "low man on the totem pole" views himself powerless. We rarely consider the potential for power in all positions.

Power is an *elusive* concept, difficult to pin down. Yet, it connotes pressure; it represents a force in the social system that causes people to behave in desired ways. Power as a conceptual force is never constant; it is in a real sense a capacity, a potential, a latent phenomenon. It is activated and relaxed by men who can control it. In any social system, even the school, it can be readily identified in its overt and authoritative forms. However, in its less obvious and more subtle forms it is often a more intuitive feeling and is sensed. In this form it is more evasive and more difficult to handle. Power in this form can be an *illusive* concept, for one can easily conjure power where it may not exist.

It is always helpful to be able to categorize or classify phenomena, particularly something as abstract as power. We might think of power in two forms—*formal* and *informal*. Formal power as it is manifest in the actual positional hierarchy can be used by those in higher power positions to dominate or manipulate those in lower positions. The power to do so is inherently prescribed in their role descriptions. Also, the formal power in an institution is often perceived since the incumbents of these positions may never manifest it. Nevertheless, perceived power, even though latent, can be an influential factor in the behaviors of subordinates. In this sense, formal power is quantitative. This doesn't really mean that the higher the position the more power one has. It means merely that one has potential power *over more people.* This hierarchical power must be actualized to become real power. For example, the principal's position in the school contains more power potential than that of the school counselor. This power is latent until the principal actually uses it. While a counselor may perceive the power of the principal by his higher position in the hierarchy and may therefore hesitate to encounter him, the principal's power remains to be actualized. And until he manifests his power with the school counselor, it is only potential. Once he has used his power to influence the behavior of the counselor, it is real.

Much of the power within the social milieu of the school is informal. It emerges largely as a result of interpersonal communication. It is often psychological. For example, one individual may have interpersonal power over another person or group of people. Sometimes it is sociological in that its source may be located in another social system with which the individual is involved. Membership in a bridge club or a church may provide an individual with the potential for informal power in the school. Informal power is the product of action between individuals. Thus, one may have power over another person as a result of his own charisma or because of some trait or combination of traits in his own personality (psychological) or because of a relationship in some other group in another setting (sociological). Informal power arises to meet the needs of individuals that the formal power structure does not provide.

Power has its qualitative aspect, too, and this is most obvious in the informal use of power. This is not a case of over *how many* people one has power but more a matter of over *whom.* While the school principal presumably has more power over teachers (formal), it is conceivable that a teacher or small group of teachers, through the informal power structure, may actually manifest more power over other teachers than the principal.

Power is also situational. It is at these times that power is most elusive or illusive. In other words, a person may have power in one situation but not in another. As a counselor you might have more power with one group of teachers than with another. Or you might have a degree of power with a group of teachers until another teacher (with some informal power) joins the group. At that point, the power dynamics may shift.

Informal power is often used to combat institutionalized power. In observing and assessing an existing institution's power structure one must consider the network of psychological relationships among its personnel and their informal groupings in relation to the actual formal structure of power as it exists in the positional hierarchy of the organization. This involves examining the power relationships among individuals and groups. It assumes that, in addition to the formal power vested in authority positions, there is a differential distribution of power among the many individuals and groups of individuals in an institution. This latent power, then, can be activated whenever these individuals interact.

Power stems from many bases and it is exerted in both its latent and active forms. John French and Bertram Raven identify five bases of power —coercive, reward, legitimate, expert and referent.[2] While power seldom stems from one discrete source or base, it is most frequently understood when one can assess the combinations of bases that occur in any given situa-

[2] John French and Bertram Raven, "The Bases of Social Power," in *Studies in Social Power,* Dorwin Cartwright, Ed. (Ann Arbor: University of Michigan, 1959), pp. 155–165.

tion. In order to understand these combinations of power, we should become familiar with these power bases.

Legitimate power is a source of power that is closely allied with the formal power structure. It is associated with the perceived power that stems from role definition (via professional role statements or role stereotypes) including all the role expectations that are associated with the position. One can use his position in exercising power as long as he remains within the perceived legitimacy of his position. If the developmental counselor were to incorporate role behaviors that exceeded the perceived role expectations of his public, he could anticipate some resistance. To the extent that he is denied legitimacy by those he serves, his legitimate power is restricted. It is easy, therefore, to see where the use of legitimate power is very restricted in attempting to modify or change a work role.

Coercive power is employed wherever one perceives that he will be deprived or punished if he does not conform or "go along" with the attempted or desired behaviors that are being induced. Coercive power is readily achieved in the formal power structure through the threat of punishment and denial. In the informal power channel, coercive power is often accomplished by the threat of psychological deprivation (such as being ignored, having information withheld, or being excluded from significant projects).

Reward power is often used to gain the support of individuals in achieving a goal or accomplishing a task. When an individual believes that he can acquire some desired goal if he behaves in a prescribed or desired manner, he is usually responding to some type of reward power. It is allied with the formal power structure, since the power hierarchy commonly controls most of the rewards and sanctions in the social system of the school. On the other hand, reward power can be used in the informal power structure and is often employed between people (or among persons in a group) when they indicate the worth of a person and the importance of his ideas. Seeking information or opinions from a person, extolling the worth of an activity for which a person was responsible, or commenting on the value or appropriateness of a remark a person made at a faculty meeting are examples of ways that people use reward power in the informal power structure. Reward power is a kind of reinforcement that is effectively employed in the school system.

Expert power is employed when an individual is perceived to have some special knowledge or expertise that can be shared with others. Expert power is often based on special information or skills that others in the system may lack. This expertise contains the potential to reach and influence others in the school system. When expertise is within the legitimate role expectations, such power is readily actualized in working with others. However, when this expertise is not perceived as being within the legitimate domain of the role, it is more difficult, but not impossible, to activate. For example, a school counselor may have little difficulty communicating with a teacher about a pupil with whom he is in a counseling relationship. This is probably within her perceptions of his expertise. On the other hand if he were to offer his services in exploring with her ways of accommodating the mental growth of individual learners and of dealing with individual styles of learning he would probably experience some immediate resistance since she might believe his consultation in this area to be both outside his function (consulting) and his area of knowledge (knowing about mental growth and individual styles of learning). In this case, then, the counselor must establish the legitimacy of his role in this area as well as his expertise in the area of knowledge concerned. Even when little role resistance is encountered, employing expert power relies on the skill of the counselor in having his public utilize his knowledge and skills.

Referent power (which we might call "relationship" power) has the broadest base in that it has potential for actualization between any two or more people in the system. Essentially, referent power relies on an individual's identification with another person and on his aspirations to believe, or to behave, or to be like this other individual. Referent power, therefore, finds its strength in human relationships and in the ability of an individual to have others seek to be more like him. The developmental counselor, with his many publics, has an opportunity to establish a wide base of referent power including administrators, teachers, students, and parents. To the extent that he is able to use his referent power, he is able to extend the range of his influence. To the extent that he is able to extend the range of his influence, he is in a position to use the informal power structure to effect changes in the system and in the way things are done in the system. At the same time, and in the same manner, he can change the image of the school counselor role, creating one that is more in tune with the needs and goals of developmental guidance. To the degree that he is involved in all these changes, he is an agent of change. To the extent that he is an agent of change, he is engaged in the process of renewing the sphere and influence of developmental guidance.

While there are many implications of the use of power in effecting change, perhaps one of the most important is the school counselor's ability to use it in ways that will enhance the learning environment of the school. When the school counselor works only within the legitimate power confines of his role, he is not only restricting his role but limiting greatly his own power and his potential to use it in the change processes of the school. Power is a resource that he simply cannot afford to waste. The dynamic of power *is* at work in the school system and the counselor must convert its use to his advantage. He must become aware of it and learn to utilize it in constructive and positive ways.

ENACTING THE DEVELOPMENTAL
GUIDANCE ROLE

There are a number of concerns and encounters that are pertinent in enact-ing the developmental guidance role. Perhaps these are not unlike those faced in more traditional guidance programs, but they are certainly to be encountered more frequently and in more pervasive ways. How these en-counters will be handled by the developmental counselor will be determined not so much by specific guidance techniques and practices as by his ability to use his knowledge of the concepts of role and power. While many of his day-to-day confrontations cannot be avoided and necessitate on-the-spot re-sponses, the developmental counselor must never lose sight of his longer term objective: to establish an environment that will allow him to engage in the functions that are vital to implementing his beliefs about develop-mental guidance.

Some Concerns in the Developmental Guidance Role

A few of the major concerns that differentiate the developmental counselor from his more traditional counterpart are enumerated below:

(1) He will be concerned with the environment of the school as it facilitates the learning-maturation process of each individual. To this end the school counselor is concerned not only with the learner and his growth and de-velopment and with his uniqueness as an individual but with the behaviors that are to be learned and with the conditions in which this learning will take place. This necessitates more attention to the learning environment of the school as well as every classroom in it. It means that the develop-mental counselor will engage himself more actively and directly in work-ing with teachers and administrators toward evolving a curriculum and conditions that will facilitate all aspects of the learning-maturation process.

(2) He will become more involved in working with teachers to facilitate the preventive aspects of developmental guidance. While he may remain in-volved with the more traditional emphases that have involved school coun-selors in remediation and crisis guidance, he will focus on greater teacher awareness of their own contributions in helping students with variant and deviant learning difficulties. This will necessitate not only an extension of the consulting function but one with a different emphasis—one that in-volves the counselor in helping to improve and to extend the influence of the teaching-learning process. This extension of the consulting function marks a most decided change in the role of guidance in the secondary school. The developmental counselor will be concerned with developing the nature and extent of his involvement in the educative process. He will

be working toward the necessary changes in the expectations of his role to accommodate the role modifications in an expanded and differing consulting function.

(3) He will be concerned with the role expectations of others as these are communicated to him by individuals or groups of individuals in the vast public he serves. Since he will be extending his role beyond some of the established or traditional stereotypes of his work, he is apt to be confronted with a variety of role expectations to which he is no longer committed or to which he has less commitment. The clearcut instances of role disagreement will challenge the very best of his interpersonal skills, demanding the utmost from his understanding of role and power in his judgments in responding to these role pressures.

(4) He will be concerned with the potential power that he has in his role as a school counselor. He will want to learn how to use this power within the formal and informal power structure of the system in which he is employed. He will want to help others in other roles to use their potential power. He will want to defend himself from the forces of power that can reduce his capacity to effect changes in the system or that can delimit his function to the disadvantage of developmental guidance. He will want to establish himself as a force for the positive use of the power motive. The trend in the larger society toward bureaucracy and professionalization is having powerful effects on education. Within the formal organizational hierarchy the developmental counselor has about the same potential power as a teacher. Yet, his much larger public, his expertise in communication and interpersonal relations—all facets of human interaction—and his knowledge and understanding of the power structure can be combined to actualize his power potential.

(5) He will be concerned with the evaluative possibilities inherent in the role expected of him, recognizing that the degree to which he meets or does not meet these expectations can affect the way others measure his effectiveness. He must recognize that his own concern for his evaluation by superiors induces role behaviors that are incompatible and sometimes undesirable to the developmental guidance role. When this occurs the counselor feels the pressure to engage in activities that limit or inhibit his job performance. He must recognize the ways in which he responds to the various types of power. He must be aware of the various psychological forces (fear, anxiety) or personal priorities (family, geographical preferences) that interfere with his ability to use whatever sources of power are at his disposal. This is not to infer that job evaluations can be readily dismissed, for they obviously cannot; rather it is to indicate that other forces and priorities do cause counselors to submit readily to unreasonable job demands.

(6) He recognizes that role conflict is inevitable. He is concerned with such conflicts as they arise from role expectations that are in disagreement with his own role preferences or from contradictory expectations in his public

(where one teacher might expect him to perform a certain activity while another teacher would expect him to refrain from involvement in that activity). Further, he is concerned about role conflict that emerges in areas where work roles may overlap. While there is the possibility for role conflict with other pupil personnel service workers (school psychologist, school social worker) in certain guidance efforts of a remedial nature, his focus on the learning environment and the teaching-learning process—the preventive efforts—make him equally vulnerable to similar role conflicts with other instructional and administrative personnel.

(7) He is concerned that the probability and possibility for change in the school guidance role, coupled with a certain amount of tentativeness and experimentation, can result in a considerable amount of role ambiguity. Since most role statements can only contain a degree of specificity leaving a good deal of leeway in the actual role enactment to the judgment and inclination of the developmental counselor, he is free to opt for developing aspects of his role for which there is no precedent or about which there is less specificity. As change accelerates, modifications in the guidance role will be demanded continually. This ever-changing, adaptive feature of the school counselor role mandates an open and continuous means of communication between the school counselor and his public. Since the developmental counselor is ever in the process of renewing his role both verbally and behaviorally, he must identify his own feelings in these situations and develop ways of dealing with them that are satisfactory to the idiographic dimensions of his role and at the same time helpful to the particular individuals who are involved. The attempt to assess his own feelings and to deal both with them and with the feelings and actions of others toward him will, to a large degree, determine his success in the developmental guidance role.

(8) The developmental counselor is aware of the judgments that he must make relative to the *direction* of his role and the *intensity* of his involvement. He is aware that the role of the developmental counselor is not sufficiently specified or detailed to provide him with personal security or to preclude his need to make judgments about his role. He must still make judgments with reference to the direction of his role (should he or should he *not* engage in an activity). He must still make judgments concerning the intensity of his involvement (the depth or degree of attention focused on an activity). He must determine the activities that he feels are absolutely essential, those that are desirable, those that would be helpful, and those that are inappropriate to developmental guidance.

(9) He is concerned with his own motivations for involvement in the guidance role. This causes him to deal with a number of pertinent questions. To what extent does he view school guidance as a step "up" in educational advancement? To what extent is he using guidance as a stepping stone to school administration? We knew that guidance has been viewed by many as an advancement in the system and that it has been used as a means to

obtain administrative positions. When the school guidance position is viewed in these ways, there are obvious implications for the counselor's role behavior. How does he respond to the role expectations of superiors in the power hierarchy? How does he respond in situations of role conflict and role ambiguity? In what ways does he use the formal and informal power structure of the system and for what purposes? The personal needs and goals of the school counselor are most assuredly involved in the behaviors he exhibits.

SUGGESTED READING

BENTLEY, JOSEPH C., *The Counselor's Role, Commentary and Readings* (Boston: Houghton Mifflin, 1968).

CARTWRIGHT, DORWIN, Ed., *Studies in Social Power* (Ann Arbor: University of Michigan, 1959).

DUBIN, ROBERT, Ed., *Human Relations in Administration* (Englewood Cliffs, N.J.: Prentice-Hall, 1961), Second edition.

GETZELS, J. W., and GUBA, E. G., "Social Behavior and the Administrative Process," *The School Review* 65:423–441, Winter 1957.

GROSS, NEAL; MASON, WARD; and MCEACHERN, ALEXANDER, *Explorations in Role Analysis* (New York: John Wiley, 1958).

KAHN, ROBERT L.; WOLFE, DONALD; QUINN, ROBERT; SNOEK, J. DIEDRICK; and ROSENTHAL, ROBERT, *Organizational Stress* (New York: John Wiley, 1964).

WILSON, L. CRAIG; BYAR, T. MADISON; SHAPIRO, ARTHUR S.; and SCHELL, SHIRLEY H., *Sociology of Supervision* (Boston: Allyn and Bacon, 1969).

SEVEN

THE COUNSELING FUNCTION

Counseling, whether viewed as an element of a guidance program or as a function of the school counselor, has been reputedly one of the more important activities, if not the most important one, of a school counselor. Its primary significance is implied in the job title "school counselor." When one comes to grips with the total role of secondary school guidance, this label is somewhat misleading. I do not wish to quarrel with the importance of the counseling function nor do I wish to debate its priority status. Rather, I would hope that we can recognize the limitations that may accrue from this occupational title as well as the benefits. Certainly, in theory and in practice, other functions are performed and the legitimacy of these can be supported. Those involved in developmental guidance need to be able to distinguish among their various functions.

Counseling Defined

To define counseling to everyone's satisfaction is akin to being responsible for selecting a faculty retirement gift for a beloved colleague. You inquire from ten people and you get ten suggestions. In the end you use your best judgment and hope that all your friends on the faculty will agree with your choice. This is what I have done in attempting to define counseling here. I have made some choices from the many definitions available, definitions that have meaning for me and, I trust, for you as well.

One of my favorite definitions of long standing is that proposed by E. L. Tolbert. He defines counseling as

. . . a personal, face-to-face relationship between two people, in which the counselor, by means of the relationship and his special competencies, provides a learning situation in which the counselee, a normal sort of person, is helped to know himself and his present and possible future situations so that he can make use of his characteristics and potentialities in a way that is both satisfying to himself and beneficial to society, and further, can learn how to solve future problems and meet future needs.[1]

Roeber, Walz and Smith, more concisely define counseling as ". . . purposeful communication in a personal (one-to-one) atmosphere of mutual acceptance and understanding."[2] Sometimes we tend to forget that our relationship in counseling should have purpose. It is doubtful if counseling can occur unless there is some purpose. Short of purpose, I rather suspect we have conversation, not counseling.

Lest we are overcome with the one-to-one aspects of counseling, Stefflre's definition reminds us that counseling can occur among persons as well as between two people. He provides the following definition:

Counseling denotes a professional relationship between a trained counselor and a client. This relationship is usually person-to-person, although it may sometimes involve more than two people, and it is designed to help the client understand and clarify his view of his life space so that he may make meaningful and informed choices consonant with his essential nature in those areas where choices are available to him.[3]

The last definition speaks more to the process and the goals of counseling than to the relationship. It has a different emphasis than the others and serves to add to our cumulative understanding of the term. Blocker, an advocate of developmental counseling, defines counseling within a developmental frame of reference as follows:

Developmental counseling . . . aims at helping an individual become aware of himself and the ways in which he is reacting to the behavioral influences in his environment. It further helps him to establish some personal meaning for this behavior and to develop and clarify a set of goals and values for future behavior. Out of such awareness and understanding of his past learning history and his environment, an individual is better able to identify those environmental influences that will best facilitate the kind of future development that is goal-oriented for him.[4]

[1] E. L. Tolbert, *Introduction to Counseling* (New York: McGraw-Hill, 1959), p. 3.
[2] Edward C. Roeber, Garry R. Walz, and Glenn E. Smith, *A Strategy for Guidance* (Toronto: Collier-Macmillan, 1969), p. 71.
[3] Buford Stefflre (Ed.), *Theories of Counseling* (New York: McGraw-Hill, 1965), p. 15.
[4] Donald H. Blocher, *Developmental Counseling* (New York: Ronald Press, 1966), p. 5.

You can easily find other definitions—almost as many as there are textbooks—on counseling. Other definitions may have more meaning for you. Those that I have included here have had considerable meaning for me and for my approach to the counseling function in developmental guidance. There is sufficient commonality in each definition to identify the relationship aspects of the function and, yet, enough diversity to allow for some consideration of the process and goals.

Counseling as a Human Relationship

Counseling is essentially human interaction. While it is often referred to as a helping relationship I prefer to think of it as a *human relationship.* The most direct concern of the school counselor for another person is expressed through the counseling function. It is a human relationship foremost. If the outcome is "helping" to another person, so much the better. We enter the relationship with the hope that it will be helping but we know that we cannot always help. We can always be human!

In the one-to-one relationship, or in the group relationship, the counselor can demonstrate his caring; he can evidence his regard for the other person; he can be himself. Utilizing his professional understandings and skills in a human relationship where counseling can occur, he can provide an opportunity for others to examine their feelings, attitudes, values, and beliefs and the manner in which they express these in their day-to-day behavior. In counseling he can encourage and help others to deal with matters and concerns of significance to them. He can create an atmosphere which is supportive and open. He can provide conditions of acceptance, understanding, and trust. We don't do these things just in a counseling cubicle: we try to be a person, and most of us try to relate to others in these *human* ways. Counseling could occur, then, anywhere, any time. When my students begin to clamor about when they are going to start "counseling," I remind them that they can start anytime—tonight, tomorrow; or any place—in their home, at their desk, or in the men's room; or with anybody—their spouse, their uncle, their next door neighbor. While they can be ready to engage in counseling, they need to be able to distinguish this from conversation. And here is where purpose has meaning. The other person has to have purpose— that is, he has to be involved. Purpose does not necessarily have to be definitively stated. Sometimes it just occurs. For example, I mentioned that students become anxious to get started in counseling. I often suggest that they start with their wife or husband or a friend. Sometimes this works well for those who have the basic relationship (the human aspects) and the necessary conditions (acceptance, understanding, and trust) going for them. The other person becomes involved and they are soon dealing with a significant part of the other's life. But sometimes it doesn't work so well (though it proves to be a real learning experience), for the spouse or the friend, conditioned to the behaviors of the other, is shaken by these human behavioral changes or is overwhelmed by the condition of experiencing greater acceptance or trust.

There is not a one among us who could not try to be more human or who could not improve upon the conditions of his human relationships. Since these are so basic to the counseling relationship and so much a part of the process, it seems like a most logical area for the beginning counselor to explore. You, too, can begin right now!

The Human Aspects of the Counseling Relationship

Now we are thinking of the counseling relationship as a human relationship. There are a number of considerations that can guide our understanding of it. First, it is important to think of the relationship as one that has real meaning, or real potential for meaning, for everyone involved. Since the counseling relationship is frequently a person-to-person relationship, I will discuss it from this frame of reference, though you should recognize that very often more than two people are involved. Second, the relationship involves two people—two human beings regardless of age and age differential, sex, status or relationship (teacher, principal, counselor). While it is true that the school counselor is generally much older, may be of different sex, may represent some authority or status figure and is in the counselor-counselee relationship, these differences need not necessarily interfere.

The reality of any or all of these differences, as they exist, should be recognized. You can't pretend they don't exist. But neither do you need to magnify them. Actually you as a counselor are working with another person and you can approach this other person, regardless of any of these or any other differentials that may exist, on a human basis. True, in the course of your human interaction you may both, as humans, need to deal with these differentials as they may interfere. But you don't have to start out with thoughts such as "I'm his counselor, now what do I do," "He's just a kid who doesn't know," "I'm mature so I should have his respect" or "He's not wise to the ways of the world yet." There are so many ways in which we play up these differentials—verbally and non-verbally—while we mean really to play them down. Simply, what we try to do is to think of the counseling relationship as a human relationship between two people. The more we live like this, the easier it is to behave like this. Now let us examine some of the ingredients that help us to build a bond with another person.

Caring. It is important that the counselor care. To care implies that you have some feeling for the other person—that you are concerned about him and his life. Caring involves a willingness to become involved with another person. It presumes some measure of responsibility for developing or maintaining the relationship even when the interaction begins with the complexities of helping the counselee to communicate with you. Caring is rarely an "I do" or "I don't" proposition but rather one of degree. Obviously it involves both people in the relationship, and the mutuality of their caring in a large measure influences the depth of their interaction and the strength of the relationship.

Positive regard. When Carl R. Rogers speaks of "unconditional positive regard" he means ". . . an outgoing positive feeling without reservations, without evaluations."[5] Carkhuff and Berenson seem to equate positive regard and respect. They state, *"Respect* or positive regard in interpersonal processes is defined at minimally facilitative levels by the first person's communication of a *positive respect* and concern for the second person's feelings, experiences, and potentials."[6] Since respect, in my opinion, suggests some differential in status or role which can inhibit as well as enhance a counseling relationship, I would prefer to think of positive regard as representing one's recognition of the worth and dignity of the other. This can be a platitude readily and easily agreed with but ever so difficult to apply in the counseling relationship. In my experience I have found that it is most difficult for people to be "unconditional" in the Rogerian sense. On the other hand, a counselor who is aware of the concept of positive regard can be always evaluating his own feelings of regard for the other; he can become conscious of the conditional nature of this regard. In this sense, to the extent that a counselor chooses to be "unconditional," he is always in process of becoming.

Openness. This is a difficult and often confusing term. Openness is often equated with complete self-disclosure. It is often confused with frankness. Openness, as I would define it for the human relationship in counseling, is a condition more than an act. It allows for the counselee to explore his own feelings and experiences within the limitations of his own defenses and social forces, leaving him to reveal those parts of himself and those facets of experience that he is able to communicate to another. In the counseling relationship, the counselor can help the counselee to become more open to his own experiences and more able to risk authentic self-disclosure. The condition of openness that exists from the very beginning of the relationship is ever in process and the counselor must learn to be sensitive to

[5] Carl R. Rogers, *On Becoming A Person* (Boston: Houghton Mifflin, 1961), p. 62.

[6] Robert R. Carkhuff and Bernard G. Berenson, *Beyond Counseling and Therapy* (New York: Holt, Rinehart and Winston, 1967), pp. 5–6.

the other individual and his freedom or ability to become more open as the relationship evolves. In the secondary school, particularly, the counselee may find it very difficult to discuss himself and his life. Such a condition is frequently encountered with an adolescent who, for the first time, has been provided with an opportunity to explore with another person (a professional counselor) the inner aspects of his own being.

Genuineness. To be genuine in the counseling relationship is to be *real.* This eliminates role playing or acting in the counseling session. Beginning counselors often attempt to *play the role* of a counselor (their perception of the counselor role). It is only as they learn to use their real selves in a counseling relationship that they begin to experience what it means to be genuine in the human relationship of counseling. Rogers talks about genuineness in the counseling relationship as follows: ". . . I have not found it to be helpful or effective in my relationships with other people to try to maintain a façade; to act in one way on the surface when I am experiencing something quite different underneath."[7] In one sense, being genuine in the counseling relationship is just *being*—that is, being what you are, being aware of what you are experiencing and how you are behaving. The possibilities for discrepancy between what you are experiencing and how you are behaving in counseling have caused Carkhuff and Berenson to differentiate between the construct of genuineness and facilitative genuineness. They qualify genuineness in the counseling relationship, indicating that when the counselor's

. . . only genuine responses are negative in regard to the second person, the therapist makes an effort to employ his responses constructively as a basis for further inquiry for the therapist, the client, and their relationship. . . . Therefore, while it appears of critical importance to avoid the conscious or unconscious facade of "playing the therapeutic role," the necessity for the therapist's expressing himself fully at all times is not supported.[8]

While this may appear contradictory to the idea of being real or genuine in the counseling relationship, it remains consistent with the idea of a human relationship that is helpful rather than hurtful.

Conditions of the Counseling Relationship

Certain conditions characterize the counseling relationship. These are acceptance, understanding, and trust. While they represent in one way an ex-

[7] Rogers, *op. cit.,* p. 17.
[8] Carkhuff and Berenson, *op. cit.,* p. 29.

tension of the human aspects of counseling we have just discussed, they can be considered conditions, for the character of the counseling relationship is dependent upon the mutuality of their existence. That is, the extent to which two people are able to develop these conditions, the more likely a relationship can exist and the greater the possibilities for human growth.

Acceptance. A primary condition is the feeling of acceptance demonstrated by both individuals. Each must be willing to accept the basic nature of the other. It is important for both the counselor and the counselee to *behave* in ways that express "I accept you." The counselor has the advantage in demonstrating his acceptance of the counselee. He may be more adept at blending his caring, his regard, his openness, and his realness in an attitude that conveys clearly his acceptance. His counselee may be less able to do this as readily or as easily. While this smacks of role playing, that is *not* what I mean. I am simply suggesting that the counselor can express his basic feelings in a fashion that is conducive to expressing his acceptance rather quickly. If he does not feel this acceptance for one reason or another, he will have considerable difficulty in masking his true feelings or in faking false acceptance. Attempts to cover up feelings which you do not want to make known, acting the counselor role, or talking down to the adolescent (all behaviors common to beginning counselors) make it more difficult to talk with him, for by his very nature he seems particularly able to fathom these behaviors rather quickly. Thus while the counselor can use his knowledge of himself and of the counseling process to his advantage, it is more natural and human to be straightforward in dealing with a counselee.

For example, the adolescent may appear very nervous about coming to the counselor's office. It may be quite appropriate to deal with this at the outset rather than to try to ignore it or to hope that it will pass with inconsequential talk designed to put him at ease. In the earlier days of counseling, this was called establishing rapport. The idea was to make meaningful communication possible. The establishment of rapport was presented as a task of the counselor—something that he did to or for the relationship. While the counselor can assume responsibility for enhancing the conditions of the relationship, the idea of acceptance as a condition of counseling assumes the involvement of both people.

Trust. A second condition, and one that is akin to acceptance, is the feeling of trust. Trust is an abstract concept, one that is particularly difficult to understand and deal with. Trust involves confidence in another person. In one sense it involves an investment in him, for to trust him is to believe in him and to be able to risk with him. A counselor must be trusting—that is, he must be able to trust others. If he is unable to trust others in his own living, it is difficult to transfer this lack of trust outside the counseling relationship to one of trust in it. It is likely that he will behave in the counseling relationship much as he would in other relationships.

This feeling of trust, then, is something that the counselor must experience himself in order that the other person can feel free and able to reciprocate and respond in the process of communication. Many beginning counselors distinguish between their feelings of trust for adolescents and adults, indicating that the former are not old enough or wise enough or worldly enough—in short, they lack enough "enough"—to be trusted. Such a lack of faith or confidence in another person, whatever his age or condition, can be exceedingly detrimental to the relationship. Again, as with acceptance, adolescents are quick to determine feelings of trust or the lack of it. Counselors don't have to wait until they begin to function in the cubicle to test their capacity for trust. They can assess it in their day-to-day interactions with people of all kinds.

The secondary school counselor works with many people—teachers, parents, pupils—and he is responsible to all these "publics." When he is working with a tenth grade student, he has some responsibility to the teachers and the parents of this individual and to the administrator of the school. It may well be that he will be in a position where he needs to communicate about the pupil to the school psychologist or to some other pupil personnel service worker. In effect the counselor, recognizing the importance of trust and its impact on the counseling relationship, is constrained at times by the recognition of his responsibility to other people with whom the youth is associated.

Adolescents are often less able to trust when they are aware of these multiple allegiances. When an individual is aware of a counselor's relationship to either his teacher or his parents or both, it is more difficult to establish a trust which can survive all these other relationships yet allow the counseling relationship to be a meaningful and satisfying one for both. While this aspect of the counseling relationship can create ethical problems, raising the issue of confidentiality, it does seem possible that the counselor can deal with this as he would other human encounters. If the counselor creates an atmosphere of acceptance and trust, one in which the individual feels free to express himself fully and openly, then the counselor must recognize the conditions that have allowed the individual to feel able to participate fully in the relationship.

Under these conditions of acceptance and trust, the counselor is unable to divulge information which he has obtained unless he has received permission from the counselee to go beyond the limits of their relationship in passing this information to the other people in his public. It does not seem that there is a "right" or "wrong" in dealing with these kinds of situations.

There are no answers for the counselor who raises the question "What do I do now?" or "How free am I to divulge this information to other people?" The freedom of the counselor is restricted by each relationship and the conditions, especially the trust, which have been established in each.

Thus the answer to these kinds of questions rests on the *judgment* of the counselor and his assessment of the situation. Only he can judge how free he is to reveal certain information related to him by his counselee and to whom such information can be released.

Understanding. The presence of mutual acceptance and trust make possible an understanding of each other's behavior and feelings. Understanding, like acceptance and trust, is a difficult concept to comprehend. Understanding is more than listening; it is more than hearing the content or feeling of another's experience and understanding it after it has been screened through the experiential world of the counselor. As Rogers said, "It is only as I *understand* the feelings and thoughts which seem so horrible to you, or so weak, or so sentimental, or so bizarre—it is only as I see them as you see them, and accept them and you, that you feel really free to explore all the hidden nooks and frightening crannies of your inner and often buried experience."[9] Rogers talks about allowing (permitting) himself to understand another person. He states, "Is it necessary to *permit* oneself to understand another? I think that it is. Our first reaction to most of the statements which we hear from other people is an immediate evaluation, or judgment, rather than an understanding of it. . . . Very rarely do we permit ourselves to *understand* precisely what the meaning of his statement is to him."[10] In counseling the adolescent, it is so important to understand. While some may refer to this as empathy, or as empathic understanding, the term is not important, the condition is.

DIMENSIONS OF THE COUNSELING PROCESS

While it is possible that a counselor and his counselee may meet only once and that in this meeting counseling may occur, it is generally recognized that the types of concerns which secondary school students bring to the counselor may require—and usually do—a number of meetings. In the secondary school the counseling process begins when the counselor and the counselee meet for the first time. They may find it necessary, depending upon the needs and the concerns of the counselee, to meet regularly for a period

[9] Rogers, *op. cit.,* p. 34.
[10] *Ibid.,* p. 18.

of time or perhaps periodically over a longer span of time. On the other hand, they may find that such meetings may be very sporadic and unplanned. Others may seek incidental or occasional sessions with a counselor two or three times during the year. Some may not wish to see the counselor at all. However the counseling contacts occur, the advantage of the counselee's being able to work with the same counselor over a period of time (two or three years or more, if possible) is the single most important consideration.

Continuity, allowing for the development and continual evolvement of a human relationship, should supercede almost any other factor in the determination of counseling assignments or loads. Not only does the factor of continuity have meaning for the ongoing nature of the counseling process, it has implications for the efficacy and effectiveness of these relationships. Nothing can replace the human aspects of any relationship, and its conditions which two people have carefully established over a period of meetings.

The Internal vs. the External

During any period in the process of counseling, the relationship between the counselor and the counselee will touch upon many facets of the counselee's life and behavior. It will weave among the external or environmental influences which comprise the realities of his life existence and relationships. At other times it will concern itself with the internal aspects of his being—his own beliefs, values, attitudes, and needs, as these are expressed in his experiencing—his sensing, his feeling, his believing, or his striving. All of these are significant components of the individual—the inner workings that make him an individual. In their total combination, we account for the individual's behavior.

In the counseling relationship these are important internal variables that need to be examined by the counselee and often reexamined by the counselor. At least, he needs to be aware of those facets of himself that cause him to react as he does to his counselee. We should assume that a counselor, in his program of preparation, has become more aware of who he is and how he functions. Now let us examine some of these internal variables that we often encounter in the counseling process.

Beliefs. While one's beliefs can often be identified and enumerated, the term is often an abstract one, which makes it difficult to deal with until we have something specific to examine in relation to one's behavior. In general, our beliefs are represented by those opinions, ideas, or concepts we accept and use in our day-to-day living. They may be abstract, such as one's ideas about the freedom of man or one's opinions about the existence of God; they can be concrete, such as too much candy is bad for the teeth or

Ron is a good Student Council president. A belief is something that we have confidence in, that we trust. A belief has been reasoned; it represents some deliberate thought. An opinion can be equated with a belief although it may be more readily subject to change. It does represent reason and thought.

An idea is something that one has assimilated and thought about though it may not be so internalized that it influences our behavior. Beliefs, including opinions and ideas, are an important part of one's internal reference and they are continually used in our day-to-day behavior in the many life situations and tasks which we encounter. Beliefs emerge in the counseling process in many ways but typically easy ones to identify often begin with such phrases as "I think," "I disagree," "As I see it," or "In my judgment." Both the counselor and the counselee may find themselves verbalizing beliefs in the form of convictions, sentiments, points of view, ideas or concepts.

Values. The social, moral, and ethical standards of our society, to which we have all been partially exposed but which none of us has completely experienced, have in one way or another contributed to the development of our own particular value system. It is important to remember that each of us is continually being exposed to different standards and values as these are represented by different groups in the social strata. Mores and customs differ widely in our culture—and yet we sometimes forget that not all Americans are alike. As our lives come into contact with these varying values, we learn more about what others consider desirable and important.

Every counselor has his own value system. He has considered aspects of worth in many different areas such as family, religion, work, love, politics, money. Our values in these areas are represented by those aspects that we find desirable and worthy. Raths, Harmin, and Simon contend that valuing involves three processes—choosing, prizing, and behaving.[11] These processes indicate the manner in which the individual selects from the many alternatives available those things which he believes are of worth to him. Those which he has chosen, which he comes to value or esteem, he prizes. These individually represent a value and these, in combination, represent our value system. The priority of any value, that is the worth that we attach to it, the place we accord it in our total value system and the manner in which we act on it, very definitely affects our behavior.

Since our society is represented by a number of core and alternative values, it is easy to understand why we might have great variation in individual value systems. In counseling, both the values of the counselor and the counselee are constantly in operation: both value systems are being

[11] Louis E. Raths, Merrill Harmin, and Sidney B. Simon, *Values and Teaching* (Columbus, Ohio: Charles E. Merrill, 1966), p. 30.

tested and explored. The counselor is constantly faced with values and behaviors which are the same as his, different from his, or foreign to him. Thus he is constantly reacting internally to the expression of values of the other person.

While there may be less difficulty with acceptance or understanding when both hold the same values, there may be some problem in the basic conditions of the relationship (that is, the acceptance, trust, or understanding) when the counselee's values differ from those of the counselor. These differences are often noted first within the context of the counselee's behavior. Very often in counseling the counselor helps the counselee to gain insight into his behaving by helping him to examine the process of valuing in reverse. That is, he helps the counselee to look at his own behavior, to identify the things or ideas that he prizes, and to consider or reconsider the alternatives available.

Attitudes. English and English define an attitude as "an enduring, learned predisposition to behave in a consistent way toward a given class of objects; a persistent mental and/or neural state of readiness to react to a certain object or class of objects, not as they are but as they are conceived to be."[12] Newcomb, in *A Dictionary of the Social Sciences,* defines an attitude as follows:

An *attitude* is the individual's organization of psychological processes, as inferred from his behaviour, with respect to some aspect of the world which he distinguishes from other aspects. It represents the residue of his previous experience with which he approaches any subsequent situation including that aspect and, together with the contemporary influences in such a situation, determines his behaviour in it. Attitudes are enduring in the sense that such residues are carried over to new situations, but they change in so far as new residues are acquired through experience in new situations.[13]

One distinguishing aspect of an attitude is its more persistent or enduring quality. Another feature to be reckoned with is the integrative or organizational conditions since an attitude may be considered an internal set, consisting of those combinations of data which together form a disposition toward a certain object or event. The complexity of these integrative conditions has puzzled psychologists for years. Yet we know that attitudes very definitely

[12] Horace B. English and Ava C. English, *A Comprehensive Dictionary of Psychological and Psychoanalytical Terms* (New York: David McKay, 1958), p. 50. Used by permission of David MacKay Company, Inc.

[13] Julius Gould and William Kolb (Eds.), *A Dictionary of the Social Sciences* (Toronto: Collier-Macmillan, 1964), p. 40.

influence behavior. In speaking of the cognitive aspects of attitude formation, Asch states,

It becomes necessary to understand the major directions or premises of the individual's outlook, the cleavages that may exist, and the functions of a given attitude within its context. Because it is a semi-autonomous system, we need to study its formation and change in accordance with conditions directly relevant to it. Because it is a dependent part of a wider system, it is necessary for us to see its place and function in the person's scheme of things, to see how it takes shape and changes in a medium of already functioning views. We may, for example, find that the formation of a given attitude will encounter resistance if it contradicts the wider system that tends to equilibrium, or that it will take shape to conform to the system. On the other hand, a change in a very cogent part may start a process that alters the system as a whole.[14]

This may help us to understand better the development and influence of an attitude and the manner whereby an attitude is integrated into the total system which comprises the character of the individual.

Needs. Needs, in a psychological sense, have been categorized in a hierarchy by Maslow in a theory of human motivation that he promulgated some years ago and which he has expanded in the intervening years. Maslow's hierarchy of needs from the most basic to the most complex and self-fulfilling is as follows: (1) basic physiological needs—water, food, sleep, etc.; (2) security and safety needs; (3) love and belongingness needs; (4) self-esteem or prestige needs; (5) aesthetic needs; and (6) the self-actualizing needs.[15] Maslow's concept emphasizes the growing, developing, maturing needs of man as an individual and as an individual who depends on others, as well as himself, for the satisfaction of his needs. It is not clear whether this society is yet fully able to subscribe to the concept of self-actualization, yet it is clearly obvious that our society readily admits to a policy which emphasizes the maximum utilization of our human resources. Part of the difficulty in obtaining fully self-actualized people seems to lie in the ability of society to accept (or to yield to) individual behavior as opposed to conforming behaviors. In industry, for example, where the self-actualization of the worker is most important to the effectiveness of the worker on the job (from assembly line production tasks to high level policy setting or policy implementing executive positions) there remains the matter of keeping the individual subservient to the company and its profit

[14] Solomon E. Asch, *Social Psychology* (Englewood Cliffs, N.J.: Prentice-Hall, Inc., © 1952), pp. 581–582.

[15] A. H. Maslow, *Motivation and Personality* (New York: Harper, 1954), chapter 5.

motives. Thus we must deal with the idea of individuality and self-actualization within the realm of conformity in the form of the "grey flannel suit." Schutz provides another way of looking at the needs of man. He proposes a theory of interpersonal relations based on the wanted and expressed needs of human interaction. His theory states that each human has needs for inclusion, control, and affection of both a wanted (incoming) and expressed (outgoing) nature. He contends that interpersonal relations must account for these needs and that the compatibility of people is dependent on the mutuality of these wanted and expressed behaviors.[16] In the counseling relationship, human needs must be considered, both in terms of the relationship as it develops between the counselor and counselee, and, in terms of the help that can be afforded the counselee in assessing and understanding his own needs and their effect on his behavior. For example, within the relationship itself, a counselor's need for acceptance, for satisfaction, for domination or control or for closure can be noted through analysis of his communication with a counselee. Likewise, these can be observed in the counselee as he reports on his own behavior and on the behavior of others toward him. Further, such needs and behaviors can often be spotted within the counseling relationship.

Abilities. The abilities one has and how he perceives his abilities can be a very important aspect of helping a person look at himself. Of the internal considerations we have discussed thus far, this is one that is more frequently dealt with in high school counseling. Abilities are most often examined from the standpoint of intelligence or scholastic aptitude, beginning with one's general capacity to learn. In recent years considerably more attention has been given to some of the more specific components of intelligence such as numerical reasoning, verbal fluency, mechanical reasoning, memory, abstract reasoning, and others. These areas have been isolated for measurement in standardized testing and are often considered individually as aptitudes. Many of these, separately or in combination, relate to the ability to think or reason but can be isolated with reference to specific mental tasks such as the ability to think with words or the ability to think with numbers. In the counseling process, consideration of one's abilities has been considered important in relation to various aspects of educational-vocational planning. Most secondary school counseling has been directed toward interpreting standardized test data permitting students to make comparisons among their own abilities and the abilities of others. Obviously, the interpretation of standardized tests is best represented by the *external* aspects of

---

[16] William C. Schutz, *The Interpersonal Underworld* (Palo Alto, California: Science and Behavior Books, 1966), chapter 2.

the counseling process in which outside information is brought to bear on the student's understanding of himself. While external data, such as standardized test results, has its import in the counseling process, the internal dimension of examining one's perception of his ability in these areas is equally, if not more, important. For example, while the standardized test may indicate that a student is "above average" in verbal fluency, if he does not view his ability that way it is important to note the differences between the external data and the internal perception of the student. Our concern here for which is "right," the student or the test data, can cause us to lose sight of the potential for growth in self-assessment and self-understanding.

Interests. Interests are often expressed in the counseling situation. Self-expressions of one's likes and dislikes taps the internal frame of reference providing many avenues of self-exploration to follow. Standardized measures of interests such as the Kuder Preference Record or the Strong Vocational Interest Record are often used to help students identify areas of interest leading to vocational considerations. All too often, however, these interests are too quickly equated with occupational possibilities—a disturbing and somewhat unfortunate use of these instruments. While such tests may help a student to identify or validate an area of interest, the occupational relationship rarely, if ever, takes into consideration many of the other internal dimensions we have been considering here.

Likes and dislikes are an important part of the internal being of an individual, and the professional counselor can easily help the student examine these in some detail. For example, with regard to a student's statement "I like social studies," the counselor can help the student to pursue what it is that he likes about the subject—history, government, geography, sociology, anthropology, or economics—for social studies is a little of all of these. To like social studies could mean to find enjoyment or fascination with all of these areas, but it is more than likely that the student, in indicating an overall feeling of "like" for social studies, means that he likes the component areas in differing degrees. Perhaps he even dislikes one or two of them.

It takes some time to help a student process an interest, or a lack of interest. In a subject matter area, or any other category of interests for that matter, if we are going to help students get on with the task of self assessment we are going to have to break through the highly generalized statements of "like" and "dislike" as well as the broadly categorized areas of interest measurement. It is only as we commit ourselves to helping students make the general more specific that we can move them toward a better understanding of their own interests, the ways in which they express them, the relationship of these interests to other facets of their being, and their potential for future development and use.

The Feeling vs. the Content

While at first this dichotomy may seem like another way of referring to the internal-external dimension (it is in some ways), there are some important differences of which the counselor should be aware. The internal-external dimension deals with the individual (internal) and with his environment (external). The feeling-content dimension derives from the fact that an individual is concerned with his feelings about himself in his environment (feeling) and with his experiences in his environment (content). These are reported in a number of interesting ways in the counseling relationship. If a student reports on an episode in an English class in which he was involved, it may begin with a description of what actually happened in the classroom. This necessarily requires that the counselee report the *content* of the episode indicating what happened, who said what, who was involved, and so on. Content descriptions and discussions are essential and often necessary to establish a base for the communication process. But an individual's feelings about the event and about what was said are equally important to explore. Sometimes, in the excitement of recounting an episode, a counselor can read much feeling while the student is telling what happened and, very frequently, the content of the story will be punctuated with significantly direct statements of feeling. The counselor learns to utilize techniques that help the counselee to express both feeling and content. More important than the actual communication techniques is the counselor's judgment in determining (or helping to determine) at which level, content, or feeling the session is best directed at any given point. Most counseling sessions will move back and forth between feeling and content. The number of times this will occur, of course, will depend on the topic being discussed and the depth of the counselee's feeling. The expertise of the counselor is based as much on his ability to judge how to help the counselee explore the situation as on the techniques which he employs in moving the session along.

There are a number of interesting aspects which the counselor can observe in himself as he uses his professional skills and tests his sensitivity in helping the counselee explore both the content and the feeling levels of his problem or concern. When a counselee is describing an incident, the curiosity of the counselor can oftentimes cause him to lead the counselee to describe more than is necessary about the incident or cause the discussion to be elaborated simply to satisfy his own curiosity. I have counselors tell me in their practicum that they really didn't need to know about a certain aspect of an episode or incident but that they were curious about the different responses and behaviors of the people involved. Curiosity is a human characteristic and I don't feel that a counselor should be punished for being curious. However, I think he should be extremely aware of his curiosity and should know how it is affecting the process of his human relating. Oftentimes curiosity lies at the root of what the counselee perceives to be prying, probing, or snooping into his affairs. This type of behavior, of course, can decidedly affect the character of the human relationship and the direction of its evolvement.

The Self and Self-disclosure

Much of individual counseling is directed at helping the individual explore his own self. This requires a good deal of self disclosure covering many areas and touching different levels of depth at different times. Many beginning counselors feel that counselees should be able to expose themselves readily. This is evidenced frequently by the counselor who is quick to provide the conditions for self-exploration with a "You are free to talk about whatever you wish in here." This, like "Are there other problems you would care to discuss?" usually draws a blank! Self-disclosure is a very slow, continual process that depends on the human aspects of the relationship and the manner in which these are characterized in their counseling relationship. So time, while important, is secondary to the humanness which is eventually experienced by both the counselor and the counselee. Studies have shown that students are selective in their self-disclosure depending on to whom and about what they are disclosing. In the secondary school there are so many topics that could be explored—physical growth and development (and all the very personal areas of consideration associated with it), social and personal relationships, vocational plans and aspirations, to list a few. These come out in many different ways, but usually in relation to problems involving achievement, family, money, sex, love, work, friends, personality. Students can talk about all of these topics but with different people and at differing depths. As one of these people the school counselor will find that his counseling clientele will deal differentially with him on these topics.

COUNSELING PRACTICE

Now that we have examined the human aspects of counseling, the conditions of the counseling relationship and selected dimensions of the counseling process, let's look at the actualities of counseling practice. I have divided the practice of counseling into three significant aspects: the communicative, the structural, and the positional.

The Communicative Aspects of Counseling Practice

Communication in counseling can be both verbal and nonverbal. Verbal communication is most often discussed in textbooks as "leading" thus inferring some responsibility to the counselor. Some years ago Francis Robinson cited *leading* as one of four important dimensions of the counseling process, proceeding to show how the counselor, by skillfully varying the nature of his communications, can more precisely guide and control (lead) the counseling process.[17] His fourteen techniques of leading were arranged in order of their degree. Leading, as Robinson presents it, is a continuum of counselor involvement from statements that embody acceptance and understanding (such as those that reflect or deal with what the counselee is saying) to responses that increasingly incorporate the counselor's judgment and interpretations.

His fourteen leads and the order in which he considered them as leading, are as follows:

(1) silence
(2) acceptance
(3) restatement
(4) clarification
(5) summary clarification
(6) approval
(7) general leads
(8) tentative analysis
(9) interpretation
(10) urging
(11) depth interpretation
(12) rejection
(13) assurance
(14) introducing a new (and apparently unrelated) aspect of a problem.[18]

The degree of lead in each of these techniques is somewhat evident. For example, one can see where an interpretation would involve more counselor judgment than restatement or clarification. It would affect the process of counseling, for an interpretation would necessitate that the counselor add new data to that already supplied by the counselee while a restatement would flow from the essence of the counselee's remarks. Most counselor education programs recognize the importance of leading in counseling and provide for counselors to learn about these techniques and to practice using them.

Nonverbal communication is best represented by a number of forms of

[17] Francis P. Robinson, *Principles and Procedures in Student Counseling* (New York: Harper & Bros., 1950), pp. 80–82.
[18] *Ibid.,* pp. 82–95.

behavior which can be noted in every counseling session. Gestures, position of the body, body movements, and facial expressions are but a few of the forms of nonverbal behavior which add to the process of counseling. The nonverbal behavior of both the counselor and the counselee is usually associated directly with their relationship and their feelings about it. The counselor can glean much evidence to help him assess the nature and depth of the relationship by observing the movements of the counselee, eye contact, the position and use of the hands, the facial expression, and other counselee expressions of comfort, hostility, or nervousness.

While no one behavior can be used to determine what has really occurred or is occurring between them, an assessment of all these behaviors over a period of conference time will help the counselor to understand better and to deal with what he assumes to be the experience of the counselee in the relationship. Gladstein has developed a chart which indicates some of these non-verbal behaviors. His chart identifies several types of behavioral characteristics, which he combines into three groups:

(1) body movements,
(2) voice qualities, and
(3) vocalizations.

He then proceeds to show how these can be used in leading, citing these three general categories:

(1) neutral acceptance or understanding,
(2) mild approval or disapproval, and
(3) strong approval or disapproval.[19]

The Structural Aspects of Counseling Practice

Most human relationships have some purpose or goal. Friends may get together for an evening of cards or a day of hunting; workers combine forces to accomplish a task; people assemble to discuss an issue. So it is with counseling. While a counselee may find himself in the counselor's office for any number of reasons (he was told to go to the counselor, he was sent for by the counselor, he decided himself to go to the counselor), either the counselor or the counselee usually has some purpose in mind for the meeting. Even if there is no stated purpose or goal in the mind of either party (and this may

[19] Gerald A. Gladstein, *Classification of Non-Verbal Leads,* College of Education, University of Rochester (Rochester, N.Y.), mimeograph. pp. 1–5.

occur), there are structural elements that need to be considered in relation to the practice of counseling.

The initial interview. The initial interview represents the first encounter between the counselee and the counselor. It is the first opportunity for these two people to relate within the context of the counseling relationship. They may be new to each other, or their relationshp at this time may consist of previous meetings or interactions at other times for other purposes. They commence with their perceptions of each other based on whatever they have experienced together or, if they have not met, on what perceptions they may have formed based on hearsay or reputation. There are some assumptions that can be made about the process of counseling in the initial interview. It can be assumed (1) that the counselee wants or needs help; (2) that nothing specific needs to be accomplished beyond the structure required by the counselor; and (3) that the initial session is merely a stage—more frequently a beginning one—in a relationship between two individuals. The initial interview represents the foundation of the counseling relationship even if the relationship does not extend beyond this first contact. While the manner in which this session is conducted will vary with the theoretical orientation of the counselor, some purposes or objectives have been cited for the first session. Tyler suggests three objectives for the counselor: "(a) getting a sound counseling relationship started, (b) opening up the psychological realms of feeling and attitude within the person, and (c) clarifying the structure of the helping process."[20] On the matter of priority, Tyler adds, "The order in which these have been stated corresponds to their importance. In individual cases one should always sacrifice number three for number two, and either of them for number one."[21] Buchheimer and Balogh divide the initial interview into three phases:

(1) the statement of problem,
(2) exploration, and
(3) closing, and planning for the future.
This approach, they feel, "represents a purposive and goal-directed approach to counseling."[22]

However, they too caution against rigid adherence to the three sequences, encouraging counselors to consider the three as guides only.

[20] Leona E. Tyler, *The Work of the Counselor* (New York: Appleton-Century-Crofts, 1969), third edition, p. 63.
[21] *Ibid.,* p. 63.
[22] Arnold Buchheimer and Sara C. Balogh, *The Counseling Relationship* (Chicago: Science Research Associates, 1961), p. 15.

Representing quite a different approach to the initial interview is the position of Cottle and Downie. They list four primary purposes, stating

one of these is to establish a good working relationship between the counselor and the client which will last throughout counseling. Another is to validate and expand the data about the client collected prior to the interview. Still a third is to observe the client directly and to collect information which will show client feelings about values, interests, attitudes, and goals. In addition this first interview is used to establish the structure within which counseling will take place."[23]

As you become more sophisticated in counseling theory, and as you become more familiar with the philosophical and psychological beliefs that undergird the counseling process, you will be able to distinguish more clearly among these expert opinions on the purposes or goals of the initial interview.

Structuring the counseling relationship. The counselee arrives at the counselor's office with little knowledge about the process of counseling and a myriad of expectations and perceptions. And he is probably more than a little apprehensive. Just as every counselee comes with his own self, so does every counselor. To talk about structuring the counseling relationship in one sense seems to violate the human aspects of two people working together. Yet this need not occur if the counselor has worked out his approach to counseling in a fashion that works best for him. This assumes, then, that the counselor has considered his own "self" and has adapted a counseling posture that accommodates this self, making him more comfortable and natural in his approach to people. Assuming that there is a good deal of variance among counselor style and approach, the need for a certain amount of structure within the relationship is obvious. How the counseling relationship is developed, then, is dependent upon the counselor's approach. How he handles the structuring of their relationship is dependent upon how he sees himself and a particular counselee relating and working together.

Structuring takes into account several areas and the counselor determines which of these will be considered and when, since structuring is often an on-going activity and may occur at various times in a relationship. We may think of structuring as a means of accommodating the "person" of the two people involved in the relationship. We may think of it as helping both people understand how one another functions.

Some counselors may wish to deal with the nature of the counselee's referral (self, teacher, counselor request). Others may wish to talk about the

---

[23] William C. Cottle and N. M. Downie, *Procedures and Preparation for Counseling* (Englewood Cliffs, N.J.: Prentice-Hall, 1960), p. 59.

counselee's expectations in the counseling relationship or his perceptions of it. By obtaining some notion of what the counselee expects or how he perceives the relationship the counselor is able to ascertain discordant expectations or perceptions that may need to be dealt with in the course of developing the counseling relationship. Whether he chooses to deal with them immediately in the initial encounter, later, or from time to time as they both find it necessary to communicate about what is happening between them, is basically a counselor judgment. This occurs frequently with regard to matters of responsibility. The counselee may expect the counselor to ask the questions, diagnose the problem, and provide resolutions. If the counselor doesn't function this way—that is, if the counselor expects the counselee to accept some responsibility for these activities, then we can expect that the discrepancy in their views of the operational aspects of the counseling relationship may need to be discussed several times.

Counselors sometimes elect to clarify how they proceed in the counseling relationship at the very beginning, working out the specific operational problems as they arise. Thus the counselor may, depending upon his own theoretical frame of reference, wish to obtain more information about the counselee's expectations or perceptions of counseling and proceed to elaborate on aspects of responsibility in approaching the problem, clarifying how he sees matters of responsibility being handled in the communication and decision-making processes that will be employed. Or he may wish simply to get on with the task of human relating, leaving the structuring (if any is necessary) to occur at appropriate occasions in the course of their relationship.

The duration and termination of counseling. Counselors, both new and experienced, frequently raise questions concerning the duration of the counseling relationship and the frequency of contacts with counselees. Questions of this nature are particularly significant for the harried secondary school counselor who may be trying to reach as many counselees as his load will permit. Certainly the assignment of a secondary school counselor is quite different from that of the typical counselor in a counseling agency or center. In most secondary schools the counselor is assigned a particular group of students, as many as three hundred or more. He may work with this group for a long period of time, perhaps as much as three or four years, depending on the organization of the school and the program for shifting students from one school level to another.

Where the counselor has the same group over a period of time, the opportunity for an extended counseling relationship with many of these students is possible (assuming, of course, that the counselor elects to counsel as opposed to numerous mechanistic or clerical functions in which he could engage). With this many students he, quite obviously, can be working with only a small fraction at any one time. Yet each student whom he meets establishes a relationship, and the possibilities for communication indicate an on-going, though not necessarily active, relationship. These relationships vary considerably from weak to strong; this will be so as long as school counselors remain so busy: it would be humanly impossible to maintain three hundred actively strong counseling relationships. But at any one point in time a counselor could be working with a number of these students. In the secondary school, I suspect the question of frequency is far more urgent than the question of duration. Certain students need to be seen regularly for a given period of time. Some may need biweekly or monthly contacts, a few may need sporadic, irregular conferences, and most probably need a counselor only a few times in any one year. Some may never need one. Questions of frequency of contact, prolonged counseling, premature termination, or of no progress are considerations that require the best professional judgment of the counselor.

Certainly a counselor worth his salt would be available to his students and, over a three- or four-year period, should be able to establish a counseling relationship with a goodly number of them. Adjusting his student contacts to the developmental needs of youth seems to hold promise for more effective counseling relationships than the more common practice of routinely interviewing each student every year at some point convenient to the schedule of the counselor. We have tried this latter plan for nearly twenty years with little success! Certainly we need to look at the potential in other approaches.

The school counselor has the advantage of testing his judgment regarding the frequency and the duration of contacts since he never *really* terminates a counseling relationship. Errors in his judgment can be more readily identified and, with his clientele so easily available, he can reestablish a contact or reactivate a relationship whenever such action seems appropriate.

Counseling notations and records. Counseling notations may be considered a working record of the counseling relationship. In some instances the counselor may wish to incorporate these, or a summary of them, into the student's record. Counseling notes are helpful for their recall value to some counselors. They can help in remembering the general tenor or the essence of the previous session, in recalling a specific conversation or topic, or in noting any special insights, understandings, or progress which may be particularly meaningful to either the counselor or the counselee. Sometimes the notation is merely a record of the meeting and the date. Record notations are particularly helpful in secondary school counseling as evidence of the contact and the nature of it. When counselors are relating to students in a developmental program as opposed to routine or scheduled interviews such a record can be particularly helpful. It is extremely difficult to recall all the meetings and the most significant aspects of each one when one is maintaining a relationship with two or three hundred students!

The Positional Aspects of Counseling Practice

The following aspects of counseling practice I have dubbed "positional," since the manner in which the counselor approaches these aspects of his counseling will depend on his theoretical beliefs—his position. Many people who begin a program to prepare them for counseling look for specific techniques to guide their practice. They are surprised to find several theoretical points of view. They are even further confounded to find that they can customize these views to accommodate their person. While this can be construed to mean that individuals can select "a little of this and a little of that" in building a point of view about counseling, that is not the actual case. They should establish a theoretical position that combines constructs in which they believe, but the various ingredients of the position must be fundamentally consistent and compatible. The areas which are discussed in this section represent some of those that every counselor should think through carefully.

Diagnosis. The very word "diagnosis" suggests a search for a cause. Most people immediately associate the word with medical practice. When you visit your doctor with a physical condition not readily identified (diagnosed), he asks questions that amount in the long run to a medical history. He may perform tests, require x-rays, and otherwise engage in activities that are primarily diagnostic. In time, and sometimes more by the process of elimination, he may ascertain the nature of your condition and prescribe treatment. On other occasions he may make a tentative diagnosis, trying one or more approaches to treating what he believes may be your difficulty. Most people have had enough contact with a physician to be familiar with diagnosis as it is practiced in medicine.

In counseling the construct is the same but the approach varies considerably. Some counseling points of view apply processes very much akin to medical diagnosis, with the responsibility for the diagnosis being essentially the counselor's. Others are less cause-oriented, with the approach being a shared responsibility of the counselor and the counselee. From a strictly problem-centered point of view counseling would focus on cause and effect; from a more developmental point of view, the maturation of the individual and his own self-awareness and self-identification would be more central. The problems he faces are more likely to stem from his striving for equilibrium and his search for self-identity than from a condition so distressful as to make him dysfunctional. Nevertheless, much emphasis has been given to diagnosis as a counseling activity and interest in it has waxed and waned over the years.

One of the early counseling texts, *How to Counsel Students*,[24] describes in considerable detail several features of the process of diagnosis. Williamson's chapters "Analytical Techniques" and "The Art of Diagnosing" are thorough in their application of diagnosis to student counseling. In fact, many of the techniques and procedures which are described in that book can be readily identified in many secondary school guidance programs today. The bulk of the book deals with types of student problems in the areas of personality, educational orientation and achievement, occupational orientation, financial, and health areas.

Bordin[25] suggested five diagnostic categories based on causes that prevented the client from solving his own problem or reaching his own solution. His five diagnostic categories: (1) dependence, (2) lack of information, (3) self-conflict, (4) choice anxiety, and (5) no problem.

Apostal and Miller[26] developed a two-dimensional diagnostic classification plan based on the formulation of earlier classifications of problems. Combining the types of problems ("problem-goal") and the causes, they developed a way to code all cases diagnostically. Their problem-goal dimension consisted of (1) vocational, (2) emotional, and (3) educational categories, while the cause dimension included (1) lack of information about or understanding of self, (2) lack of information about or understanding of environment, (3) motivational conflict within self, (4) conflict with significant others, and (5) lack of skill.

While the advent of client-centered views has tended to counteract the earlier concerns with individual analysis and problem identification, these activities are still very prevalent in counseling and guidance programs. Diagnosis remains an important part of the counseling process. The questions of its purpose and use, and its significance in the establishment and maintenance of the counseling relationship, are important considerations for every counselor.

The use of educational and occupational information. A lack of information is very often associated with student problems. To know how to

[24] E. G. Williamson, *How to Counsel Students* (New York: McGraw-Hill, 1939).

[25] Edward S. Bordin, "Diagnosis in Counseling and Psychotherapy," *Educational and Psychological Measurement* 6:169–184, Summer 1946.

[26] Robert A. Apostal and John G. Miller, *A Manual For The Use of a Set of Diagnostic Categories* (Columbia, Mo.: University of Missouri Testing and Counseling Service, 1959), mimeograph.

handle student needs for information is a demand of the counseling function, one that must be faced squarely by the counselor and one that he must learn to handle adequately. Students will demand information of all types in relation to the many concerns and conflicts they encounter.

What do I mean by the counselor having to face this matter squarely? Simply that some counselors do not wish to engage in the process of helping others locate and use information. Such involvement, they claim, is too routine, too trivial. It's hard to believe that a counselor would deny the information-giving function, and most do not. Rather, within their beliefs about counseling, they identify a position that details how, when, and by whom information is transmitted to the counselee and how the counselee is assisted in making use of the information in relation to his decision making or self-directing activities. In short, information-giving can be more than a counselor responsibility. It can be a responsibility shared with the counselee but rarely can he be left to shift all by himself.

If any counselor was prepared to handle at any given time all of the questions he was asked, or to supply all the demands for information placed upon him, he would have to contain an encyclopedic fund of knowledge. In the first place, he could not accumulate all the information, either in his head or in his files, even if he deemed this one of his primary responsibilities and a vital part of his counseling function. Secondly, with information changing at a rapid rate, it is doubtful that he could keep his information accurate and up to date at any given point in time. Thus he is faced with the selective aspects of what he knows, what sources he has available, and their accuracy and usefulness. Nevertheless, the counselor is expected to be able to handle the many information gaps with which his counselees are faced.

Fortunately there is sufficient commonality in the informational needs of adolescents to make it worth his time and effort to keep up to date or to maintain current and timely resource materials. Even then he is faced with the question of responsibility—of how and when to dispense it. Does he secure the material and give it to the counselee or does he simply indicate its availability and its location, leaving the counselee with the responsibility for obtaining it? The counselor is faced not only with the matter of identifying and using informational resources but, more importantly, with the process of the counselee's subsequent integration and internalization of the information. It is one thing to locate information and another to use it in problem solving or decision making.

Information can be processed and used in different ways. Simple facts are helpful by themselves but some types of information have to be analyzed, compared, or synthesized with other data. How does the counselor help the counselee to process data in ways which are meaningful to the counselee? Some counselors are prone to stop with the dispensing of information finding the personal assessment and integration of the information difficult and time consuming. Yet this is the essence of professional counseling, the heart of the process, and the source of helpful and beneficial assistance. All too frequently, I fear, we have rested the case for the uses of information with the location of resources or the provision for experiences which will fill the informational vacuum. The follow-up counseling in which the counselee has to deal with the data in terms of its meaning for him, the contradictions it may pose, the uncertainties it may rear, or the discrepancies it may raise is very crucial. Information giving is not all answers and resolution. For some adolescents it can be quite the reverse.

The selection of tests and the interpretation of test results. I do not mean to imply immediately that every counselor uses tests. Whether or not he does, or how he does and when he does are basic to his position on the use of tests in the counseling process. Every counselor needs to work through considerations relative to the use of tests; on the other hand, the questions of counselee participation in test selection and test interpretation may be a straw man for the secondary school counselor. Most schools have a standardized testing program, which includes many of the types of tests commonly utilized in the counseling process. Since these tests are administered to whole classes of students, the student has little choice in the selection or administration of such tests. Rather, he is expected to take the tests and to take them on the dates when they are administered. While this may be a fact, this does not preclude the counselor's exploring with a counselee the possibility of taking other tests that would provide different or additional data. Nor does it preclude a possible change in the development and conduct of testing programs in the secondary school in the years ahead—changes that may be more in accord with the efficient use of tests in the counseling process rather than the mass use of test data in the counseling program.

The interpretation of tests is a reality in many school programs. The fact that standardized tests are administered is a form of mandate for their interpretation. With the extensive use of standardized tests in the secondary school, a stereotype of the school counselor has evolved which commits him heavily to an involvement in the program (often in the selection and administration of such tests) and particularly in the interpretation of test results. This has happened more by default than by design. Few counselors have considered their position on the interpretation of test results. The failure to establish their position, coupled with an attitude of resignation, has caused them to accept a role in the school testing program as a part of their counseling heritage. Despite "what is," it remains a responsibility of the counselor to examine the role of test data in the counseling process and to determine his position. Certainly this condition will force those who elect not to use tests, or to use test data sparingly, to deal with the disparity between their position and the more common role expectation that they do use and interpret tests.

The use of test data with a counselee requires a great deal of skill and understanding. Current practices involving the use of profile sheets and other homemade devices which make test results more meaningful to students are to be encouraged. Individual interpretations provide an opportunity for a student to react to the interpretation, to raise questions about aspects of the results which remain vague, and to talk about the results in ways which will help him to internalize the data for future reference and use. In some schools where counselors interpret test scores, group test interpretation sessions are conducted and in some instances students are merely advised of their results and given a copy of the completed test profile. The use of test data in this manner can hardly be condoned, yet it is rarely condemned (probably because the data remains meaningless to students and therefore harmless). In interpreting tests to students, it is essential that the student understand the following:

(1) the purpose of the test and its significance or relevance to him at this time
(2) the *general* nature of the test (interest, intelligence, aptitude, achievement, personality) and its meaning
(3) the *specific* nature of the test and its meaning including the meaning of all the various subtest measures
(4) information about the norm group and the comparative aspects of the results
(5) explanation of how the results are presented (percentiles, stanines, or by high, average, and low categories)
(6) presentation of results including part and total scores
(7) comparison of test data with expressions of self evaluation
(8) discussion and integration of test data with other information which the student has.

These eight areas are not necessarily steps to be followed in order. They are guidelines to insure that tests and tests scores are adequately covered and thoroughly discussed with the student.

Legal and ethical considerations. Imposing on the work of the counselor are a number of legal and ethical considerations. There is little actual legislation to govern the work of the counselor though the legal aspects of counseling differ from state to state. Each counselor should become familiar with the educational law of the state in which he is employed. More apropos

are the legalities involved in judicial rulings and the precedence established
in court decisions. Many of these court decisions, while generally applicable
to everyone in education and consequently affect counselors as well as
teachers and administrators, serve to establish a legal code for the practice
of counseling in the schools.

Professional ethics is a matter of individual responsibility almost
wholly dependent on the sensibleness and judiciousness of the school counselor. The *Ethical Standards* of the American Personnel and Guidance Association serve as the guidelines for the professional behavior of the secondary school counselor. These standards establish principles in six areas:
general ethics, counseling, testing, research and publication, consulting and
private practice, personnel administration, and preparation for personnel
work.[27] These standards do not dictate behavior, they guide it. As such, the
counselor's behavior is largely a matter of his conscience, common sense, and
judgment. The *Ethical Standards* establish the professional responsibilities
and obligations of the counselor in a general way. They are more precaution-
ary than explicit in delineating the boundaries of responsible, professional
behavior. Within these rather broad limits, then, the counselor has a great
deal of leeway in making judgments about his behavior as a counselor. The
school counselor will find that the standards for the profession are generally
broad enough to allow him to make decisions that are consistent with his
own philosophical and psychological beliefs and with the theoretical basis
that he has established to guide his practice.

Judgments of an ethical nature are encountered almost daily as the
counselor ponders about his competence to handle a particular counseling
situation, thinks over a request for information about a student from a college admissions officer, contemplates the confidentiality of a communication
from a student. His professional behavior and the manner in which he assumes responsibility for it will influence the behavior of other colleagues.
There will be times when he may find it necessary to evaluate his own conduct in relation to its influence or effect on other colleagues, and there will
be occasions when he may need to assess the behaviors of other counselors in
terms of their demands or influence on him. The ethics of his behavior is
further complicated in many ways by the many different people with whom
he deals—students, teachers, parents, administrators. His primary allegiance
to those students with whom he counsels, and whose confidence and trust he
has earned is often severely and crucially tested as he valiantly tries to maintain this status while helping these others who equally value his counsel and
service.

[27] Ethics Committee (APGA), "Ethical Standards," *Personnel and Guidance
Journal* 40:204–209, October 1961.

GROUP COUNSELING

One of the more complex counseling situations is working with groups of students. The elements of the group situation are much the same as those defined for individual counseling relations. As was suggested earlier in the chapter, the bonds that build human relationships must be present: caring, positive regard, openness, and genuineness. In the group situation the opportunities for these to enhance human interaction are magnified by the increased number of interrelationships possible. On the other hand, the group situation, with its "amongness" as well as its "betweenness," relies more on a group expression of these human qualities and their emergence is often more gradual and subtle. The counselor or group leader now has the responsibility of gauging not only the more simple, and perhaps more obvious, one-to-one interactions, but a multiple set of human interactions.

The conditions of the one-to-one relationship are also important in group counseling—acceptance, understanding, and trust. In some respects these are easier to obtain in the group primarily because the leader is likely to be the only individual who represents another point in time or another era. Peers in the group are more likely to be in tune with the times even though they will probably not agree among themselves. The mutuality of life experiences, to say little of the similarity of their problems, can aid in the development of group interaction and help to establish more quickly some of the human bonds that will allow the group to work together more effectively.

While there are several texts devoted to the topic of group counseling (and students who are interested in group counseling are encouraged to read or browse through a number of these publications), it may help to highlight a few of the more unique dimensions of group counseling and to distinguish it from the more conventional one-to-one relationship.

Group members as counselors. Perhaps one of the more advantageous aspects of the group situation is the potential for all members of the group to be of help to one another. Within the group, ideas and beliefs can be expressed and exchanged, ways of approaching particular situations can be described, and a variety of alternative solutions to problems can be identified. Each group member in his own human way, within the confines of his own life experiences, can be a force in helping the other members of the group.

Safety in numbers. It is often much easier to raise a concern or to deal with a personal problem when there is the possibility that others in the group may have experienced, or are experiencing, the same problem. One doesn't feel quite so different or so foolish with the thought that others may have the same concerns; one can anticipate some understanding and acceptance almost immediately. Even though understanding and acceptance are possible in a one-to-one student-counselor relationship, most adolescents feel safer with their peers. Even if one's peers fail to understand, it's still less difficult for some adolescents to accept criticism or disagreement from a peer than to risk not being understood with an adult. Above all, one doesn't feel so alone.

The matter of goals. The goals or purposes of group counseling are many and varied. Some groups are formed with very general objectives usually related to the growth and development of the individual and are designed to enhance his own understanding of himself. These groups focus on self-realization and the insights and understandings that can help an individual to identify better his own being and becoming. Other groups have more specific objectives designed to deal with very definitive facets of educational growth (e.g., underachieving), social development (e.g., dating behaviors), or personal problems (e.g., getting along at home). Groups are often formed when a number of students are presumed to have a similar kind of problem (such as problems with drugs or sex). While groups with specific goals are not always formed to meet problem situations, they are for the most part problem-oriented and therefore have a remedial rather than a preventive emphasis.

The need for limits. Unlike individual counseling, where the limits of human interaction are more likely dealt with as they occur, the group situation will gain from an early discussion that establishes the limits of member behavior. Usually group members are cautioned against physical outbursts that disregard property or person. Equally important are matters concerning the confidentiality of individual and group considerations. The helpful rather than the hurtful aspects of group behavior are often emphasized thus providing some necessary safeguards for the feelings and attitudes of all who participate in the experience.

Group size. Authorities on group counseling differ in their recommendations on the size of groups. Groups of at least four persons and not more than fifteen are the usual minimum-maximum numbers cited. Most seem to consider a group of eight to twelve people the most desirable size. Perhaps more important than the size of the group is the actual interaction that occurs among the participants. Whatever number of people are participating, the basic conditions of human relating and human interaction must be present. Group size is better determined by its ability to allow for these human ingredients to emerge in the process of their human communication. The larger the group the less likelihood there is of meaningful communication among the participants. Certainly the larger group is more difficult for the leader since he has many more human dyads or combinations of interactions to observe, making the leadership function much more complex. Group members are likewise apt to have less opportunity to become actively involved. Also, as size increases there is a tendency for the interaction of the group to rely more on the group leader and for communications to be directed either to or through him.

Group selection and composition. Membership in the group is dependent on the goals or objectives of the group counseling situation. Commonly, however, the selection of group members involves consideration relative to the individual's needs, motivations, abilities, and sex. Since groups are formed for a variety of purposes and needs, group membership characteristics, insofar as selection and group composition are concerned, are best considered in light of the goals for the group. Within this framework, then, one must decide on matters of member heterogeneity-homogeneity. The commonality of member problems and the question of same or mixed sex groups, for example, must be considered.

There is a growing body of research that can help the counselor in considering some of the combinations of member characteristics that appear to be most conducive to productive results. One factor seems to be fairly well substantiated: group members who are highly motivated and who seek participation voluntarily are more apt to gain from the experience, to remain in the group experience, and to contribute to the group than are those who are referred or are persuaded to participate.

The group and human learning. Perhaps one of the more important contributions of the group (and one that is frequently overlooked) is the manner whereby the group can enhance the thinking and learning of the individual. The group counseling function often gets pointed in the direction of problem solving and the success of the group is often judged or evaluated on the basis of its effectiveness in achieving precise outcomes in the form of behavioral or attitudinal changes. While these forms of evaluation are important, nonetheless, we should not minimize the significance of the group as it can enhance the individual's ability to process information—that is, to *think.* The group can contribute to the problem-solving or decision-making abilities of the individual. While we have little evidence to support the group counseling activity as a model of human learning, we do know that individuals engage in a variety of thinking operations in group counseling under conditions that are quite different than those they experience in the more formal atmosphere or climate of the classroom. In the group situation, members are engaged in a variety of mental processes—analyzing, synthesizing, observing, comparing, describing. They are learning how to think and how to use these thinking processes in their daily lives. Though some would reject these outcomes as too general or as unmeasurable, if we accept the experience as one that has developmental, facilitative potential, then we should consider its potential for the intellectual growth of the individual and its applicability for individuals in dealing with life situations.

Group counseling in relation to other types of group experience. There are many different types of group experience many of which are often confused with the group counseling experience. In some instances, the inability of counselors to differentiate among these various experiences has created some difficulties with school boards, principals and parents who seek and desire more specific details about these experiences before allowing such programs to be established or, as in the case of parents, before they permit their child to engage in the experience. These requests are reasonable and the counselor should be able to distinguish rather clearly among these group experiences. Group work can take many forms and some of the following are frequently confused with group counseling.

(1) *Discussion groups* usually emphasize the presentation and exchange of information and opinion, the development or improvement of skills (such as study skills), thus being highly task or topic oriented. Although exchanges among members of the group may become emotional, the process of the group rests on mutual respect and tolerance and the tenor of the experience is primarily in the cognitive realm of human experience.

(2) *T-groups* emphasize interpersonal relationships and communication skills and represent one of the earlier forms of sensitivity training. The emphasis is on the affective experiencing of the group members, encouraging them to examine their own feelings and attitudes and the manner in which they use themselves in human relations. The T-group experience relies on very little structure and the use of stress or tension in obtaining group member involvement, although it remains more similar to group counseling than to group psychotherapy.

(3) *Encounter groups* emphasize the self and sensory awareness with the almost exclusive purpose of self-growth and self-understanding. The encounter experience is more psychotherapeutic in design in that it tends to probe and penetrate more deeply the affective domain of human experiencing, emphasizing the past of the individual as well as the present and the future, seeking through greater self-awareness attitudinal and behavioral change. The process involves more individual confrontation among and between group participants frequently employing techniques

that rely on physical and sensory encounters among participants. These are most often of a short-term nature such as an encounter weekend or "marathon" experience.

Group counseling is essentially different from each of these. It is not solely a cognitive experience for it does draw on the affective aspects of the human experience. It is more than a discussion group, though it may utilize many of the verbal techniques that allow individuals to exchange ideas and experiences. Unlike the T-group and the encounter experience that capitalize more heavily on individual tension and stress as factors of participation, group counseling tends to maintain or reduce the level of participant stress or tension. More like the T-group, it is not psychotherapy-oriented and deals more with the present experiencing and feelings of participants without attempting to examine the why and wherefore of the past.

Group counseling utilizes structure as necessary to encourage individual participation by reducing the anxiety of its members. It does not employ sensory awareness or physical contact techniques. Group counseling, at least in the secondary school, is an extension of the individual counseling relationship where students can examine together, with the help of the counselor and other group members, those topics of concern and interest important to their own growth and experiencing.

Thus group counseling is a way whereby all adolescents with the normal concerns of growing and living can come together to help one another examine these aspects of growing and living that are of mutual concern, where they can help one another to learn how to face these life situations, and, as necessary, to examine the underlying attitudes or manifest behaviors that will affect their living and working.

THE COUNSELOR: HIS PERSON AND POSITION

The Counselor as a Person

Over the years the counseling literature has been replete with descriptions and lists of personality traits which have been considered by one group or another as essential to the counseling function. At one time it was deemed important to identify those characteristics a counselor should possess. While such characteristics could be endlessly arrayed, such traits as fairness, sincerity, interest in people, intelligence, and alertness were considered important to success in counseling. More recently, however, less emphasis has been placed on what personal characteristics and attributes the counselor should possess while more attention has been directed toward the way he uses himself in his human communication. Leona Tyler speaks directly to the rethinking that is current. She says,

It may be that we have been approaching the problem from the wrong direction. The assumption that there is a certain combination of personal characteristics which is optimum for counseling may be unsound. It seems possible now that men and women of a wide variety of personality types can function successfully in this situation. If we give up the belief that there is *one* standard relationship that should be created in every case, we can relinquish along with it the requirement that the counselor be any *one* type of person. . . . Perhaps it would be better if we all assumed that any personality pattern which permits rich and deep relationships with other human beings to develop is satisfactory.[28]

Weitz[29] contends that the counselor's personality traits and the ways he communicates these traits to his clients will determine his effectiveness as a counselor. He says, "Counseling involves the interaction of two personalities through the medium of speech and other symbolic behavior. It is reasonable to suppose, therefore, that the structure of each of these personalities will have a marked influence on the interaction."[30]

Speculating on the kinds of personality traits that can facilitate counseling, Weitz nominates three: security, sensitivity, and objectivity. Security, states Weitz, is a ". . . sense of self-acceptance. This involves a frank recognition of strengths *and* weaknesses."[31] The secure person, he adds, ". . . accepts other people as they are, recognizing within the limits of his perceptions their needs, and expects to be accepted on the same terms by them, and he usually is."[32] The sensitive person, according to Weitz, ". . . is capable of understanding and appreciating a wide range of psychological behavior."[33] This must be construed to include both the cognitive and affective levels of human understanding. Thus, for example, the sensitive counselor can sense the sadness of a counselee; he does not necessarily have to be told. Lastly, Weitz characterizes the objective person as ". . . capable of distinguishing between objective and symbolic behavior, yet understands the intimate relationship between these two."[34]

The objective person finds it easier to refrain from making judgments about another person. As a counselor he is able to transcend the certainties and uncertainties of his own life and to deal with those of another person as they are perceived and manipulated by him (the counselee).

[28] Leona E. Tyler, *The Work of the Counselor* (New York: Appleton-Century-Crofts, 1969), third edition, p. 200.
[29] Henry Weitz, "Counseling As a Function of the Counselor's Personality," *Personnel and Guidance Journal* 35:276–280, January 1957.
[30] *Ibid.*, p. 276.
[31] *Ibid.*, p. 277.
[32] *Ibid.*
[33] *Ibid.*, p. 278.
[34] *Ibid.*

The counselor's need for self-understanding becomes increasingly important as counseling becomes more a human than a mechanistic function. The counselor, secure in his own identity, is conversant with many facets of his own internal being—his beliefs, attitudes, values, needs, interests, abilities. He is able to distinguish between his own internalizations and those expressed by his counselees. He is able to deal with differences in ways which are facilitating to the counseling relationship and satisfying to the counselee.

The counselor must be capable of making judgments, many of these spontaneously. Counseling can be, and usually is, a rapidly moving, dynamic interaction in which the counselor continually finds himself responding to verbal and nonverbal cues. Judgments relative to direction, responsibility, and involvement remain available to the counselor's manipulation. These judgments hinge on his combined assessment of the many dimensions we have discussed in this chapter. The measure of his success or failure in the human relationship is determined in part by these judgments; the extent to which the relationship becomes a helping one is even more dependent on them.

Obviously, he must learn to evaluate his own judgments and to rely on them. To err in judgment is human and he will learn that an error in judgment, an emotion not sensed or a remark overlooked, at any point in counseling, can usually be dealt with when the oversight is recognized. To err in these ways consistently or too often can be detrimental. Such counselors do not remain in counseling very long. Judgments such as content pick-up, selection of lead, assessment of counselor behavior demand complete human involvement in the process.

The counselor can only put into a session all that he is—no more. In most instances that is usually enough, for the counselee senses that too, and accepts it. But for a counselor to bring only a part of himself is just as quickly captured by the counselee. That, like role playing or acting counselor, is sufficient to produce less than a counseling relationship demands. As a person, then, the counselor represents what he is; he uses all that he is. This does not standardize the counselor as a person, nor does it reflect, beyond the interactional qualities that have been suggested here, the personal characteristics he must possess. Rather, it suggests a person who knows himself and who is willing to use himself in warm and real and human ways.

The Counselor and His Position

The American School Counselor Association *Statement of Policy* states,

The counselor is dedicated to the idea that most pupils will enhance and enrich their personal development and self-fulfillment by means of making more intelligent decisions if given the opportunity to experience an accepting, non-evaluating relationship in which one is helped to better understand himself, the environment he perceives, and the relationship between these. Counseling is essentially such a relationship. The school counselor views himself as the person on the school staff with the professional competencies, behavioral science understandings, philosophical orientation, and position within the school necessary to provide such help to pupils.[35]

Inherent in this statement is the fact that the counselor will establish his own philosophical *position*. If the counselor is to understand and evaluate his own operation, then he needs to develop and organize the basic beliefs that undergird his own selected method of operation. In this activity the counselor formulates and organizes his own ideas to guide his counseling practice. He gets his ideas from the theoretical formulations of those who have preceded him. He may advocate and follow a particular theoretical system of counseling, or he may choose to blend a variety of theoretical constructs into one system which he perceives to fit him.

Whatever he selects and however he does it, the position he evolves will be primarily his point of view or his position. These are his beliefs. This is his system. This is not eclecticism in that wildly unsystematized, "let's see what works best" approach. This is a thoughtful, individual search. It is a process in which one seeks out the ideas and concepts he can believe, unifying and blending them with his own individuality, his own background of experience and understandings into his own unique counseling point of view—his position.

In establishing his position the counselor is faced with several problems. First and foremost, any ideas which he hopes to accept for his own must be tested using his own self. In the process—initially an intellectual one—of selecting and testing theoretical formulations for his own use, the counselor-in-preparation learns a great deal about himself.

Second, the counselor-to-be is likely to conceive of the position building process as entirely an intellectual one. He may see this in more simple terms as merely a matter of familiarizing himself with the theories, and selecting those ideas which he intellectually believes will make him the most effective counselor. While there is a great deal of intellectualizing in the position building process, differences that exist (or seem to exist) among the theories, when combined with a number of other ideas in practice, ofttimes produce quite different feelings from what the neophyte had anticipated. Thus his experience sends him back to reconstruct and realign his

[35] American School Counselor Association, *Statement of Policy for Secondary School Counselors* (Washington, D.C.: American Personnel and Guidance Association, 1964), p. 3.

formulations. Often too he finds that it is not so much a faulty or unworkable formulation as it is one with which he is not comfortable. Ideas and beliefs that fit well on paper are often unsuitable to the counselor in practice. This too can set him to reexamining facets of his position.

Last, it is important to recognize that establishing a position in counseling is a long and ever-changing process. The counselor-in-preparation must begin with what he is and what he knows and from there proceed toward what he wants to be. In doing this he must move through the world of the unknown, the insecure, and the unsafe. He must explore new domains of human relating. He must discover and expand those resources and potentials that lie within himself; he must test himself and his ideas as he grows to be what he has chosen to be—a school counselor.

SUGGESTED READING

CARKHUFF, ROBERT R. and BERENSON, BERNARD G., *Beyond Counseling and Therapy* (New York: Holt, Rinehart and Winston, 1967).

GLANZ, EDWARD C. and HAYES, ROBERT W., *Groups in Guidance* (Boston: Allyn and Bacon, 1967), second edition.

JOURARD, SIDNEY M., *The Transparent Self* (Princeton: Van Nostrand, 1964).

OHLSEN, MERLE M., *Group Counseling* (New York: Holt, Rinehart and Winston, 1970).

PATTERSON, C. H., *Theories of Counseling and Psychotherapy* (New York: Harper and Row, 1966).

ROGERS, CARL R., *On Becoming A Person* (Boston: Houghton Mifflin, 1961).

SHERTZER, BRUCE and STONE, SHELLEY C., *Fundamentals of Counseling* (Boston: Houghton Mifflin, 1968).

STEFFLRE, BUFORD (Ed.), *Theories of Counseling* (New York: McGraw-Hill, 1965).

TYLER, LEONA E., *The Work of the Counselor* (New York: Appleton-Century-Crofts, 1969), third edition.

EIGHT

THE CONSULTING FUNCTION

To suggest a consulting function for the developmental school counselor poses several risks. The counseling practitioner, already bogged down and overworked, might shake his head and ask "When and with whom?" The school administrator could raise his eyebrows and inquire "Why?" The teacher, already in so many instances alienated from guidance and counseling, may grin and promptly retort "Not with me he won't!" And so on through the realm of the school counselor's public. I presume for those who will reject this notion there are as many who will accept it. At least they will listen and perhaps move toward experimenting with it. I surely hope there are counselors in this group.

In a recent interview C. Gilbert Wrenn reported that he had little evidence about the role of the counselor in other countries in effecting change in the operation or organization of schools and community agencies. He added,

I have evidence that in this country the counselor can act as a change agent as well as the counselor of an individual. He can modify the environment; he can be both counselor and consultant. But I think we've just gotten to the point in this country, after a great many years experience, of assuming that the counselor can work on changes in the school environment as well as helping the person change himself. We've been a long time getting there.[1]

Now that we are beginning to view the possibilities of a role for the developmental counselor in educational change, we can begin to test some of the role relationships and expectations we have established over the

[1] C. Gilbert Wrenn (in an interview), "International Guidance: A Conversation with C. Gilbert Wrenn," *Caps Capsule* 3:3, Fall 1969.

years. Changing these in directions that are favorable to the consulting function will be a most difficult and challenging but not at all impossible task.

The friction between instruction and guidance in many schools is widely recognized. This schism seems to widen with time and school counselors have been beside themselves in an attempt to patch this growing rift. To propose that teachers and counselors work jointly on matters concerning the teaching-learning process and the educational environment could be considered by some parties as a heretical one. I refer to this breach mainly because we cannot close our eyes or turn our backs on it, for it is a condition that does exist in varying degrees in enough schools across the nation to cause concern. This need not detract from the promise of the consulting function nor need it deter its implementation in the guidance role. The teacher as a major consumer of the consulting function will be crucial to its development.

The school counselor has frequently been identified with the administrative unit of the school. To engage him in consulting functions could result in solidifying the perceptual alignment of the school counselor with the school administration. Thus we need to consider the outer limits of the consulting function and the authority (power) invested in it as well as the interpersonal implications involved. It is to these and other considerations that the remainder of this chapter is directed. My intent is to deal with the conceptual aspects of the consulting function, to establish some guidelines for consultive activities, to differentiate it insofar as possible from counseling, and to consider its possibilities for educational change. In later chapters, specific opportunities to engage in the consulting function will be cited.

A BASIS FOR THE CONSULTING FUNCTION

The overwhelming emphasis that has been afforded the counseling function is understood readily. The ASCA *Guidelines for Implementation* section of their *Statement of Policy* states, "The school counselor's primary role is in counseling. He assumes other roles such as consultant, resource person, researcher, etc., and educator, but only as those roles support the primary role of the counselor."[2] While we have labored these many years to establish counseling as the primary function, we may wish to reconsider this priority

---

[2] American School Counselor Association, *Statement of Policy for Secondary School Counselors* (Washington, D.C.: American Personnel and Guidance Association, 1964), p. 7.

in the years ahead. Youth presently need much more counseling assistance than is provided and the prospects for the future would indicate an even greater need for individual counseling. Some of these needs can be better accommodated right in the classroom, the focal point of the individual's learning-maturation. Teachers do have very real relationships with students —human and helpful ones. The potential for assisting teachers to carry out this responsibility lies in the consulting function, primarily, perhaps, for helping them to feel comfortable in developing such relationships with their students. The possibilities for further teacher involvement of this nature I have explored in another publication.[3]

The school counselor either is expected to perform or already is performing a number of activities that suggest the consulting function or aspects of it. The guidance role, whenever it has been delineated, is replete with statements that enumerate expectations that a counselor "encourages," "collects and disseminates," "furnishes," "interprets," or "provides"—and occasionally that he "consults"! Or consider another common approach to role, that which delineates his "assistance to parents" or "assistance to teachers." All this is to show that repeated allusions to the counselor's consulting responsibilities have been implied these many years. We have expected him to consult with teachers but this has been more inferential than actual. Nevertheless, the potential for the actualization of the consulting role has been present.

On the other hand there has been a cautionary and limiting restriction that may have been influential in keeping the consulting role in its rather dormant state. Much of his assistance to teachers has not been related to the teaching-learning process or to the promotion of educational change but rather restricted to the information he could furnish about students or the interpretations of their growth and development. His more expansive role in assisting teachers with activities that would enhance the individual's learning exposures and experiences, and thus the teacher's influence on the learning-maturation process, has seldom been inferred and rarely stated. It is toward this more expansive role that the developmental counselor can focus a great deal of his effort.

The most direct reference to the school counselor's consulting function is contained in the relatively recent ASCA *Statement of Policy for Secondary School Counselors* in the section suggesting *Guidelines for Implementation*. They cite staff consulting as one of ten professional responsibilities elaborating on it as follows:

[3] Harold L. Munson, "Guidance and Instruction: A Rapprochement." In *Guidance for Education in Revolution,* David R. Cook (Ed.) (Boston: Allyn and Bacon, 1971).

The school counselor works closely with members of the administrative and teaching staffs to the end that all of the school's resources are directed toward meeting the needs of individual pupils. In staff consulting the counselor—

   a. Shares appropriate individual pupil data with staff members, with due regard to confidentiality.

   b. Helps teachers to identify pupils with special needs or problems and keeps teachers informed of developments concerning individual pupils which might have a bearing upon the classroom situation.

   c. Participates in in-service training programs, staff meetings, and case conferences through which he discusses his own role, interprets a child-centered point of view, and encourages effective use of pupil data in teaching activities and guidance services given by teachers.

   d. Assists teachers to secure materials and develop procedures for a variety of classroom group guidance experiences.

   e. Provides materials and information concerning such matters as the characteristics and needs of the pupil population, pupil post-school behavior, and employment trends for use in curriculum study and revision.[4]

This statement helps to establish his consulting efforts with other school personnel. It recognizes more clearly the importance of the consulting function in secondary school guidance. However, it only suggests the expansive possibilities of working with teachers; it only hints at the assistance which the school counselor can afford the teacher in improving and enhancing the teaching-learning process. As we shall see it opens the opportunities for the school counselor to more actively engage in consulting of a "first level" type. ("First level" consulting will be explained later in this chapter.)

Consulting in the Secondary School Setting

Teacher-pupil contacts in the departmental organization of the secondary school will range from 120 to 150 students. That represents a lot of teacher attention and responsibility, especially when we are talking and thinking of more rather than less individualized learning. If a teacher really cares about his relationships with students, a load of 150 students is a lot of "caring," a lot of human relating. Such an intense involvement with each and every pupil is, of course, an impossibility. Students, on the other hand, are involved with seven to ten teachers. It is feasible that they can handle this number of day-to-day intimacies with teachers. With four or five academic subject contacts and another four or five special teacher contacts, every student ought to be in a position to find one or more teachers with whom he can relate and whose approach to learning can be tolerable.

The departmental organization of the secondary school results in

[4] American School Counselor Association, *op. cit.*, p. 9.

several work environments for both the teacher and the student. With a teaching load of four or five classes, the secondary school teacher finds himself with as many learning environments. Each class has its own identity even though any one teacher may tend to establish a similar learning milieu in each of his classes. This occurs even if the teaching is focused on a particular age-grade level, on the same curricula, and even though the teacher approach to each class is more consistent than different.

Both teachers and students in the secondary school labor under conditions that tend to serve the curriculum and the fulfillment of its prescribed experiences. Subject matter and concerns for covering the content have more than a passing influence on the teaching-learning process. Teaching strategies and the environment of the classroom reflect these concerns. The objectives of education and the concern for the individual in the learning activities are often neglected. Adolescent growth and development and all our knowledge about it become frequently forgotten in a race that pits the curriculum against the school calendar. Learning is content-oriented, task-centered; learning loses its excitement in the routine and meaninglessness of rote and recall. To many teachers those are the expectations of their role; for many students these are the realities of their school existence. And in this environment, the very essence of the learning-maturation process is lost or undermined.

Secondary education, like other levels of the educative process, is facing revolution and change. Some educators, many parents, and most students are disillusioned with the drudgery of present-day practice. All seem to be hopeful of promise in some of the educational changes that are being proposed and tried. And yet the overriding reluctance to become involved, prompted by attitudes of let's wait and see, results in much the same classroom behavior year after year after year. There remains far too much schoolmaster complacency. Despite known weaknesses in the educative process, some educators are threatened by forces that seek to change educational practice. Guidance workers who will choose to embrace a developmental approach can expect to encounter some resistance, perhaps a good deal of it in some systems, in a role that includes a more expansive consulting function. This "leave me alone and let me teach" (or administrate, or guide) attitude can deter the development of programs that can enrich the learning-maturation of youth. The school counselor in activating the consulting function will find that such attitudes are more superficial than profound. While their intensity will vary from individual to individual, the counselor will be able to penetrate the underlying resistance in most instances over a period of time.

The secondary school counselor represents young people. He is concerned with them as individuals in the process of learning and maturing.

This means he must be oriented to their present experiencing. Sometimes, as we know, counselors deal with adolescents solely in terms of their future —an orientation that often overlooks the very significant concerns of the adolescent in the here and now. He can and must be prepared to share in shaping and reshaping the educative process. He is concerned about the learner *now* and involved in matters that deal directly with the behaviors he is expected to learn and the conditions of his learning.

The consulting function incorporates helping the school—and the community if need be—to face and to deal with many aspects of the educational dilemma. It embodies helping teachers to examine their own classroom responsibilities and behaviors. Through the consulting function, in a quite different but possibly more effective way, the developmental counselor serves the learner. In this way he is putting his knowledge about human learning and human development to work for the benefit of everyone, and particularly for the student. He is helping teachers to expedite the learning-maturation of every student.

His efforts can be viewed in terms of their facilitative, developmental focus. In this manner he helps the school to accommodate the variant learnings that occur in the normal, everyday process of an individual's living and learning. Thus, the consulting function takes on a more encompassing purpose than the narrower, more restrictive views that have been associated with it.

His consulting activities need not conflict with his primary allegiance to youth nor with his concern for the individual learner. The fact that he may be communicating more directly with teachers about what *they* are doing and how *they* are doing it, rather than just communicating information about students, could reduce the bind that often occurs when a counselor is communicatively trapped between the student and the teacher. It will not eliminate this from happening but it has possibilities of alleviating the student perception of the counselor as the pipeline to teachers.

Neither should it detract from his ability to expend himself with youth in a human and helping way, nor should it interfere with his ability to serve the uniqueness of the individual learner. In fact it supports his work with youth. It portends more potential; certainly it recognizes the singly important role of the teacher in the life of youth—and tries to help the teacher deal more effectively and more humanly with it.

Consulting As a Process

There is a dearth of information about the consulting process. As a process it involves many of the same characteristics as one commonly associates with the process of counseling. It is another form of human, helping relationship. We are learning a great deal about consultation as it is increasingly employed in a new work role in education—the elementary school guidance specialist. In a few years, as the process of consulting becomes the focus of more intensive study and research, we may consider our present views and formulations quite antiquated and naive. This has occurred in studying the process of counseling and I believe we can anticipate some new directions for consulting. As it achieves more consideration in secondary school guidance and as the developmental school counselor utilizes consultation procedures and processes, I suspect we shall learn even more about the possibilities.

One of the more helpful and extensive treatments of consultation is contained in *Concepts of Mental Health and Consultation* by Gerald Caplan.[5] The process and techniques Caplan describes have been developed within a highly specialized program having been established ". . . for consultants who were psychiatrists, psychologists, or social workers, and consultees who were mainly teachers or child-care workers."[6] While he cautions about generalizing from their approach, some of the principles and many of their experiences are applicable to the consulting function in secondary school guidance. Certainly, even if one chooses to be cautious, they are worthy of consideration and trial. To build on the experiences of other disciplines, particularly on one whose goals are so compatible, is far wiser than to continue the hit or miss experimentation that is so prevalent today.

The consultation function, like the counseling function, is based on communication and human interaction. The relationship between the consultant and the consultee is basic. Acceptance, trust, and understanding are essential. The relationship can be short-term although greater benefits lie in the long-term relationship. Consulting is essentially problem centered, and the consultee seeks the help of the consultant. In the process of consulting, then, we need to be concerned with the process aspects of initiation, maintenance, duration, and termination. Consulting as a function of secondary school guidance has promise of extending assistance where it may be most needed—in improving the learning environment of the school and in enhancing the teaching-learning process. It has promise of promoting and effecting change—of helping consultees (teachers in particular) to deal directly and comfortably with new directions in the educative process.

[5] Gerald Caplan, *Concepts of Mental Health and Consultation* (Washington, D.C.: Children's Bureau, U.S. Department of Health, Education, and Welfare, 1959).

[6] *Ibid.*, p. 119.

The Consulting Relationship

There are two very basic, closely related questions to be considered with regard to the consulting relationship. First, can the secondary school counselor serve in both the consulting and counseling capacity with the same personnel? I believe he can serve both functions, as I shall explain later. Second, can the secondary school counselor engage in both functions as a full-time member of the staff?

Caplan speaks directly to this question of dual function. He indicates,

I used to think that it was advisable for the consultant not to be a member of the staff of the consultee institution. I thought that as a staff member he would be influenced by the field of forces within the institution to such an extent that he would be hampered in his role as consultant. But I am no longer sure it is impossible for the consultant to be a member of the staff of the consultee institution.[7]

He goes on to qualify, however, ". . . although the consultant might possibly be a member of the staff of the institution, he should under no circumstances hold a position of administrative responsibility in relation to the consultee. This restriction is essential because consultation demands an accepting, noncritical, permissive attitude, which is incompatible with the administrative role."[8] Lippitt is more exact indicating that ". . . the consultant is an 'outsider,' i.e., is not a part of any hierarchical power system in which the client is located."[9]

Both Caplan and Lippitt, however, clearly perceive the necessity for the consultant to be free of association with authority, making it possible for him to establish relationships based on needs rather than by force or domination. However, this restriction seems to be categorical referring to positions in the formal power structure. In suggesting the notion of power and its use we shall later need to look at the consultant's use of power to foster change within the more informal dynamic of power in the system.

It is essential that the school counselor in developing his consultive activities create an image that reflects his concern for teachers and students rather than one that appears supervisory or management-oriented. The developmental counselor's position is a staff position, freeing him from affiliation with the administrative hierarchy; this is important for it allows the counselor to identify readily with the instructional staff. Free of authority,

[7] *Ibid.,* p. 120.
[8] *Ibid.*
[9] Ronald Lippitt, "Dimensions of the Consultant's Job," *Journal of Social Issues* 15:5, 1959.

he can use his own interpersonal skills to establish the kinds of relationships with teachers that are necessary and vital to the further growth and improvement of the teaching-learning process.

First-level consulting relationships with teachers. The consulting relationship can be conceived as one that builds continually from the first contact. These beginning experiences are usually teacher-initiated. Caplan advises that once the lines of communication are open ". . . the consultant should come into the consultee's field in response to an invitation based on some need felt by the consultee."[10] These first-level relationships originate with teacher needs that are usually external in nature. The consultation may be concerned with a specific teaching technique or with more general matters pertaining to the teaching of a certain subject such as an approach to the teaching of mathematics or science. It may deal with a special curriculum problem such as the development of a unit in English or it may be concerned with a particular unit activity such as a field trip or a special film that could be used. It may involve an individual or a group of individuals in the classroom.

Generally the consultant is contacted because the teacher needs some help in dealing with a specific aspect of the teaching-learning process. Sometimes the consultant is used simply to supply a specific kind of information that will enhance teaching or learning. A few teachers will refuse to use a consultant. Some teachers may approach the consultant cautiously at first, while others will view the consultant as one who can be of assistance and one who will not threaten the teacher's position in the school or her relationship with her class. The consulting relationship may range from a simple request by one teacher for information that can be given in a few moments to a series of meetings for a group of teachers where a number of significant teaching-learning problems can be discussed. Generally the consulting function involves one or several short-term relationships with the teacher in which his or her immediate needs are reviewed and filled insofar as possible.

With regard to these initial requests Caplan states,

If the consultant is to establish a fruitful contact he must at first accept his assignment at its face value and refrain from making his own contradictory ideas explicit. In other words, if one is invited in to talk about a child, one must talk about the child, even though it is very clear the real reason you have been invited in is that this particular . . . school teacher . . . is very upset about something or other.[11]

[10] Caplan, *op. cit.,* p. 121.
[11] *Ibid.,* pp. 121–122.

Where teachers seek consultant aid in dealing with a student or a group of students, it is generally with some type of problem in mind. Under present practice the teacher is quite likely to view the school counselor as the person to whom she can refer a student for assistance or remediation. Sometimes the teacher contacts the counselor seeking additional information of all types about a student. In such instances the teacher is usually seeking advice (and sometimes support) on ways to deal with the pupil in the learning environment.

In some school situations, depending upon the teacher's interpretation of the counselor's role, the teacher will avoid consultation by sending the student directly to the guidance office, by suggesting that he visit the counselor, or by requesting that the counselor call him in for a conference (usually requiring that the teacher complete a referral slip but not always mandating any other communication between teacher and counselor). Most often these types of referrals are associated with students who are causing disciplinary problems or who are exhibiting behavioral difficulties. The nature and extent of these referrals have meaning for the counselor since they indicate teacher expectations of the school counselor and communicate to him their perceptions of his role. In being aware of this *sent* role, he can deal directly with role conflicts that may emerge if he does not oblige or if he compromises. In these instances, he may need to define his perceptions of his role, leaving himself available for future discussions.

If the school counselor is primarily interested in developing his consulting function around activities that are going to result in more effective learning situations for *all* children, he will need to make skillful and astute judgments relative to each teacher request. Again, as is so often the case where judgment is involved, one cannot categorically state, "He does it" or "He doesn't do it." Rather, it is an instance where his judgment will take into account the kind of image he hopes to develop and the need, at that time, to meet the expectations of those in his role set.

First-level consultation can be directed toward helping teachers identify pupils with particular learning needs or problems, interpreting pupil information including information about special learning abilities of students or other significant pupil data, providing material which may be helpful in classroom learning experiences, or conferring with school personnel on particular curriculum developments and improvements. The opportunities for involvement with teachers at this level are many and varied. They offer the school counselor a chance to work more closely with teachers, and they provide a base from which he may later become more deeply involved with teachers and the educative process.

Second-level consulting relationships. While first-level contacts are external to the teacher and therefore safe and nonthreatening, they can be used to develop more personally significant relationships and enable teachers to feel capable in areas where they are less secure. Teachers may, for instance, be willing to try new ideas and techniques; they may feel free to risk more of themselves with youth and others. They may be motivated to operate in any number of professional or personal ways that can not only improve their relationships with others but encourage others to become involved as well. Caplan speaks to this second-level relationship as follows:

The continuing link between consultee and consultant is provided by the emotional relationship which is built up between them. This not only motivates the consultee to maintain the contact but is the vehicle for the consultation process itself. To build up this emotional bond as quickly as possible, and to be constantly aware of its nature, is a basic responsibility of the consultant.[12]

It is at this second level of consultation that the more creative, innovative practices in education can be encouraged. Assuming that the consultant is aware of and concerned about his relationship with the consultee, he can begin to intervene in ways which can result in a positive influence on the learning environment. He must depend on *his* judgment of the strength of the relationship that has been developed with the consultee in deciding what action to follow such as suggesting, interpreting or proposing. He functions very much as he would in a counseling relationship. He reads feelings, he encourages the expression of feelings, he is aware of attitudes. He is involved with the teacher. He is concerned with his or her growth. He cares. Under these conditions, and most likely *only* under these conditions, will the more dynamic and long-range changes in the teaching-learning process occur.

Compulsory consultation probably won't work; but intervention may have possibilities. This will be one of the most difficult areas of the consultation process to assess. Without the teacher's involvement, any participation would be deemed unnecessary, irrelevant or undesirable. In short, if the school counselor were to press the teacher, he would probably be told that it is "none of his business." But assuming that undesirable learning situations should be the business of education, it does become somebody's concern.

First and foremost it should be the concern of the teacher involved. There are those that would recommend that the school counselor withdraw

[12] *Ibid.,* p. 122.

from the situation and deal only with the teacher concern that caused her to interact with him in the first instance. While to retreat may be a very likely judgment in some instances, it does not seem appropriate in all cases. It would seem that the school counselor would need to involve the teacher insofar as possible in activities likely to result in increased teacher receptivity to changes in her classroom organization and behavior.

In recent years school administrators have attempted to change teacher behaviors by employing different approaches to the teaching-learning process. For example, team teaching and modular scheduling have been employed in some instances, not only because they appear to be more effective approaches to learning but because they have inherent within them the need for teachers to change. In some school systems initiating teacher personnel to different approaches has worked successfully, resulting in some significant changes in teacher attitudes and teaching styles. These have had a dynamic and important impact on student learning. In other systems teachers have resisted a changed approach to classroom instruction and have resented modifications in the school organization. They have continued their "old" ways in the "new" organization. As a result very little change has occurred in the teaching processes employed and classroom environments have remained essentially the same.

The secondary school counselor must learn to understand and work with the resistant teacher, the doubting teacher, the content centered teacher —in short, with any teacher who in essence refuses to examine her own teaching methodology. In some instances the school counselor may find it possible to confront the teacher directly and seek ways together in which they could modify the classroom toward a more efficient and helpful learning environment. In other instances it has been more desirable to continue to work with the teacher in ways that could help her become less threatened and more trustful of his consultant function and the type of assistance he can provide. With some teachers he may need to continue his efforts in regard to individual pupils or groups of pupils about whom the teacher is concerned. And, let's face it, there are some teachers he will be unable to reach at all.

Third-level consulting relationships. This is a very personal relationship. It is actually a counseling relationship with a teacher. I identify it to indicate the degree to which the consulting relationship can be extended. I label it to differentiate it from the second-level relationship. Caplan, from his experience with consultants who were not members of the school staff, indicated, "If you have a long series of interviews with an individual consultee, your work is apt to develop into either mental health education or psychotherapy. These are both potentially valuable in their own right, but only if planned for and defined as such."[13] While Caplan recommends that psychotherapy be avoided (and I agree), the school counselor through his relationships with teachers is always vulnerable to a counseling relationship with them. While I do not wish to differentiate between counseling and psychotherapy (such differences have been made sufficiently clear in a number of counseling theory textbooks), I am suggesting that the school counselor be prepared to deal with the personal problems and the self-understanding concerns raised by consultees. It is not uncommon to identify teachers who are in need of personal counseling. It is not uncommon to find teachers whose personal concerns are affecting the ways they deal with children in their classroom. A counseling relationship with a teacher is a natural outgrowth of effective interpersonal communication within the first two levels of the consulting function. If the school counselor has been effective in his interaction with teachers with regard to consultation activities at either the first or second level, it is quite possible that the conditions basic to a productive counseling relationship have been established. These will permit the teacher with personal concerns to seek his help. The following are some examples:

(1) Tim J. was a first-year teacher. The counselor had heard via the grapevine that Tim had difficulties with classroom control. Not too many weeks passed before the counselor and Tim were in communication. Tim indicated that he presumed his lack of classroom discipline was the talk of the school but he added that he felt *control,* as many teachers understood it, was coercion and he didn't want any part of that. The second time the counselor had an opportunity to talk with Tim, Tim told the counselor that he really didn't want to teach. While teaching had been an aspiration of some standing, the actual experience had dampened his enthusiasm. Frankly, Tim admitted, he continued in teaching because it kept him draft exempt. As Tim and the school counselor continued to discuss the draft, Tim revealed his plans to leave the country, adding that these thoughts bothered him to the point that he was not able to function well in the classroom. During a third meeting a few days later, Tim indicated that he appreciated this relationship with the counselor, stating that he actually had no one to confide in since his mother was dead and his father, with whom he lived, was gone a great deal. He expressed the need and desire to meet a girl, indicating that he had been unsuccessful although he had been in love with one girl, who had given him the "cold shoulder." And so it went.

(2) Mrs. P. had been working with the school counselor in reference to several activities and they had conferred very briefly on several occasions and at

---

[13] *Ibid.,* p. 126.

greater length four different times. One day Mrs. P. simply approached the school counselor requesting some time to talk about a personal problem. Although Mrs. P. appeared very tense, she readily moved to the point of the session. Her own problems, she felt, interferred with her teaching and she added that she focused too much attention on her own needs and neglected her classes in the process. If she was going to do anything about her teaching, she simply had to have some help with her own concerns and problems. As her story unfolded the counselor learned that her husband had left her two years previously with two teenage daughters. While she felt she had a fairly good relationship with them, they were more than she could handle. Basically, she experienced loneliness and rejection. At times she wanted to establish relationships with other men but the fear of rejection by her own children prevented her from doing so. These feelings even permeated her relationships with her colleagues at school and she talked about her feelings of rejection by other younger teachers. In her perception they looked upon her as an "old bag" desperate for attention.

(3) Mrs. T. had had a rough day and, for that matter, so had the school counselor. The school counselor happened by Mrs. T's classroom and seeing Mrs. T. sitting at her desk staring into space thought he would drop in for a moment. Hardly had he passed through the door when Mrs. T. began to sob. "I'm so glad you came by," she said, "for I simply can't hold out much longer." And then it all poured out—the difficulties with her husband, the fights and the unpleasantness of the past year. Now, with her husband asking for a divorce, what was she to do?

Counseling relationships (or third-level consulting relationships) can be extremely time consuming and costly. But if these relationships can effect positive influences for the educative process they may in the long run be more effective, less costly, and exert greater results. In many school situations consulting efforts may indicate the necessity for dealing with the "system"—its structure and its limits. To effect these changes, the consultant must be involved with a number of consultees over a period of time. He must be involved with the school and its personnel. It is hardly likely that he can visit a school on a part-time basis and become involved in changes that will facilitate communication and human interaction and in program modifications or extensions that will improve the education of boys and girls.

While there is always the possibility for a counseling role with teachers to become complicated by other interactions and activities with which either the teacher or the school counselor may become involved, it would seem that they can work through any differences or misunderstandings that may occur *if* they have developed a real working counseling relationship—that is, if as two persons they have truly developed a relationship that *exceeds* the levels of understanding, trust, and acceptance essential to consulting at the first two levels. While it is important to recognize that teachers do *not* expect the school counselor to engage in the counseling function with them (counseling with teachers is not a commonly identified guidance role expectation), its availability seems to outweigh any disadvantage that may arise as a result of overlapping or contradictory endeavors.

I realize that by equating the third-level consulting relationship with the counseling relationship I may be confusing rather than clarifying the two functions. However, I feel it is essential to do so at this time so that we can better understand how both the counseling and consulting functions are eventually fused. Yet at the same time it is important to show how they differ. The third-level consulting relationship with teachers (or the counseling relationship with teachers) might include a wide variety of concerns but these can be reduced to two types.

First, teachers may bring to the school counselor personal problems that involve outside-of-school concerns stemming from family, social or economic difficulties and conflicts, particularly as these may be related to or interfering with the teacher's interpersonal functioning with children. In the second type, teachers may seek assistance in self-evaluation and self-examination. These teachers may be more concerned with the kind of person they are and the implications of this for their classroom behavior. The school counselor should be able to help teachers deal effectively with these problems or to assist them in seeking other forms of professional assistance. In some circumstances the school counselor may feel uncomfortable (but should feel free to express his uncomfortableness) when teachers seek his assistance with regard to professional or interpersonal conflicts they are having with other members of the school staff. Even for these situations, which can be worked through, it doesn't seem necessary to differentiate between roles. The human relationship may prove to be more crucially useful than the role relationship.

CONSULTING AND EDUCATIONAL CHANGE

Employing the concept of consulting as a continuing professional relationship places the school counselor in a unique position within the school hierarchy to encourage and support innovative change. When defining their goals most school systems strive for a delicate balance between the maintenance of certain accepted behaviors and ideas and the innovation of potentially beneficial practices that have won the support of educators and/or the public. In actuality, schools, like most bureaucratic organizations, remain resistant to innovation and change. Teachers, who have enjoyed decades of autonomy within a system which has become larger, more diversified, and more bureaucratic, are particularly reluctant to relinquish their real freedom within the four walls of their individual classrooms. The increasing size of the student population, necessitating more personnel and thereby adding to the number of intermediate positions between the teacher and the policy-makers at the top of the bureaucratic ladder, further complicates the issue of innovation and change within any system.

The school counselor by virtue of his unique position in the school bureaucracy, albeit a staff position, may be able to bridge the increasingly wide gap between teachers and administrators, particularly in the area of innovation in the school. Because his responsibilities involve him in activities with both teachers and administrators, he is in a position both to evaluate the need for change and to help school personnel implement innovations. The school counselor who recognizes this aspect of his role is in a position to preserve the very best of the status quo and at the same time to serve as a catalyst for creative change.

The Interpersonal Dynamics in Change

Education, like many other professions, provides the stimuli for helping its personnel recognize the possibilities for change. School personnel are encouraged to attend conferences, workshops, and other meetings where new ideas are presented and the need for change is discussed. Within the institution of the school itself, in-service programs that focus on the particular problems of a school district are offered. School personnel are encouraged to take courses at local or area institutions of higher education and many districts offer salary increments as an inducement to keep its personnel up to date.

Yet for all these opportunities and experiences the educational process often remains essentially the same. The pressure for change originates with enlightened school administration; sometimes this occurs within the teaching ranks. Pressure downward frequently meets with resistance and many such efforts fall short of instituting a difference in the classroom—the actual center of the educative process. In part this can be explained by the failure of the institution to provide the teaching force with the kind of assistance that enables people to actually introduce these changes and to deal with the day-to-day problems they incur in implementing these new directions.

Lippitt speaks directly to the role of the consultant in this regard. He says,

Often the consultant offers diagnostic help and arrives at certain recommendations for improvement or change, but offers no continuity in the actual working through of the meaning of the diagnostic findings for changing procedures, practices, and interaction patterns. This dropping of the relationship with the client system at such an early stage in the process of changing often results in disruption and demoralization because of the inadequacy of the client-group to cope with the implications for change without further technical help from a consultant.[14]

Two points are very clear. First, the consulting relationship cannot be a hit and run affair: its effectiveness lies in the measure of its continuity. Associated with this continuity is the interpersonal dynamic of one person helping another to make whatever transitional adjustments are necessary to the change in process. Such adjustments often involve more than superficial, external changes in behavior; they can involve changes in attitudes or modification of ideas or beliefs. The school counselor is in a position to be helpful since he can be available on a long-term basis. He can contribute to the continuity of the change process through the consulting function as it is a part of it. Others are certain to be a part of the total effort making the school counselor one of several team members.

Second, he brings to the situation of change, the interpersonal skills that allow for the kinds of help an individual needs in making the professional and personal adjustments basic to the implementation of change. He can evolve with teachers a consulting relationship with potential at any of the three levels of consulting previously detailed. This is not to infer that the school counselor will evolve higher level relationships with all teachers. Rather, it is to indicate the potential for such relationships to develop, to emphasize his availability as a helping person, and to point out his competencies in matters both professional and personal.

Thinking of a school counselor whose expertise in the human relationship can be utilized in a consulting manner is a natural point of emphasis. The consulting relationship, evolving in much the same fashion as the counseling relationship, has every potential for a human relationship that can foster the type of human growth that foments change rather than resists it.

Consulting in the Change Process

Lippitt is explicit in citing seven phases of consulting in the change process noting that the consultant must be prepared to make changes in his behavior as these different phases of the consulting relationship are encountered. These seven phases are as follows:

[14] Lippitt, *op. cit.*, p. 9.

1. The development of a need for change.
2. The establishment of a consulting relationship.
3. The clarification of the client problem.
4. The examination of alternative solutions and goals.
5. The transformation of intentions into actual change efforts.
6. The generalization and stabilization of a new level of functioning or group structure.
7. Achieving a terminal relationship with the consultant and a continuity of change-ability.[15]

His characterization of the consultant's role in the change process emphasizes the long-term, on-going aspects of helping others to effect change. The first three phases suggest the concerns of initiating change and the personnel involved. Matters of leadership and the processes used to inaugurate change are, of course, significant here.

Perhaps one of the most difficult aspects of the whole change process is getting it started. Overcoming the forces that resist change and rallying those that start it are not easy. Obviously this is not a one-man responsibility; but the developmental counselor, through the consulting relationship, can help in surmounting resistance and in mustering support. Change does not have to flow with the formal power structure—that is, from the top down. In fact, as we have noted, the forces of resistance often make these attempts at change futile. Yet the counselor, to the extent that he can employ the informal power system of the school, can initiate the change process. Adroitly used with individuals and with groups (yet without employing deception or misrepresentation), those who are less willing to accept new ideas or practices, can be influenced, coerced, or sometimes manipulated into "going along" with change.

While at first glance these uses of power may seem underhanded, they are positive ways of moving into the change process. For example, two teachers, hesitant about accepting a new idea, may succumb under group pressure, even if reluctantly. Or one teacher may be able to convince another of the value of an idea. If these seem too commonplace, too representative of the everyday behavior of people then you have grasped the idea of how power, even though informal, is employed all the time. Consider this understanding in a positive light—that is, look at these behaviors with reference to the welfare of the school and its potential for influencing the learning-maturation of adolescents—and you have a picture of how and by whom change is accommodated.

Also, it should be noted that while the school counselor is often

---

[15] *Ibid.*, p. 10.

actively at work as a stimulator, a provocateur, an idea man, he is not always the leader of change-oriented moves, nor is he always responsible for the decisions, determinations, or actions of an individual or a group of individuals. His part may be dependent on a variety of factors including his relationship to others involved, his relative status, and the means employed to initiate the change process.

In any event, there must be involvement of all concerned and within the procedures for initiating the change process there must be tolerance for a variety of behaviors on the part of those affected. These can range all the way from acceptance and involvement in the process to outright hostility and resistance. These behaviors become readily apparent in the behaviors of persons affected such as the enthusiasm shown and the cooperation extended by those involved. The consulting relationship during this period can cater to the needs of the group (clarification of goals, explication of need for change, etc.) and to the development of processes for effecting the changes.

Obviously, the very nature of these early phases of change would point to the involvement of others in planning and effecting change. The role of school administrators, outside consultants, teacher committees in working through the many facets of these early stages and their responsibilities here are quite explicitly detailed in many publications devoted to the process of change.

In initiating change the developmental counselor may have cause to help the group or an individual deal with resistance as it becomes obvious in their uncertainty about change or in their ambiguity about its goals, their fears about performing in new or different ways, or their lack of participation in the decision to have these changes. The school counselor can help in dealing with feedback, goal clarification, understanding of the need for change, or with individuals who essentially are threatened by the whole process (assuming they feel sufficiently positive about their relationship with him and free to raise these concerns to him).

The last three phases of the consultant's role refer more specifically to the transitional behaviors and problems which are involved in actually effecting change. Here is where continuity is most important! Here is where the interpersonal relationship between the consultant and the consultee is severely tested. Here is where consistent, understanding help is most urgent. Here is where the consultant may need to alter his behaviors to accommodate the needs of an individual immersed, or about to be, in the process of change. And finally, here is where much of the change possibilities in education have broken down in the past. Teachers who are all fired up as the result of a workshop, an in-service meeting, or a seminar, may want to try their new ideas, yet certain factors tend to restrict exploration. Thus without support and encouragement, or lacking help in coping with the problems that arise from first exploratory attempts, their enthusiasm fades until the next meeting kindles another passion.

Lippitt, Watson, and Westley list four sources of resistance to change. One or more of these forces are associated with people who often aren't as resistant as they are afraid. They say,

Perhaps the four most frequently noted sources of resistance to the idea of help are (1) reluctance to admit weaknesses, (2) fear of failure or awkwardness in trying to initiate a new practice or behavior pattern, (3) a fatalistic expectation of failure instilled by previous unsuccessful attempts to change, and (4) a fear of losing some current satisfaction (for example, power, dependency, and so forth).[16]

The school counselor could be very active, for example, in helping teachers who were trying to get from here to there in their approach to a classroom, a subject, or a student. The working through of needs and attitudes is a likely way in which the counselor can help with the process of change. The latter phases may last for some time and may lead the counselor into helping the individual teacher with many other aspects of his or her professional work not necessarily directly involved in the actual change that caused them to work together initially.

The counselor's role in the change process is not a definitive responsibility that he and he alone assumes. Not at all. The consulting function contributes to educational change and innovation as a rather natural part of the school counselor's concern for making the educative process a more meaningful, productive, and relevant experience.

To the extent that he observes processes which need changing or that he becomes aware of conditions which could be improved, he moves forward to help in initiating needed attention or intervention. To the extent that he can assist others who seek to improve the teaching-learning process, he uses himself. Within these realms, he acts as a member of a team designed to make educational innovation a reality instead of a textbook platitude. In this sense, then, he uses his consulting competencies to act as an agent of change and to the extent that he is successful, he *is* an agent of change.

SUGGESTED READING

BENNIS, WARREN G.; BENNE, KENNETH; and CHIN, ROBERT, (Eds.), *The Planning of Change* (New York: Holt, Rinehart and Winston, 1969).

[16] Ronald Lippitt, Jeanne Watson, and Bruce Westley, *The Dynamics of Planned Change* (New York: Harcourt, Brace and World, 1958), pp. 180–181.

CAPLAN, GERALD, *Concepts of Mental Health and Consultation* (Washington, D.C.: Children's Bureau, Department of Health, Education, and Welfare, 1959).

LIPPITT, RONALD, "Dimensions of the Consultant's Job," *Journal of Social Issues* 15:5–12, 1959.

LIPPITT, RONALD; WATSON, JEANNE; and WESTLEY, BRUCE, *The Dynamics of Planned Change* (New York: Harcourt, Brace and World, 1958).

NINE

THE COORDINATING FUNCTION

The ASCA *Statement of Policy for Secondary School Counselors* cites a number of professional responsibilities including pupil appraisal, educational and occupational information, referral work, placement, parent help, and local research.[1] While aspects of these responsibilities are likely consumed in the counseling or consulting function, many facets of these areas suggest a coordinating function. The coordinating function contains within it some managerial and organizational responsibilities. The coordinating function, like counseling or consulting, is based on communication and interpersonal relationships. In some ways the coordinating responsibilities of the secondary school may be only an extension of the counseling and consulting relationships that he has established. In other ways these coordinating responsibilities are fundamental to the smoother operation and the fuller implementation of the counseling and consulting function. In short, without a measure of coordination to provide the needed organizational structure and to manage certain basic resources, the guidance program could lose some of its potency.

THE COORDINATING FUNCTION
AS A ROLE HERITAGE

There are a number of responsibilities which the school counselor has inherited. They may be just as valid as any new ones that are proposed, or, more likely, some are more appropriate to certain approaches to secondary school guidance than others. It may be high time that we review the appro-

[1] American School Counselor Association, *Statement of Policy for Secondary School Counselors* (Washington, D.C.: American Personnel and Guidance Association, 1964), pp. 7–9.

priateness of some guidance responsibilities with respect to the modern demands of secondary school guidance and to the approach which the school is trying to implement.

It is rather common to find school counselors heavily involved in some of the following activities: collecting and filing occupational information materials; arranging and planning field trips to local businesses and industries; preparing the school standardized testing schedule; orienting teachers to administer standardized tests; supervising or arranging for the scoring of standardized tests; collecting and filing information about colleges and other institutions of higher education; maintaining pupil personnel records; preparing college transcripts; writing recommendations for college. Experience has shown that these activities consume a large amount of the counselor's time and energy; in some positions they are major responsibilities. Yet the sphere of responsibility for some of these activities could be questioned. Certain aspects of these activities, if not the entire activity itself, could be an administrative or instructional responsibility. Are these guidance responsibilities? If so, are they primary or supplementary responsibilities?

In viewing his coordinating function, the school counselor must examine most carefully the nature and direction of his efforts as well as the time he allots to it. Much of his coordinating activity utilizes a different set of competencies. His organizational-managerial skills are more directly employed in most of these activities than are his interpersonal skills, though admittedly these too are involved. These are jobs that can be counted and accounted for and the satisfaction in their completion is a tangible one for the school counselor. While their coordination requires a certain amount of other school personnel involvement, for the most part their enactment can be accomplished by decisions in the guidance office. A counselor needs to assess his own needs as these are fulfilled by his participation in such activities as opposed to the more ambiguous accomplishments in the human relationships of counseling and consulting.

The school counselor needs to think about his coordinating function in terms of work priorities and balance. He can begin by asking himself several questions. Do his coordinating functions have more priority in terms of student needs than his other functions? How can he apportion his coordinative effort with his own two functions? Is the coordinating function more important than the others? What are the role expectations of others with regard to his coordinating function? Since he is very apt to be the only member of the pupil personnel staff who is working in the school on a full-time basis, it is quite likely that many of the managerial activities associated with records, meetings, and informational resources will be expected of him. The counselor will have to be most selective of those activities for which he accepts primary responsibility. Despite a heritage of mechanistic and clerical routines, some of which are associated with the coordinating function, he is in command of the distribution of his efforts among his three major functions in the performance of his role.

In the years ahead, in view of the expanding and differing responsibilities for the school counselor, we will need to consider the modification and alteration of the school counselor's role. Some activities will become mechanized, others will become less vital. New responsibilities will emerge, others will be dropped. Many of the activities that will become mechanized or less vital will probably be of a coordinating nature. It is more than likely that many of these functions will become the province and responsibility of the paraprofessional in guidance. Others will be modified by our advancing technology and the changing nature of all work roles in education.

Many of the activities to be discussed in this chapter are, in my opinion, the prime consumers of the counselor's time and energy. Some are the activities he professionally disclaims but actively practices. A few already should be regarded as role "discards." Traditional involvement has stymied the school counselor who is unable to deal with outmoded role stereotypes in the enactment of his position. It seems best to recognize all these activities, to assess the traditional role expectations for them, to inform the inquiring student of guidance about them, and to determine the nature of these activities. Yet the potential counselor should be alert to the necessity for assessing their validity and applicability in the future role of the secondary school counselor. Beyond this, I would further suggest that future counselors examine carefully the coordinating aspect of these activities being aware of the acute difference between coordinating and enacting an activity. School counselors in the past have, I fear, equated coordination and performance preferring to *do* the job rather than to *coordinate* its doing.

PUPIL APPRAISAL ACTIVITIES

The pupil appraisal process in the public schools centers basically around three major practices.

(1) *The maintenance of individual pupil personnel records*—containing basic information about the student, his family and his home; his growth and development (teacher anecdotals); his activities record; his standardized test results; notations about his health; notes on interviews with him and conferences with his parents; and other miscellaneous information about him obtained through rating scales, autobiographies, and questionnaires.

(2) *Standardized testing programs*—designed to provided data about the student's abilities, interests, aptitudes, and achievement.

(3) *The academic record* (the central office "permanent record")—consisting of a year-by-year record of the student's academic performance in all subject areas.

Pupil Appraisal in the Educative Process

The approach to pupil appraisal in the schools is both accumulative and longitudinal. It presumably takes place over the period of the pupil's enrollment in the school and is accumulative in that additional data about the pupil is being assembled each year. While much of this data is presumably available for pupils, and supposedly directed toward helping the pupil identify his strengths and weaknesses, very little use of this type is made with the data until his first program planning session with his counselor. At that time school achievement data and test data are generally taken into consideration in helping pupils and their parents plan a program of study for high school and beyond. Even then such conferences are usually held but once a year and are of a short duration (seldom more than an hour, with most conferences lasting approximately 30 minutes).

The pupil appraisal process is usually diagnostically centered and is generally launched when students evidence some learning difficulty or behavioral problem. At that time the data in the pupil folder is often reviewed by the counselor or by the counselor and the teacher in an attempt to make some sort of diagnosis of the student's problem and to formulate plans for resolving it.

Administrative appraisals. The administrator uses data about pupils to describe various dimensions of his student body. Standardized test data, in particular, is used to describe the performance level of students in the district and to compare the performance of students in the system with that of students in other school districts in the state and nation. Within the district, comparisons can be made among building populations, for example. Such data, therefore, have basically evaluative and descriptive uses. Building principals sometimes use the individual pupil personnel folder in making a decision about a student or in justifying one in a parent conference. Such uses are occasional and administrators tend to rely on the interpretations of pupil data from the pupil personnel specialists.

Instructional appraisals. Teachers differ widely in their use of individual pupil records. Some teachers spend a great deal of time perusing pupil records while others never review them, preferring to formulate their own judgments about the student. Many use the record to obtain a particular bit of information about the student. Teachers often seek help in understanding a student, particularly those who pose behavioral or learning problems, by studying the pupil's folder. The folder is frequently the one source containing all standardized test data allowing for comparison of results.

Some teachers find these folders helpful in planning and modifying curriculum experiences for a student or group of students or in capitalizing on an individual's strengths and interests. Standardized test data is often used in planning remediation efforts for an individual or a class or in identifying areas of the instructional program where additional emphases could contribute to the development of necessary skills and understandings.

Pupil personnel service appraisals. The pupil personnel specialists rely heavily on the individual cumulative record folder for background data about a pupil. The school psychologist, attendance teacher and school social worker, in particular, find these data helpful in diagnosing student difficulties and in understanding student behavior. The school counselor tends to use such data for informational purposes maintaining that it helps him to understand students, offers cues to follow in counseling sessions, and provides data which can be employed in validating student decisions and plans.

With such a myriad of uses for pupil data, it is readily understood why the maintenance of pupil data is a common educational practice in our schools. With practically all school personnel making use of these data it could be readily presumed that such a venture would be a cooperative one in which all school personnel were involved. In order to maintain the kinds of data which are helpful to the various personnel involved, the collection of such data could be a joint responsibility involving not only teachers and pupil personnel service workers, as it usually does, but students and their parents as well.

In most schools, the pupil appraisal process begins at the time the parent registers the child for entrance into kindergarten and continues throughout the school life of the child. Thus, each year an expanding record of data is maintained and accumulated. This growing record of information about the student has been traditionally referred to as the cumulative record, though the term "pupil personnel record" has been introduced of late as the concept of pupil personnel services has become more common to educational practice. Other terms such as the individual inventory or the anecdotal record have been used to denote the individual pupil record.

The School Counselor and Pupil Appraisal

The school counselor has been frequently involved in the formulation and development of the school's system for maintaining individual pupil records. In many instances, particularly during the years that guidance was emerging, the school counselor was the force behind their instigation. For example, as a practicing guidance counselor during the emerging years of guidance, I helped to initiate pupil records in two school systems. I presume my successors have continued to assist in the maintenance and modification of these records over the years. In retrospect, at the beginning of the guidance movement there was perhaps good reason for the involvement of guidance personnel in this aspect of pupil appraisal. And perhaps not. Regardless, we have developed a heritage which the modern counselor must reassess.

The development of pupil records. In most schools today the individual pupil personnel record is a fact. It exists and counselors, either individually or as members of school committees, are often in leadership positions with reference to them. This has come about primarily from their insistence that such records be kept in the guidance office or in a nearby one. Changes are continually being made in the forms of such records and in the process of maintaining them, necessitating leadership in keeping school personnel up to date in these changes and in any responsibility they share in contributing to or maintaining them. Counselors very frequently assume or are assigned this task.

The collection of data about the pupil. This is often a guidance responsibility or one shared with the school administration. The collection of pupil data requires helping teachers learn about the nature and type of information they can contribute, the form in which such information is desired, as well as the materials they will use. In some systems, particularly in the elementary schools, teachers are required to write about the growth and development of each student in their charge. Such information, usually in the form of written anecdotes, describes the student's social interaction, his interests and abilities, his progress and achievements (or lack of), the teacher's perception of his home and family environment, and any other significant data which the teacher decides to enter on his record. Teachers usually write about their students near or at the end of the school year and this record is filed in the pupil's folder.

A variety of other information is gathered from time to time such as information about the student's involvement in school clubs and organizations, his awards, or his participation in community organizations (Scouts, church groups, etc.). Counselors sometimes request autobiographies (usually written in connection with an English class), administer questionnaires, or circulate rating scales requesting teachers to judge an individual student on a number of traits or characteristics. These data, year after year, with some annual review, eventuate in quite a student dossier.

The maintenance of pupil records. Maintaining such records can become quite a responsibility. There are the more simple problems of an administrative nature such as keeping the routine information current (home address, etc.), storing the folders, and making them available to teachers. Then there are the more difficult questions of accessibility (who can use these records), confidentiality, and appropriateness of data for inclusion. Almost daily any number of decisions or actions must be faced regarding the maintenance of these folders. In some schools, counselors use conference time to update pupil folder data. In other situations, special forms are used to gather current data, or homeroom teachers are held responsible for securing and adding the needed information.

The interpretation of record information. The culmination of all the data collecting processes lies in its use and we have examined earlier some of the administrative, instructional, and pupil personnel uses. School counselors are generally responsible for interpreting pupil record data to school personnel, parents, and pupils. In practice, members of the school staff often request pupil personnel help in interpreting the data, especially in analyzing or synthesizing these data in ways that contribute to a teacher's understanding of a student. Frequently such data is analyzed and interpreted to help in identifying the cause of a learning or behavior problem.

Pupil data, except for standardized test results, is rarely used with parents. In New York State, for example, parents can request to see such information but such data must be interpreted by a school counselor or a professional designated and authorized by the school. Of the voluminous information available, the standardized test data is the most commonly requested interpretation. This information is now made available to both parents and students either through uniform interpretations to groups, by individual interpretation in high school program planning conferences, or upon special request.

Pupil Personnel Records—A Note of Caution

In a study some years ago, the staff of the Division on Child Development and Teacher Personnel of the American Council on Education analyzed a number of teacher cumulative record entries concluding that they contained very little information about any student. They reported that teacher comments were more general and summarizing than factual, were more evaluative than descriptive, and were more judgmental than objective.[2] They identified four factors that influenced the nature of teacher statements.

[2] The Staff of the Division on Child Development and Teacher Personnel, *Helping Teachers Understand Children* (Washington, D.C.: American Council on Education, 1945), pp. 3–4.

. . . (1) the child's success or failure in mastering the content and skills prescribed as learning tasks for particular grade levels; (2) the problems met in
controlling the child's behavior so that it accorded with the local school code
and the teacher's personal conceptions of "good" and "bad"; (3) the standing of
the child's family in the community and its relation to the teacher's own social
status; and (4) the attractiveness and sympathy-winning power of the child
(or his repulsiveness) in terms of the teacher's individual background of experience, personal needs, and values.[3]

These findings, reported over 25 years ago, are as valid today as they
were then. We need to face the basic question of accumulating information
about the pupil. If we believe that such information can be helpful and useful, we need to examine carefully the kinds of information to be obtained
and the best means of obtaining it. If teacher notations are to be a part of
this record then we need to help teachers to understand and report the behaviors of children. Prescott and his staff made note of their optimism and
demonstrated how work with teachers could improve the caliber of cumulative record notations. Teachers, with help, can better understand and describe
pupils. But they do need help! The school counselor can assume some responsibility here but it need not extend to the actual collection and maintenance of these data. The point is, however, that unless we can improve these
records—unless we can get beyond the general, the evaluative, and the judgmental—whatever we maintain is worthless!

One final word of caution: many textbooks have contained chapters or
sections on anecdotal records, citing their value in pupil appraisal practices.
The confidentiality of these records has been stressed. Despite the known
weaknesses of records, over the years we have continued to employ their
use and to extend the range of their significance. Seldom have we examined
their limitations; rarely have we deplored the inherent dangers in our present
pupil data collecting methods. Therefore, where records exist and however
they are used, an analysis should be made of the manner in which the information was collected, the help provided for teachers in preparing their
contributions, and the general tenor of the data collected. In short, to para-
phrase a currently popular admonition—Caution: Record Writing May Be
Hazardous to a Pupil's Growth.

ORIENTATION ACTIVITIES

Orientation activities to help students prepare for and adjust to environmental changes in their educational experience is a rather recent educational phe-

[3] *Ibid.,* p. 5.

nomenon. In the days of the little red schoolhouse when all the children in a district attended school in the same building, there was very little need for any kind of orientation. It is only recently, as school districts have grown and expanded, that the need to help students make the change from one building to another has been necessary. The common breaks—traditionally—have occurred at the end of the elementary school (usually grade 6 or grade 8), at the conclusion of junior high school (between grades 9 and 10), and at the conclusion of high school (with a job or higher education immediately ahead). Of course the point of orientation need varies with the organization of the district. At whatever level, readiness is usually a concern of guidance personnel.

Why Orientation?

Change is difficult for everyone. It's accompanied by feelings of strangeness and uncertainty. One becomes anxious and apprehensive. Students experience these feelings very deeply both prior to and during a change of schools. They are concerned about their life in their new environment and they usually dread the period of adjustment. At the same time, they anticipate the change and they recognize that the move is evidence of their progress toward adulthood. Yet with all these fears and anxieties they are able to face the move with courage and determination.

Orientation does have a significant part in the process of helping students to feel more comfortable about changes in their educational environment and eases the strain in adjusting to them. Providing them with information and experiences helps to reduce the uncertainty and insecurity which they feel. An oreintation program should not be a haphazard affair. It should be a well organized activity involving school personnel at both the sending and receiving levels.

Orientation can provide continuity to the educative process; it can be facilitative in that it can help students to adjust more readily to a new environment and to new procedures more readily; it can reduce problems of adjustment; it can contribute to student needs for safety and security.

The Three P's of Orientation

While every school district has its own peculiar orientation problems and needs, orientation activities, in general, should be designed to expose pupils to experiences and information about the school *plant,* the school *program,* and the school *personnel.*

The school plant. The list of things a student should know about the new school plant are endless. And the questions they will raise, both before and after the move, are numerous and extensive. Students want to know all about the new building—where they will be housed, where their homeroom will be located, what the gym is like, where their lockers will be located, may they ride bicycles and if so where they will park them, the location of the nurse's office, where they eat, etc. Some of these concerns can be talked about; others are best approached by providing an opportunity for the student to visit the new school in the spring before they enter it.

There are all kinds of activities which can be planned to help students obtain information about their new building. Some of these include having students from the seventh grade visit the sixth grade, conducting tours of the new plant, asking student panels to discuss some typical problems of junior high school pupils, or by preparing fact sheets which can be distributed to the students both before and after they enter the school.

The school program. Here again the concerns of pupils cannot be left to chance or incidental coverage. Their concerns and questions must be dealt with in a forthright and direct manner. They want to know about their courses of study, the school clubs and organizations that are available to them and how to join them, the length of the school day and the length of classes, athletic and intramural programs, information about departmental organization, special classes in which they will be enrolled, and school rules and regulations. Here again pupils can be provided with information through student handbooks, visual aids, assembly programs, and demonstrations.

School personnel. Students are always anxious to meet their new teachers, their new principal, and any other personnel with whom they may have contact during the year. This is a time when the school counselor may introduce himself and explain his role in the school. And then there is always the matter of unfamiliar faces and the need to make new friends. Some schools have incorporated a "big brother–big sister" program to help students become not only acquainted with the plant and the program but with other students in the school.

Techniques for introducing new school personnel and for helping students to become acquainted with one another are numerous. Special school personnel can visit classrooms via closed circuit television or by personal visits to each classroom. If neither of these is possible, they can be introduced at a very early assembly program, or special messages which need to be conveyed to students can be taped and played in individual classrooms. The techniques for helping students and the school staff to become better acquainted are only limited by the ingenuity and creativity of those in the school.

THE CASE CONFERENCE

The case conference is essentially a remedial activity, focusing generally on students with some type of learning or behavioral problem. School personnel who have direct contact of a continuing or periodic nature with the pupil are usually invited to participate in the case conference. The general purpose of the case conference is to bring together those members of the school staff —administrative, instructional, and pupil personnel—who might be able to provide additional information about the pupil or who might be able to assist in any effort designed to help the pupil more effectively with his school environment.

Case conference activity generally includes three phases:

(1) collecting and synthesizing information from existing school records and from members of the school staff who have current, up-to-date information about the pupil;

(2) inviting all school personnel who are involved with the pupil to attend and participate in the meeting; and

(3) conducting the meeting. Case conferences usually follow this or a similar pattern:

   (a) stating the reason for the meeting
   (b) identifying the general problem or difficulty of the student
   (c) presenting information about the pupil including pupil data covering his interests, abilities, achievement, home background, and school performance
   (d) encouraging teacher reaction to the data and eliciting current, up-to-date observations of the pupil in the school setting from members attending the case conference
   (e) seeking suggestions and reactions to the information and encouraging the exchange of possible ways in which the student can be assisted by the faculty members participating
   (f) planning and assigning interventional activities designed to help the pupil
   (g) planning follow-up activities designed to observe and follow pupil progress and adjustment.

The school counselor often plays a major role in coordinating the case conference. He can assume a major responsibility for each of the case conference procedures delineated. On the other hand, he may choose to play a less dominant role and assume only minor coordinating functions in which he might share the responsibility with other pupil personnel specialists or members of the school staff. While this activity is often considered an important and vital part of the school program (and he will soon discover a number of role set expectations that will lead him to feel a major role responsibility here), the school counselor will need to gauge the extent of his responsibility in relation to the time and effort he feels appropriate to this aspect of the program.

If he chooses to involve himself in a large number of remedial efforts, he will probably assume more responsibility in coordinating the case conference activities of the school. If he chooses to deal more with the developmental and facilitative aspects of the students with whom he works, then he may choose to engage in less case conference coordination. While this leaves the school counselor in a position to make judgments about his coordinating function, it does not free him completely of any responsibility in the case conference activity. He will need to participate in case conferences frequently and he may find that this activity is one of those areas in which his participation could be a contributing and vital influence in the life of the school. He may find, further, that this is one of the ways in which he can establish more firmly his consultant relationship with teachers.

RESEARCH AND EVALUATION ACTIVITIES

The American School Counselor Association's *Statement of Policy* states that guidance research ". . . is concerned with the study of pupil needs and how well school services are meeting those needs."[4] The school counselor is expected to assume a leadership role in initiating, conducting, and reporting needed research. This could be another significant coordinating function leading to dynamic developments of benefit to students as well as other possibilities associated with changes in the counselor's role and the teaching-learning process.

Schools historically have been noted for their lack of research endeavor. While there have been short periods of hope, as there was a few years back when federal support monies were available for research projects, the level of interest in school research has been exceptionally low. Ironically, the research endeavor, the one area of guidance that the counselor has persistently avoided, contains the potential for freeing him from the routine tasks he so emphatically deplores.

In these rapidly changing times the school will need to become increasingly involved in research and will need to identify needed studies that can be accomplished in its own environment. The school counselor may consider the involvement of school personnel in educational research as one of his more important coordinating functions. It may be a very wise use of his time to become engaged with other members of the school staff in planning

[4]American School Counselor Association, *op. cit.,* p. 9.

and organizing research activities. Research and evaluation efforts can enhance the knowledge of the staff about educational practice and can be utilized to provide more efficient and effective programs. While lack of time and money have been used as excuses for not becoming involved in efforts of a research nature, the time has come when schools cannot afford to avoid becoming engaged in research.

The number of research opportunities in which the school counselor can become involved are bountiful. To research and evaluate the processes of the school and its program have implications for the counseling-consulting function of guidance and for the teaching-learning process. These studies can provide meaning for and direction to future changes in the school.

EDUCATIONAL AND OCCUPATIONAL INFORMATION SERVICES

The work of the school counselor in the collection and dissemination of educational and occupational information is a well established responsibility. Most basic guidance texts devote at least a chapter to the necessity for handling educational and occupational planning matters. Many state certification agencies specify courses in occupation information as a qualification for licensure. To ignore this aspect of the guidance role would be evidence of professional neglect; to obscure its importance would be a gross misinterpretation of its value and significance in the guidance of our youth. On the other hand, to overemphasize its significance or its impact for the choices and decisions that youth face, particularly those related to the choice of an occupation, would be to exaggerate its real and potential value. Each school system and every counselor must examine very carefully the nature and scope of this activity in an attempt to make judgments about and to affix values to its importance in relation to all the other activities in the guidance and counseling program. This will be difficult; it will force school counselors to make judgments and decisions about their own behavior in dealing with this particular activity.

While I seem to be pushing a somewhat "middle-of-the-road" course, I do not intend quite that interpretation. I do not feel that this responsibility can be ignored. I recognize the involvement of the school counselor in the development of informational services. However, unlike some high school guidance situations that do exist, I do not agree nor do I encourage the overwhelming attention and emphasis directed toward the provision for and the dissemination of occupational and educational information. Rather, I would call for school counselors to weigh very carefully their efforts in this activity as compared with those devoted to other counseling and guidance services in an attempt to achieve a balance which they feel would better serve the needs of all youth in their schools. Whatever the balance among guidance activities, any position is tenable provided the school counselor can demonstrate and support that his position best serves the needs of the youth in his school.

The collection and use of educational and occupational information is very thoroughly and definitively covered in a number of publications. The school-counselor-in-preparation will probably become familiar with these publications in the course of preparatory experience. He will learn more about the factors to be considered in making judgments and decisions about the coordination of the informational services.

In the following sections I have summarized a few of the important areas of informational activity and some of the related considerations leaving the reader to examine other matters pertaining to the informational services in other publications. Also, in another section of this book, specifically the chapter concerning the vocational development of youth, matters of particular importance in educational and occupational planning are covered.

Information About Institutions of Higher Education

Much of the work of the school counselor is directed toward assisting pupils to obtain information about opportunities in higher education. The informational needs of young people range all the way from a consideration of the values of higher education and the types of higher education opportunities available to the actual selection of an institution, including how to seek admission and how to finance and prepare for attending it. To attend to these informational needs is no small matter indeed. Perhaps this is why so many guidance programs have seemingly overemphasized the preparation for college aspect.

Considerable effort involving the counseling, consulting, and coordinating functions is placed on matters pertaining to selecting and getting into college in the last year or two of the high school program. Much time and energy from the time the student enters the secondary school, and certainly from ninth grade on, is devoted to the discussion of post-high school plans. Most of this discussion centers around planning for higher education. For a good many students these are interesting discussions but far less meaningful than some of their immediate concerns, and it is only as graduation nears that they find a real need for such information and the opportunity to discuss it with someone.

In recent years, with admission to college becoming increasingly difficult, high school students have experienced more pressure (from parents, teachers, and counselors) to get at the task of deciding about college. These pressures have become increasingly significant in the lives of pupils as high school populations have bulged, as more persons seek admission to college, and as colleges become increasingly selective in applying their admissions standards. The increasing pressures to attend institutions of higher education, as well as the increasing need for higher education and the increasing social desirability of college attendance, have created a high degree of anxiousness or "acceptance anxiety."

Counselors as well as students and their parents feel these pressures, pressures which have caused counselors to insure that adequate and accurate information is made available to students and caused them to alert students to the need to obtain and use this information early. At the same time, alerting students to get started early and making them aware of the selection and admission process has created tensions and raised anxieties. It seems as if, for some students anyway, the school counselor has confounded the very conflict and stress situations he presumes to reduce.

Counselors seem to vary in their approach and in their involvement in college placement activities. Some make the information available to students, leaving the student to accept the responsibility for insuring that he makes all the necessary arrangements for the tests, the interviews and the transfer of credentials. Some counselors are very active in this process as well, double-checking with students and making sure that they complete the necessary requirements on time. Here again, counselors need to make sound professional judgments about their own participation in this activity and the extent to which they are willing to assume a share of the student's responsibility for the actual filing of applications and the submission of necessary data.

Educational information materials. A number of different types of informational materials can be helpful to students and their parents. College reference books and directories are very helpful in the initial identification and screening stages. There are a number of such directories which can be made available for students and their parents who need a general description of an institution and its program. Other directories contain information about scholarships, freshmen profile data, and other specific facts often pertinent to a student's consideration.

Most schools also have a college catalogue library. These catalogues, as most people know, contain specific information about the college, its scholarship and financial aid programs, as well as detailed information about entrance requirements and courses of study. While students are usually encouraged to visit the campuses of the colleges they are considering, the catalogue is a good source for information about size, type, departments, degrees offered, costs, facilities for room and board, scholarships, admission requirements, student services, and student activities. Some schools maintain scholarship files, which provide important information about the sources of scholarship and other financial aids for those who need some kind of financial assistance in order to make higher education a reality.

Using educational information materials. Such informational materials are frequently used within the context of counseling or educational planning conferences. Students are either encouraged to obtain such material on their own or the counselor may elect to help the student in locating needed material. Time should be extended to allow students an opportunity to discuss their findings and reactions and to seek any such additional help as may be necessary. Students do seek information from counselors and counselors should be prepared to assist students in locating needed information.

An increasing number of schools are developing guidance resource centers which house information making it possible for students and their parents to engage uninterruptedly in locating and using informational materials. Some schools house these educational materials in the guidance office or in the school library. The accessibility of such materials, as well as their availability, is an important consideration in determining the location and arrangement of such material. Such information can also be incorporated within the curriculum of the school. The relationship of many high school courses of study to college offerings can help to make a high school course of study more relevant provided such relationships extend beyond a mere "you will need this if you are planning to take a biology course in college."

Teachers can relate the content of their particular subject to post high school programs and courses of study. They can make relevant and meaningful associations perhaps more readily than the school counselor. They can help the student identify institutions that have advanced programs and courses in a particular area of study. For example, in a secondary school mathematics course, the teacher could identify typical programs of study in higher education (architecture, engineering, statistics, accounting, computer programming) and could discuss such information as the high school preparation required and recommended, the length of such programs, and the nature and scope of courses commonly taken in a given program.

Teachers could develop this information from the general to the specific by using actual catalogues and brochures or directories, arranging for on-campus visits, making contacts with alumni or with students currently attending the institution, or even asking other teachers in the school who are familiar with specific college programs to visit the class and present their views of the institution and its program. Such information not only has relevancy but it has motivational value as well!

Information About Careers

Most people identify the work of the school counselor with vocational guidance and specifically with the school counselor's responsibility for providing occupational information which can be used in the vocational planning of pupils. Most high school programs devote a considerable effort to collecting and providing occupational information for student and parent use. In comparison with educational planning, most students are not under as much pressure to make specific choices about their future careers.

While some parents equate the selection of a college with the selection of a career, many parents do not require, nor do they pressure, their children into making a hasty decision about their future occupations. These parents are usually content to delay such decisions and allow their sons or daughters to enroll in a general or liberal arts program. This type of parent behavior has the effect of reducing the student's need to decide about his future career. It has been my experience that such students are less likely to utilize the occupational information services of the school.

While it is important to recognize this and other factors, this does not minimize the need for a career information program. There are still many students who at one time or another are in need of information about the occupational structure and career fields in the world of work. While students differ in their need for information and in the pressures they experience to make a career choice, most students are curious at one time or another about a certain career opportunity and seek information such as the duties or nature of the work involved, the employment outlook, the qualifications and preparation for the occupation and the salary or compensation it provides.

Although such information attends to the external considerations involved in the career decision making process, students often seek information about the psychological and social factors. Students often want to discuss how an occupation will comply with their own personalities, needs, values, and attitudes. They are concerned about the relationship of the career to their own social identity and status and its effect upon home and family life, as well as the social implications and influences which may utilimately affect their own value systems and attitudes. Such considerations constitute the internal and are highly individual and personal.

Occupational information materials. Sources of occupational information are numerous although the counselor is cautioned against the wholesale use of such information without some prior appraisal or evaluation. One of the most common types of occupational information is provided through the career literature, which is available in books, monographs, fact sheets, occupational briefs, and pamphlets. These publications tend to describe one occupation or a few occupations of a similar nature. Also available are a number of handbooks, references, and directories that usually describe many careers or many career clusters. These publications tend to be very helpful for the student who is exploring the range of career opportunities in the world of work. Films, film strips, and other audio-visual sources of occupational information are also available.

Written materials are usually filed alphabetically or according to some plan which utilizes an alphabetical or coded arrangement. The most common coded filing plans are based on the *Dictionary of Occupational Titles.* Some schools have developed tape recorded work interviews designed to provide "live" occupational information. Such interviews usually rely on local participation and represent job opportunities available in the community or region.

Using the career information materials. School counselors have found that it is often difficult to get students to use the many different sources of information they have accumulated, even when such information is readily incorporated in the counseling session. Counselors have found that students are often too "busy" to read the materials provided. Also students frequently report that they find the information "boring." This problem is closely associated with the manner in which such materials are prepared and the reading level at which they are written. Career information is often stored in files and is usually available in the school resource center, the library, or school guidance office.

While the school counselor can play an important part in the dissemination of occupational information, I have long believed that the classroom teacher is the catalyst in motivating and activating students to seek and obtain information of an occupational nature. I have further believed that the involvement of the classroom teacher should focus directly on the occupational implications of their particular subject matter field. Teachers can introduce, in a planned or incidental way, information about occupational opportunities which are related to their course of study or about employment opportunities in which knowledge of their course of study is either essential or helpful. Thus, through most courses of study in the secondary school, a number of occupations or groups of occupations could be examined and discussed.

PUPIL REFERRAL TO OTHER SCHOOL AND COMMUNITY RESOURCES

The resources of a community can be considered an important adjunct to the program of the school. These resources include all types of services and sources of help. They can range from social agencies designated to provide a specific service (rehabilitation for handicapped, family counseling, employment) to business or industrial concerns that are in a position to accommodate a particular need or problem (consultant, field trip).

It is quite likely that the combined knowledge of the entire pupil personnel staff about referral resources in the community or region is extensive. Within any given school year it is quite possible that a large number of instances will occur when pupils or parents will need to utilize the services of a wide variety of community resources. While the number and availability of community agency personnel will be dependent upon the locale of the school, it is important that the school establish a liaison with these agencies in order that they become fully aware of the nature and scope of the resources and the types of services they provide. Some localities have developed directories that list these community resources and provide information about the location of the agency, the names of contact personnel, the nature of the agency and the types of services it provides. Someone in the school should know about these community resources and the means for utilizing them.

It is often suggested that school personnel establish a liaison with these agencies by visiting them and becoming acquainted with their services prior to the need of them. This would insure that the school would be aware of the range of services provided. Such visits could help make an initial referral or an inquiry more easily accomplished.

It is feasible that referrals could be made by any staff person in the school depending upon the nature of the referral and the extent of the difficulty involved. It is easier to establish contacts when the personnel in both the school and the agency are known to one another. It is also possible that when a number of people in a given school system are known to the agency equally effective referrals can be made. The block to the latter approach rests usually with school policy dictating who, when, and under what circumstances a referral can be made.

This policy rests, in most schools, with the administrator. When a number of people are in contact with an agency, more extensive communication within the school and between the agency and the school is necessary in order that those involved will have some idea of the number of cases being handled by any given agency at any point in time. Obviously, then, appropriate procedures need to be established for any policy.

While there is very little doubt about the school counselor's involvement in pupil referral activities, his responsibility in the chain of referral considerations is more a matter of local school policy and procedure. A great deal of the school's staff involvement is apt to be a product of individual judgment and individual interest. Much of the *action* in referral procedures will result from the role perceptions and expectations that exist among school personnel. While policy and procedures may exist, the potential for role ambiguity and role conflict among referral matters must be considered. In fact, rigid policy in such matters can have detrimental effects in program development. Just as a lack of procedures can result in chaos and confusion. Some guidelines to staff roles are necessary and helpful; too precise policies can stifle and inhibit the effective use of referral resources both in the school and in the community.

What Is a Referral?

Referral consists of assisting people—anybody, but primarily pupils and parents—to make contacts with other people who have the competency to help an individual with a particular problem or concern. Students ~~and their parents~~ are often referred to the school counselor because he is assumed to have special professional competencies that others do not presume to have.

The referral of an individual to another person can result from a situation as simple as a need for information or as complex as behaviors which interfere with learning efficiency. If we were to examine the referral process in a school, we would find a very complex network of referral in which individuals are routed from one to another for a variety of reasons and purposes. While a referral can be a very rewarding and helpful experience, it can be an equally frustrating and confusing one. Individuals can be sent from one to another with little help ever provided. When this occurs, the individual who is being referred is often forgotten in the shuffle of referrals. Unless the person originating the referral keeps in touch with the individuals, it is possible for the latter to get lost in the process. Or the help that he needs may be too long delayed.

Referral, therefore, should incur some responsibility for the person initiating it to follow through with the individual to insure that the needed help is provided and provided within a reasonable amount of time. Without this responsibility, a referral can soon become another method for passing the buck or a means of getting an individual off your back. While we tend to reject these attitudes of referral, we cannot ignore their repeated occurrence. Further, whether purposeful or not, we need to recognize that people who are referred are frequently left with no help or with no possibilities for getting it. Anyone who has worked in community agencies will attest to these possibilities no matter how noble the intentions may be.

The school is a network of helping agents, and helping people to get help is a daily affair. Referral, while often associated only with the troubled or the sick, can be viewed from its more frequent usage—just helping two people get together. The school counselor as a member of the school staff is involved, but his special knowledge of community resources may cause many—teachers, students, ~~parents~~, even citizens in the community not connected with the school—to tap his resources. This is the facilitative aspect of referral!

Referral also has its remedial aspects. School personnel see the school counselor and other pupil personnel specialists as referral sources for those students and parents whose needs for assistance extend beyond their ability to deal with them. And pupil personnel specialists have many such cases referred to them. Some of these require competencies that extend beyond *their* ability; others present problems or conditions that exceed the bounds of their responsibility. In these cases the pupil personnel specialists are usually in a position to help the individual locate other sources of help.

Identifying these human needs and helping people make contact with personnel and agencies who are prepared to provide assistance is an important responsibility—one that is commonly shared by *all* school personnel and one that often befalls the school counselor because of his very special interest in and responsibility for the growth and development of all youth in his charge.

Referral Readiness

The decision that a particular problem extends beyond one's competency or that it exceeds one's assigned responsibilities is primarily a matter of professional *judgment*. Many instances are clear cut and the decisions or judgments can be quickly and surely attained. Many, however, are not so readily made, falling in an indeterminate zone that we often refer to as the gray area. When in doubt, school counselors, rather than stay with the situation until a more substantial judgment can be arrived at, tend to choose a safe course of action (at least the safer alternative for them)—the referral.

From my experience with school counselors, students ~~and their parents~~ have been often referred to others when the counselor himself could have been effective. A decision to refer too quickly is as much a matter of professional incompetency as to refer belatedly. I suspect we have far too much over-referral in guidance practice. This could, and probably does, stem from the caution exercised in the counselor's education which warns him of becoming involved with students whose problems extend beyond his competency as a counselor.

There is a real difference between working with a student in order to make a more appropriate referral and actually becoming involved in the case. It is time we became concerned about the professional judgments of counselors who tend to refer at the proverbial drop of a hat. This is the type of professional behavior we need to examine more closely in our programs of preparation. We need to emphasize the judicious referral rather than the wholesale. This means helping counselors to develop confidence in their ability to make timely and appropriate referral judgments.

A referral is of little value if the person being referred either does not understand or accept his need for help of the type to be provided. The carte blanche use of referral under these circumstances is a needless, wasteful use of everyone's time. Most pupil personnel workers in schools and agency workers in the communities are already carrying heavy case loads and in many instances have waiting lists. The referral process should involve helping the individual see more clearly how the professional involvement of another worker could be of assistance to him.

The individual being referred can be helped toward accepting some measure of his own responsibility in the matter. Therefore, while knowing the referral resources available and how to use them are a part of the counselor's practice, making judgments about a referral and helping the individual to understand the referral are often more important in referral readiness.

PLACEMENT ACTIVITIES

Placement activities have been ascribed a place in the guidance program. In fact, James E. Allen, Jr., in a newsletter to New York State school superintendents, cited placement as one of the elements of a sound guidance program. In it he defined the purpose of placement as follows: "to assist pupils in carrying out their educational and vocational plans—assistance in securing admission to appropriate educational facilities and/or employment, in joining extraclass and leisure activities and in fulfilling service obligations."[5]

The ASCA *Statement of Policy for Secondary School Counselors* cites placement as one of the professional responsibilities of the school counselor indicating,

The counselor's role in providing placement services for individual pupils involves assisting them in making appropriate choices of school subjects and courses of study and in making transitions from one school level to another, one school to another, and from school to employment. Placement thereby involves the informational services of educational and occupational planning, pupil appraisal, and counseling assistance appropriate to the pupil's choices and progress in school subjects, extracurricular and community activities, and employment.[6]

[5] James E. Allen, Jr., "Good Guidance—And Enough of It" (Albany, N.Y.: The State Education Department, December 2, 1957), p. 2.

[6] American School Counselor Association, *op. cit.,* p. 8.

Although precedence has established placement as a specific activity, it is more an extension of other services and other relationships. Many facets of what has been historically treated as placement are consumed more legitimately as a part of the counseling or consulting function. Any residue may be quite managerial, tending to fall therefore in activities of a coordinative nature. To continue thinking of placement as a discrete element of guidance may only tend to promote many role responsibilities for the counselor that are more legitimately those of youth and their parents.

Changing concepts of secondary school guidance in the future will eliminate, hopefully, the specificity of these activities and the responsibility for them from the school counselor role. For the present it seems appropriate to consider these activities at this time as a part of the coordinating function.

Planning the high school program. The school counselor is expected to assist pupils and their parents in planning the high school program of study. In most schools the counselor meets individually or in small groups with the pupil and his parent(s). This occurs commonly in the eighth or ninth grade and reviews of the student's plans and his progress are scheduled annually thereafter. Parent participation in these subsequent reviews varies widely among programs though presumably any parent could participate upon request.

We have very little hard data to indicate whether this practice merits the time it consumes. We have many years experience with the practice and the following are some of the observations I have made and the conclusions I have drawn.

Individual conferences must, of necessity, be limited. Unless the student is sufficiently prepared, he is asked to make course and program choices based on very limited knowledge of himself and of the opportunities available to him. More than likely subjects are recognized by name only and the nature of their demands on him are vague and superficial. He could make these same choices in a large group, in his home room, or in the leisure of his home. Many students do not need help but those that do should be aware of its availability.

Most school administrators approve of this activity, viewing it as an excellent public relations vehicle. Many parents feel positively about these sessions and they frequently express their gratitude for the counselor's interest in the child. Many parents benefit from the opportunity to talk about their son or daughter and his or her progress and potential. On the other hand, many parents resent these meetings, feeling that they could accomplish this planning with their offspring at home. Even with these planning conferences, many high school programs are later realigned or altered (a positive practice) so that such planning conferences cannot be considered to reduce or prevent late and last minute changes in the program.

Certainly the school is interested in the child and there are many ways it can express this concern—many that I feel would utilize the talents of the counselor in far more effective and meaningful ways than the now traditional yearly interview. Unless we can find some solid support to continue the practice, it would seem wise to abandon the family interview in favor of other approaches.

Classroom grouping and program tracking. The school counselor's role in the assignment of students to particular groups within the school has been extended well beyond what might be considered a desired role responsibility. In fact, there is some cause to question the practice of program tracking and classroom grouping. Grouping is *not* a pupil personnel responsibility any more than it is an instructional one. The fact remains that it is primarily an administrative responsibility and the extent to which the administrator seeks the involvement of others, including the school counselor as well as teachers, is an administrative prerogative. Traditionally, the counselor, because of his ready access to pupil data and his real or presumed knowledge about the pupil's abilities and interests, is quite often accorded a role in decisions about the classroom placement of students. Teachers are solicited for opinions about pupil placement in groups and are often requested to supply information about the pupil and his academic progress. Counselors have all too frequently been cast as the coordinators of these data with responsibilities ranging through collecting the information, deciding about the placement of the individual, and even in many instances, establishing classroom groups. While a counselor may have a responsibility for contributing to the establishment of classroom groups or to the placement of a pupil in a group or school program, he should be able to distinguish very clearly between any coordinating activities in which he might engage and the actual decisions about student placement in classroom groups or school programs.

Counselors are involved in providing information to pupils and parents about various programs (such as the accelerated, the college-bound, and the vocational). They often help them by interpreting information that can be helpful in making choices and decisions about these programs. In addition, the counselor often provides information relative to the establishment of new courses and modifications or changes in program sequences. Few would dispute the involvement of the counselor or the teacher in these matters.

College application and admission. As indicated in the earlier section on educational and occupational services, the counselor has been accorded a major responsibility for assisting in the process of helping students move from the high school to institutions of higher education. His involvement in the placement of students in these institutions after high school has been extended well beyond his information giving and collecting concerns. He spends much time conferring with college admissions personnel and arranging for students and their parents to visit with them. He spends an even greater amount of time in helping students arrange for on-campus interviews and in completing applications for admission to these institutions.

In many schools he acts as a high school registrar. He oversees the forwarding of transcripts and the collection of any data for them. He is charged with completing that portion of most certifying forms which requires a written statement of recommendation. These efforts, many of which are clerical and few of which could be considered professional, consume valuable time that could be devoted to other functions.

While the stereotype of college placement continues, it is difficult to believe that the counselor has done much to change the direction of his responsibilities in the college application-admissions procedures. That he labors assiduously in writing college recommendations is a fact; that he will continue to do so until he challenges this role is another fact. That his involvement in writing college recommendations has so infrequently been challenged is an enigma. Of all the personnel in a school who are capable of attesting to a student's performance in college, the counselor is far less capable of commenting on a student's performance in his more remote relationship to learning than any of a student's several teachers who are working every day with him.

Seeking and applying for work. For several years now the criticism has been directed at school counselors that those seeking employment do not receive the same attention as those in the college-bound group. In fact there has been some concern that these students have been sloughed off to state and private employment agency personnel. Many fine cooperative programs have been developed between the school and the local state employment agency. For those seeking jobs, these programs have been helpful.

If we were to compare the involvement of the counselor—that is, his actual effort and attention to both groups—we would find that the criticism has considerable validity. Yet, his coordination of the job placement program with outside agencies appears to utilize his professional competencies more than the clerical aspects of his college placement effort. The current dissatisfaction with his role relative to both groups indicates rather clearly a real need to reexamine such programs and practices.

Counselors flock to a college open house, an alumni dinner, or a college round table discussion (an annual program activity in one state conference for counselors). And in almost equal numbers they appear at industrial tours, business-industry dinners, and special workshops on labor market trends. They indicate little bias in their search for professional enlightenment. Could it be that they are responding on the job to the pressures and the forces of our times? Could it be that they, along with students, feel more urgently the mounting pressures of college admissions? Could be.

In Summary

There will be some who will resent the classification of certain historical guidance practices as coordinative. Associating them as I have with a different set of counselor competencies (the managerial-administrative syndrome) is a different approach from that commonly followed in guidance texts. Hopefully, it will raise questions and not tempers. If we ever mean to do something about the role of the school counselor, we must soon be about the task. It will not be accomplished in the textbooks for, as I have suggested in other chapters, changes in the guidance role will be started and continued, *ad infinitum, by* counselors *on* the job *in* the schools.

That so much of our present-day practice should be compressed in a chapter describing the coordinating function is sufficient reason to cause us to look at our field and our relation to youth. That many of these activities are worthwhile is not the question. That these are the role of the school counselor is. That these activities should be accomplished to the exclusion of others raises questions concerning work priorities and role balance among the three major functions.

I presume my biases are by now quite clear. I hope I have left an impression of legitimacy with the coordinating function. At the same time, I hope I have challenged counselors to consider a balance among all three functions—counseling, consulting, coordinating.

SUGGESTED READING

American School Counselor Association, *Statement of Policy for Secondary School Counselors* (Washington, D.C.: American Personnel and Guidance Association, 1964).

HOPPOCK, ROBERT, *Occupational Information* (New York: McGraw-Hill, 1967), third edition.

PETERS, HERMAN J., and FARWELL, GAIL F., *Guidance: A Developmental Approach* (Chicago: Rand McNally, 1967), second edition, Chapters 5, 6, 7, and 14.

PART THREE

THE DIMENSIONS OF
DEVELOPMENTAL GUIDANCE

Developmental guidance in the secondary school caters to the adolescent. It is logical that its dimensions would flow from the affairs of the growing, developing young person. The development of each individual is a unique and variant proceeding which has been designated as the learning-maturation process. For some adolescents this process is very gradual and smooth—a somewhat natural, progressive one. For others there are periods of strain and peaks (or points) of short duration when the uncertainties and the complexities of life are almost intolerable. For many this is a most difficult period characterized by struggles with tensions and stresses that torment the individual and interfere, in small or gross ways, with his learning-maturation.

For all adolescents it is a time when they are finding a *personship,* when they are building a selfhood that will be fundamental to their life style for several years to follow and more than likely for a much longer period—possibly their lifetime. It is a time when the stirrings of an approaching maturity begin to emerge in many forms and the individual asks himself not only "Who am I?" but "What has meaning for me?" For the first time the adolescent is serious about matters of identity and commitment and he searches valiantly, though not always logically nor rationally, for answers and solutions. It is the beginning of a quest that has no end. But how fully each adolescent engrosses himself in the task. And how exciting to be helping him!

This section concentrates on five aspects of the adolescent's learning-maturation from which the dimensions of developmental guidance derive. Each chapter is pointed toward the work of the developmental counselor within the broader context of the educative process. In combination, the five dimensions represent an interdisciplinary integration of research and theory as a basis for the strategy and thrust of developmental guidance in the secondary school.

These dimensions follow very closely those that I have suggested for elementary school guidance in another publication. The content of these chapters have been developed specifically to strike at the learning-maturation of the adolescent in the secondary school years. Where the background of research and theory applied equally to the adolescent and the work of the secondary school, I have borrowed from this earlier work.

In some chapters I have drawn generously from the same sources and the same concepts but always in accord with the needs of the adolescent and the endeavors of the secondary school. Any similarities between the elementary and the secondary school guidance effort lie in their *raison d'etre*. Some ideas and beliefs apply equally well to both levels though the method and content of their implementation might be quite different.

Each chapter ends with a partial listing of illustrative functions in which the developmental counselor can engage. These are grouped according to counseling, consulting, and coordinating functions. While the list of functions for any area could be expanded, those that are suggested should serve to provide a base from which the counselor can translate theory into practice. The creative developmental counselor will have little difficulty in effecting this last step once he has control of the theoretical base from which he is operating.

Chapter Ten, Physical Maturation: Learning About Growing, employs a broader interpretation of physical development going well beyond the concerns commonly attended to in the school health services. Different aspects of adolescent growth are reviewed in relation to their impact on the individual's learning-maturation and with reference to their meaning for the teaching-learning process. Some emphasis is placed on sexual maturation and the importance of sex education.

Chapter Eleven, Mental Maturation: Learning About Learning, presents the newer conceptions about mental growth within the context of others that have emerged earlier in this century as they have been incorporated in present educational practice. Helping youth to think and learn—to learn how to learn—portends tremendous possibilities for the teaching-learning process. Related areas of learning and wanting to learn are touched lightly in overviews of creativity and curiosity.

Chapter Twelve, Social Maturation: Learning to Socialize and Value, examines the processes of socialization and valuing. The inner dynamics of these processes are explored through the internalization sequence as the adolescent moves toward establishing his social identity. The contribution of the school to social maturation is viewed in relation to the school and classroom environment and in consideration of the adolescent culture.

Chapter Thirteen, Self-Maturation: Toward Self-Realization and Utilization, highlights the development of the concept of self and the adolescent's quest for identity and commitment. Educational practice and concerns such as school marks and achievement and the maintenance of student records are considered for their effect on the self-concept and its development. Ways of helping the adolescent to become aware of and to understand his emerging "self" and to actualize his being are the focus of this chapter.

Chapter Fourteen, Vocational Maturation: Learning to Make Decisions, emphasizes helping the adolescent in matters of readiness and responsibility for the choices and decisions he will make in formulating his career plans. The significance of changes in the meaning and nature of work, newer concepts of vocational development, and the concept of vocational maturity are explored, particularly with reference to their implications for developmental guidance in the secondary school. Modifications in approaching career development are suggested.

TEN

PHYSICAL MATURATION:

LEARNING ABOUT GROWING

The potential for developmental guidance in the secondary school years as it is related to this dimension alone—helping youth achieve physical maturity —is sufficiently staggering to overwhelm a program. To dwell on the tremendous importance of these years in the growth of the human organism is superfluous, for the many changes in these years of extreme and rapid growth are well known. On the other hand, the need to deal more directly and more significantly with the concerns which youth face during these years remains a crucial area for development throughout secondary education. Secondary school guidance must involve itself increasingly in these matters not only as a discrete and separate aspect, but as a shared responsibility with the total school effort. While every facet of individual learning-maturation during this period is extremely critical, attending to the individuality and the uniqueness of the individual mandates responsibilities for all school personnel. This responsibility has been recognized in part through the provision for physical education as a formal, required course experience and for a variety of other learning experiences in special units or courses dealing with personal and public health, human anatomy, nutrition, and the like. Most school systems have made real attempts to provide educational exposures in a number of these and other areas. The health services provided by most schools add another important dimension to the school's involvement in the physical growth of the student. These school health services, as represented by such personnel as the school nurse, the school physician, and the dental hygienist, are directed toward the general health of the individual and also provide special attention to individual health problems or physical handicaps. These services are essential and their contribution over the years has been significant.

The school counselor represents another person who can help. Many times, despite annual physical examinations, he is among the first to note some physical difficulties that may be interfering with an individual's normal academic performance or physical development. Where the school counselor has reason to suspect some physical malfunction or some health aberration, he works closely with the health services bringing these conditions to their attention or by encouraging students to seek some type of medical evaluation. His front line activity in the referral of health problems, as well as his efforts to coordinate these services with appropriate instructional activity, is well documented in past guidance efforts. But beyond these situations there lies an uncultivated focus of guidance effort which has only been viewed incidentally and superficially. Helping the individual to understand his unique physical development and helping him to synthesize his own feelings about his physical growth and development with other aspects of his learning-maturation suggests a whole segment of human maturation that has been rarely attended to in any depth. Simply, it's a matter of helping youth examine how they view the physical aspects of their being and to integrate these perceptions with other phases of their learning-maturation. Some of the basic information that youth need, in part at least, is provided through courses, units and services already established in the school. Even considering these and other exposures, most students still have a myriad of questions regarding their physical development. Anyone who has worked or lived with an adolescent is familiar with the areas of concern and the range of questions which they have. And a lot of these are directly related to their body, their physical growth, and their physical maturation. What is less understood and experienced, however, is the impact of this information on the student's concept of himself. We've established the ideal—a strong body, a shapely figure, etc., but we have seldom been concerned with the feelings and the attitudes of those many young people who, in one way or another, fall short of the ideal. How they deal with these feelings about themselves or how they relate any new information with the feelings they already "own," as well as the effect of this on their behavior, is an important part of their maturation. To help a youth with the more internal aspects of his physical development is to provide him with further insights into himself and his behavior as he grows. Some of these internal feelings are most difficult for the adolescent to cope with and they are often even more difficult for him to discuss. If he can talk about them it is usually with a very trusted few—peers or adults—in his life. Yet within this sphere the developmental school counselor can become one of these individuals. He can be that somebody who cares, who can be trusted to help.

Physical Maturation and "Normality"

The developmental program of guidance can very easily lose its perspective if it focuses too directly on those developments which are expected to occur at a given age or point in time. The concept of developmental stages represents an expectancy that certain developments in the human organism are expected to happen within a given period of time to the average child. These expectancies are built on data which represent or constitute the average or the norm for a group of children. These normative expectations for human growth and development have been helpful in planning the learning experiences of the school.

School personnel have found, however, that they cannot operate rigidly according to these normative expectancies, for some children develop more rapidly than the norm and some develop more slowly. Students at all age and grade levels are very conscious of their own growth and compare their growth with others. They are quick to note any discrepancies between their own physical growth and the more typical growth pattern of their peers. Take, for example, the seventh or eighth grade boy who finds himself considerably shorter than most of the other boys in his class. Think of all the important people who can respond to his height—himself, of course, his family, his teachers and his peers. His own feelings about his height are very important and how he feels about this can affect his behavior. How others respond to his height influences his perceptions which, in turn, influence his behavior.

Nicknames based on physical attributes, while seemingly harmless, can have life long implications depending on how they affect an individual. "Shorty," "Red," "Fats," or "Squeaky" can result in both positive and negative reactions. Teachers, too, often become involved in the normative, responding in terms of the normal growth expectancies rather than to the state of the individual's growth. For example a teacher, without thinking perhaps, might remark, "When are you going to start growing?" While this may seem insignificant, or too exacting, it can have tremendous meaning for the child.

Physical development is the most obvious clue to the growth of an individual. It is the one most frequently used by others in judging an individual's maturation. By comparing an individual with his age peers, using observations, health data, etc., others can draw some generalizations about an individual's progress in physical maturation. These generalizations, whether global or specific, can be helpful in the educative process.

The school has become quite adept in dealing with the external and normative aspects of physical maturation. Teachers and parents in particular have gained insights into and understanding of a student's development through the help that has been available. In fact it might be suggested that teachers and parents often have insights and understandings which the student himself does not possess.

Few people in the school are prepared to deal with the individual and his feelings about his rate of development and any special differences he may experience. As we mentioned earlier, the school health program is prepared to cope with health deficiencies and physical handicaps. Other differences are noted with only occasional attempts to deal with them, and when they are dealt with it is usually because they are believed to be associated with irregularities in behavior or in academic performance. In these instances the concern originates with others—parents or teachers primarily.

Dealing with physical maturation by this approach is different than dealing with it by involving the student directly as a result of his own referral. A developmental program should focus on relationships that foster the self-referral, that deal with the internal and personal aspects of achieving physical maturity. Such a focus would be facilitative. The cause-effect emphasis that characterizes the identification and remediation of differences, as judged by others, may be a part of such a program but it would not constitute all of it. In fact it might be only a small segment of it.

It is important for us to have and to use information about the typical growth patterns of individuals but it is important that we remain aware of its normative base. Within this concept of normal growth expectations we must recognize not only the individual differences that may occur in physical growth, but the variant learning-maturation that results from one's reactions to and feelings about his life experiences. It is this constellation of individual differences as reflected in just this one aspect of development—the physical —that brings clearly to our attention the need to concern ourselves with programs that attend to this facet of learning-maturation, both alone and in relation to the other aspects.

PHYSICAL MATURATION AND DEVELOPMENTAL GUIDANCE CONCERNS

The range, extent, and duration of concerns, problems, or "small troubles" that stem directly from the physical maturation process are sources of great anxiety and bewilderment both to adolescents and to the adults who share their life. It is no small wonder that adolescents are a continual source of amazement to their elders. Sometimes it is a wonder that they survive at all. One would think that adults, having experienced adolescence and all its changes, would understand the process and consequently be able to deal effectively with it. If we were only dealing with the straight physiology of physical maturation, this would help. But each adolescent experiences these years in different times under varying and changing conditions. In the future these conditions will be increasingly different and varying, making it more difficult for everyone. Societal standards and mores may no longer provide adults or adolescents with sufficient guidelines and direction. The disappearing generation gap may leave us with little to depend on. This may be frightening but it remains, nonetheless, not just a possibility but a probability.

The sections that follow are devoted to looking at some of the developmental concerns to which the school must direct its attention now and in the future. That developmental guidance must be a part of this forward look is without doubt.

The Body Image

One's perception of his body—one's body image—can have all kinds of implications for his life. It is important, then, as the child matures physically that we devote some attention to the body image which he develops. His image of his body may well set the pattern for his whole manner of presenting himself to his world. While it is not essential that every young male see himself as tall, dark, and handsome nor that every female see herself as a future Miss America, it is important that every individual build a positive image of his body and that he learn to use this image in ways that can be enhancing to him and helpful to others.

Schilder, several decades ago, produced a volume that opened many avenues of thought concerning the body image.[1] Combining concepts from physiology, neuropathology, and psychology, he explored the body image emphasizing its interrelationship with perception and personality. In a unified approach, Schilder drew on phenomenological, gestalt, and psychoanalytic principles to explain body perception and its influence on individual behavior. He indicated that "the image of the human body means the picture of our own body which we form in our mind, that is to say the way in which the body appears to ourselves."[2] While few have followed the theory of Schilder, his work has served to highlight the topic and to encourage other research efforts.

In the intervening years since Schilder the research on body experience has diverged in two directions. The first is concerned with the neurological and physiological aspects of perception and has led to several interesting conceptualizations about perceptual development. The other direction remains basically oriented in psychological constructs and focuses on the

[1] Paul Schilder, *The Image and Appearance of the Human Body* (London: Kegan Paul, Trench, Trubner, 1935).
[2] *Ibid.*, p. 11.

individual's perception of his body and his body experiences as they influence his psychological self.

Secord and Jourard[3] investigated body-cathexis to determine an individual's satisfaction with parts of his body, relating these feelings about one's body to feelings about the self. Body-cathexis was measured using an instrument listing 46 parts of the body (such as hair, hands, body build, legs, sex activities, height, and chest), each of which were rated by subjects on a five point scale from positive to negative feelings. The self-cathexis scale consisted of 55 items (such as taste in clothes, moods, love life, popularity, capacity for work, memory, and creativeness), which were rated on the same five point scale. A third instrument, a homonym test, was employed to measure an individual's anxiety or preoccupation with his body. Subjects were college males (70) and females (56). They found that feelings about body correlate with feelings about the self. They report that females tend to more extreme body-cathexis in either direction than do males. Beyond the relationship between body-cathexis and self-concept, their findings indicate that low body-cathexis, or negative perceptions of one's body, are associated with anxiety and insecurity.

In another study Jourard and Secord, using these same body-cathexis and self-cathexis scales and actual body measurements (height, weight, width of shoulders, circumference of chest and of biceps), examined the relationship between body-cathexis and body size. Using 62 college males, their findings suggest that positive body cathexis is associated with large body parts. They report:

With the exception of body weight, the findings reveal that cathexis for body characteristics pertaining to "masculinity" is related to the size of relevant body parts. Large size is apparently a desired quality among males, and its presence or absence leads to contrasting feelings toward related aspects of the male body.[4]

In a similar study with 60 college females, Jourard and Secord explored the relationship between body-cathexis and the ideal female figure.[5] In this study the investigators concentrated on the five body parts believed to be of most concern to all women—height, weight, bust, waist, and hips. They found that the reported measurements and the actual measurements of the

[3] P. F. Secord, and S. M. Jourard, "The Appraisal of Body-Cathexis: Body-Cathexis and the Self," *Journal of Consulting Psychology* 17:343–347, October 1953.

[4] S. M. Jourard, and P. F. Secord, "Body Size and Body-Cathexis," *Journal of Consulting Psychology* 18:184, June 1954.

[5] S. M. Jourard, and P. F. Secord, "Body-Cathexis and the Ideal Female Figure," *Journal of Abnormal and Social Psychology* 50:243–246, March 1955.

subjects were almost identical. Further, they report that the ideal size for these subjects tended to be smaller than their measured size except for the bust where the ideal size was larger than the measured one. Both of these studies emphasize the influence of the "ideal" on one's satisfaction or dissatisfaction with his body parts.

In an article summarizing and integrating several body-cathexis studies, Jourard and Secord[6] suggest

that a person's security—his felt self-acceptability as well as his acceptability to significant others—is related in some way to his feelings about his body. Perhaps the explanation of this relationship is that a person in our culture perceives his body appearance as a tool for impressing others, whose approval he has come to need for his self esteem.[7]

Their data repeatedly point to the extreme importance of one's perception of his body in relation to his self-concept. Apparently the cultural standards for the body parts are more influential than we may have recognized. Certainly they appear to be the base from which self-satisfaction or dissatisfaction with the body stems.

Franklin C. Shontz[8] maintains that the components of the body image concept are not sufficiently established to provide more than propositional commitments. In what Shontz terms "one last wild fling" he details two steps that are necessary in reconciling the perceptual and personality aspects of the body image concept. According to him, these steps are as follows:

the first is to recognize explicitly that more than one kind of experience is derived from the body. The second step is to stipulate that the several kinds of body experience ordinarily function together without essential conflict or disharmony. Having taken these steps, it is necessary to describe more fully both (a) the kinds of experiences that must be taken into account, and (b) the ways in which these experiences are integrated.[9]

This suggests a broader, more encompassing concept of physical maturation —one that attends to the evolvement of the body image and its integration with other experiences.

We have sufficient ideas about the structure and form of the body image concept to begin applying these concepts in our work with youth. In expand-

---

[6] S. M. Jourard, and P. F. Secord, "Body-Cathexis and Personality," *British Journal of Psychology* 46:130–138, May 1955.

[7] *Ibid.*, p. 137.

[8] Franklin C. Shontz, *Perceptual and Cognitive Aspects of Body Experience* (New York: Academic Press, 1969). Copyright © 1969 by Academic Press.

[9] *Ibid.*, pp. 201–202.

ing our concept of physical maturation we should incorporate body perception as well as body development. Shontz indicates that "The most fundamental form of body experience is the experience of the body as a single object with a specific locus in space," adding,

. . . it is inconceivable that self-identification can occur until after the self has been globally localized. A child cannot differentiate himself psychologically from his environment unless he can at least locate himself somewhere within that environment. Only when spatial localization has been achieved is it possible to think in terms of egocentric spatial coordinates such as up-down, near-far, before-behind.[10]

As the counselor works with youth in the secondary school he becomes aware of the body percepts and values which an individual ascribes to various parts of his body. During the period of adolescence, then, we might anticipate any number of very significant feelings and behaviors. For example, the adolescent girl who has just undergone a spurt in growth may need time to reorient herself perceptually, i.e., to adjust to a different height or longer arms and so on. We speak of the period of adolescent awkwardness but seldom do we provide youth with opportunities to talk about these changes, how they feel about them, or how they feel about the way others respond to them. Rather, I presume we often provide the momentum for the development of *less than positive* body percepts with statements like "you awkward thing" or "you're all arms."

Youth are frequently exposed to embarrassing experiences causing them to feel inferior, wanting, or sad. In a total sense, though it is relatively easy to translate this to its component facets, the high school athlete is reinforced for his physical attributes even though he may be exceedingly large (football) or frightfully skinny and tall (basketball). These body percepts, under such successful conditions, can be positively internalized and such experiences can contribute to a strong positive body concept. Yet athletics is only one vehicle and a very limited one in terms of the students it can reach. The physical education program can be employed as a positive force if the instructor is alert; on the other hand, it can be a deterring one if, for example, the teaching style is so stereotyped that a few people are *always* among the last to be selected by their peers when teams are being chosen.

Considering the many aspects of one's physical growth and the many, many experiences incurred in the process, it is no wonder that the development of the body image is a vast and complex process. Crooked teeth, acne, body scars, even the texture of one's hair, to say nothing of its distribution over the body, only serve to illustrate but a very few of the possible imme-

[10] *Ibid.*, p. 202.

diate and external sources of individual anxiety and concern. To mix these with all the other varieties of body concern and experience, and to relate these body concepts to the development of the self-concept, points to an important area of adolescent growth that somehow or other has been relegated to a domain of lesser importance. The increasing attention to services and products for the adolescent which cater to the body parts—creams, orthodontia, makeup, oils, etc.—is some evidence that the "teenage market" *is* an extremely significant and important one.

Masculinity and Male Stereotypes

Boys are concerned about becoming men. They are concerned about their masculinity. Boys are schooled, early and repeatedly, on what it takes to be a man. The societal concept of masculinity, even though it differs somewhat among various subcultures, is a combination of stereotypes that have evolved over the years. Even though the adult male role has historically been centered around the roles of husband and father, one must be a man first. Thus the male learns to identify first with the social view of male behavior. From an early age, boys are assuaged with "big boys don't cry" or they are cautioned "that's girl talk (or play)." These many familiar admonitions remind us that societal role expectations can be as effectively communicated by word as by deed.

The ideal masculine stereotype is characterized in men who are strong, muscular, active, adventuresome, brave, reckless, handsome, bold. The adjectives which describe the male are endless but they surely don't include gentle (as contrasted to a gentleman), loving (as contrasted with being a lover), sensitive, thoughtful, or emotional. Granted these are qualities which he may have in moderation, or which he may have for display at an appropriate time, but they are usually "reserve" behaviors which should not interfere with the male "front." The similarities in the stereotypic male and the adult male role lie more in matters relating to attracting, winning, and cohabiting with a female. Any discrepancies that appear to exist are accounted for in the assumption that the male will grow into his adult role and come to understand and perform it. This assumption could be reviewed in light of certain societal changes and trends such as the "unisex" movement or the pill.

The male learns about being a man in school just as much as he does at home. Boys are by nature more aggressive and noisy—at least the masculine concept would assume boys to be more aggressive and noisy. While the school caters to the development of the physique and provides for the athletic interests of males, the classroom, in which the greater amount of time is spent, exacts behaviors from boys which are quite contrary to the masculine image.

In the American classroom boys are expected to be quiet and conforming. In fact if they are not, they are punished. This "double standard" of masculinity poses a very genuine concern for many boys. It tends to confuse rather than clarify the growing American male. On the other hand it may be that the school provides a dimension to masculine development which is badly needed and which cannot be provided elsewhere. We need to examine more closely our beliefs about masculinity and to provide more adequately for their development.

Patricia Sexton speaks directly to this problem. She writes,

A primary concern here is that our society, its institutions, and its citizens, still cling to old and inaccurate sex stereotypes. . . . Thus sex role stereotypes, which result in serious discrimination against women and ambivalence in men, create a fissure that runs throughout the society, dividing it, and diminishing its vigor and humanity.[11]

Later, she adds,

Old sex stereotypes need to be replaced by rules that permit the natural expression of the individual's inner self and the assertion of both aggressive and humane impulses. Men are neither lions nor lambs. Being human, they should be permitted to grow in ways most natural to their species and their individual temperaments.[12]

Femininity and Female Stereotypes

There is more consistency in our approach to developing the feminine nature of the female and the stereotype of the American woman. Girls from birth on are oriented to their future roles of wife and mother and are allowed activities which are more consistent with these adult roles. Girls are permitted activities both at home and in school that help them to develop positive attitudes toward becoming a wife and a mother.

The feminine stereotype is as difficult to define as its counterpart. Yet there are qualities which are ascribed to the female. Women are, or are expected to be, neat, clean, mannered, kind, gentle, affectionate, sensitive,

[11] Patricia C. Sexton, *The Feminized Male* (New York: Random House, 1969), p. 18.
[12] *Ibid.,* p. 199.

understanding and, to a degree at least, deferrent or submissive. They are actually able to participate more widely in activities of all kinds—indoor and outdoor. To be a "tomboy" carries far less social disfavor than to be a "sissy." This carries over to school as well.

In school girls are rewarded for their feminine dispositions and behaviors. The female stereotype affords them more opportunities to study since school work is often perceived as more feminine than masculine, thus they tend to achieve well in school. Some studies indicate that they tend to receive better grades than boys, not because they have actually learned more, but because of behaviors and attitudes which are viewed more favorably by the teacher.

Girls, too, are concerned about their attractiveness to boys and their sexual development. Within the female stereotype they strive to accept their relations and relationships with boys. Since girls mature earlier it is not uncommon to find the junior high school girl trying desperately to win the attention and favor of her less inclined and less interested male counterpart. The difference in the development of the male and female results in one or two very awkward years (usually these involve grades 8 and 9 or grades 8, 9, and 10) while the girls "wait" for the boys to achieve sexual maturity.

During these years, it is not uncommon to find girls, usually within the feminine stereotype, moving more aggressively to attract male attention. While the boys remain somewhat dormant, the girls are primping and dressing and acting in ways they hope will attract boys to them. It is important that adults, and institutions such as the school, recognize and understand these behaviors and, more importantly, that they help youth, particularly girls, to understand the facets of their growing and the meaning of their life experiencing.

While there has existed more consistency in the evolvement of feminine feelings in girls, there is currently a trend in our society that may have great meaning for the future of female youth. As an adult woman whose role traditionally has been wife and mother, the modern adult female, as we noted in Chapter Two, is increasingly embracing a work role at some point in (or before) her married life. While girls will remain in mother and wife roles, the female has sought and gained in this society an equality with the male that becomes increasingly obvious not only in occupational and marital affairs but in political, economic, and social matters. As women compete with men in all aspects of life, the female stereotypes will be tested. These new work roles and the responsibilities which they carry will require in many instances a woman who will be aggressive, controlling, self-confident, ambitious, tough. As women assume these traits, so long associated with the male, we will have more evidence of our changing mores.

Personal Appearance and Grooming

Much attention is given to the personal appearance and grooming of adolescents in the school situation. Units of study within the school curriculum
often focus on the details of grooming and dress. Such attention is often
more predominant in subject matter areas in which primarily girls are
enrolled, such as business education and home economics, although such
units do appear in other courses such as health and physical education
where both boys and girls are enrolled.

Another way in which the school directs considerable attention to
dress and grooming is through school regulations, which usually emphasize
the types of clothing and dress that are disapproved by the school administration. Attention to grooming and dress taboos has been accelerated in
recent years as long hair styles, beards, tight pants, slacks, and mini-skirts
have become fashionable. As these modes of dress and grooming have become increasingly popular among adolescents, school administrators and
communities have deemed it necessary to establish more precise codes of
dress and style. The increasing number of school regulations regarding
dress, and the accompanying number of violations, have resulted in a
number of student suspensions, raising questions of legality and infringe-
ment on individual rights and freedoms.

In New York State, for example, Acting Commissioner of Education
Ewald B. Nyquist, in the matter of Daniel Cossey, a Schenectady (N.Y.)
sophomore who was suspended for hair worn in a manner that violated the
dress code of his high school, ruled that the suspension was unlawful and
ordered Cossey readmitted. In his decision Nyquist states,

There is no question that social norms and standards are essential, and that each
individual must be made aware of the social consequences of his failure to abide
by them. There is also no question that learning to accommodate oneself to the
standards laid down by a group of which the individual is a member constitutes
a valuable social experience. But the issue in this case is not the value of such
standards or the desirability of adherence to them by the individual. The issue
is whether the rights of the individual in matters of dress and appearance are
subject to legally enforceable regulation in accordance with the wishes of the
majority.

Commissioners of Education have held repeatedly that the matter of a
student's appearance may not be regulated by administrative order where
fashion or taste is the sole criteria. Regulations must relate to a specific educational purpose, such as health, safety, or full participation in various activities.[13]

[13] In the decision of Acting Commissioner of Education (N.Y.) Ewald B. Nyquist in the matter of Lillian E. Cossey, appellant versus the Board of Education of
the City School District of the City of Schenectady (N.Y.), respondent, July 25,
1969.

This particular decision is most interesting in that the code referred to in the case was initiated by the student organization in the high school attended by Daniel Cossey, and adopted with support of parents, faculty, and the student body. In a society where a person may find decreasing opportunities to express his individuality, matters of personal taste in dress and appearance may become paramount.

Two important factors seem to undergird adolescent behaviors in matters of grooming and appearance. Their desire for peer approval and acceptance is primary. This infers adherence to codes of dress and conformity to current styles. Yet there are those who need neither approval nor acceptance but who, for whatever psychological or social reason, seek to flout the normative and to behave in their own individual ways regardless of their nonconforming nature. It is quite possible that we may observe more of this in adult behavior in the years ahead. Peer pressure and influence may become less a factor in individual behavior. The need for people to express their own uniqueness and individuality may challenge even our most enduring beliefs about human behavior.

A second but perhaps less influential factor is related to the student's body image, his perception of himself, or to the immediate feelings which he needs to express. Dress and appearance offer an opportunity for him to express new feelings and to try out different ways of appearing to others, testing at the same time their reactions to him. Some boys are anxious to grow beards and long hair more to test adult and peer reactions than to satisfy any inner strivings or desires. Some girls wish to test their attractiveness with very tight or very short skirts. The myriad of personal factors which cause adolescents to do what they do and to appear as they do are many and varied. If we wish to understand these behaviors we should go directly to the individuals involved and trust that our relationship with them will allow for the kinds of communication that can facilitate understanding and acceptance.

The school has confronted these situations essentially from two approaches: acceptance (but not necessarily approval) of the situation, and rejection. Most schools have accepted the situation attuning school policy and regulations, within reason, to the tenor and fashions of the time. A few schools, on the other hand, have elected to stand on principle or custom, remaining less flexible and adaptable. The arbitrary decision to impose adult values or to maintain existing standards has resulted in legal entanglements or in the eventual erosion of the decision.

In most instances the school policy has, in time, adjusted to accord with current trends. In such cases the school district has invited these difficulties by choosing to ignore or to circumvent the more basic issues of adolescent learning-maturation. If school systems believe in individuality and freedom of choice, and if they claim to contribute to the development of individual responsibility, then school officials and school personnel need to direct more attention to the general tenets of adolescent development and societal directions and less to institutional idiosyncrasies and societal traditions. In other words, schools must become more humane and less hidebound; they must become future-oriented rather than past-dominated.

Sexual Maturation and Behavior

No other facet of adolescent development causes as much concern and frustration, both for the individual and the adults in his life (including school personnel), as the arrival of puberty and the ensuing process of sexual maturation. The adolescent's concern begins with his need for information about the body and the sexual aspects of reproduction. The adult's concern begins, appropriately, with his role in dispensing such information. Naturally this responsibility would appear to be best accommodated in the home with the father or the mother, or both, assuming a major role in providing not only basic informational needs but helping to establish the fundamental attitudes toward sex and sexual behavior.

That many homes have failed in this responsibility is generally recognized. That the community and the church have been poor substitutes is also commonly acknowledged. That the schools have been unwilling to accept this responsibility is a generalization (open, of course, to some debate) that has some basis. The current debate in many communities regarding sex education in the schools is evidence of the reluctance of the home, the church, and the community to relinquish certain responsibilities to the school. In some communities this has been debated with varying positions represented. For example, in Rochester, New York, the parochial schools (in this particular instance the schools of the Catholic diocese) proposed a program of sex education developed under the direct supervision of the diocese, only to encounter tremendous resistance from parents and others in the community. In this case the church, through its school system, recognized the need of adolescents and attempted to assume a responsible role.

Probably few curriculum matters have received as much community reaction and discussion as have attempts, by one group or another, to establish sex education in the school. While some progress in dealing with the void in sex education has been made in isolated areas across the nation, adolescent needs in the process of sexual maturation have remained primarily a prerogative of the home. To translate this obligation into an actuality or to transfer it to other responsible institutions is a number one issue.

It is not my purpose to establish individual or institutional responsibility for the sex education of our youth. I merely intend to describe the conditions that exist and to point out the need for adolescents to have someone to whom they can turn, with confidence and trust, not only for basic information (which currently is only incidentally handled, if at all) but, more importantly, for assistance in examining their feelings and concerns about their sexual development and behavior.

Regardless of the programs that are or are not established, the developmental counselor could act as one of the adults to whom young people could turn. Again, in our studies of the school counselor role, the greater emphasis on educational-vocational matters has left little if any time for the school counselor to act effectively with adolescents, either individually or in groups. All too often the adolescent is expected to deal with decisions about his proposed courses of study or his post-high school plans when his energies, interests, and concerns are almost entirely tied up in matters concerning his own physical maturation. As most teenagers are quick to announce, they can handle by themselves most of the immediate aspects of high school or college planning, but in facing the concerns of their own development and maturation they can use help. Furthermore, to even begin to deal with the future when you are quite unsure about the present seems a bit unrealistic (for adults as well as adolescents).

Adolescents seek a very strong and significant relationship (a safe one) in which to raise and discuss their very individual and personal sex problems. Such a relationship is presumed to exist for most adolescents with his parents, his clergy, his counselor, or with other significant adults in his life. Research investigations of sources of sex information would indicate that such relationships serve an informational purpose. However, the very personal nature of integrating and internalizing attitudes toward sex and the personal aspects of individual sex behavior are often unattended. Students should be encouraged to communicate with people they trust, and the school counselor should have a sufficiently strong relationship with enough students to be of help with their most pressing concerns.

Sexual maturation involves many avenues of sexual knowledge and experience. Sex information surveys show that many adolescents wish to seek help but are fearful and embarrassed about doing so. Lacking an adult with whom they can communicate, they turn to peers. This leaves their education to chance, and it increases the chances of receiving misinformation and forming misconceptions. Further, the need for such information and the timing of it are crucial considerations. Information too soon or too late is of little value or help.

Beyond the informational, opportunities to discuss sex problems, experiences, and attitudes should be possible at the time the student feels the need to discuss them. This is the time to help, not next week—perhaps even the next day would be too late. Basic to the involvement of teachers (as significant and trusted adults) or counselors in providing help is their own feelings about their sexual role, their own knowledge of sexual development, and their own attitudes about sex behaviors. Their own assessment of their knowledge, beliefs, and attitudes toward sex is an essential ingredient of any role in which they might engage.

Let's look at just a few of the more common areas of sex development about which adolescents seek information and help. While the areas discussed in the succeeding section represent only a fraction of those that may be raised, they do suggest to the teacher or the counselor, the kinds of knowledge, and the personal attitudes which he himself needs to examine.

Sex education includes both the provision of accurate information and the development of positive attitudes toward sex and sex behaviors. Like so many areas of our life today, our information about sexual development and sexual behavior has changed and is changing as we learn more about human sex and human sex behavior from the research available. Our information about sexual matters must be accurate and up to date. We cannot afford to pass along misinformation to young people or to promulgate myths about sex.

Undergirding sexual behavior are those values and beliefs that are accepted by the individuals or by the society in which the individual lives. We must recognize both in our consideration of sexual behaviors. Society has established standards of acceptable sexual conduct. Individuals are expected to perform within the limits of these standards imposed by society. Within these standards of sexual conduct, however, there is considerable room for individual beliefs and values. The alternative behaviors to guide the sexual life of a person are varied and we must recognize the range and the extent of these alternatives and the beliefs and values that they represent. Thus the range of alternative behaviors available to any individual, as well as the societal standards, should be included in the sex education of our young people.

Further complicating sex education programs and our work with young people are the changing mores and beliefs of a society in eternal transition. The societal standards for sex behavior, as well as the laws pertaining to sex behavior, are undergoing constant review. Our changing ideologies, as well as our scientific and technological advances, have produced a continual alteration of the standards for sexual behavior resulting in considerable flexibility in individual beliefs, values, and attitudes that undergird sex practices.

For example, the introduction of the pill has resulted in a modification of the standards for premarital relations among unmarried couples. That such standards are in process of change, if only among the young unmarrieds, then an influence has been effected. That the pill has influenced or is influencing the sexual behavior of married couples is a known fact. These kinds of change cause some people to reconsider basic tenets in other areas of their life as well. Even societal institutions such as the church have been caused to reexamine their dogma.

We simply cannot ignore these changes. The recognition of sex as a vital, integral, healthy part of modern American life is more universally accepted than ever before in our history. Sex is no longer the secretive and mysterious domain of human behavior that it has been. This in itself represents a major change in our approach to sex education. It should influence most significantly our approach to helping the adolescent with his sexual development.

Seeking sex information. Individuals become very concerned about their sexual development and spend a great deal of time thinking about sex and seeking information so that they can better understand what they are experiencing. Not only are they concerned about the growth and size of their genitals or their breasts, they are interested in comparing their own bodies with those of their peers.

His sexual curiosity heightened, the adolescent explores all possible avenues for obtaining information—books, pamphlets, and people who might be able to help. That he is seeking such information is often not readily revealed since young people, at least in the past, have been reluctant to make known their curiosity. In fact it should be recognized that thinking about and exploring sex has been accompanied by much anxiety, guilt, and fear. These feelings alone are cause for some concern and should be an integral part of our approach to helping students. In fact as sex becomes a more open subject for discussion in the future, it is possible that we may be able to reach young people earlier and in more meaningful and personal ways.

Interpersonal relations with the opposite sex. During the adolescent period, individuals become concerned about their relations with the opposite sex. Beginning with the basic question of relating to the opposite sex and accepting this interest, boys and girls go on to become concerned with each other with regard to such areas as popularity, dating, petting, and sexual relations. Their concern with these matters begins initially with their own assessment of their feelings and attitudes and their equating of these with what they regard to be the "normal" pattern of interpersonal relations between boys and girls. Thus from feelings of indifference and repulsion regarding the other sex, the individual moves to an acceptance of and an association with the other sex, to dating (including going steady), and finally to courtship and marriage.

As we know, this range of experiences occurs over a very few years for some while for others it is a more gradual one. Much reading material is available for young people regarding their questions and concerns during each of these periods, but there is an even greater need for opportunities to talk things out with knowing adults who will accept and understand them. Society—and the school in particular—has been able to deal more directly with the concerns and needs of boy-girl and courtship relationships, matters that arise later in the learning-maturation sequence.

Sex identification. Both boys and girls are concerned about the growth of and development of their bodies and about the relationship of this growth to their masculinity or femininity. Girls are afraid they may be too tall and boys are often fearful that they may be too short. The boy whose voice "breaks" becomes embarrassed, or the boy whose voice is late in changing wonders if his voice will retain its high pitch. Adolescents are in a hurry to develop—often unaware that the maturation process is a slow and continual one. Being told to wait or to give it time does not always reduce the anxiety or the fear which they are experiencing.

Also, as I discussed earlier in this chapter, there is the problem of developing roles appropriate to the masculine and feminine stereotypes which exist. Boys and girls frequently exhibit behaviors consistent with these stereotypes in order to prove appropriate sex identification to themselves and others. This sometimes gets them into trouble as in the case of a male who becomes overly assertive and bold.

Questions and problems of sex identification in the physical maturation process are often discussed at the adult level and included in the professional preparation of people who work with adolescents. That such matters are seldom discussed with adolescents is another of our major shortcomings.

Masturbation. Masturbational exploration in early childhood is a frequent occurrence, and one that causes a great deal of parent consternation. Such exploration is normal but how the parent deals with it has meaning for the future and the sexual maturation of the child. Male sexual maturity is attained with the release of semen. The male most commonly experiences this by masturbation or by nocturnal emission (commonly referred to as a wet dream). Both can be cause for alarm in the young male.

Masturbation can be accompanied with guilt or shame or fear, depending on what the young man has been taught or has heard. The myths of masturbation, such as that which contends that the practice of masturbation can lead to insanity, have been fairly well destroyed and more healthful attitudes toward the practice of masturbation are replacing them. Most boys, at one period or another, engage in masturbation until they learn how to cope with the feelings and tensions of sexual maturity. Some continue to practice masturbation until marriage and beyond, while others discontinue it as other means of sexual release are discovered. For most young men, however, there is a period extending from several months to several years when he needs help in the form of information about this practice and in discussing feelings associated with it. Some boys wish for help in interpreting the new sensations and different feelings that accompany sexual maturation.

Menstruation. For the female the menarche, or initial menstrual period, can be a surprising and shocking occurrence or it can be happily anticipated depending upon the information provided the girl in advance. Many girls have been informed about menstruation and the physical aspects of the menstrual period. However, much of a girl's attitude toward menstruation will be conditioned by her education. Whether she considers menstruation as a "curse" or as a normal aspect of her femininity will depend upon the information and the attitudes she is assisted in developing.

While school health programs have contributed greatly to this aspect of sexual maturation in girls, very little has been done to assist girls in dealing with the ensuing menstruation questions and problems and in integrating attitudes about the menstrual function with other attitudes and problems related to their sexual development.

Homosexuality. This area, while related to the individual's concern for appropriate sex identification, poses more specific questions and concerns relative to sexual conduct and behavior. This topic has long been "hush-hush" and is more often omitted than included in the usual sex information program. The adolescent in the process of sexual maturation may frequently raise with himself the question of his own sexual identity. While homosexuality may not be an equally important topic for all adolescents in terms of their own development, it is a topic about which they could all use more information and a behavior which they could all better understand.

The question of homosexuality is not an either-or question since we have come to understand better the continuum of sexual behavior ranging from heterosexual to bisexual to homosexual. But it is one facet of sexual behavior that has heretofore been considered unlawful and deviant. Homosexuality in whatever form or degree is an aspect of human sexual behavior that individuals should not only know more about but should be free to discuss. Since this topic is difficult for adults to deal with, they may need to explore their own underlying feelings and attitudes about homosexuality before attempting to handle this topic with adolescents.

Recently legislation in some states has been relaxed so that homosexuality among consenting adults is no longer a civil offense. Such legislation is another illustration of the changing standards of our society and of the changing beliefs that undergird it.

Sex Development and the Educative Process

Sex education in the public schools remains a controversial topic. In an issue of *Life*[14] citizens of a midwestern community were shown mobilizing in support of sex education while others were preparing to protest it. Most school systems that have dared to initiate such programs have faced similar consequences. Yet it is only a matter of time before more schools will become deeply involved in the sex education issue. Only part of the problem rests in the debate as to whether the home, the church, or the school should assume this responsibility. An important facet of the controversy lies in a number of social trends which have highlighted the double standard in our attitudes toward and exploitation of sex. No matter how communities choose to contest the issue, the sign of the times will persistently point to action. The school program will eventually be charged with a good share of this responsibility.

The arguments against sex education are well known: To educate youth in the ways of sex is to create problems that otherwise wouldn't exist. Such a stand is reinforced or supplemented with arguments relative to possible intrusions on religious positions and the lack of qualified personnel to lead sex education programs. Despite these arguments against sex education, a good deal of research substantiates a need for well-thought-out programs.

Adolescent needs for sex education extend well beyond mere information. The sheer dissemination of information about sex falls far short of their requirements. To be effective, programs must not only provide information but they must allow students to review it, react to it, and internalize it. This means dealing with all aspects of sex and sex behavior, presenting alternative views and behaviors. This also means providing for the development of healthy attitudes toward sex that students can use in guiding their sexual conduct.

When we think of the misinformation which students have, and the myths about sex that have been promulgated, we realize more fully how badly we need these programs. On top of this, of course, are the scientific advances leading to cultural adaptations which will have a direct bearing on sexual attitudes and behaviors. Further, some areas of information contributing to sexual maturity have, heretofore, been considered taboo.

[14] Facing the "Facts of Life," *Life* 67:35–41, September 19, 1969.

To pretend, as some people or programs do, that any sexual activity other than intercourse in marriage does not exist is to close our eyes to the realities of our society. Youth are not that stupid. Mass communication media as well as their own observations have made them well aware of premarital and extramarital sex relationships, prostitution, homosexuality, and other varieties of sexual conduct. They are not only aware of but concerned about these behaviors and the societal issues and problems related to them such as abortion, venereal disease, and the sex deviant. These topics are not only significant in physical maturation but central to an informed and involved citizenry.

In dealing with sex development, adolescents want straight talk. Multisyllable medicalese and gross technical explanations are deplored and often become the subject of ridicule and jest. This is not to encourage—nor even allow—vulgarity and filth. It is simply to adjust our language so that we communicate meaningfully. When we insist on only the "proper" terminology, we sometimes fail to transmit our message.

I believe we need to deal more directly with young people and to use the popular expressions (and I do not mean those straight from the gutter) which have meaning to them. I am inferring three levels of sex talk: (1) the technical and the medical; (2) the popular or the colloquial; and (3) the vulgar. If our goal is to educate, then clear, concise statements, worded so that adolescents can understand and interpret their meaning, seems to communicate more than the fancy, formal, highly technical presentations which are so characteristic of past efforts.

IMPLICATIONS FOR DEVELOPMENTAL
SCHOOL GUIDANCE

The relationship of developmental school guidance to the many aspects of physical maturation is clear indeed. In dealing with students, parents, teachers, and others the school counselor must be ever aware of this expanded view of physical development and its import not only for the growth of an individual but for its meaning in the teaching-learning process. In the day-to-day business of guidance, he will engage in a constellation of activities ranging from the corrective-adjustive (remedial) to the facilitative-developmental (preventive). The relationship of these efforts to the variant-deviant continuum of learning was developed in Chapter Four. Students may wish to review this concept again relating it specifically to efforts in this specific dimension of developmental guidance practice.

The developmental counselor will become involved with problems of physical maturation in many different ways. He may find himself working with a number of other school and community personnel. Some problems may be primarily concerns of a physiological nature which can be remedied through appropriate health or medical facilities. We have referred to some of the more common physical conditions which can cause an adolescent some stress or anxiety. While health personnel can be of great help in dealing with the actual condition, the school counselor is often the person who can help the individual to examine the stress or the anxiety that he is experiencing. It does not seem necessary or wise to categorize these functions by saying, for example, that the school nurse or physician deals with the physical health while the counselor works with the mental health of the individual. Such divisions are so broad that they are often worthless. Rather I believe both work with the physical aspects of any problem—the school health authorities emphasizing remedial efforts while the school counselor spearheads the preventive.

Developmental guidance is concerned with the internal needs and feelings of an individual as these are associated with his physical maturation. All that an adolescent feels and experiences may be quite normal although he may not perceive what is happening to him as normal. Further, if he is sufficiently bothered, being *told* that his condition is common or being advised that the condition will change or get better in time is very often of little help or relief. Trivial, unimportant, and troubles they must learn to face, some would exhort—adding that we simply don't have the time, the personnel, or the financial resources to deal with such small, everyday problems.

Are we saying, then, that we just don't have time for adolescents? Are we ignoring the very essence of the adolescent experience? Are we failing to recognize the relation of any concern to the more encompassing and complex aspects of helping adolescents to maintain personal equilibrium at a very critical point in their development? Obviously the counselor who accepts a preventive approach to guidance and who is concerned with the facilitative-developmental aspects of his program would reject this point of view.

Adolescent problems associated with physical maturation are not always easily identified by either the counselor or the student. This brings us to another level of involvement with them. Counselors, in dealing with students whose concerns seemingly originate in other areas of life (academic performance, social relationships, life planning), discover that aspects of physical maturation are often contributing segments of a more comprehensive problem.

Sometimes these concerns are not brought out until the counselor has had several meetings with the student. Students themselves are sometimes caused to feel that they should be able to deal with these problems by themselves. Others are too embarrassed or too fearful of revealing these concerns. While focusing on any phase of physical maturation may not resolve his more complex problems, the student can still be assisted in placing it in perspective in relation to his problem and his growth. This of course depends upon the ability of the counselor to help him to talk about it and to examine the various dimensions of it.

Since the physical aspects of maturation, particularly the problems of sexual development, are so common to most youth, the developmental counselor may find this an area in which group counseling can be particularly effective. Counselors have found both same sex and mixed sex groups beneficial to students who are willing to engage in this type of group experience.

Because most young people are hesitant to raise concerns about their sexual development or their sex behavior with an adult, the peer group situation provides a safe atmosphere to explore and deal with problems of this type. Often a counselor may find that students simply lack reliable, current information, which can be readily supplied. On other occasions arrangements have been provided for speakers or discussion groups as a supplement to the group counseling activity.

Working with students in this setting, particularly in times of changing moral values such as these, the counselor can use this opportunity to learn more about the problems and behaviors of young adults as they search for ways to cope with the scientific advances of a changing world (the pill, for example).

One final consideration seems appropriate. In view of the stereotypes of guidance and the general nature of past guidance efforts (as these were elaborated in Chapter One), physical maturation has received comparatively little attention. Yet as I have repeatedly tried to emphasize, this dimension of the individual's learning-maturation is fundamental to other maturational aspects and intimately a part of them. This dimension holds considerable promise for cooperative planning between the instructional program and the pupil personnel services.

Within the existing curriculum of most high schools, innumerable opportunities are available to incorporate discrete experiences, units of study or entire courses concerning personal health and grooming, mental health, physiology, family living, marriage, and community health. Some of these topics, though limited in scope, are an integral part of the adolescent's school experience, although in many schools their availability is restricted to a small segment of the total school population.

We could expand these opportunities by utilizing more effectively our existing programs in English, social studies, mathematics, science, and language, as well as those that have been always active in areas related to physical maturation (home economics, health, and biology). Attention to body perception and awareness activities in physical education is illustrative of a classroom opportunity that is almost completely unexplored. And there are many, many other classroom opportunities for meaningful exposures of this type. Within the consulting function, the developmental counselor can assist teachers and curriculum specialists in planning for these experiences and he can help them to become more comfortable and secure in implementing them.

Some of the functions delineated in the following sections suggest a point of departure for the counselor who wants to become active in practicing this dimension of developmental guidance.

The Counseling Functions

(1) Counseling with individual adolescents or with small groups of adolescents who are experiencing concerns originating in or associated with the process of physical maturation.

(2) Counseling with parents (individually, as a family, or in small groups) on problems associated with physical maturation—sex role identity, sex problems, physical variations or handicaps, body perception.

(3) Counseling with individual teachers to help them in clarifying and understanding aspects of their own physical maturation and to help them relate and use these understandings in their classroom teaching and student relationships.

The Consulting Functions

(1) Assisting teachers in their understanding of the concerns which adolescents encounter in the physical maturation process.

(2) Helping teachers to create appropriate learning experiences that will contribute to an adolescent's understanding of physical maturation and particularly to the adolescent's perceptions of his growth toward physical maturity.

(3) Helping teachers and curriculum specialists to develop, sequence, and implement units and courses which have relevance for the physical maturation of youth.

(4) Conferring with parents whose children are experiencing difficulties in physical maturation.

(5) Helping teachers to identify adolescents whose learning experiences are being disrupted by problems originating in or associated with their physical maturation.

(6) Conferring with appropriate school personnel, parents, and community leaders about possible new school courses or programs such as sex educa-

tion, body perception, human development. Initial action may have to depend on school and community readiness—a factor that the counselor must consider in all his consulting efforts.

The Coordinating Functions

(1) Assisting in the appraisal and referral of adolescents with physical maturation problems.

(2) Participating in case conferences concerning adolescents encountering physical maturation difficulties.

(3) Planning and conducting research activities to provide information that can be useful in assessing school policy and practice as it relates to the physical maturation of the adolescent (school organization, school codes and regulations, curriculum modifications and additions, special services).

(4) Assisting in the planning of in-service meetings for teachers to provide information about new ideas and recent research on topics appropriate to the physical maturation of the adolescent and the teaching-learning process.

(5) Conducting parent information meetings and seminars on aspects of the physical maturation of the adolescent.

(6) Identifying community resource personnel who can serve in referral capacities for students with problems of physical maturation, or who can participate in school programs or activities to provide for the physical maturation of youth.

SUGGESTED READING

COLE, LUELLA and HALL, IRMA N., *Psychology of Adolescence* (New York: Holt, Rinehart and Winston, 1964), sixth edition.

FISHER, SEYMOUR, "Sex Differences in Body Perception," *Psychological Monographs: General and Applied,* Volume 78, No. 14 (Washington, D.C.: American Psychological Association, 1964).

FISHER, SEYMOUR and CLEVELAND, SIDNEY E., *Body Image and Personality* (Princeton: Van Nostrand, 1958).

GESELL, ARNOLD F.; ILG, FRANCES; and AMES, LOUISE B., *Youth: The Years from Ten to Sixteen* (New York: Harper and Row, 1956).

SEXTON, PATRICIA, *The Feminized Male* (New York: Random House, 1969).

SHONTZ, FRANKLIN C., *Perceptual and Cognitive Aspects of Body Experience* (New York: Academic Press, 1969).

ELEVEN

MENTAL MATURATION:

LEARNING ABOUT LEARNING

Much of the theorizing about the nature of intelligence has occurred quite apart from the mainstream of education. A great deal of the theory has been ignored because it has been viewed as having little practical value for the teaching-learning process. Educators have been prone to "wait and see" or to "let the other fellow try it." Some have been interested in experimenting with and researching these new ideas but have had little direction in applying them to the process of education. Yet, the implications of these newer ideas about the intellect and intellectual development are vast and far-reaching and present broad new challenges to education.

We have arrived at a point where education can no longer remain ignorant or indifferent to ideas that hold so much promise. Educators need to steep themselves in information about the nature of intelligence and the processes of cognitive growth. They need to synthesize their information and apply it to the educative process. They need to examine and study the mental processes of human thinking and learning and the environment that best facilitates these processes. To put it another way, education needs to emphasize less to what extent an individual has the ability to learn and to emphasize more how the individual learns to learn.

There is little question but that developmental guidance will be right in the middle of these new developments and challenges. If it isn't, it *ought* to be! The developmental counselor with his concern for the learner *as an individual* (the *uniqueness* of each individual) and for the individual *as a learner* (the *variant* nature of each individual's learning-maturation) mandate that he become involved in fostering new approaches to learning and in encouraging new ways of studying the learning styles and growth of each individual.

EMERGING CONCEPTS OF INTELLIGENCE IN THE TWENTIETH CENTURY

As an aid to understanding the present situation (and the present need to deal directly and forcefully with outdated concepts and methodologies), the following synthesis of past developments and an interpretation of their meaning for future directions in education may be useful.

Two Significant Developments

Two concurrent developments have been influencing our approach to the intellectual development of children. First, since around 1900, psychologists have been speculating and theorizing about intelligence. They have attempted to define and describe it. A number of significant concepts of intelligence have emerged. These hold considerable potential for the educative process and we shall examine them in more detail later in this chapter. To date, however, they have had far less impact on education than a second development, the mental testing movement.

Mental testing, while rooted in definitions and concepts of intelligence, is the measurement of intelligence. It presumes a theory of intelligence. Intelligence testing is a standard practice in our schools; in fact, most children experience it several times in their school life. Unfortunately the mental testing movement has *not* influenced the techniques or the methodologies of the teaching-learning process, at least not in ways that have meaning for the cognitive growth of youth. Tests have been used to help label children (bright, dull, average) or to support teachers' hunches. They have been used for a number of administrative, instructional, and pupil personnel purposes.

However, in some respects, while appearing to promote our understanding of the child and our ability to foster his mental growth, the development of mental tests has hindered our progress and stultified the potential of the theory. Perhaps some historical accounting of the mental testing movement will help us to understand better where they have influenced education and how.

Intelligence as Unitary and Fixed

In 1916 Terman published a new measure of intelligence based on the premises and test patterns of Binet called the Stanford-Binet Scale. It was this instrument that introduced the concept of the intelligence quotient (IQ), which has remained a standard concept of intelligence testing to this day. Terman obviously held to the fixed, unitary aspects, since the test provided one IQ score. The scale was revised in 1937 and again in 1960. Its survival these many years would qualify it as a landmark in mental measurement. Its common use in schools today (with increasing reference to its use "when we need a reliable IQ on a pupil") reflects the minimal effect of the more recent and perhaps more potential concepts of differential intelligence. In this instance, then, the mental testing movement has not been a force for change. In fact, one might say it has retarded it.

Since these earlier instruments were individual tests necessitating a trained examiner and considerable time for administration and scoring, the challenge of utilizing manpower efficiently in World War I led to the development of group tests of intelligence. A group intelligence test, the Army Alpha, based primarily on work done by Otis, was used with thousands of recruits and heralded the beginning of a vast testing program in America. Whereas earlier intelligence tests had required individual administration, the development of a group instrument encouraged massive test programs involving thousands of children.

For the next half century, abetted by World War II, a great many group tests were developed. With rapid administration and scoring, an IQ on every child was readily available to school personnel. Teachers soon learned about the IQ; it became common to pupil records and school practice (although it contributed little to changing teaching practice). Parents then learned about intelligence tests and many demanded (and still do) to know how their child scored. The intelligence quotient (IQ) became (and in many schools still is) the standard index of measuring the child's *ability to learn* (a basic premise of most of these instruments).

Schools throughout the nation have developed testing programs, K-12, that administer a number of group intelligence tests during the school life of the child. Some, for example, test for intelligence every two or three years. With the IQ such an integral part of the teacher's armament and with parents nowadays so "tuned in" to its meaning, it will be most difficult to alter these understandings and to change current practice. The concept of intelligence as a fixed and unitary entity, as a measure of one's ability to learn, has taken over fifty years to "set"—but set it has!

Intelligence as Multiple and Differential

Just as World War I spearheaded group intelligence tests, World War II provided the impetus for the development of multifactor tests. Again, with many young men entering military service, the research opportunities for test development were fertile. In the decade following the war, a number of multifactor intelligence tests were made available. Some schools, even though they were well imbued with the IQ concept, were convinced by test publishers and their sales representatives of the greater use and value of these tests.

At about the same time, a new type of test—the aptitude test—became available for group administration. There was much confusion initially among school personnel as to the difference between an aptitude factor and an intelligence factor. There still is! Thurstone postulated about twelve "primary mental abilities." The PMA (Primary Mental Abilities) test developed by the Thurstones was released in the late 1940s and the initial version measured seven of these (perceptual speed, space, reasoning, memory, numerical comprehension, verbal comprehension, and verbal fluency). This was later reduced to five. At about the same time, several new multifactor aptitude tests were purporting to measure the same factors (numerical, verbal, etc.).

A close examination of the test manuals would have helped to determine more precisely what was being measured, but the average school principal or newly trained guidance counselor (guidance in the secondary school was gaining a foothold and with its early vocational emphasis, these aptitude tests were a program "must") didn't have the background in measurement to make these necessary distinctions.

Over the last fifteen years, however, there has been some progress, though slight. School counselors have been prepared to deal with the differential concept of intelligence. The rank and file classroom teacher and school administrator are increasingly aware of the multifactor concept; they have learned to use the IQ with some facility and caution. And as for parents, they are just becoming comfortable with an understanding of the IQ; they do not understand much about the differential nature of intelligence.

We shall probably always have several differing levels of understanding of intellectual growth. Counselors should be more aware of newer concepts than teachers and teachers more so than parents. A consensus on the nature of the intellect should defer to progress. The task of moving dynamically forward to incorporate newer ideas and concepts is a tremendous undertaking. Yet to delay is to delude.

NEWER THEORIES ABOUT INTELLECTUAL DEVELOPMENT

Guilford's Structure-of-Intellect (SI)

Perhaps one of the most comprehensive attempts to establish a theory of intelligence and to define the factors of intelligence has been accomplished by

Guilford.[1] His structure-of-intellect (SI) model provides for 120 possible factors, of which around 80 have been identified. Although Guilford considers each factor to be distinct, certain classifications can be made to facilitate an understanding of their relationship to each other. He has perceived three different categories: *content* (categorizing the general varieties of information available to an individual); *operation* (classifying the specific processes or operations that the individual uses in order to organize the raw items of information confronting him); and *product* (categorizing the ways an individual organizes the information available to him).[2]

Guilford's model provides us with a dynamically different way of viewing the intellect and its development. It causes us to become less fixed on the strength of the ability to learn (that is, how much ability does an individual have) and more concerned with the factors of intelligence and their operations in intellectual development. When one examines the many varieties of intellectual patterns that can emerge in the mental growth of an individual, one can readily respect the complexities of the mental processes and the distinctly unique and individual nature of their development.

Guilford's structure-of-intellect model provides a base (or at least one point of view) for recognizing the *developmental* aspects of intellectual growth. His theory not only identifies those factors he associates with the intellect, but describes how these factors relate and how they are interdependent in the development and use of the intellect. The implications of his theory for the teaching-learning process (and for variant learning in particular), for the mental testing movement, and for the future of developmental guidance are vast.

Jean Piaget

Jean Piaget is one of the most prominent of the contemporary developmental psychologists. His theoretical views on the growth and development of the child are complex and his formulations difficult to understand. A great deal of the interest in Piaget is very recent (beginning in the fifties), and his ideas are just beginning to infiltrate educational thought in the United States. His contributions remain uncertain, but his impact appears promising.

Since Piaget had an early and continuing interest in biology, it seems entirely appropriate that his conceptions of intellectual development relate biological and psychological mechanisms. Piaget emphasizes the importance of early motor activities as the first indications of intellectual functioning and the basis for the developing mental processes. The significant aspect of

[1] J. P. Guilford, *The Nature of Human Intelligence* (New York: McGraw-Hill, 1967).
[2] *Ibid.,* pp. 61–65.

this concept is its emphasis on the early stages of sensory-motor functioning as a part of—a period in—the *intellectual* development.

Clearly this conflicts with the notion of a fixed intelligence, incapable of environmental influence. It rejects the frequent separation of *motor* and *mind*. Essentially, Piaget's developmental concept of cognitive growth emphasizes that the formal patterns of thinking and reasoning (what we are gradually coming to refer to as the "higher thought processes") develop from experience with concrete, overt activities.

You may recall in Chapter Three the summary of the four periods that Piaget identifies in the development of the child: the sensori-motor, the pre-operational, the concrete operations, and the formal operations. Piaget's concepts of intellectual development are most relevant, since they speak to the developmental nature of the intellectual processes. His ideas about mental growth, of a progressively emerging and developing capacity to think, are contrary to our common use of intelligence test measures (the IQ score) that establish learning expectations and limitations for the students in our schools. There is a real challenge for the educative process when we consider the dynamic of teaching for thinking. It expands the responsibility of the school beyond that of helping the student to accumulate facts and to develops kills. It involves them directly and responsibly in the mental maturation of the individual. This would necessitate more than the traditional programs emphasizing mental discipline, memory, and performance. It mandates an active, experiential program that favors nurturing the natural development of the mind.

In the development of the individual, according to Piaget, two functions remain continuous and central: *assimilation* and *accommodation*. These functions occur within the internal structure of the individual and involve taking in new situations (assimilation) and accounting for needed changes (accommodation). Assimilation involves receiving new information from the senses and incorporating these new bits into the already existing structure of knowledge. Accommodation is the internal modification of existing structures making the individual more able to adjust to these new conditions. The two functions operate sympathetically for the benefit of the self, the entire process being termed *adaptation.*

Piaget postulates that these two functions contribute to a constant process of input, feedback, and internal reconstruction that causes the growth and change in the behavioral structures. An individual, in moving through the periods and stages described by Piaget, develops his intellectual processes as he interacts with his environment, assimilates through his senses the constant flow of stimuli impinging upon him, and through accommodation modifies his own structure of knowledge.

Such functions are not fully activated in passive learning situations nor are they truly operative where memory storage is the prime mental activity. In fact, these situations tend to stifle the thinking operations and to deflect individual interest and motivation. When students speak of irrelevancy they are referring to learning content and tasks that have little or no meaning to them. For learning to have meaning, it must activate the process of adaptation and in some way cause the student to have to deal with the incoming stimuli within his existing structure of knowledge.

CONCEPTS OF INTELLIGENCE AND EDUCATION

One of the more powerful and consistently reported concepts on the nature of intelligence is that intelligence is developed in a gradual but specific and defined manner. A child does not simply acquire new and larger amounts of information as he grows, thereby increasing his storehouse of knowledge. As he grows his thought processes *themselves* change. Although children seem to move from the simple and concrete to the more complex and abstract in a developmental pattern, the structure of the mental processing is uniquely individual, depending on hereditary factors and environmental experiences.

Teachers have been prone to think of a child's intellectual capacity as a fixed and static entity. They have tended to recognize the influence of hereditary and environmental forces on intellectual capacity, but they have seldom considered the influence of *their environmental stimulation* and the experiences they afford. After all, teachers holding a fixed, unitary view of intelligence (and an IQ to prove it) tend to think of the environment as more a product of the home and the community than of the classroom.

The newer ideas that we are far too slow in comprehending and incorporating into educational practice indicate that we need to focus far more attention on the multiple and differential aspects of intelligence and the processes involved in its human expression. The cultivation of intellectual processes should lead educators to deal more directly with the ways children think and process their information.

It is time schools questioned *seriously* their continued allegiance to mental tests that provide an IQ. While this has become a means of making the teacher secure (somewhat like giving a baby his blanket), can he or she continue to deal with the varied aspects of the intellectual growth of children with such limited and restricting information? These instruments are limited not only in the factors they measure (emphasizing memory and cognition as defined in the SI model), but they often require intellectual manipulations the child has not developed.

While many schools have abandoned intelligence testing in the kindergarten and primary grades (on the basis that the results were not reliable), this has stemmed more from their dissatisfaction with the test results than from knowledge about intellectual development. There is no reason for continuing to use the available intelligence tests unless we can validate their time and the cost in better educative practice.

Much of our learning focus is on the process of recall. We have been concerned with knowledge input and with what Guilford calls *replicative recall:* (". . . brings back stored information in its original form, or essentially so, in response to cues in connection with which it was committed to memory storage. . . .")[3] There is little question but that the school curriculum and teaching methodologies are not offering the variety of mental processing experiences that cultivate and nourish all the factors of the intellect. Schools are decidedly overemphasizing memory and convergent production at the expense of more experiences that engage divergent production or evaluation operations.

There is little doubt that most children's intellectual experiences in school afford a narrow range of thinking processes, and their learning consequences have been rote and repetitive (drill). This may be an unfair indictment of an educational system that has made it possible for children to read and write and speak fluently, of a system that has increasingly improved its ability to teach "skills" and to transmit "content."

Guilford also speaks of *transfer recall*. He defines transfer recall as ". . . retrieval of information instigated by cues in connection with which the information was not committed to memory storage."[4] This implies learning experiences that draw upon and involve what was referred to in Chapter Four as the *inner* process of human learning; as the *continuing* nature of learning whereby the increasing complexity of personal meaning and the many and varied transfer manipulations lead the learner in many directions, not just one; as the *individual* or personal character of learning is reflected in *variant* learning.

It has become a cliché to talk about the increasing rapidity and unpredictability of societal change. Education is faced with the complex dilemma of trying to prepare young people for a future world that is changing at an incredibly fast pace. Our advances not only in science and technology but, more recently, in the human condition (affluence, values, individuality) have challenged the existing structure. Our task in education becomes increasingly clear each year: to prepare youth for the *process of change* itself. We can no longer effect procedures that help a person to understand and adjust to changes from *this* to *that* but to understand and adjust to—to live with—*the process.*

[3] *Ibid.,* p. 303.
[4] *Ibid.,* p. 303.

In a world, then, comprised of so much uncertainty and change we need to move (or at least begin to make the effort) toward an educative process that allows an individual to assimilate new ideas and concepts and accommodate them in his own internal mental structure.

Since the essence of living is actually the product of our intellectual development, to focus on the development of the mental processes of thinking and learning is an ever more challenging task for education.

Teaching for Thinking

One practical example of an attempt to translate the theory of mental processes into practice is the recent publication *Teaching for Thinking*.[5] The authors state,

Thinking is *a way* of learning. Thinking is one way of inquiring for facts, and if the thinking is to some purpose, the facts so found will be relevant to that same purpose. We then have purposeful learning, and a person is maturing when his activities are disciplined by purpose.[6]

They elaborate fifteen thinking operations that can be encouraged by teachers, and provide practical suggestions at both the elementary and secondary school level for incorporating these operations into the school curriculum. In encouraging their use at *all* school levels, they are attempting to promote teaching practices that will contribute to the development of the child's mental processing capabilities. Their approach is based on the following belief:

The concept of *higher mental processes* may suggest to some that the mental processes operative in high school youth are quite different from those carried on by children in the elementary school. When one finds, however, that nearly all of these operations may be observed in the very early grades of elementary school, it raises a question about what is meant by higher mental processes. It probably means processes which distinguish human beings from lower orders of animals. It does not mean uniquely different processes for different age levels in the development towards maturity. Children in the elementary school, adolescents in our secondary schools, and the older students in our colleges all need continuing practice in these thinking operations.[7]

[5] Louis E. Raths, Arthur Jonas, Arnold Rothstein, and Selma Wasserman, *Teaching for Thinking: Theory and Application* (Columbus, Ohio: Charles E. Merrill, 1967).
[6] *Ibid.*, p. 3.
[7] *Ibid.*, pp. 29–30.

The fifteen thinking operations they describe and apply are comparing, summarizing, observing, classifying, interpreting, criticizing, looking for assumptions, imagining, collecting and organizing data, hypothesizing, applying facts and principles in new situations, decision-making, designing projects or investigations, coding, and coding other papers. The authors do not imply that these constitute all the thinking operations. This represents an attempt to translate psychological theory to educational practice. We need more such efforts and we need to test them in our schools.

Teaching the individual how to think is akin to teaching him to learn. Helping the student to learn how to process information, that is, how to think, is a way of teaching that will extend the usefulness of the educational experiences for an individual—perhaps for a lifetime. Such teaching can survive facts that become out of date or beliefs or values that become outmoded. In an age of "planned obsolescence" and change, a person needs an education that can help him to live and move with the times. His thinking abilities can help him to examine the issues and events of his time and to seek the adaptations they may demand.

Much of the theory about intelligence that has been presented in this section does not refute individual differences in the ability to think or learn. It goes well beyond these differences emphasizing the aspects of an individual's ability to think—to "process the data" that he receives. It encourages an educative process that enhances his ability to employ the many different thinking operations. It strives for an education that permits man, after his formal years of schooling, to continue to know and to grow because he knows how to learn.

CREATIVITY

Creativity has long interested teachers and other educators. But it is only within the last decade that the research and conceptualization have gained sufficient momentum to have an impact on the schools.

For a good many years creativity was narrowly construed as a distinct trait or ability. A person either had "it" or he didn't; he was creative or he wasn't. Another prevalent view, more recent in origin, explains creativity as a part of giftedness and associates it with the ability to learn. Most recently these and other earlier ideas have been modified to a point where there is considerable acceptance of the principle that all individuals have some degree of creativity and that creativity is associated with the development of the mental processes. Creativity, in this sense, has become a quality to be developed rather than a quality innately possessed.

David Ausubel represents those who still view creativity in its more narrow and restricted interpretation.[8] He deplores the broader concept of creativity, indicating that it equates creativity with general intelligence, which is "continuously and normally distributed." Ausubel feels that creativity exists in all humans to some degree but emphasizes that the creative individual is one who is capable of unusual, original, and unique discoveries of a kind that have never been made before. Creativity, by his definition, would be in accord with the more traditional descriptions of a talent or unique ability in which the individual excels. One either has this kind of creativity or he hasn't. Under this definition there seems little for the teaching-learning process to do except to encourage the talented and to provide them with whatever opportunities the school can offer.

E. Paul Torrance, on the other hand, is one of the exponents of a concept that conceives of creativity in a general and universal sense. Torrance speaks of the creative growth of a person, distinguishing the talented as highly creative. All children, therefore, have creative potential which the educative process can develop.

One of his earlier publications, *Guiding Creative Talent,* discussed creative thinking abilities, the creative personality, and creative development.[9] Torrance links classroom practices and teacher behaviors closely to the development of creativity in children, showing how everyday life, in school and out, affects the creative development of the child. For example, he cites societal "sanctions against divergency," showing how these can inhibit creativeness.

Whether or not one accepts this broadly-based approach, aside from the semantics of defining creativity and the scientific questions of research, it is necessary that teachers recognize that children do *threaten* them with "way out" ideas and that individuals do not share their ideas for *fear* of ridicule. Situations such as these all too often characterize the American classroom, where convergent-conforming thinking is rewarded and divergent-creative thinking is punished. In essence, Torrance encourages teaching for creativity, using what many would term a mental hygiene approach.

Guilford, whose SI model was examined earlier in the chapter, identified the "divergent production" operation, an operation he relates to creative thinking.[10] While he is extremely enthusiastic about the possibilities of *relating* these two concepts, he is equally cautious of *equating* them. The divergent production operation involves abilities (fluency, flexibility, originality, elaboration) that are closely associated with creativity.

[8] David P. Ausubel, "Creativity, General Creative Abilities, and the Creative Individual," *Psychology in the Schools* 1:344–347, October 1964.

[9] E. Paul Torrance, *Guiding Creative Talent* (Engewood Cliffs, N.J.: Prentice-Hall, 1962).

[10] Guilford, *op. cit.,* Chapter 6.

Thus, while Guilford's SI model appears to contribute to earlier descriptions of creativity, tending toward isolation of the creative "ability," it actually extends the concept to include a wide variety of mental ability combinations and permutations. Further, if creativity is so closely allied with the thinking processes, it should be possible to foster creativity in the classrooms. This would support those who would encourage the development of creativity through the classroom, using techniques that focus on the development of the thought processes—particularly, insofar as creative thinking is concerned, those utilizing divergent production.

Wallach and Kogan, dissatisfied with the experimental models of earlier investigations, chose to explore the continuum of creativity, including as many possible combinations of creativity and intelligence as possible.[11] They describe what they term an "associative concept of creativity."[12] Basically, creativity is the use of one's behavioral repertoire in an associational process of generating new and unique ideas.

Their model is most interesting since it acknowledges factors of intellect but emphasizes the process of thinking. They explain that while one must draw on his intellectual reserves, the important considerations are the atmosphere provided and the time allocated for the creative process to occur. They state,

. . . it is quite possible that more frequent associations will occur earlier and more unique associations later in a sequence, so that individuals who are able to produce a larger number of associations also should be able to produce a greater number of unique ones.[13]

To really distinguish the creative individual, time should be sufficiently long and conditions sufficiently relaxed to allow the individual to generate responses that are less stereotyped and usual but more unique. Thus in their study ample time was provided for the development of associations and considerable effort was expended to insure a relaxed atmosphere.

The creativity research, while inconclusive, points to a need to consider more seriously than we have the *process* aspects of creativity and the environment or *conditions* in which this occurs. While children think in differing modes, they do think creatively. Thus the process of creative thinking appears to be established. It apparently can be fostered. It appears to be an extremely important facet in the development of the intellect and in the evolvement and refinement of the mental processes employed in thinking and learning.

[11] Michael Wallach and Nathan Kogan, *Modes of Thinking in Young Children* (New York: Holt, Rinehart and Winston, 1965).
[12] *Ibid.,* pp. 13–20.
[13] *Ibid.,* p. 14.

CURIOSITY

Psychologists have long pondered over concepts of curiosity. They have attempted to isolate it as a human factor, to equate it with creativity, and to relate it to motivation. Some have even proposed theories of curiosity. Although we need to continue to examine the concept of curiosity in scientific ways, the classroom teacher must utilize whatever knowledge she has about it in her daily contacts with youth. She can learn to recognize it, to encourage it, and to use it as a means of helping children to learn, and more importantly, to *want* to learn. In this very brief mention of curiosity I wish to accomplish two purposes: to indicate the importance of this concept in the development of the mental processes, and to mention a few of my own notions about it and their relevance to the teaching-learning process.

The *wonder* of a child—of any person for that matter—is one of our most pleasant and delightful experiences. The mystery of the unknown, the secret in a surprise, the enigma of a riddle, or the anticipation of a first day at school all tap in one way or another that human quality we have labeled curiosity. Our need to know, our urge to explore, our desire to seek answers are ways whereby we evidence our curiosity.

The child who ponders, who wonders about his world and the people in it, and who asks his teacher about these things only to be turned off with a sharp "that's not important now" experiences dissatisfaction, perhaps discouragement, until something soon sets him to pondering and wondering again.

Curiosity is a natural and normal experience. It has the element of inquiry that triggers action. In a school classroom it could cause children to want to learn. Teachers often say that some children don't want to learn, usually qualifying this by pointing to some specific task or skill. Yet curiosity can be a key to learning. It can be one of our strongest motivators. Our colorful books, our diverse materials, our elaborate instructional strategies as well as our techniques and tricks to motivate the learner, assuredly have a place in the teaching-learning process. They are "lures" to initiate wonder and exploration, to whet the curiosities of children, if they are used appropriately and timely. They direct a child to a learning situation.

Perhaps where we have failed with our materials is between the naturally curious expressions of a child—the spontaneity of wanting to know and the awesome but challenging task of discovery—and the presumed curiosity in the fixed and established behaviors to be learned in the classroom. While it is quite possible that some children, part of the time, do not want to work or study, I can hardly believe that they do not want to know. The impatient, enthusiastic, indeed curious, youngster awaits eagerly his first day in kindergarten. He is more than willing to explore the mysteries and marvels of living.

However curiosity is eventually identified we know it to exist in the everyday expressions of adolescents. We need only to listen, to hear, to lead them in ways that will satisfy them now, yet encourage them to move further in their quest to learn.

The research dealing with the concept of curiosity, while difficult to apply to general educational practice, tends to indicate that curiosity and motivation are interrelated elements in human behavior. There is some evidence that some affective states such as fear, anxiety, and frustration inhibit curiosity, making any attempts to employ curiosity in the motivation of learners futile and unsuccessful.

IMPLICATIONS FOR SECONDARY
SCHOOL GUIDANCE

So much of our newer knowledge about intelligence and learning challenges our educational practice, especially our views on the appraisal and assessment of intellectual capacity. Unless we can recognize and accept these differences in degree and direction, any efforts to improve or modify the teaching-learning process will be fruitless. Let's not believe for one minute that we need to reject all that we have learned about or to jettison all that we do in education. We have effected many positive practices and we are continuing, albeit slowly, to make improvements.

What the newer concepts about intelligence and the development of the intellect seem to imply is a change in some of our basic approaches and in certain of our basic assumptions about mental growth. These vary widely not only among school systems but among school personnel. The reconstruction of the teaching-learning process to incorporate these ideas and attitudes has to begin from these bases. We know that individual differences in ability to learn exist among people. And it has been helpful to know about these differences in a general way. What seems to be implied in the newer ideas is a reduction in our emphasis on the differences in individual abilities to learn and a magnification of our accent on the thinking processes used in learning.

As Bruner has so aptly stated in concluding one of his discourses on cognitive growth, "What is significant about the growth of mind in the child is to what degree it depends not upon capacity but upon the unlocking of capacity by techniques that come from exposure to the specialized environment of a culture."[14]

[14] Jerome S. Bruner, "The Course of Cognitive Growth," *American Psychologist* 19:14, January 1964.

We find that the secondary school years correspond with the development of the so-called "higher thought processes" or with that period, as Piaget has labeled it, of formal operations. The individual is able to think more abstractly and more symbolically. He is able to interpret and synthesize more adroitly. It is on the development and improvement of the adolescent's ability to process information and ideas, *to think,* that our educative process should focus.

This, then, represents a shift in emphasis and a change in direction. We are changing direction—or at least altering it—when we begin to facilitate the student's thinking operations by emphasizing those that are central in solving problems and making decisions (interpreting, hypothesizing, generalizing). We are shifting our emphasis when we help him employ these in deciding whether or not to take biology or geometry as opposed to making a decision that rests primarily on an appraisal of his general scholastic ability. We are implementing these shifts where they really count, in the teaching-learning process and in its ultimate effect on individual learning-maturation, when teachers incorporate these thinking processes in daily classroom methodologies and establish subject matter objectives that enrich their development.

Student evaluations and appraisals of their mental growth are often based on their capacity to learn and on evaluations of their achievement in the learning process. The sources of this information are very narrow and limited, consisting mainly of standardized test measures and school grades.

Unfortunately, school marks are all too often simply appraisals of the student's ability to store and recall information. While subject matter tests may require a number of thinking processes, there is little to validate how a youngster thinks so long as he is able to respond correctly—to check the "right" answer. Under these conditions it is little wonder that many students become discouraged and disillusioned with themselves as well as with the educative process.

The developmental counselor can help in shifting the teaching-learning process to accommodate an emphasis on the thinking operations. By working with teachers he can help plan learning episodes and experiences that will foster mental growth. He can work toward helping both teachers and students to view learning in its more encompassing forms. He can help them to expand the base of their learning appraisals so that they include not only the capacity to learn but the operations used.

One immediate implication of this shift, insofar as the individual student is concerned, is the opportunity afforded the individual to examine his growth developmentally. It provides hope and encouragement where the present system only implores him to exert more effort—to "try harder"—in an approach that emphasizes competition with others rather than himself.

We are moving rapidly to the understanding that our secondary school curriculum may need a major overhaul. We are beginning to see more clearly how we can provide for the mental growth and development of the individual as opposed to filling his warehouse. As knowledge expands in all subject matter areas we may be forced to this position, since the burgeoning content of the curriculum is already unwieldy both for the student and the teacher. There is a limit to what can be covered contentwise and the decisions to include or exclude material are becoming increasingly difficult.

Further evidence of a limited view of mental maturation can be noted in the assistance provided students in assessing their mental abilities—a practice long accorded to the guidance effort and one that has been implemented largely in educational planning (for high school and for higher education). Scholastic ability, achievement, interest, and multifactor or aptitude test data comprise the assortment of test profiles that must be synthesized by the adolescent in making these decisions.

Some schools provide the student with an extensive analysis of these data. Others tend to use only those scores which are considered most helpful in making a particular choice. These appraisals of ability relate to capacity primarily. Thus a student learns about his measured capacity to learn (intelligence) or about certain factors such as his verbal reasoning, numerical ability, or abstract reasoning.

While these are helpful, the newer conceptions of mental growth offer opportunities to work more expansively with individual "abilities." Placed in the context of learning-maturation, an individual can be provided assistance in exploring his mental maturation, which could readily include how he thinks and learns. It could help him in assessing how he processes information—how he employs the various thinking operations.

Specifically, guidance as a means of helping youth in decision making and problem solving has its own processes which require that they apply these thinking operations in dealing with the choices and problems in their own lives. In this way, students become really involved in examining their mental development and their perceptions of it. In the past, students have relied on these outside measures and in some cases have attributed more meaning to these results than they deserve.

Traditional guidance programs have tended to follow a standard line of operation emphasizing progress in content mastery (achievement) in relation to ability (intelligence), allowing for some consideration of individual aptitudes (multifactor or aptitude). While standardized tests have made it possible to differentiate ability to learn among the school population and while refinements in methods for reporting results have been effected (profile sheets, explanatory pamphlets, etc.), the appraisal and evaluation of mental capacities remain relatively restricted and narrow.

Although we have promise of real breakthroughs in understanding mental growth, we have far to go. We have been very carefully and repeatedly schooled in the dangers of moving too fast with an idea. As a result, I fear we fail to move at all. I would urge that school counselors, in consort with their colleagues in other areas of education, move forward with efforts that will produce classrooms where children are encouraged to learn how to learn.

That such changes are already underway is of little doubt. Leaders in curriculum development and instructional supervision are encouraging new approaches and practices. Guidance, too, can play a major part in helping to foster changes that will enhance the mental growth of the adolescent. A number of possible ways for the developmental counselor to become involved are suggested in the sections that follow.

The Counseling Functions

(1) Counseling with children individually or in small groups to help them understand better the modes of thinking they employ in approaching the learning tasks of the school and the choices and decisions in their own living.

(2) Counseling with individual children to help them relate the cognitive and affective aspects of their learning experiences.

(3) Counseling with individuals to help them examine and assess their own intellectual development in relation to their individual styles of thinking and learning and their use of various thinking operations.

The Consulting Functions

(1) Assisting teachers in becoming better acquainted with a variety of thinking operations (observing, summarizing, interpreting, hypothesizing) and in engaging these processes more adequately in the teaching-learning process.

(2) Helping teachers to understand better the nature of intellectual development in the adolescent and the individual nature of its expression in thinking and learning.

(3) Helping teachers to examine their individual approach to the teaching-learning process and to assess their style in relation to its potential for fostering mental maturation in adolescents and for developing the various types of thinking processes.

(4) Helping teachers to assimilate and accommodate new ideas and technologies in ways that will facilitate thinking and learning and contribute to the intellectual development of the adolescent.

The Coordinating Functions

(1) helping to plan and conduct in-service meetings and workshops to help teachers understand and initiate new or different ways of fostering the development of the thinking operations in the classroom.

(2) Planning information meetings and seminars for parents to help them understand better the processes of mental growth in the adolescent years and ways in which they can enhance this development.

(3) Developing case study materials and other demonstration devices to use in exploring with teachers ways of accommodating the mental growth of individual learners and of dealing with individual styles of learning.

(4) Reporting to school personnel and to parents new ideas and research findings on all aspects of intellectual development and related areas (creativity, curiosity, motivation) offering, when appropriate, suggestions for implementing these ideas in the classroom and the home.

SUGGESTED READING

BRUNER, JEROME S., "The Course of Cognitive Growth," *American Psychologist* 19:1–15, January 1964.

FLAVELL, JOHN A., *The Developmental Psychology of Jean Piaget* (Princeton, N.J.: Van Nostrand, 1963).

GALE, RAYMOND F., *Developmental Behavior* (New York: The Macmillan Company, 1969), Chapters 10 and 11.

GUILFORD, J. P., *The Nature of Human Intelligence* (New York: McGraw-Hill, 1967).

RATHS, LOUIS E.; JONAS, ARTHUR; ROTHSTEIN, ARNOLD; and WASSERMAN, SELMA, *Teaching For Thinking* (Columbus, Ohio: Charles E. Merrill, 1967).

TWELVE

SOCIAL MATURATION: LEARNING

TO SOCIALIZE AND VALUE

The social maturation of individuals has always been a school concern but, in many systems, it has not always been considered a responsibility. More frequently it is viewed as concomitant to education rather than an integral part of the educative process. No one has really denied the importance of the social development of the student though those who argue for a return to an emphasis on the 3 R's would treat it quite differently. Educators express their interest and involvement in the socialization of youth in a variety of ways. When they speak of social interaction, peer group culture, social maturity, popularity, or leadership potential, they are, in one way or another, referring to or describing an aspect of the process of socialization. As we learn more and more about education, and particularly about human learning, we tend less and less to consider it a by-product of the educative process or an entity to be considered apart from it. We have reached a point where we are better able to view it as a significant component of the teaching-learning process and to integrate it rather than to isolate it. To gear it to the educative process means, of course, that we can examine its discrete nature. That is part of our purpose in this chapter—to look separately at the process of socialization and to view its integration in the education of the adolescent. The involvement of the teacher and the school counselor rounds out our intention.

THE PROCESS OF SOCIALIZATION

Socialization, the complicated process whereby children learn to interact successfully with adults and peers in their immediate environment, begins with birth. During these early years before an individual goes to school his world is a gradually expanding but restricted one. At first it is in the environment of his home, from his immediate family, that his orientation to social interaction is provided. Through his family he learns to communicate with others and to control and to be controlled by others. As he grows older, he moves from his home to his community—from his family to others outside the family unit. The individual's introduction to the world outside his home is a gradual one. He leaves his home unaccompanied, to visit at the home of a friend, to go to the store, or to attend a party. With his family he attends meetings, goes shopping, or visits relatives and friends. As his circle of experiences widens he learns more about communicating with others. He learns through all these experiences the basic patterns of social conduct. His social development is well underway by the time he enters school. Lest we confuse social development and socialization, let's pause here, as the child is ready for school, and examine the meaning of socialization.

The Meaning of Socialization

Elkin has defined socialization as ". . . *the process by which someone learns the ways of a given society or social group so that he can function within it.* Socialization includes both the learning and internalizing of appropriate patterns, values, and feelings."[1] McCandless, in treating social and emotional development, defines socialization as ". . . a learning-teaching process that, when successful, results in the human organism's moving from its infant state of helpless but total egocentricity to its ideal adult state of sensible conformity coupled with independent creativity."[2] The latter definition reflects the psychological aspects, the Elkin definition emphasizes the social. Both need to be considered.

The social aspect of socialization involves the environmental, the external, and the transmission of societal mores as they have been established. It involves exposure to the "givens." It is concerned with the facts, the "knowns," about the way a society has chosen to develop. In this sense then it is concerned with the past. In this way it is static in that the emphasis is on having to learn the "oughts" and the "rights." But it is actually more than learning how to respond and how to behave. It is more than learning right from wrong (though these controls do exist) and good from bad.

The psychological aspect of socialization is concerned with the individ-

---

[1] Frederick Elkin, *The Child and Society* (New York: Random House, 1960), p. 4.

[2] Boyd R. McCandless, *Children: Behavior and Development* (New York: Holt, Rinehart and Winston, 1967), p. 421.

ual and the internal. It is that part of the process wherein the individual (his preferences and values) and his environment (in this instance the culture and its mores, including whatever controls these may include) seek balance, making it possible for the individual to express his uniqueness yet exist in a satisfying way within the limits established by his culture. Socialization, then, to the degree that one believes man has freedom of choice, is a matter of choosing what one will believe (and value) and how he will behave, making these decisions within the cultural standards in such a way as to provide for his personal needs and satisfactions and for his social utility.

Inherent in the whole socialization process is the matter of individual freedom of choice. Socialization could be equated with conformity; with the maintenance of the status quo. Conformity is a form of social control. It rests heavily on individual obedience or acquiescence. Conformity does not necessarily imply acceptance. An individual can be told to conform or else (dictated behavior); or he can be cajoled into conformity—both representing processes of socializing a person against his will. He can be moved to social compliance for any number of social or psychological reasons (needs for approval, inclusion, etc.). Such compliance is usually the decision of the individual—either by reason or by default. It is to be hoped that the process of socialization would allow for sufficient individuality as to allow a society (or a culture component) to incorporate new ways of believing and behaving. The growth of a society is dependent on the introduction of new ideas and the reconstruction of older ones. A society to continue must be able to integrate new thinking and new ways of doing and being. These flow from individuals who dare to be different, who are not afraid to risk, who are willing to explore the unknowns. It would be sad not to allow this freedom. We must be careful that we do not equate socialization and conformity and that we do not confine the socialization process to indoctrination.

Socialization and Internalization

Socialization has both its social (external) and its psychological (internal) elements. The cognitive aspects—that is, the knowledge and understandings of a society—would be somewhat more readily transmitted if they could be disassociated from the affective elements. This is almost the same as saying we could socialize faster and with more certainty if we did not have to be concerned in the process with the inner dimensions of an individual's learning. But we do. It is through our understanding and acceptance of the internalization continuum that we are able to encompass the psychological dimension. The *Taxonomy of Educational Objectives, Handbook II: Affec-*

tive Domain[3] describes the internalization process in five hierarchical categories or levels: (1) *receiving* (awareness and attentiveness); (2) *responding* (responsiveness and involvement); (3) *valuing* (acceptance and commitment); (4) *organization* (integration of the phenomenon with others previously accepted); and (5) *characterization* (one's total beliefs [one's philosophy] that guide his behavior and characterize his being).

While Krathwohl et al. have developed this continuum primarily to assist teachers in establishing and classifying instructional objectives, we can use these levels to understand the steps in individual internalization.[4] The first level, *receiving,* consists of three subcategories: (1.1) *awareness,* (1.2) *willingness to receive,* and (1.3) *controlled or selected attention.* These subcategories represent movement into the internalization process although the individual can stop attending to the phenomenon at any of these points. Awareness is represented best by an individual's conscious recognition of an object, idea or situation. Recognizing it—his willingness to give it his attention—does not mean that he accepts it. From this he moves to selected attention, meaning that he can selectively give it his attention, that he can sort it out from among other incoming stimuli.

The second level, *responding,* also contains three subcategories: (2.1) *acquiescence in responding,* (2.2) *willingness to respond,* and (2.3) *satisfaction in response.* This level, of course, presupposes the first and establishes a higher level of internalization. Acquiescence in responding involves continued attending to the phenomenon although it infers some individual reserve in commitment to it and suggests that pressure or threat could be applied to achieve response. The second subcategory, willingness to respond, represents voluntary commitment and is based primarily on the individual's choice or desire to respond. Beyond this, satisfaction in response denotes not only willingness but pleasure and enjoyment in responding. Until this point there is little if any individual involvement of an emotional nature. The authors of the *Taxonomy* make special note that this satisfaction, in the form of an emotional component, frequently occurs here but that it could be delayed until a higher level. Thus one would not necessarily experience or need to experience satisfaction at this point for the internalization process to continue. Obviously if it does, it would add to the individual zeal with which the third level is approached.

Valuing, a topic we shall discuss in detail later in this chapter, repre-

[3] David Krathwohl, Benjamin Bloom, and Bertram Masia, *Taxonomy of Educational Objectives, Handbook II, Affective Domain* (New York: David McKay, 1964), pp. 95–175. Used by permission of David McKay Company, Inc.

[4] The following descriptions of these five levels and the subcategories of each have been adapted from the *Taxonomy of Educational Objectives, Handbook II, Affective Domain, op. cit.,* pp. 176–185.

sents the third level—also with three subcategories: (3.1) *acceptance of a value,* (3.2) *preference for a value,* and (3.3) *commitment.* At this level, we might say that the individual is getting serious about his relationship with the phenomenon. He has received it and responded to it. This phase actually represents the process of committing himself to it—at least for a period of exploration and testing. In the first instance, acceptance of a value represents a willingness to be identified with it and a tentative commitment to it.

Preference for a value goes beyond acceptance but falls short of certain commitment. Commitment, the highest level in this category, represents individual conviction and certainty. These three categories describe the process whereby *an* attitude, *a* belief, *an* idea, *a* value is internalized (or formed). Over a period of time an individual may internalize a number of specific attitudes, beliefs, ideas, or values. These are a part of an individual's internal frame of reference. They are sufficiently internalized, to the point of being valued, that they can be used to guide the behavior of an individual. In situations where he is caused to draw upon his beliefs and attitudes, he will probably use them consistently and consequently exhibit his valuing in his behavior.

The fourth level, *organization,* is concerned with the integration of these separate values, beliefs, ideas, or attitudes. This step involves the individual in the complexities of establishing relationships among those things he has internalized thus far, and of interrelating them in a configuration which represents a more complex organization of values and ideas to which he has committed himself. As Krathwohl et al. state, "Thus necessity arises for (a) the organization of the values into a system, (b) the determination of the interrelationships among them, and (c) the establishment of the dominant and pervasive ones."[5]

The first subcategory, (4.1) *conceptualization of a value,* permits the individual to test, in an abstract or symbolic way, a value (or a belief or an attitude) in reference to others which he may hold. Obviously, as he becomes aware of values that are in contradiction or that conflict with others he may be considering, he will need to reformulate his value complex, eliminating those that he can no longer accept.

The other and higher subcategory, (4.2) *organization of a value system,* is represented by the individual's continuing search for internal consistency and harmony. This involves integrating and ordering values and establishing these relationships into a system of values that will help him to direct his life and to deal with his life situations. This is represented in individual learning-maturation as one seeks both personal and social bal-

[5] Krathwohl et al., *op. cit.,* p. 182.

ance. The inconsistencies and incongruities that an individual encounters in this conceptualizing and organizing represent the conflicts and anxieties that he experiences in this phase of his internalization. Throughout an individual's life, this organized value complex is constantly being realigned and reevaluated. For the adult, then, this represents change. For the adolescent in process of establishing his value complex, this represents learning-maturation.

The highest and last level, *characterization by a value or value complex,* is best described by Krathwohl et al., who say,

At this level of internalization the values already have a place in the individual's value hierarchy, are organized into some kind of internally consistent system, have controlled the behavior of the individual for a sufficient time that he has adapted to behaving this way; and an evocation of the behavior no longer arouses emotion or affect except when the individual is threatened or challenged.
The individual acts consistently in accordance with the values he has internalized at this level, and our concern is to indicate two things: (a) [5.1 *generalized set*] the generalization of this control to so much of the individual's behavior that he is described and characterized as a person by these pervasive controlling tendencies, and (b) [5.2 *characterization*] the integration of these beliefs, ideas, and attitudes into a total philosophy or world view.[6]

This last level represents the final stage of internalization when the value complex is set. While an individual can and does change, such change often must begin with this characterization of self. The adolescent is striving for this identity; he has rarely achieved it. Thus the secondary school years and the manner in which the internalization process is attended to in the educative process during these years is crucial. Adolescents are intimately involved in this process. In this sense to say that they are in transition from childhood to adulthood is quite accurate.

When we consider the psychological aspects of socialization, with specific reference to the internalization of values, ideas, beliefs, and attitudes, we are considering both the society and the individual and the individual's resolution of these in the form of a social identity. Helping adolescents develop a social identity, then, is not peripheral to learning in the secondary school; rather, it is integral, allied with all the other facets of adolescent growth.

Socialization and the School

Now that we have examined the meaning of socialization and the process of internalization as it contributes to it, let us examine the school as a pri-

---

[6] *Ibid.,* p. 184.

mary agent in the development of social identity. In the school the individual student becomes involved with many people who really count in his life. The importance of peers, the pressures they incur, the responses they induce, and the controls they inflict, have a deep and abiding influence on the individual and his behavior. He no longer has the degree of freedom which he earlier experienced and he finds himself in a constant state of adapting from one situation to another, from one person to another.

No teacher will deny the effect of just one child, a group of children, or the total group on the thought and action of any given individual in a class. In addition the child now finds other adults who can and do direct his life, who can reward or punish him, who can accept or reject him. From the time he is greeted in the morning by the bus driver, teacher or friend, until he departs for home, the school as an agent in the socialization process is at work.

Helping teachers to realize the magnitude of the socialization process, not only in its broader aspects as reflected in the teacher's objectives, in the content of lessons, in class participation or group interaction, but also in the more subtle and indirect aspects of the child's experiencing, is a formidable task. Much of the process is teacher-induced and we cannot ignore the actual influence of "sit down," "be quiet," "stand in line," "that's fine," "good boy" and other verbal or nonverbal conditioners.

These very real day-to-day experiences of students are often a great deal more influential in the process of socialization than are the make-believe activities that comprise a large portion of curriculum exposures. We presume to expose the student to the heritage of our culture and to inculcate the democratic ideals of our society. We build our curriculum toward these goals. Yet, under the guise of group control, school safety, or social "good," *we tend to promote these goals in a most highly totalitarian, dictatorial environment.*

Our classroom discussions may speak of tolerance and love, yet our actual classroom practices may be discriminatory and indoctrinating. These attitudes are not always obvious. Teachers are often unaware of their attitude toward an aggressive boy or of their need (or the school's) to have things continually neat and clean. Yet these attitudes and needs, as expressed in classroom behaviors, often have more influence on the socialization of the child than any discussion of how things ought to be.

Educators are apt to emphasize the importance of the home and family relationships, to stress an individual's relations with peers in the group. The school is often equated with the home, as if it were one big happy family. And, finally, educators seem to think the school is a wonderfully happy place to be. In fact, they have presumed to be quite knowledgable about these forces and quite vocal in acting upon them.

Many educators are just beginning to recognize that some children find the home more accepting and loving than the school. They are just beginning to comprehend the intricacies of the school as a social system and the influence that its network of social relationships, including matters of control, power, status and communication, exercises over the learning environment (making it sometimes far less desirable than it should be). They are just beginning to realize that the behaviors of one teacher can significantly affect those of another. They are just beginning to understand the power struggles that exist in the instructional and administrative hierarchy. They are just coming to realize that the environment of the school, the climate of the classroom and teacher-pupil interaction, as well as pupil-pupil interaction, are immensely significant variables in the social development of children.

Socialization requires participation in the society. Human interaction is a key. In the school, the teacher, through her classroom behavior and interaction with pupils, demonstrates social behaviors. While we often think of the teacher as setting an example, I would like to think of the teacher as providing an opportunity for the child to view an adult social being. In this sense, then, the teacher does not have to set an example for all children to emulate but instead provides a model of social action to which children can react, accepting or rejecting as they wish.

From this point of view the teacher provides conditions for socialization to occur but does not necessarily determine the precise direction of behaviors. There are some, on the other hand, who believe the teacher should set an example that should be emulated by the pupils, that it is the teacher's function to determine the nature and direction of the socializing process.

Many teachers and administrators still would rather point the finger of blame at the home, the church, or the community for any student shortcomings. It is still quite common to hear teacher discussions of children punctuated with "Well, if you could see his home, you'd understand," "He's just like his father," "If the taxpayers would provide us the service," or "That's the responsibility of the home (or the church)." Yet these teachers are concerned. They search for "right" things to do. They seek help, but they persist in viewing the problems as if all were well within the school. They cannot quite bring themselves to examine the internal aspects of the school.

One day I would hope to hear teacher discussions include such statements as "We need to study the kind of environment *we provide* in this school," or "I'd like to change the way *I speak* to my children." This kind of awareness is not likely to arise spontaneously. It is toward the development of this understanding that the developmental counselor is committed. In this way will he be able to assist teachers and administrators in bridging the existing gap between statements of objectives and the socialized man.

Socialization and the Teaching-Learning Process

The school cannot expect socialization to occur simply by helping students to acquire facts or by providing students with opportunities to gain skills. The teacher as a role model, as an adult with authority and power, as a person who can, if she chooses, control and dominate, can influence significantly the direction and nature of the socialization of youth.

Starting in the elementary school, teachers do influence children with such comments as "We listen to our teachers," "We always try to do our best," "In this room we work hard and we don't have much time for play," which, while made in an attempt to motivate or control a group of children, do represent direct but subtle ways of socializing a child. In the same context and under the same conditions children learn to be quiet through a variety of teacher verbalizations that range all the way from "shush," "be quiet," or "shut up," to more subtle approaches such as "We can complete our workbooks more quickly with our mouths closed." Children therefore soon learn the rules and regulations of socialized group behavior. They soon learn too that if they do not conform to these rules various forms of punishment will be administered for violations.

These learnings are socialized learnings. Some are dictated learnings, others represent learning by acquiescence and compliance. For some children these exposures are readily rejected at the first or second level of the internalization process. For many children while these experiences are initially rejected, repeated compliance soon conditions their behavior. For too many children these become lifetime behaviors.

Whether we can afford to continue this type of socialized learning is doubtful. While these examples do not allow much freedom for rejection, there are many classroom activities where students do have an opportunity to react to ideas, beliefs, values, and attitudes. Where these opportunities exist, they can attend and respond to these phenomena and, if they choose, they can adopt them as their own.

The school curriculum offers many opportunities to contribute to the development of an individual's social identity. Educational objectives and methodologies can be readily attuned to the internalization sequence as proposed in the *Taxonomy*. The wherewithal *is* available, leaving the translation of the curriculum to actual classroom practice as it emerges from the heads and hearts of teachers. It is parodoxical that teachers often overlook or fail to take advantage of these opportunities. In some instances teachers are reluctant to provide much individual freedom.

It is always interesting to hear teachers and school administrators talk about student government and then to listen to the students discuss it. Sometimes you wonder if they are all in the same school. What is freedom and a self-governing body to one group is just plain totalitarianism to the other. And yet, through student government in our schools we have an opportunity to practice democratic government. I fear we have made a mockery of social studies lessons. This is an example of our failure to meet our objectives through actual, observable behaviors.

The school counselor, in focusing his concern on the adolescent in the process of developing his social identity, must consider and examine the day-to-day influences affecting this process. He is concerned about the conditions of learning and, in particular, the atmosphere of the school. The climate of the classroom—including both teacher-pupil and pupil-pupil relationships—has direct bearing on the nature and direction of socialization within the school.

Every student can hardly be expected to respond in the same way to these elements, for the uniqueness of each individual will cause a wide variety of individual response patterns and behaviors (variant learning). The school counselor can help the staff of the school to interpret these influences and their effect on youth, since he is concerned with the adolescent's reaction to his environment as viewed by both the individual and his teachers. He is concerned about the manner in which the adolescent demonstrates, as well as verbalizes, socialized learnings. He is interested in how the adolescent views his school and his interaction with others and how both of these relate to his social development.

All of these concerns are vital, for they represent the degree to which he is developing his own social identity as opposed to the extent to which he is merely conforming. As Elkin has stated,

The pupil on his part learns the patterns of the school system and, to some unmeasurable degree, those of the society at large. He consciously studies certain subjects; he observes what happens in school to himself, his fellow students, and the authorities; he participates in various activities and experiences accompanying feelings. In order to know what is expected and desired of him, he also imaginatively takes the position of his teachers.[7]

Children can learn to conform by choice; they can learn to conform by force; they can learn to conform by faking it. Socialization by force and deceit, while possible, is *not* what the school is seeking.

VALUING IN THE SOCIALIZING PROCESS

Valuing, as we have seen, is an integral part of the internalization process. It is helpful to think of valuing as a part of the total socialization of the

[7] Elkin, *op. cit.,* p. 62.

individual. Though we try not to lose sight of the more encompassing process of socialization, we very frequently are engaged in a segment of it —that which deals specifically with values and value formation, called valuing.

Society and Values

Societies and the cultures within societies have values. While the sources of these values are sometimes forgotten, they do exist. Value usually connotes usefulness or worth. In the socializing sense, then, we might think of a societal value as having some usefulness and worth. Linton defines culture as "social heredity."[8] Our values come to us through the culture of a society. Linton describes the content of a culture in three categories. Two of them—the *universals* and the *alternatives*—are helpful in understanding values. Linton defines universals as ". . . those ideas, habits, and conditioned emotional responses which are common to all sane, adult members of the society."[9] His universals would include those core values held in common by all members of the culture.

To live in the society one would have to ascribe to these values. His alternatives consist of ". . . a considerable number of traits which are shared by certain individuals but which are not common to all the members of the society. . . ."[10] Alternative values would represent the socially acceptable beliefs and behaviors available for individual choice. These beliefs range from those commonly accepted, such as a particular religious preference, to those uniquely individual, such as the behaviors of vegetarians and hermits.

Core values remain central to a society for a long period of time. They are the foundation beliefs, the bedrock of society's existence and maintenance. Any change in the core values of a society must be very slow, wearing away gradually as a river erodes the land along its bank. Generations can exist with little change in the universal beliefs that comprise the heart of a society. (While this is the way it has been, we must recognize that our society now has the means to change these ideologies in a relatively short period of time if it chooses to do so. That this is in fact occurring is part of my reasoning in the earlier discussion of the disappearing generation gap in Chapter Two.)

On the other hand alternative values representing individual choices and preferences can vacillate from acceptance to rejection depending on the

[8] Ralph Linton, *The Study of Man* (New York: Appleton-Century, 1936), p. 78.

[9] *Ibid.*, p. 272.

[10] *Ibid.*, p. 273.

whim of individuals. Some come and go and these may merely represent fads. Many are more durable and withstand the test of time. Some alternative values eventually become so prevalent that they are considered universal values. In the past, such changes have taken years to occur. Alternative values represent the wide world of individual belief.

An individual's behavior is predicted to a large extent on those choices he has made in forming his beliefs. To smoke or not to smoke represents a behavior based on alternative beliefs. A person can choose from the many beliefs available to him and his behavior will reflect the values he has chosen. His beliefs can change and will alter his behaviors accordingly.

The social acceptability of an alternative does influence individual choice and its societal frequency can determine in a large measure its availability for choice. This availability can and does change, as we noted. For example, smoking some forty or fifty years ago was common among men but very few women smoked. Some twenty to thirty years ago a number of women smoked but very few smoked in full public view. Today a large number of women smoke, most of them in public. Over the years the availability of smoking as an alternative value for women has increased. Research in recent years linking cigarette smoking and cancer may eventually have an impact on the availability of smoking as an alternative. It has already changed the beliefs of some individuals, who have behaved by giving up smoking. Others have altered their behavior and now smoke only cigars or pipes. Many too have been unsuccessful in quitting the habit—but that's another story. Thus our beliefs about many things have changed and will continue to change, with our rapid means of communication accelerating any changes we want to occur.

This changing nature of alternative values is one of the more difficult resolutions in a society and its approval-disapproval of human behaviors. We are all influenced in our beliefs by our experiences. We form many of our basic values in the earlier years of our lives from the alternatives available to us during those important years. While people can and do change, the stability of these basic values is often expressed in the so-called generation gap. This is actually another way of referring to the changes in the alternative value patterns exhibited by a majority in our society. Thus, some alternatives available to one generation are not available to the next.

The availability is often cyclical. Long hair and beards, acceptable a century ago, have not been available for several generations but are increasing nowadays. Today more than ever, many of the alternatives offered are new ones, never having been experienced by humans young or old. Thus men of all ages stand to learn from one another—the old from the young as well as the more traditional pattern of young from old. This is but another evidence of our disappearing generation gap. The implications of alternative values, their changing nature, and their availability for choice has rather obvious implications for the school and its role in the socialization and valuing processes. It has considerable importance too.

The School and Valuing

The role of the school in valuing has been examined and approached from different points of view. Any disparity in these views surrounds the involvement of the school with reference to *value indoctrination* (inculcating values without consideration for individual acceptance or preference) or *value orientation* (making children aware of the wide range of values available to them). The controversy quite possibly can be resolved by insisting that the school pass on those values which are believed universal or core to a democratic society; those which are constituted as essential to the welfare of the nation; those which are consistent with democratic ideals and the freedom of the individual. On the other hand the many alternatives in human existence should be examined. One should be free to choose those ideas, beliefs, and behaviors which best represent the nature of his existence and the direction he would choose for his life. Our schools have perhaps overinvested in value indoctrination.

This is not to say that schools should never engage in value indoctrination, nor that the values of teachers should never be made known. The point rests with knowing in what kind of valuing we are engaged. Teachers often inculcate their values. For example, youth are expected to keep their lockers clean and some schools conduct periodic inspections (just prior to which there is always a flurry of cleaning activity). This represents a cleanliness or orderliness value.

I do not suggest that this is an undesirable value, but neither is this illustration meant to imply that storing food in lockers for days on end is to be encouraged. It is simply to show that youth have little choice about the condition in which they keep their lockers. They learn that neat, clean, orderly lockers are good. They are rewarded. Those who merely conform complain about it outside the school. Those who rebel are punished. It is just one of many examples of student indoctrination in our schools. To the extent that we are engaged in these activities, we should be aware of the basic nature of the practice.

Earlier we detailed the valuing level and its subcategories as it appears in the *Taxonomy of Educational Objectives*. These goals suggest a direction for the school, one that has been identified as "value clarification" by Raths, Harmin and Simon in their publication *Values and Teaching*.[11] They de-

[11] Louis Raths, Merrill Harmin, and Sidney Simon, *Values and Teaching* (Columbus, Ohio: Charles E. Merrill, 1966).

scribe the process of valuing (arriving at a value) as involving seven requirements utilizing three processes. These are:

CHOOSING: (1) freely
               (2) from alternatives
               (3) after thoughtful consideration of the consequences of
                    each alternative
PRIZING: (4) cherishing, being happy with the choice
               (5) willing to affirm the choice publicly
ACTING: (6) doing something with the choice
               (7) repeatedly, in some pattern of life.[12]

Looking at the process of valuing within this framework makes it
easier for those in education to clarify and develop values. The actual
value(s) identified become less significant than the process. In other words,
the teacher helps youth to engage in the process of valuing by providing
the conditions for students to engage in the choosing, prizing, and acting,
and is only incidentally involved, if at all, in the value(s) they actually
identify as their own. Raths et al. contend,

Somehow or another the idea is held by adults that their chief function—in
relationship to children—is to *tell* them things: to tell them what to do, when
to do it, where to do it, how to do it, how often to do it, and when to stop
doing it. . . . The real problem is that almost no one sees the necessity for
helping a child to make some order out of the confusion which has been
created inside his head. Almost no one sees the necessity for questioning a child,
to help him sort out and examine all those confusing ideas.[13]

In a society that demands increasing human flexibility and adaptability
it is important that we encourage and assist adolescents in the process of
developing and clarifying their values. Adolescents need freedom in making
choices for which they can be responsible, rather than have adults impose
values that have already been selected by role models or predetermined
through school rules and regulations. An appproach to value formation that
is characterized by techniques of persuasion and urging and imposes limitations on the number of alternatives available to them will be less meaningful, less valuable, and in the long run less apt to result in internalized values.
Allowing adolescents the freedom to test from these alternatives and to
choose freely requires of them less pretense and makes them less likely to

[12] *Ibid.,* p. 30.
[13] *Ibid.,* p. 24.

engage in deceitful and questionable ways of dealing with the activities and requirements imposed upon them. The freedom to make intelligent and thoughtful choices requires of them responsible behaviors that are more likely to be genuine and honest.

Counselors are increasingly becoming involved with the disadvantaged. More than with other groups in our society, the counselor finds himself face-to-face with a student whose value complex is often very different from his own. His counselee tends to express or exhibit values that are quite opposed to those of the typical middle class counselor. Not only does the counselor have to recognize any basic value differences, but he must also help his counselee clarify and distinguish his own.

In these adolescent years, the time of value clarification, when the young adult is busy with the complexities of sifting and sorting value alternatives, of engaging in the valuing process of synthesizing his value complex in all aspects of his identity, he needs a counselor who can understand the process of valuing and the discrepancies between the values of his environment outside of school and those in the school. He needs a counselor who can aid and abet the clarification of his values and their integration and organization into his personal being. He needs a counselor who will not press him to accept only the values of his school or of middle class society.

The dilemma of the disadvantaged child in a school where the values of the dominant ethnic group are imposed is a real one. Youth are confused when they are caused to deny the values of their own reference group in favor of those which represent most usually a white, middle class society. It makes sense to begin by helping these youth to understand and clarify the values indigenous to their own people. This seems to be the basic point from which the counselor can operate or from which the teacher can communicate. Then, helping these young people to understand the values of the school or of the larger society can be accomplished within this context. While it is difficult, this at least prevents a youth from having to deny his own being and his own world of experience. It offers him an opportunity to live and to grow by both standards.

The school can play an important part in helping boys and girls in the valuing process. The school can help the student to identify the available alternatives and can provide an atmosphere in which he is free to choose from these available alternatives those which he feels are most meaningful to him. It can help him to examine the consequences of any alternative he has chosen, and can provide him with an opportunity to test the consequences of alternatives when these are unknown to the student. Perhaps most importantly, it can provide an atmosphere where students can learn about the variety of alternatives that have been chosen by their peers, and where they can match some of their choices with those of the models provided in the school. It can encourage the valuing process and provide an atmosphere conducive to free expression and intellectual respect.

The developmental counselor can make significant contributions in helping school personnel to understand better the nature of the process, to provide conditions in which the process can occur, and to suggest techniques and practices they can employ in carrying out activities of a valuing nature.

I am partial to the value clarification techniques of Raths, Harmin, and Simon. The approach and the twenty-one clarifying strategies they describe are appropriate to valuing and socializing activities in the school. Further, students enjoy the techniques they encourage and their methods are easily adapted to regular classroom procedures. Teachers can readily learn to engage in the valuing process with youth.

THE ADOLESCENT AND SOCIAL IDENTITY

In Chapter Two I presented the idea of the disappearing generation gap based primarily on the effects of mass media communication which result in constantly changing ideologies and mores. There are many implications for education in the sociological changes of our times. The society in which adolescents live is very different. When we consider their life exposures up to age twelve with those of any adult over thirty, we can identify many differences which make it difficult, for example, to compare the life experiences of the typical adolescent from 1950–1955 with that of an adolescent in 1970 or 1975, so great have been the changes and so different are their worlds. In a few more years, as I suggested, the so-called gap will disappear. We will be less sure of those values and ideas that identify *a* generation. So much for the past and what has been. Though the remnants of these concepts are still with us in large measure, our concern must turn to the future.

The School Environment and the Adolescent Society

In 1961, James S. Coleman reported on the world of the adolescent in *The Adolescent Society*[14] using the results of a study of adolescents in ten schools in the late 1950's as the basis for his analysis. Although his very comprehensive study has been most helpful and widely used, we need to continually reexamine and reassess the adolescent world. Coleman's study does suggest a number of areas, however, that are crucial in the socialization of the adolescent, such as the climate of the school and the factors in status and status attainment. Coleman refers to the effect of the adolescent society on its own members, stating:

[14] James S. Coleman, *The Adolescent Society* (Glencoe, Ill.: Free Press, 1961).

The means through which the adolescent society has these effects is primarily the rewards and punishments it dispenses among its members. These rewards and punishments include popularity, respect, acceptance into a crowd, praise, awe, support and aid, on the one hand, or isolation, ridicule, exclusion from a crowd, disdain, discouragement, disrespect. As in the larger society, these rewards and punishments, coming from others who are important to a person, exert a powerful influence on his subsequent efforts, and can have a powerful effect upon his psychological equanimity.[15]

In this respect the adolescent culture has a powerful psychological impact. And this will increase as other agents, like the home and family, become less able (or less likely) to maintain their previous dominant position.

As we have noted in a number of ways, the adolescent as an individual has the tremendous task of maintaining some semblance of personal equilibrium. His growth toward social maturity is no exception. Here once again he is faced with ambiguity and conflicting standards. The discrepancy between his world, the adolescent culture, and the social system of the school poses hurdles and raises doubts that tend to aggravate his social growth. At the very least he is caused to make tentative choices and judgments which could be, under other circumstances perhaps, delayed without interfering with his development. Most glaring is the dichotomy between the school and the adolescent world in defining achievement.

The social system of the school values academic achievement. It emphasizes marks through its well-established system of reward and punishment—the marking system. Students strive for these rewards in varying degrees. On the other hand, the adolescent culture does not always value the scholar. In fact in some schools it doesn't pay socially to be a "brain" or a "grind." Adolescents have several ridiculing accolades for those who strive to achieve academically. The adolescent world rewards individuals for different achievements. It ascribes status to those who are athletic, good looking, or sharp dressers. Some schools, in recognizing this, have attempted to resolve this discrepancy or to alleviate unnecessary anxiety by adding more and more activities. "Something for everyone" is a worthy cause but it does not necessarily square with the issue.

The school today focuses largely on the past and the future. The curriculum content is drawn from what has been. It emphasizes knowledge and knowing. It assumes a major function in the transmittal of our heritage. It is future-oriented in that students are urged to project several years ahead to their future adult roles as citizens, parents, workers, and, perhaps most frequently of all, as students (with reference to post-high school education). It regales students to accept much of their learning on faith, with admoni-

---

[15] *Ibid.,* p. 314.

tions that "you will need this information in college" or "when you have your family. . . ."

The adolescent world, however, is built around the present, the here and now of each day. Adolescents are almost totally immersed in the new discoveries they are making every day about themselves and others and with the new feelings and emotions they are experiencing. Erikson speaks of a period of "psychosocial moratorium" following puberty defining it as ". . . a psychosocial stage between childhood and adulthood, and between the morality learned by the child, and the ethics to be developed by the adult."[16] While it acts as a period of delay, akin to the Freudian period of latency, it occurs in the later phases of adolescence providing time for the individual to integrate and order his identity and to give meaning to his existence.

The psychosocial moratorium is not a period of inactivity or dormancy. Quite the contrary, for the adolescent in his search for identity, is busily engaged in the internalization process involving the higher levels of organization and characterization. These consume much of the adolescent's time and energy and his interest focuses largely on topics related to his identity—love, friendship, morals, family, personality, work, money. He spends many hours just talking and thinking and experimenting. There is little doubt that for many adolescents the search for identity continues well beyond the high school years and, in view of societal trends, that it will continue to elongate as life becomes more mechanistic and restrictive.

The real world of the adolescent, then, is filled with these concerns so intimately a part of his internalizing a set and forming a character. He is involved primarily with his own self and the finding of this self both personally and socially. The business of writing themes, memorizing facts, or reading textbooks is far less vital, exciting, or challenging.

The task lies in the merger of these two worlds, in the recognition that something must be done. The school is attempting to make learning more palatable. Burdened with a commitment to pass on the heritage and a charge to provide youth with a foundation upon which the future demands of further study and work roles can be built, the school has been forced to turn from the psychological issues of social identity. Thus the social issues at best get the preponderence of attention and even these are often geared only to the other, more central, tasks the school has assumed.

The adolescent, in the throes of his own need to find identity, has pleaded for less on faith and more relevance in his education. He has sensed his own needs for exposures to learning which will help him to value and to

---

[16] Erik H. Erikson, *Childhood and Society* (New York: W. W. Norton, 1963, second edition), pp. 262–263.

conceptualize and organize his values in a way that will accommodate and define his social self. He has argued in his own way for meaning in his learning experiences. He has shown by his behaviors his acceptance or non-acceptance of the tasks that the school has heaped upon him. There is some hope for diminishing this discrepancy if the school can tailor its classroom learning to accommodate the nature of its clientele, the adolescent, and the processes of his socialization.

Socialization and Character Types

Peck and Havighurst, as the result of a longitudinal investigation of the nature and development of character in which they studied a group of children from ages 10 to 17, have elected to describe five basic character types: (1) amoral, (2) expedient, (3) conforming, (4) irrational-conscientious, and (5) rational-altruistic.[17] They propose these types as a maturational hierarchy ranging from the very unstable, less consistent, impulsive nature of the amoral character to the rational-altruistic type who demonstrates a high level of character integration, moral stability, and social identity. These classifications, they caution, are not discrete and final categories into which a person can be pigeonholed. Rather they are categorical gradations describing themes of character formation.

Peck and Havighurst found that individuals tend to demonstrate in their psychosocial maturation characteristics which are predominantly associated with one of these types. While this allows for general character typing, one is reminded that an individual can evidence personality formations of other types even though these are of a more subordinate nature in the overall character formation.

The two authors note "increasing ego strength" and "increasing strength of conscience"[18] as two common themes in the hierarchy from amoral to rational-altruistic types. This suggests the possibility of working into the socialization process, activities and experiences which would contribute to the development of the ego and the conscience assuming, of course, that we wish to encourage the development of youth who exemplify the rational-altruistic character. One is prompted to view the school as it inclines young people toward conformity with its emphasis on obedience and people-pleasing behavior.

On the other hand there is reason to consider how much *real* influence the school can exert in the socializing of individuals. Peck and Havighurst

[17] Robert F. Peck and Robert J. Havighurst, *The Psychology of Character Development* (New York: John Wiley, 1960), chapter IX.
[18] *Ibid.*, p. 170.

found that ". . . most individuals tend to maintain *the same attitudes and motives* through the years, in major aspects of morality. . . . even allowing for all the pressures and encouragement to become more independent as adolescence progresses."[19] Of family influence on character formation, they add, "Character, as defined in this study, appears to be predominantly shaped by the intimate, emotionally powerful relationship between child and parents, within the family."[20] These findings, in combination, while having perhaps even greater relevance for elementary school guidance, do imply several possibilities for action in the secondary school. For the adjustive-corrective (remedial) efforts, closer and more frequent involvement with families may be indicated.

Helping families to deal with their own patterns of interpersonal relationships may be one very significant way for the school to help. The growing interest in family counseling finds considerable support in this regard. Further, while we need to continually assess the impact of the home on character formation, the changing nature of the family as a unit may necessitate more liaison between the school and the home based on developmental as well as remedial efforts. In the facilitative-developmental (preventive) realm, it would appear that the front line of action is the teacher and the classroom. To the extent that the teaching-learning process can focus on experiences which will cause youth to consider and reconsider the values and attitudes they hold—to view their own valuing and the organization and set of these values—our prospects for contributing to the social maturation of the individual increase.

Achieving Social and Self-Identity

So far we have emphasized the psychological and sociological aspects of socialization with reference primarily to the individual's learning—his internalization. We have talked about his exposures (receiving), his preferences (responding), his choices (values), and his integration (organization) as leading to his identity (characterization). This is a simple way to describe what is actually a complex and life-long process. Also, we examined this internalization continuum as it is influenced by the learning experiences the school provides. Let us examine in more detail some of the more personal and psychological elements of this socialization.

Earlier in the chapter, in defining socialization and its meaning, we spoke of the individual's seeking balance with his environment. Later, in discussing the organization and characterization categories of the *Taxonomy*, we spoke of accommodation. Accommodation is closely allied with this

[19] *Ibid.*, p. 165.
[20] *Ibid.*, p. 175.

balance, or personal equilibrium. We do not always understand the very personal nature of this, especially since we tend to view the person by the behaviors he exhibits and our reaction to these, and not by what he is feeling and experiencing. We are seldom aware of how he is dealing with the matter of his equilibrium. Let me explain this further.

A child we have come to consider as neat and orderly suddenly begins to exhibit behavior we consider sloppy. His homework papers are messy. We might say to him, "That's not like you," or "You never had a messy paper before." We are reacting to his behavior. We have noted it as different behavior for him. We view it as conflicting since it is at odds with our perception of his usual behavior. We could also be disturbed, disappointed, or confused. If the behaviors were reversed (from sloppy to neat) we would note it as different behavior but we would probably be pleased.

While we can't ignore *our* reaction, what is more important and more central to socialization is the internal experiencing of the child. We have observed outward evidences of his exploration. These behaviors may be part of his trial-and-error experimenting, and could represent any level of his internalization. He could be in process of testing neatness as a value, or it could be that he is accommodating. Perhaps some new value that he has recently accepted is interfering, causing him to hurry with his homework. At whatever level and for whatever purpose, changes in the behavior of youth could be evidence of the internalization process. Where one's behavior seems out of character, it is likely that he is internalizing at higher levels.

In the socialization process we need to recognize both the child's experiencing and our reaction to it. We have been emphasizing the latter (the sociological aspect). For example, it is easy to see how pleased the teacher will be with the neat homework paper (her reaction). She will probably reward him with "that's good" or with a higher mark if that is possible. Or in the reverse situation (neat to sloppy), the child will be "rewarded" with some sort of punishment, such as having to do the assignment over. Repeated reactions of this kind can determine the socialized behavior of a child. They might eventually force him to conform.

But teacher behaviors, whether rewarding or punishing, do not account for his experiencing—his internalization—of his feelings. They do not consider the psychological elements of his socialization. And this is important if the child is to have any freedom in the values he will choose and in the identity he will establish. His *social identity* is dependent on the outcome of his experiencing. While he is in process he may exhibit conflicting, vacillating behaviors representing the confusion and the conflict that are a part of his efforts to accommodate what he believes and to integrate these into behaviors he will find satisfying. In this sense, then, he has established his identity and his social balance.

Identity is never fully achieved. We are always in process, we are always becoming. When we think about this we realize that internalization as it results in social and self identity is a life-long activity. We can understand better some of the human emotions and the behaviors that exhibit these when we consider socialization (social identity) as a process. For example, children, adolescents, and young adults experience a great deal of distress and disappointment in the process of developing their values and in integrating these behaviorally. These are the years so vital to social identity. These are the years so full of hope and optimism and enthusiasm. These are the years of activism, of rebellion. These are the years that are characterized by degrees of stress, fear, anxiety, and conflict; of faith, joy, and love.

The adult, when one seeks to plumb the depths of identity and to ferret the meaning and purpose of life, experiences these same emotions but perhaps over longer, more enduring periods of time. With his value complex more firmly established and with facets of his identity more clearly developed and known, his identity with himself and with the human condition seems more fixed and more difficult to change. These years can be characterized by more enduring feelings of love, happiness, and security; by more intense despair and apathy. But the adult years are another story.

SCHOOL AND CLASSROOM CLIMATE

It is relatively simple to relate our examination of the process of socialization and the adolescent's growth toward social identity to the objectives and tasks of the secondary school. The conditions of classroom learning are not so readily identified and yet we are coming to recognize that the atmosphere of the school and the climate of classroom learning are very important to the accomplishment of educational goals. We realize that schools are different. We know that teachers vary widely in the mien of their classrooms and in the nature of their teaching. We need to learn more about these differences and their effect on an individual's learning-maturation.

The most extensive investigation of school climate has been carried out by Halpin and Croft in their school organizational climate studies.[21] Using an Organizational Climate Description Questionnaire (OCDQ), they have identified eight dimensions of organizational behavior. Four of these are teacher and four are principal behaviors. Teacher behaviors include disengagement, hindrance, esprit, and intimacy; principal behaviors are aloofness, production emphasis, trust, and consideration.[22] Using these behaviors

[21] Andrew W. Halpin, *Theory and Research in Administration* (New York: Macmillan, 1966).

[22] *Ibid.*, pp. 150–151.

they were able to describe six different school organizational climates: (1) open, (2) autonomous, (3) controlled, (4) familiar, (5) paternal, and (6) closed. While they are cautious in interpreting their results, they frequently point to the necessity of knowing more about the conditions a school provides for children's learning. Halpin states,

But above everything else, we must remember the purpose of our schools: they exist for our children. We know, too, that children interiorize their value-systems through a process of identifying with those adults in their immediate environment who provide ego-ideals that the children can respect. But what happens when the range of available ego-ideals is constricted? Or more pointedly, what is the price that a Closed, inauthentic climate exacts from the children themselves?[23]

The Halpin and Croft research provides a base from which we can at least begin to communicate about the school climate. It allows us to focus on the environment of the school and the need to look at different dimensions of the school organization. Schools do differ in their learning conditions. I once visited a school and found the only access was through the basement. The doors were locked to outsiders. Students were not allowed in the halls except between classes. Admittedly, this is extreme. I have felt differently when I visited schools and sensed, as I talked with school personnel and students, a variety of moods.

We need more research to improve our ability to identify differences in school climates and to relate these to the learning-maturation process. For the present, we are sufficiently aware of school atmosphere as a factor in learning. We can now begin to talk about it. We have long regarded the school as a castle—as an environment that, without question, is somewhat ideal. When learning goes awry, it is seldom the school or the classroom that's at fault—it's the home, or the Board of Education, the taxpayer, or the child. It is encouraging to hear a faculty discuss the climate of its school —and further, *to want to deal* with it. It is heartening to find teachers concerned with the immediate environment of children and its impact on them as individuals and as learners.

The climate of the school only suggests another equally important environment—the classroom. The classroom is the immediate environment of the student and the one in which he spends a majority of his school day. In the secondary school, the student gets to experience several differing environments in the course of a day. A great deal of the research on classroom environment has focused on pupil-pupil interaction and group relationships, using sociometric and other techniques for observing and studying

[23] *Ibid.,* p. 236.

the child's relationships and interaction with his peers. Only recently has there been interest in research about ways of analyzing and studying classroom interaction, including the most important one—pupil-teacher interaction.

Getzels and Thelen describe the uniqueness of the classroom group.[24] Their proposed model for studying classroom interaction and behavior is essentially the same as the Getzels and Guba model referred to in Chapter Six. Using the nomothetic and idiographic dimensions of group behavior, they emphasize the sociological and psychological aspects. Thus, in about the same manner as one would approach the study of role behavior in a larger, more complex institution (such as the school), one could study any number of classroom aspects, such as leadership, conflict, goals. Their model has many research possibilities for analyzing the classroom roles of teacher and students. It provides a new and different way of looking at classroom relationships.

Warren S. Williams, after reviewing a number of research studies concerned with classroom climate, cites several significant points:

(1) The primary needs of students are affective; teachers who consider these needs increase pupil concern with learning tasks and increase the possibility of positive attitudes toward school.

(2) Interpersonal anxiety reduces learning efficiency; teachers who are democratic and promote classroom interaction reduce this anxiety.

(3) The climate of any classroom will not serve all pupils equally well; teachers must seek ways of reacting to each individual.

(4) The classroom teacher is the key to classroom climate; autocratic leaders increase hostility, democratic teachers tend to reduce tension and increase interaction.

(5) Classroom climate influences the learning process; there are varying views as to the nature and extent.[25]

Obviously, we need more research. But a few generalizations about the socializing-valuing processes are worthy of mention. The importance of the teacher, of the teaching methods and of pupil-teacher interaction are recognized. Students respond to teachers whom they like and enjoy and who find time to interact with them. These teachers will influence children. These

---

[24] Jacob W. Getzels and Herbert A. Thelen, "The Classroom Group as a Unique Social System." In Nelson B. Henry (Ed.), *The Dynamics of Instructional Groups,* The Fifty-ninth Yearbook of the National Society for the Study of Education, Part II (Chicago: University of Chicago Press, 1960), Chapter IV.

[25] Warren S. Williams, "Classroom Climate," *Research and the Classroom Teacher* (May 1965), pp. 3–6.

teachers will probably have a classroom that is conducive to the learning-maturation of individuals. The affective or internal aspects of learning are related to classroom climate. Teachers cannot ignore the needs, feelings, or attitudes of students. Teachers must be aware of affect—of guilt, fear and anxiety, of belongingness, enthusiasm, and pride as it is noted in classroom behaviors. A great many pressures are caused by teachers who emphasize "getting work done," rather than the individuals who must do it. When books and themes and all the busywork in which students engage become *more* important than the individual, we have lost sight of the affective aspect of human learning.

TEACHER-PUPIL INTERACTION

A great deal of our attention in the past has focused on identifying and describing the successful teacher. We have investigated teacher characteristics hoping to identify the magical combination of traits that determine a teacher's effectiveness. We have in one sense tried to describe *the* "good" teacher, knowing very well that teaching is subject to many of the human variables that make it most difficult to measure both the traits of teachers and the act of teaching. To assess these alone is most difficult; to determine how these relate to teaching effectiveness is nearly impossible. Pupils react quite differently to different teachers and to different teaching styles. "Good" teaching may be more a matter of teacher-pupil interaction than we have heretofore recognized.

Teaching is being viewed differently than in the past. The personality and behavior of the teacher, while having always been recognized as important, are being considered in relation to how teachers utilize themselves in the act of teaching and to the style of teaching they employ. Instead of emphasizing the role of the teacher as one who imparts information and who emphasizes content as a major way of providing for the instructional program, we have begun to analyze teaching with greater reference to the human interaction—the relationship between the teacher and the students in the classroom.

Teaching has, to a degree, emphasized the autocratic behaviors of classroom management and a considerable amount of teacher domination and control has been expected. It would seem that we are less concerned with control and authority (though we recognize these as ingredients of school and classroom management) and teacher-centered methods (e.g., lectures), becoming more concerned with ways of helping teachers to use their individual personalities more effectively in encouraging and motivating pupils. We are recognizing that pupils vary in their need for classroom structure and direction. We are allowing for much greater individual pupil reaction than has heretofore been tolerated.

Our task at the present time is to generate a change in teacher classroom behaviors so that *more* democratic and individualized procedures can be incorporated in the teaching-learning process.

Flanders, in a publication entitled *Teacher Influence, Pupil Attitudes, and Achievement,* summarizes a number of earlier studies completed by Anderson and his associates:

The findings of Anderson are based on the study of preschool, primary school, and elementary school classrooms involving five different teachers and extending over several years. The imaginative research of Anderson and his colleagues has produced a series of internally consistent and significant findings: First, the dominative and integrative contacts of the teacher set a pattern of behavior that spreads throughout the classroom; the behavior of the teacher, more than of any other individual, sets the climate of the class. The rule is that a climate of domination incites further domination, and one of integration stimulates further integration. It is the teacher's tendency that spreads among pupils and is continued even when the teacher is no longer in the room. Furthermore, the pattern a teacher develops in one year is likely to persist in his classroom the following year with different pupils. Second, when a teacher has a higher proportion of integrative contacts, pupils show more spontaneity and initiative, more voluntary social contributions, and more acts of problem-solving. Third, when a teacher has a higher proportion of dominative contacts, the pupils are more easily distracted from school work, and show greater compliance to, as well as rejection of, teacher domination.[26]

Flanders, in studying the concept of teacher influence, has conducted research using classroom interaction analysis techniques. He notes the following assumptions in his analysis of teacher influence:

First, acts of influence are expressed primarily through verbal statements. . . . Second, how much teachers talk and what they say determine to a large extent the reactions of the students. This is another way of saying that the teacher is an influential authority figure. . . . Third, . . . that teachers can control their verbal participation in the classroom. . . . He can be indirect if he chooses, or direct, according to his assessment of the situation.[27]

Flanders's studies indicate (1) that students learned more when working with more flexible teachers, (2) that students learned more in both

---

[26] Ned A. Flanders, *Teacher Influence, Pupil Attitudes, and Achievement* (Washington, D.C.: U.S. Department of Health, Education and Welfare, 1965), p. 4.

[27] *Ibid.,* p. 112.

mathematics and social studies with more flexible teachers, and (3) that dependent-prone students learned more than independent-prone students when working with teachers who were indirect. He feels that teachers can accomplish more, can enhance achievement, and can develop more independence through indirect influence (accepting feeling, praising or encouraging, accepting or using ideas of students, and asking questions). Direct influence (lecturing, giving directions, and criticizing or justifying authority) tend to require more teacher involvement, increase student compliance to teacher opinion and direction, and condition students to seek assistance from the teacher and to check more frequently on their progress to insure that they are moving in the desired direction.[28]

It is possible that the greater number of teachers employing what Flanders defines as the "direct influence" accounts for student inclinations (even in graduate school) to ask such questions as, "Is that what *you* want?" "Am I doing the *right* thing?" "Is this *right?*" Continued research on teacher-pupil interaction, teacher behavior, and teacher influence and their relation to student dependence-independence, creativity, and motivation, as well as achievement, will be significant to improved educational methodologies.

To the extent that we are concerned with preparing students to live creatively, to act democratically, to evidence independent thinking, and to discover and apply new learnings to their everyday living, we must insure that they are having opportunities to engage in these activities in their daily classroom life. These are all phases of student socialization.

While the supervisor of instruction or the school principal is concerned with teaching effectiveness, school guidance is concerned with the behavior of the teacher and with the teacher's interaction with pupils individually and in groups. The counselor is concerned with the behaviors the adolescent is learning in the classroom and the relation of these to his socialization. In the interest of the adolescent and his learning-maturation, the developmental counselor must be in a position to work with the teacher and to help the teacher examine the impact of classroom teaching and teacher attitudes as they affect the student and his learning.

These ideas are somewhat foreign to the school at the present time. Our information service, the pupil inventory service, and the techniques we have used to study children (case study, anecdotal records, classroom observation) have centered on the student and the characteristics or traits he exhibits. They have focused on his identity at that time, and not on his becoming. While we continue to talk about the growing individual adolescent, we maintain the emphasis on how others view and react to him. We seldom

[28] *Ibid.,* pp. 114–117.

seek his reaction to his teacher and to his classroom environment. We seldom seek his own view of his being and becoming. We rarely move a student from a classroom environment which is not conducive to his learning-maturation. We rarely accommodate his social maturation—or any other facet of his maturation for that matter—by transferring him to another classroom where the climate may be more in accord with his needs, nature, and temperament.

For example, while classroom structure is not an either-or proposition, if a student needs less structure, or more structure, why not provide him with situations where this can be afforded? It doesn't seem appropriate for an individual who needs less direction or more at a given time in his life to have to exist in a classroom that cannot provide adequately for him at that time. This is not to say that the teacher who is unable to provide for this child is inadequate or is not a "good" teacher. The fact that a teacher can recognize an individual's needs and note his (or her) personal inability to serve them is indicative that he is alert to his students and their needs and secure in his teaching demeanor.

IMPLICATIONS FOR SECONDARY SCHOOL GUIDANCE

Two major conceptual changes are suggested in the approach of this chapter. Both have tremendous significance for the direction of secondary school guidance and the day-to-day functions of the developmental counselor. First, the concept of social development has been expanded beyond the *external*—the interactional aspects of getting along with others and the routine concerns of socializing the child to the school. The *internal* aspects of social maturation and its relation and contribution to character formation are accented in the individualized nature of developing a social identity. Thus the process of socialization has been elaborated to stress the social and psychological components with particular emphasis placed on valuing and internalization.

Second, the relevance of the teaching-learning process, including the environment of the school and classroom, has been reaffirmed with an emphasis on the inner aspects of human learning. Moving beyond the more observable dimensions of social interaction, attention is directed toward the conditions of classroom learning as these are influenced by the behavior of the teacher and the attitudes and feelings of the student. The process of socialization is viewed within the dynamics of the teaching-learning process rather than as an adjunct to it.

The School Counselor and Student Records

The secondary school counselor, as we have noted in earlier chapters, is responsible for the collection and maintenance of pupil personnel records. These records come to the secondary school with a rather complete year-by-year evaluation of the individual's growth and development in the elementary school. These anecdotal notations usually include references to the social development of the individual as viewed by the teacher. Such comments as "well liked," "cooperative," "popular," "quiet," "active," "a leader," "a tease," "bossy" are illustrative of the record notes that teachers tend to write about students. Obviously these represent the teacher's reaction to the child's behavior in her class.

In following the longitudinal social development of the child through his elementary school years, one can learn how several teachers have viewed the child, noting consistencies and inconsistencies in these teacher views. Rarely, however, do such records indicate more than generalized statements about his social behavior. Little is available about his growth from year to year or about any efforts to help him with his growth. If Mary is reported as "quiet" in second grade, it is likely that some such repetitive or similar remark will appear in her third grade notation.

Few comments ever reveal how the student views his own social development. Yet as anyone who has ever asked children about their social self will attest, they have plenty to say about their own social relations. When these records get to the secondary school, these year-by-year notes are usually discontinued simply because of the difficulty in obtaining teacher appraisals. Thus, after a year or two, about the only time these records are used is when a student may be having a problem that requires a case history. Whether or not a school chooses to maintain these records beyond the elementary school (and there is some question as to whether they should be maintained there) is a decision for the school and its staff.

If such records are to be maintained in any form, it would seem that these appraisals should represent the child's experiencing—his views as he cares to report them. Beyond the mere report of his social development, we should be getting at the inner dimensions of his social identity and the processes involved. Unless records can focus on social maturation and social identity and involve the student's considerations as well as, or instead of, the teacher's judgment, there seems little point to bother with them.

The School Counselor and Social Identity

Helping the student remains primary in the guidance effort. The student as learner should be the primary benefactor. I reaffirm this assumption because it is possible for the school counselor to become the agent of the institution, not the individual—especially in this process of socialization. Assuming, then, that the individual's social identity is primary, we can view his socializing growth as a factor in his development of personal autonomy.

Here is where we seem to block as a nation, as educators, as individuals. We voice a belief in personal autonomy but we react against it if it challenges or interferes with our own. For example, students who react against a school regulation that seems unfair or who suggest a change in school policy are often quickly silenced. Student activism reflects in part the thinking of individuals who, in the process of personal integration (as this occurs in valuing, organization, and characterization) have been caused to examine societal issues and to raise pertinent questions.

Students increasingly are becoming aware of the double standards that exist in society and the sham of democratic principles and practices that so clearly exist in segments of our society. Actions like these can be anticipated when young people have given some thought to their own convictions and to those ascribed to their society. These are the youth who dare to speak out on issues and to challenge conformity on a do-as-you-are-told basis. These are the youth who will challenge the depersonalization inherent in bureaucracy and the "establishment."

And so while we exhort our beliefs in helping youth to achieve social identity, we fear it and we are threatened by it. And there are many who consequently reject it, choosing instead to implement principles that tend toward social indoctrination.

Certainly school counselors are caught in this dilemma, yet they cannot straddle the fence and remain totally effective for long. They will need to examine the issue rather carefully and thoughtfully. I personally believe that if school guidance is to maintain its central function of assisting in the learning-maturation of the individual it cannot hedge in matters of social and self-identity. The school counselor must align himself with those beliefs and behaviors that promise to foster the development of socially useful and effective individuals.

In this regard he cannot hope to change the course of the school or of the teaching-learning process overnight. This becomes a day-to-day function in which he performs as an agent of change helping as he can, wherever he can, with whomever he can. His consulting role is significant to change the socialization process of the school and his efforts with administrators, teachers, and parents should help to move the school toward these goals.

We are moving as a society in many directions on many fronts. Probably as divisive among our citizenry as any issue of our times is the matter of student protest and unrest in our secondary schools and colleges. Reams have been written examining its many dimensions and facets. The range of response runs the continuum from complete abhorrence and rejection to alliance and full support.

Naturally, few people agree with violence and rioting or other unlawful behavior. Most demonstrations have been peaceful and orderly. The school counselor can help youth, as well as teachers and parents and others who work with youth, to understand the forces and the influences in our society that undergird the discontent and the unrest of these years. He, no more than anyone else who is conversant with this issue, has answers. But he should be attuned sufficiently to the factors involved in order that he can offer some explanations and interpretations.

In his work with teachers and parents particularly, he will find a wide range of human reactions and responses. To these he must be sensitive and understanding. He must be prepared to assert leadership leading to change. He must provide leadership within a strategy that allows for teachers and parents to move through the same process of personal integration as their exposures encompass new ideas, values, and attitudes, and are ordered or reordered, organized or reorganized, in the internalization process.

In working toward the achievement of individual social identity, the developmental counselor can become involved in ways that utilize all three functions—counseling, consulting, and coordinating. Activities in which he can engage are covered in the remaining sections.

The Counseling Functions

(1) Counseling with individual students to assist them in the general development of their social identity or with any particular facet of it for which they may seek help.

(2) Counseling with individual students or groups of students to help them understand better the dynamics of their behavior in social situations and to assess the nature of their social interaction with others both in and out of school.

(3) Counseling with small groups of students to help them in clarifying their own values and attitudes and in conceptualizing and organizing them into their own value complexes.

(4) Counseling with individual students to help them identify their values and the manner in which they apply their values to life situations.

(5) Counseling with individual teachers to help them identify their own values and the means by and the degree to which these are expressed or imposed on others in their day-to-day teaching.

(6) Conferring with parents individually or in groups relative to their approach to value development in the home, and the techniques they use in helping their child (or children) clarify and develop values.

The Consulting Functions

(1) Helping teachers to understand the processes of socialization, including internalization and valuing in particular, so that they might better accommodate the process in their teaching.

(2) Helping teachers to examine the nature of their judgments about children and the factors that may be influencing these judgments.

(3) Helping teachers to integrate concepts about the socialization process in their everyday classroom activities and to relate and use these concepts in helping pupils to assess their behaviors as they internalize and develop their own social identity.

(4) Helping teachers examine the dynamics of human interaction in the classroom with reference to pupil-pupil and teacher-pupil relationships and behaviors.

(5) Helping teachers to identify their own values, the ways in which they reveal their values both in the school and in the classroom, and to understand how they can express or demonstrate their values in ways that will help youth to engage more openly in the valuing process.

(6) Helping school personnel to identify socialized behaviors and values imposed on (rather than chosen by) students and to assess the need for, as well as the results of, these impositions.

The Coordinating Functions

(1) Promoting research activities designed to provide information regarding the learning atmosphere of the school and individual classrooms within the school.

(2) Planning research activities that will provide more information about the processes of socialization including internalization and valuing.

(3) Planning in-service seminars and workshops for school personnel to help them understand better the components of the socialization process, the relation of school and classroom environment to learning and social identity, and the dynamics of teacher-pupil and pupil-pupil interaction.

(4) Planning parent education programs to discuss societal trends and issues with reference to home, school, or community roles in promoting the development of an individual's social identity.

(5) Providing reviews of research and current literature pertinent to the involvement of school personnel in the socialization process or components of it.

SUGGESTED READINGS

COLEMAN, JAMES S., *The Adolescent Society* (Glencoe, Ill.: Free Press, 1961).

ERIKSON, ERIK H., *Identity: Youth and Crisis* (New York: W. W. Norton, 1968).

ERIKSON, ERIK H., *Youth: Change and Challenge* (New York: Basic Books, 1963).

FLANDERS, NED A., *Teacher Influence, Pupil Attitudes, and Achievement* (Washington, D.C.: U.S. Department of Health, Education and Welfare, 1965).

KRATHWOHL, DAVID R.; BLOOM, BENJAMIN; and MASIA, BERTRAM, *Taxonomy of Educational Objectives, Handbook II, Affective Domain* (New York: David McKay, 1964).

PECK, ROBERT F. and HAVIGHURST, ROBERT J., *The Psychology of Character Development* (New York: John Wiley, 1960).

RATHS, LOUIS; HARMIN, MERRILL, and SIMON, SIDNEY, *Values and Teaching* (Columbus, Ohio: Charles E. Merrill, 1966).

THIRTEEN

SELF-MATURATION:

TOWARD SELF-REALIZATION

AND UTILIZATION

Imagine yourself as a member of a high school faculty. You are attending a high school assembly program to induct new members into the National Honor Society. The program begins with an address by the President of the school's Chapter of the National Honor Society. He steps to the podium and begins.

Let me open by dispelling any fears which you may be harboring about this segment of the induction. I come to this platform today not to impress you with a speech on the virtues of scholarship, service, leadership, and character. I come not to relay second-hand facts and worn-out opinions about some distant conflict or problem. I come not to impress you with beautiful language about some deep philosophical debate. I am before you today to protest a very real situation which affects every individual present in this auditorium: the tremendous over-emphasis on grades and the excessive and inhuman workload on the shoulders of the serious high school student.

Grades: that one-syllable word of the English language holds more meaning and power than any other single factor in the high school today. Students do not find a desire for knowledge as the main driving force behind their efforts. Rather, it is the goal of the golden "A" or "B" on the report card that sends individuals into a frenzied scramble of work at the end of each marking period. Evidence of this drive for grades is readily available. Students, for example, talk of success in a course in terms of the grade printed on the report card not in terms of the amount of material being absorbed. The question is always "What did I get?" not "What did I learn?" Grades often force many individuals into the awkward and embarrassing position of "grade-grubbing." "Grade-grubbing" is the humiliating process of begging teachers for extra points on tests and assignments in order to raise the mark on the paper. A student searches feverishly on his papers for ambiguous responses which might be accepted as correct or half-correct answers. The student does not look for what is wrong in his answer; rather he searches for any minute faults in the teacher's evaluation which might get him an extra one and a half points. After quickly combing his test paper for those elusive points, comparing his answers with those of his neighbors', the grade-conscious student timidly raises his hand and asks "Will this change my mark?" The teacher, of course, becomes furious with the student for "mentioning grades at a time when I'm trying to teach," and rejects his plea as being petty and trivial. The teacher has differentiated mentally between grades and the learning process and feels that his teaching atmosphere has been interrupted. Today's student, on the other hand, finds the achievement of grades and learning to be synonymous concepts.

Grades have become so important that students shape their educational careers around this false focal point. The courses that are traditionally associated with a high number of failures are immediately rejected even though the student may have a desire to experiment in this field. Students give opinions as to the relative merits of a teacher based on how hard a marker he is, not on how well the teacher presents his material. Knowledge is secondary; grades come first.

Another aspect of this tremendous pressure is the excessive amount of work demanded of students. Many parents and teachers do not realize the enormous amount of time and effort that the serious high school student devotes to his school work. A noted professor stated last month that the conscientious student puts in a 17-hour day of classes, school activities, and homework. Of course, there are variations from this number and there are individuals who coast through high school with very little work outside of class. The serious student, however, is expected to and must devote more and more time to his occupation as high school student. As a consequence, he has become one of the most over-worked members of our society.

This heavy workload has a very detrimental effect on the individual. First of all, he misses the freedom and joy of being a teenager in our society. It is my belief and that of philosophers and literary giants of many ages that the period of youth should hold a special quality for its members. Youth should be a period of exploration, freedom from responsibility, creativity, and enjoyment. It should be characterized by vibrant expression in art, music, and literature. The pure bliss of wasting an afternoon doing absolutely nothing should be known to all. Young people should have this brief span of time as a glorious splurge of living, away from the responsibilities, problems, and anxieties of adulthood. For all too soon the sandcastles and velvet blankets of youth are crushed by the harsh reality of existence in our society. Then youth becomes a memory—a golden segment of life, a blurred memory of sounds, faces, laughter, tears, strong hates and even stronger loves. And yet the constant burden of endless hours of homework is turning today's young people into frustrated, nervous, and exhausted old men. For many members of our generation there will be few of these memories.

I would like to draw on my own personal experience as evidence of the excessive workload and its effects. Up until the ninth grade I was able to know the joy of creativity through hobbies, music, and artistic expression. The homework load, however, reached a point in that year which forced me into an unfortunate but necessary decision; was I to continue my art and music, my only creative outlets, or was I to submit to the hours of outside work that my teachers demanded. I could not do both satisfactorily and I knew that I must make the decision between grades and fine art. I chose the grades—and that is why I am up here today. Many times I have regretted that decision and wish that I could regain the youth that I have lost over the past three years.

I am bitter when I realize that the only thing that my hands can push is a pencil and not the delicate bow of the violin or the fine shaft of a brush. I am bitter when I count the number of times I have given up whole weekends to do homework. I am weary of late nights finishing assignments of impossible length.

Who is to blame for this excessive pressure? It is my belief that parents provide the initial basis for this pressure. They know that success in the middle class is dependent on a college diploma. Early in the child's life the parent demands that the individual strive to achieve the top in academic success, which is equated with high grades. However, those children who are not gifted with the capacity to maintain a high level of accomplishment begin to fall by the wayside in school. The parents then ask teachers for more homework and pressure to make their child work. The few intellectually talented individuals respond to this added pressure and work even harder on their school work. The ones who cannot handle the workload and need special, individualized attention reject it and begin to resent the education process because it is painful and holds punishment for them. Parents even offer monetary rewards for A's and B's and threaten punishment for lower marks. The individuals who cannot come up to their parents' lofty goals begin to develop negative self-images and work even less. A vicious spiral develops with parents holding out an unreachable goal of perfection, hoping that added homework and grade pressures will somehow force the child to accomplish something he just cannot do. The teachers can assign more and more work and fall back on the excuse that it is the parents who demand the added homework. The absurd part of this spiraling workload is that the students who need it the most do the least, and the capable students, who do not need the added workload, assume the burden. If parents would only realize the actual potential of their own children and set goals for them which are attainable then I believe that many individuals will come to enjoy the learning process and not require the added pressure of excessive homework and grades. I challenge the parents to accept their children for what they are, not what they would want them to be.

Another cause of this pressure is the effect of the Cold War on American education. When the Sputnik was launched in 1957, Americans began to develop national guilt feelings over our education process. It was felt that we had somehow slipped behind the Russians and must bring our education system up to a par with theirs. The responsibility for correcting this inequality was placed on the shoulders of this generation, as are many problems these days. Perhaps the Americans felt that homework slavery and grade anxiety on the part of this generation would compensate for the failure of the last generation to build enough rockets. In any case a definite trend toward increased demands was seen after the launching in 1957. I challenge this nation to accept the fact that the way to a better future through this generation is to not crush it because of a belated fervor for world stature.

An additional cause of the pressure is the increasing selectivity of college admissions. The number of applicants has steadily risen while the available spaces in college have grown at a much slower rate. Even though each college stresses the importance of activities, character, and personal interviews, each one concludes by saying that the best measure of a student's ability to do college level work is his high school record. Consequently the pressure is on the high school junior and senior to produce better and better records of achievement. I can see no solution to this source of pressure. Unless the American public decides to spend less of its money on space shots and more on the expansion of its college educational system, these pressures for admissions will grow each year.

The most important cause, however, of the pressures rests with the teachers. Although parents, Sputnik, and college admissions are definite influences on teachers, the final decision rests with them. They are the most respected body of experts on the subject of education in our society. However, it is the distressing philosophy and attitudes of many of today's high school teachers which are the decisive factors in the mounting pressure on the students. Many teachers equate the quality of the course with the quantity of work being assigned. This attitude comes to the surface when some boast to their students of how many books are to be read, or the massive amount of work that is to be covered. I do not deny that these added burdens may be producing individuals with a great deal of factual knowledge. I question, however, the price of this knowledge. Some teachers have lost sight of the word reasonable in their demands on the acquiescent student. The value of study and homework has grown all out of proportion to its role in the development of the whole personality. Life in our society has so much to offer and yet the student is forced to glean what he can of life from the pages of his textbooks and the reams of endless paperwork he produces. Many teachers do not realize that a teenager's life should not revolve solely about the school environment. Young people have many desires for knowledge and for life which cannot be quenched by endless hours behind a desk.

Therefore, let me close with a plea to teachers. To you, the teachers, who hold the lives of so many in your hands from day to day, who have the training in the needs of young people, who are dedicated to the complex task of providing our nation with a constant supply of discerning, educated young people, I am presenting a difficult challenge in my last opportunity at Amherst: I am asking you to take the lead in a frank, drastic, and immediate re-examination of the pressures in high school; this is a challenge to re-examine those forces which are producing individuals who head for college feeling cheated of their youth and weary of learning.[1]

What is your reaction? Will you applaud Mr. Raiken and then proceed to forget about his challenge? Are you angry with him? Or will his message get to you so intensely that the rest of the ceremony will be lost in your obsession with his hurt and the school's failure? Or will you laugh and say "That's Steve for you!"? What would you do? The many times that I have read Raiken's address I have wondered after each reading if any teacher really heard him crying out and, if they did, how they heeded his alert. It has a powerful message!

Others have spoken in a similar vein. Only two months later in another setting, at the Commissioner's Conference on the Views of Youth in Albany, New York, May 15–16, 1967, youth had things to say about the curriculum, teachers and teaching, grouping and grading, guidance, and student activities.[2] Much of what they had to say was concerned with ways in which the secondary school could better serve youth in search of knowledge and meaning. As Miss Ford, the first of three student keynote presenters, said,

Education is the development of a person with inherent potential into a full, balanced person . . . intellectually, morally and physically. . . . Education (in an ideal high school) would be a growing process, in a creative atmosphere,

[1] Address by Steven Raiken, President, Amherst (N.Y.) Senior High School Chapter of the National Honor Society on the occasion of the Spring Induction Program, March 21, 1967.
[2] Report on the *Commissioner's Conference on the Views of Youth* (Albany: The New York State Education Department, 1967).

in which a person can decide who he is now, and what he wishes to become. At the same time, it must encourage him to freely and responsibly develop what is best in himself.[3]

And there are more. A rather extensive study of the reactions of several hundred high school students has been reported in *High School Students Speak Out*.[4] If we value these youth and what they have to say, why are we so reticent and so slow to move in the directions they suggest? Is this all, as Kathryn Ford suggests, only an ideal, a dream? I hope not.

Why do I begin this chapter on self-identity with the voice of youth that reacts to the gamut of educational practice? For two reasons: I value highly what they have to say and I believe their comments reflect repeatedly our need to actualize the objective of self realization in educational practice. Their comments would indicate that we are not meeting this goal by a long shot. With self-realization and self-utilization in mind, then, let's turn now to a review of the societal and educational forces impinging on the individual.

THE INDIVIDUAL IN MODERN SOCIETY

Historically, American society represents individual freedom. One has only to reexamine the freedoms guaranteed by the Constitution of the United States or to review the procedures characterizing the democratic way of life to be reminded of the importance of the individual in our society. Our nation and its form of government was founded on principles of individualism. We have fought valiantly and successfully for the maintenance of these principles when they have been challenged or jeopardized. We have expended considerable effort in helping other societies establish similar forms of government. While we have not always agreed internally on the extent of these freedoms and have not been successful in extending them to all people, we have continuously resisted outside interference in the basic tenets of individual rights. We have preserved freedom and democracy these many years.

The history of American education has been influenced greatly by such areas of knowledge as religion, politics, philosophy, and psychology. To probe the pervasive and penetrating aspects of these and other influences is the purpose of other textbooks and courses. These many points of view

[3] Kathryn Ford, "What an Ideal High School Means to Me," excerpts from her address as reported in the *Commissioner's Conference on the Views of Youth, op. cit.,* p. 3.

[4] David Mallery, *High School Students Speak Out* (New York: Harper, 1962).

have not made the task of determining the direction and purpose of education easy. They have complicated goals and methodologies, making it necessary for educators to examine beliefs about man and his society and about educational policy and practice. Educators have had to cope with matters of freedom and responsibility and the nature of man. They have had to confront the basic issues in serving the needs and rights of the individual while maintaining and preserving the interests of society. How the school chooses to deal with these issues is represented in its educational philosophy and practice. Most schools in their philosophical statements and program objectives purport to be concerned with the "self" of the pupil. The degree to which they are concerned with this self is determined to a large degree by school policies and by the beliefs of individuals in the system about the nature of man and man's involvement in promulgating and ameliorating his society.

There are several forces and factors relevant to helping the individual utilize himself in our modern world. One point of view that is frequently represented speaks of the role of the individual in relation to national defense and the importance of using our nation's manpower to maintain and enhance the strength of the United States within the world. This point of view, while allowing for individual freedom and choice, maintains that we must utilize our human resources in ways that maximize human potential rather than waste and proliferate it. Concern for the conservation of our human resources is evidenced in programs designed to reduce early school withdrawal (stay-in-school campaigns), and delinquency. Industries have been encouraged to cooperate in "equal opportunity" and school–work programs designed to encourage young people and to help them find themselves a job. Such programs are designed to assist the individual in developing his potential in order to contribute to the maintenance and strengthening of the American way of life. Inherent in such programs is recognition of the need for self-identification and self-utilization in ways that can enhance not only the individual but his society.

The Individual and Depersonalization

Regardless of our national history and the freedoms which have characterized it, we must recognize those scientific and technological advances which have tended to change the nature of the relationship of man to society. In Chapter Two many of these social forces and changes were depicted, albeit briefly. When we combine these forces and measure their impact, we are forced to conclude that it is no longer easy for man to find and maintain his identity. The role of an individual, in his work and in his social life, is changing in ways that make it more difficult for him to express his individuality and to find meaning in his existence.

The increasing technical aspects of our personal and social affairs, as well as our vocational pursuits, tend to reduce rather than enhance one's feelings of worth and uniqueness. These are readily documented in the lives of those people whose daily experiences exemplify man's continuing and expanding condition of depersonalization. It is this trend that necessitates more than ever our need to help youth in beginning to establish their identity and to find meaning in their existence. This is perhaps their most important quest. I am always reinforced in this belief when I listen to their music. Lyrics such as "I've got to be me" and "My way" are so much an indication of their striving and searching for a self-identity.

The nature of societal tendencies toward depersonalization has been a point of discussion in other sections of this book. Yet it may help to recite some of the changes which are indicative of it and to raise a few related problems in meeting the identity needs of youth. A young person used to find some identification in the transmittal of a value or a skill from father to son or mother to daughter. In these times the longevity and the utility of a value or a skill is strongly in question. What is useful one year can be obsolete the next. Even though skills and values are less apt to go out of style rapidly, our changing mores increasingly bring more and more ways of being and doing in question.

Skills are even more susceptible to change than values. A father is hesitant in transmitting his skills; his son is dubious of learning them. Values can be communicated more readily within the family unit and parents are prone to pass along their own ideals and beliefs. The young child readily accepts these and comes to value them. It is only later in adolescence that he may experience situations which raise doubt causing him to question that which he has been carefully taught. And, again, the adolescent finds himself in conflict. His rejection of family values can bring about a breach with his family. His need to reevaluate his beliefs and values causes internal turmoil and stress as he tries to seek a compromise—one that will please his family and one that will provide the needed "balance" (personal and social) for himself.

In the past the individual has had more opportunities to identify himself through his work, his neighbors and his friends. Man could delight in his uniqueness as expressed in his craft or business. His home and family provided for further expression of his individuality. Modern man, however, has less opportunity to express himself through his job and he finds his life and the values he incorporates more like those of his friends and neighbors. There is a tendency toward sameness in things and people. The sprawling suburban development is a prime example—house after house, more alike than different, with occupant individuality expressed by its color and the appendages such as its shutters and lamp post, its neatly manicured and well fertilized lawn (individuality is best shown here by the man who dares to let his lawn become ill kept), and its backyard pools. Inside these homes, families can express uniqueness in their selection of its furnishings provided their decor remains acceptably "period."

The Individual and the School

While learning is the core of education, we must never lose sight of the learner as an individual. We need to continually remind ourselves of the importance of recognizing the *self* of the individual as he engages in the learning process. In our concern for maximizing the potential of the educative process, we have frequently allocated matters of curriculum and teaching method highest priority. The doctrine of individual differences while recognized universally in theory is often sacrificed in practice. We become concerned more frequently with the group than with the individuals that comprise the group. We often compromise the individual for the benefit or welfare of the group.

Since teaching will remain primarily a group process, any consideration of the act of teaching must deal directly with the paradox of individualizing instruction to serve each individual's learning proclivities and of maintaining a group climate that benefits the learning needs of the group as a whole. There is no ready solution for this dilemma. The secondary school is a real life situation and what goes on among the inhabitants of any classroom is reality, not a representation of it or of what it might be. We are not teaching youth to live with others, they *are* living with others! Within each school and classroom, then, helping an individual in day-to-day situations seems appropriate to the resolution of this dilemma.

The American classroom is typically a matter of dealing with thirty or more individuals in a group situation. It is easy to understand why we have believed in individual differences (and talked about them in principle) but have attended to the normative aspects of teaching. The fact that we have been able to identify aspects of the developmental nature of individuals has helped us to determine the behaviors and maturational sequences that can be expected at given periods. We have been able to generalize about human growth and development and to plan and conduct an educational program based on normal patterns of human development. Within this normative framework, then, we have tried to individualize our instructional program, to employ the doctrine of individual differences in ways that will accommodate the individual needs of the learner.

There is little doubt but that there has been great variation in teacher ability to handle the individual and his needs within the generalized structure of the learning situation. Some teachers have been able to deal very effectively with individualized needs while others have been unable to deal to any extent with the individual without great detriment to the total instructional program. The instructional program is the prime target of teacher concern. Teachers need a great deal more assistance in learning how to deal with individuals within the framework of the program, which prescribes and details learnings for an entire group.

If we are going to help young people learn to recognize and utilize themselves, we shall have to begin engaging them in the process at an early age. We are going to have to help them realize more fully who they are, and how they can utilize self as they grow and develop. This is a day-to-day operation that begins early in the life of a child. It will require readjusting our self-understanding, self-direction activities, from those characterized by faith to those engaging the here and now.

As we mentioned in the previous chapter, much of our present day effort at helping youth capitalize on having them engage in activities which, it is believed, will be good for them and helpful to them in the future. This necessitates faith in what one is doing, faith that it will lead to a life of meaning and worth.

Young adults are repeatedly speaking to us of their faith in what has been selected for them to achieve. Activities that will require them to recognize and utilize self in the present (the here and now) may prove to be more effective in self-realization. Certainly such activities will engage the child in decision making earlier and more actively.

In our social studies classes we talk about an individual's rights and responsibilities in a democracy. We talk about what these involve. We talk about ways of becoming informed about major national issues so as to become an informed member of the electorate. Meanwhile the student government in the school—a here and now opportunity to employ these same principles in an important, significant and immediate way—is left to a once-a-year campaign where a few students are elected to offices in which any action they initiate is under the direction and scrutiny of the school principal. The outcome is that students are left to learn on faith and, as most high school students will tell you, the student government continues to be a mockery of democratic practices.

Sometimes we fail to move ahead because we feel inadequate or insecure seeing a task as being too involved for us. Dealing with the self of the child is one of these areas. Teachers believe there is little they can do because they don't have sufficient knowledge or background to handle it. This is understandable. And yet the self is one of those areas where teachers need only to examine the influence and the pressure they are already exerting. Teachers bring out many facets of the self just through their own caring and understanding. A few minutes here and a few minutes there can work wonders so long as the communications are genuine. They can turn students in negative directions just as readily.

Many a student has evidenced a marked change in his attitude or behavior when he has been told how well he performed or how helpful he was. On the other hand, accusations and sarcasm can result in less than positive behaviors like learning to "play it cool" or to be deceitful. These behaviors, in time, take their toll on the self-concept. Teachers don't need advanced courses or hours of in-service work to proceed in these ways to deal with youth. They need only to begin to assess their relationships with their students and to become cognizant of their impact on the growth of the student's self.

The Individual and Interpersonal Relationships

Whereas in the past we have emphasized the importance of facts in the educative process, education in the future will have to deal more directly with the self. We shall increasingly recognize the importance of interpersonal relationships. We shall emphasize ways in which humans can express and utilize themselves for, as well as with, other people. Emphasizing the humanness of the person, and his capacity to express his humanness, may be one way of helping the individual to utilize his identity more appropriately in the modern world.

We can distinguish among classroom behaviors those which permit youth to express and utilize their human capacities and those which inhibit individual expression. We can examine ways whereby the educative process can help individuals learn to express themselves more fully. In other words, our classrooms can be real living situations where students not only talk about how people should get along but where they can talk about how *they* are getting along and about how they are using or are not using themselves in human as well as social ways.

This suggests that one's individuality may find expression in his human relations—in his interaction with others—in his caring and in his being, in his learning to utilize himself in a world of people. This may differ, in part at least, from the past where one learned to express his individuality in his deeds. His deeds were his accomplishments—the things he did could be attributed to his hand or his mind. This remains an effective utilization of the self but it may not be as possible in the future. Increasingly man finds his identity in who he is—in *his* decisions, *his* actions, *his* involvement. Man is what *he* represents himself to be.

This means that all school personnel, not just the school counselor, must be aware of the nature of their relationships with students. The classroom teacher, perhaps more than any other individual, must be skillful in establishing the conditions for effective human relationships. She can create, modify, or dissipate student feelings. She can lead a student to see himself as capable or adequate, as inferior or unworthy. She can provide a classroom where pupil behavior is characterized by fear and anxiety or she can create a classroom where pupil behaviors reflect excitement and eagerness, where pupil motivation and interest are high, where pupils can be open to their experiencing, yet one where the limits have been established and where structure can, as necessary, be provided.

The Individual and Human Needs

One cannot ignore the school's past concern for the emotional development of the child. Educators have been describing the child in relation to the emotions he exhibits ("He's a happy boy," "Martha is easily excited") or the manner in which these emotions are expressed behaviorally toward other persons ("Bill seems to have a chip on his shoulder," "Sally often hits the other children"). It is not uncommon to find teachers describing children in relation to their own emotions ("Mary is a delight," "I get angry with John a great deal"). Being concerned *for* the child, then, is not new. It is the concern *with* the child that is different—with his understanding of who he is and how he uses himself. This requires quite different teacher reactions and judgments.

In the past we have tended to examine and assess emotional development from external, normative standards, and to formulate our evaluations in relation to these expected standards. We have tended to employ case study and case conference techniques to gain additional information and to provide insights into ways in which the school could help the child. We have engaged other pupil personnel specialists—school psychologists and school social workers—to work with deviant learners and their families. For some children, particularly deviant learners, we will need to continue these efforts. For the normal, variant learner the assessment and understanding of his needs and feelings remains quite an individual process. It is hardly a process that can be readily accomplished by other persons.

Maslow's delineation of basic human needs suggests an approach to self-concept development which has utility for secondary school personnel. Maslow describes man's emotional needs in a hierarchy of five levels: physiological; safety-security; belongingness-love; esteem-prestige; self-actualization. Needs at the lower end of the hierarchy (physiological, safety-security, and belongingness-love) are often most readily satisfied through immediate interaction with other individuals.[5] Those at the higher end of the hierarchy (esteem-prestige and self-actualization) are less readily satisfied in immediate situations. They are highly individualistic and basically intensely private and personal.

The self-esteem and self-actualization needs must, insofar as possible, be met in order for a person to have feelings of adequacy and fulfillment. An individual must begin to develop some sense of his worth as a person. He must have some experiences of accomplishment and achievement. To the extent that these needs are unattended and unfulfilled, the development of his self will suffer. The individual nature and the wide variety of human needs, the manner in which these needs are recognized, and the extent to which students are able to express needs and seek their gratification must be considered in the teaching-learning process. Many youth in our affluent society (more affluent each year as government programs continue to reach the deprived) are grappling for acceptable ways of dealing with the higher level needs of belongingness and esteem as their physiological and security needs are more readily satisfied.

Students will continue to express all kinds of needs. They are in process of developing and discovering a highly unique inner self. It is within this inner self—so private and personal—that one discovers the resources and potentiality that can be effectively utilized for self-actualization and self-fulfillment. The educative process by its very concern with matters of self-realization can provide experiences that lead one to examine the sources of his motivations and satisfactions. In providing experiences that can help an individual identify his needs, we help him to examine his own feelings about his experiences. We should be encouraging students to express their feelings of joy, hope, excitement, anger, fear, and guilt. We should be moving them to experience the range and richness of these emotions. We should be freeing them to live all these experiences, and to be sensitive to and aware of their experiencing. In short, we should be helping them to be human and to recognize and express their humanness.

Equally important is the prolonged impact the educative process can have on the emotional development of children. Children who experience an overabundance of fear, anxiety, frustration, and guilt in an extended learning environment are not being provided with positive conditions for self-growth. Rather, such situations can lead to feelings of inferiority, unworthiness, personal conflict, anxiety, or shame.

In our attempt to provide for the growth of the youth, we must be as fully cognizant of his experiencing and its uniquely inner nature as of the

---

[5] A. H. Maslow, *Motivation and Personality* (New York: Harper & Row, 1954), Chapter 5.

conditions in which this experiencing occurs. Thus, our best efforts to assist the individual in his own self-utilization should focus on his involvement in examining and assessing the nature of his experiences and the conditions of his experiencing. We should rely less on techniques that center around an assessment of him by "others" even though these may be more accurate judgments of his growth and behavior.

While observation of pupil behaviors, case studies, psychological tests, individual inventories, and other pupil appraisal and assessment devices may be helpful, it would seem that individual assessment and appraisal is facilitated when the student himself is involved in the process. Such involvement is also best accomplished when encouraged in day-to-day experiencing rather than at some crisis point. Further, if the pupil is to be really involved, conditions that evidence understanding, acceptance and trust must be provided.

THE SELF-CONCEPT

In recent years a great deal has been written about the self-concept and its development. The recency of this proliferation is, of course, partly due to the growing impact of the phenomenological-self-existential system of psychological thought. In this section we shall examine the theoretical base upon which much of our concern for the self-concept of the individual rests.

The Self-Concept Defined

The self-concept is defined by English and English as follows: "a person's view of himself; the fullest description of himself of which a person is capable at any given time."[6] The self-concept in a unitary sense is an encompassing one, tending to incorporate a number of more specific views of self. Or to describe it another way, it is a gestalt consisting of a constellation of many self-perceptions. An individual can describe many different facets of his own self. Combs and Soper talk about these concepts of self, stating,

Each individual, within a comparatively short time after birth, has developed a large number of perceptions about himself. These more or less separate perceptions of self might be termed "concepts of self." They are more or less

---

[6] Horace B. English and Ava C. English, *A Comprehensive Dictionary of Psychological and Psychoanalytical Terms* (New York: David McKay, 1958), p. 486. Used by permission of David McKay Company, Inc.

discrete perceptions of self which the individual regards as part or characteristic of himself.[7]

Combs and Snygg distinguish between concepts of self and the self concept thus:

Whereas the concepts of self about which we have been speaking describe isolated aspects of the person, the phenomenal self is the organization or pattern of all those which the individual refers to as "I" or "me." It is himself from his own point of view. . . . To describe the organization of those very important or central perceptions of self involved in a great deal of the individual's behavior, it is sometimes helpful further to differentiate the perceptual field to include only those perceptions about self which seem most vital or important to the individual himself. . . . We call this organization the self concept.[8]

Combs and Soper describe the formation of the self-concept as follows: "The self concept is created by the individual's inferences from his unique experiences. It is derived from observations about his own behavior and the behavior of other people toward him."[9]

The "self" is the product of a series of learned or observed perceptions resulting from interaction with other persons. If in the course of his interaction with others over a period of time he develops a number of positive concepts of self, these, in combination, comprise his self-concept, which likely will be positive in direction. Negative self-perceptions, in combination, may cause a person to feel less worthy and to view himself negatively. While it is possible for a person to have both positive and negative concepts of self, the concepts that one deems important and upon which one acts form the core of the self-concept.

It is difficult to generalize about the self-concept because its composition and nature are defined by the large number of separate perceptions that a person has gained about himself. Yet we often hear mention of a person having a positive (feelings of adequacy) or negative (feelings of inadequacy) self-concept. At best this is a generalized description of self-perception which a person might attribute to himself or which another person might attribute to him. At times it is sufficient to deal with this global, generalized self-concept. At other times it is necessary to deal with a discrete, more specific concept of self.

[7] Arthur W. Combs and Daniel W. Soper, "The Self, Its Derivate Terms, and Research," *Journal of Individual Psychology* 13:135, November 1957.

[8] Arthur W. Combs and Donald Snygg, *Individual Behavior* (New York: Harper & Row, 1959), revised edition, pp. 126–127.

[9] Combs and Soper, *op. cit.,* p. 137.

Self-identity, as it is considered in this chapter, is a composite term used to refer to an individual's identification of his own uniqueness and purpose as a person. It incorporates the self-concept but it also encompasses the meaning and significance of the self-concept with reference to one's philosophy of life. It is not sufficient to establish one's strengths and weaknesses without attaching some value or significance to these in terms of what one wishes to be or how one chooses to live.

Self-identity goes beyond knowing oneself. It provides for the individual to relate his self to others in his world and to his society, insofar as this is possible. Obviously, self-identity is a life-long concern. It is rooted in the development of the self-concept; it springs directly from it. In this sense, then, the school is concerned with the development of the self concept and with its translation in the emerging self-identity of the adolescent.

The Development of the Self

The self of a person is always in the process of evolving and changing. Beginning with birth, the human organism gradually defines itself as an individual with its own unique qualities and characteristics. This process of self-emergence and self-definition is a reciprocal endeavor involving an individual and all other individuals who share his life. The individual learns who he is from his experiences with others and their reactions to him. Thus, the defining of one's self is a learning process that takes place over a lifetime.

Naturally, every individual has more contact with some people than with others. For most individuals, mother, father, other members of the family, friends, and teachers are daily contact people. These are the "significant others" in an individual's life whose behaviors toward him and whose reactions to his behaviors teach him so much about himself. Over a period of time an individual experiences many life situations with many different people affording him many opportunities to test and retest his self.

It is relatively easy to understand how the very young child learns about objects and ideas but it is more difficult to understand what he learns about people, particularly himself. The self is an inner and private world that cannot be readily identified by others and it often remains a mystery to the individual himself. The growth of an individual toward self-identity necessitates his becoming aware of himself—physically, mentally, socially, emotionally, and vocationally. Psychologists refer to this as self-awareness. As an individual grows, he becomes more aware of his self in its many dimensions. As he experiences himself in many life situations he is able to project better the self he wishes to be and he is able to assess more accurately the self perceived by others. As he grows in self-awareness he is better able to accommodate the discrepancies he perceives between his real self (the way he experiences himself) and his ideal self (the way he wishes he were). Also, he is able to discern discrepancies between his own view of self and the view he perceives others have of him.

Every year of human growth is crucial to the evolvement of the self. Every day in the life of an individual provides an opportunity to test, to validate, or to explore new and unknown aspects of one's self. The period of adolescence is especially crucial in terms of self-maturation. As the individual moves from adolescence to adulthood, he is assumed to have a maturity which will allow him to establish himself in society. This infers that he has achieved a sufficient self-identity to permit him to fulfill work and family roles and to carry out the day-to-day responsibilities which these and other roles demand. At the same time he is assumed to be in sufficient control of his own self to make decisions and choices and formulate goals that will suit his individuality and his life style and lead him toward the fulfillment of his life objectives.

There are several ways of viewing the self that help to explain the concept of self-identity. We must remember that full self-identity is rarely achieved, for an individual, even as an adult, is always becoming aware of new facets of self and extending his experiences into uncharted regions of self. But the adult does have an advantage. He has a basic self-identity from which he can further explore self, yet at the same time he can use himself in ways that are beneficial to him and to his society.

Now let us turn to some of the dimensions of the self as these have been developed by authorities using phenomenological concepts.

The phenomenal self. Combs and Snygg, whose definition of the self was presented earlier, contend that the many perceptions which make up the phenomenal self are not ". . . a mere conglomeration or addition of isolated concepts of self, but a patterned interrelationship or Gestalt of all these."[10] In its organized form, the self is consistent and stable. There are two important distinctions among these concepts of the self, however. According to Combs and Snygg, "Some self perceptions appear to be much more central, or basically part of us than others."[11] They add, "Concepts of the self vary in sharpness or clarity. Perceptions about the self may range all the way from concepts which are vague and barely discernible to concepts which are clear and sharply in focus."[12] Despite its relative stability, the phenomenal self can be attuned or changed as new or different demands

---

[10] Combs and Snygg, *op. cit.,* p. 126.
[11] *Ibid.,* p. 124.
[12] *Ibid.,* p. 125.

make these changes necessary. Combs and Snygg, in speaking of self concept changes, indicate that "While changes in peripheral aspects of the self concept may sometimes occur fairly quickly, changes in the important or fundamental concepts of self usually change only slowly and gradually."[13]

Self consistency. A theory of self adequacy based on an organized and consistent presentation of the self has been postulated by Prescott Lecky.[14] He emphasizes the unity and the stability of the personality. According to Lecky, an individual builds a consistent view of himself and selectively admits only those values and ideas that fit his own perceptions.

We can understand this notion if we relate it to the upper levels of the internalization process. Lecky contends that an individual selectively admits into his own value hierarchy those beliefs and ideas that tend to maintain and support the individual's own value structure. Those which cannot be assimilated and integrated because they are inconsistent or incongruent tend to be rejected. Lecky does allow that the value complex can be re-conceptualized and reorganized, although this is accomplished at greater individual expense. The individual tends to resist values and beliefs that challenge the organized value complex. Learning, according to Lecky, would occur when an individual encounters situations that are in conflict with the organized self. The individual is aroused to cope with the conflict until it can be resolved in a manner consistent with the unity of the self. In facing conflict the individual can only allow change to the extent that it is accomplished while he maintains his own unity and stability.

Lecky states, "As a person grows older, and as situations change, it is expected that new values will be assimilated into the organization and old values eliminated; meanwhile the organization must be kept consistent as well as may be in the process."[15] The behaviors that define the self are consistent with these internalizations. Thus a person will behave consistently with his perceptions of himself. This self, as Lecky portrays it, would tend to be a fairly stable one—one that is capable of change, though carefully guided by the individual who must maintain the self above all else.

Self-congruence. Rogers hypothesizes a concept of congruence that he defines as ". . . a matching of experience, awareness, and communication."[16] Congruency must be considered in degree since it involves the level of an

[13] *Ibid.,* p. 161.
[14] Prescott Lecky, *Self-Consistency* (New York: Island Press, 1951), second edition.
[15] *Ibid.,* p. 187.
[16] Carl R. Rogers, *On Becoming A Person* (Boston: Houghton Mifflin, 1961), p. 339.

individual's awareness of the relationships among these. The congruent person is one who is aware of what he is experiencing thus allowing him to communicate more authentically. He is, therefore, able to be more genuine in his communicatory behaviors. He may be more facile in risking himself with others. He is one who may recognize more quickly his own incongruent behaviors. Congruency is related to self-consistency in that it depends on an internalized and organized self-identity yet it does not necessarily demand consistent behavior. Self-congruence is a behavioral expression of self-awareness and an assurance that one is developing a self-identity.

Self-actualization. In the previous section we discussed Maslow's hierarchical conception of human needs. You will recall the self-actualizing need as the highest and most self-fulfilling. Maslow describes it as follows: "It refers to man's desire for self-fulfillment, namely, to the tendency for him to become actualized in what he is potentially. This tendency might be phrased as the desire to become more and more what one is, to become everything that one is capable of becoming."[17]

In establishing his theory of human motivation based on the needs of man, Maslow notes ". . . that gratification becomes as important a concept as deprivation. . . ."[18] Self-actualization represents an ultimate in human development—a level of human behavior that perhaps few people attain. Yet everyone strives for it and perhaps many achieve a degree of self-actualization. The motivations of man, the influences and drives that move an individual are basic to Maslow's conception of the need hierarchy. Self-identity is geared to knowing, or being aware of, those needs that cause a person to move in a certain direction or to seek one satisfaction rather than another.

Toward maturation of the self. The self is both object and process. It is conceptualized through values, beliefs, ideas, and attitudes that have been both introjected (those an individual has been carefully taught) and internalized (those he has selected, valued, and acts on). It consists of all those self-percepts that have been incorporated and which, in combination, make up the structure of the self-concept.

As process, the self is experienced in the realities of day-to-day situations and interactions. This is the experiencing, active self in all its organismic responses and feelings. It consists of all the reactions and evaluations an individual experiences in the course of his living. The opportunities for conflict

---

[17] Maslow, *op. cit.*, pp. 91–92.
[18] *Ibid.*, p. 84.

between the self as object and the self in process are numerous. The degree to which conflict exists can be understood using the constructs of congruence and consistency.

To the extent that one's conceptualized self and one's experiences are in balance, little conflict is felt and one can be said to experience congruence. To the extent that these are different or in conflict, an individual experiences self-incongruence. Such incongruency often results in the expenditure of considerable energy to defend the conceptualized self—to establish, if possible, a balance. Behaviorally this may involve rejection of one's experience or resistance to the forces that magnify the incongruency. Very often this results in the rejection of one's self and the establishment of negative percepts. To the degree that one internalizes these negative experiences, one is less able to move forward in actualizing behaviors. In fact this can lead to self closure and perceptual distortion, making it more difficult for the individual to cope with reality.

Self-consistency does not necessarily imply rigidity since the consistency of self is related to the range of conceptualized self. If this self can accommodate only a very narrow band of experiences, it is apt to show in more rigid, inflexible behaviors. If it is sufficiently wide to tolerate a wider set of experiences, there is apt to be more personal fluidity and adaptability. Such a person cannot be viewed as having a loosely structured self for it may be a well organized one. It permits a broader range of human experiencing (the self-in-situation) before conflict with the conceptualized self occurs. Such a wider range can allow for more varied, even inconsistent, expressions of feeling before an individual feels threat, guilt, or fear. Such an individual can exhibit some behavioral inconsistencies (as perceived by others) without interfering with his self-structure. It is only as his experiences impose on or contradict the conceptualized self that the individual finds it necessary to become rejecting or resistant.

In either self-congruence or self-consistency, however, an individual can encounter conflict. As the individual becomes aware of this, he begins to divert his energies toward its resolution or extrusion. As his attention becomes focused on these self-discrepancies, the individual becomes more selective in his perception of his experiences, more liable to distortion, less open and more rigid in his behaving. In brief, he is not able to facilitate his self-maturation, he is less likely to risk himself, and he is unable to actualize his potential. As these are compounded, he is likely to withdraw or retreat from experiences with others.

On the other hand, as his self matures, as he is able to incorporate and accommodate his new learnings and deal constructively with such self-conflicts as may arise, he is able to move toward the further actualizing of his self. Being aware of his feelings and behaviors, and able to deal with and accept them, allows the individual to see himself as adequate, to accept failure, and to risk himself in new tasks and situations.

Since he does not have to expend his energy defending his organismic experiences, he can more freely explore his self and its unknown domains and tap the inner resources of his being. In the Maslowian sense, he is moving toward self-actualization. In doing so he is in touch with his feelings and aware of his experiencing. His fluidity allows him to move forward in more original and creative ways and to engage his own self more fully for his own fulfillment and the benefit of others.

The Adolescent and Self-Identity

Having reviewed some of the basic constructs which can help us to understand the nature of the self and its development, let's turn to the period of adolescence and some of the particular hurdles which the individual must surmount in establishing his own identity.

Adolescence is the period when many introjected learnings (values, attitudes, etc.) are tested in reality. This is the period when earlier childhood identifications (as part of the conceptualized self) are re-evaluated and tested for their worth or meaning to the individual in terms of the "self" he now envisions or strives to be. Erikson speaks to this period as a time of "identity formation."[19]

The process of finding self-identity is not without conflict. The adolescent's conflicts are intensified not only by earlier learnings and identifications but by physical changes, which add new dimensions to his organismic experience. If he has few internalized values and beliefs (those he has assimilated by his choice and of which he is consciously aware) and more of the introjected type (those he has absorbed through acquiescence, conditioning, or indoctrination and of which he may not be aware), he is very likely to encounter many situations that challenge his self as it has been structured.

This stems partly from the fact that much of conceptualization of the self has been largely a process of accepting the beliefs and ideas of others with little of his own involvement—his own thinking—in its internalization. In adolescence, then, he becomes more consciously aware of these past learnings and their influence on his behavior. He is caused to examine them and to think about them deeply. Part of the conflict of adolescence is due to these earlier identifications and introjections and the turmoil or stress from his need to reformulate his views and reconfigure the self.

[19] Erik H. Erikson, *Identity: Youth and Crisis* (New York: W. W. Norton, 1968), p. 159.

There is little question that the empirical, biological self is conditioned (past learnings) but the individual through his awareness can come to recognize these conditionings and can take action to restructure his conceptualized self in ways that are more effective for him and his self-actualization. There is a suggestion here of a rapprochement between the behavioral (the conditioned man as a reactive being) and the teleological (the purposeful man as one moving toward actualization, man becoming).

Thus, there appear to be three major considerations relative to adolescence and the formation of one's identity set. First we must recognize and understand the conflict and confusion that the adolescent experiences as he relinquishes or modifies his earlier identifications. Thus the adolescent is faced essentially with the task of not only restructuring his view of self but with accepting his right to waive earlier identifications as new identity configurations appear more appropriate to his being. Matters of autonomy, sex role identification, social and personal responsibility, value selection and formation, and personal commitment are all inextricably a part of the adolescent's task of finding himself. It is little wonder that these are years of uncertainty and confusion.

Second, it is obvious that adolescents who are unable to resolve their conflicts can be severely restricted in their learning-maturation and even ultimately in their ability to assume adult roles. The increasing tempo of modern society will no longer allow us to leave these matters to time. In a slow, evolving society, adolescent concerns could be left to time and their natural evolution; it is doubtful if the modern American society can rely on this method. We must understand and accept the challenge of the adolescent years and prepare ourselves to offer our youth the kind of assistance they need in working through the basic concerns and problems of establishing their individual identity.

Third, we must recognize the influences of societal change on the patterns of identity development. Self-identity is a concept that is rarely achieved; that is, it is a human task that is never completed. Yet there are aspects of self-identity that we might call identity set. While we have viewed this basic set as essentially a task of adolescence, it becomes more obvious each year that changes in our society have extended or elongated the process of basic self-formation.

In our present-day society, the restrictions on youth that prevent their actual experiencing of various life roles such as the limitations on work experiences, longer periods of educative exposure, delayed or limited responsibilities in the home and community, and structured activities may require us to reconsider the period of self-identity as one that extends well into the young adult years—well into the twenties and perhaps, for some, into the early thirties.

This remains, at this time, a matter of conjecture. Even if psychologists accept this contention, our society is not so structured. It expects adult behavior in its conventional forms. It anticipates adulthood as it has been legally defined. It has experienced difficulty accepting any delay in the formation of one's self-identity (the general adult rejection of the "hippy" is an example). We must remain open to a continual reexamination of the self-identity process, making our reassessments in view of our knowledge about human growth and development and the changing ways of our society.

The secondary school can begin to foster the process of self-definition and in this respect there is much to be done. Edgar Friedenberg takes a similar point of view. In speaking to the task of adolescence, he says,

This task is self-definition. Adolescence is the period during which a young person learns who he is, and what he really feels. It is the time during which he differentiates himself from his culture, though on the culture's terms. It is the age at which, by becoming a person in his own right, he becomes capable of deeply felt relationships to other individuals perceived clearly as such.[20]

THE SCHOOL AND SELF-IDENTITY

Obviously the school can and does contribute to the development of the self-concept. As a child proceeds through the educative process from year to year, he has an opportunity to learn about himself as a result of the many and varied experiences provided. Contact with a variety of individuals over a period of years yields human interactions from which an individual can form an endless number of concepts of self or self-perceptions.

It is likely that these will cluster in constellations of perceptions providing the core of the self-concept. For instance, a child may form a number of perceptions about himself in physical activities. While these may vary from positive to negative, if he has sufficient positive perceptions of these activities he will probably feel quite adequate. He will come to see himself in other developing skills—reading, number work, writing, etc.—in much the same manner. If he excels sufficiently in all skills, these combined perceptions of self should provide a most positive self-concept about his ability in the academic aspects of school. We could list hundreds of constellations that develop out of thousands of self-perceptions.

While this is a very simple explanation of the school's contribution to the development of the self-concept, it serves to show the developmental

[20] Edgar Z. Friedenberg, *The Vanishing Adolescent* (New York: Dell, 1959), p. 29.

nature of one's self-image. It shows, too, how the self-concept can change. If a sufficient number of these self-perceptions are changed through experiences in the school, that eventual facet of the total self-concept is changed. If sufficient facets of the total self-concept are changed, then the general character, or perhaps direction, of the self-concept is changed.

The school, as the center for many experiences that can influence these self-constellations, is a very real force in the direction of the development of an individual's self-concept. While a school may wish to focus on facts and skills, it cannot ignore its influence on the self-concept. The most significant "influencers" at any one time are, of course, the student's teachers and his peers.

Although everyone in the school (as well as everyone outside the school) plays an important and influencing part in the formation of the self-concept, the experiences and opportunities to make self-observations and inferences from interactions with one's classmates and immediate teachers in the school situation are numerous. These self-learnings can be viewed as a most significant part of the individual's learning experience in the school. These are learnings which in great measure contribute to his developing self-image. These are learnings which direct his behaviors, which tend to determine his way of living. These are learnings which he utilizes in directing himself toward the fulfillment of his goals and ambitions.

While the factual learning of his educational experience may provide him with helpful and essential information, it is only as he is able to use it, in combination with his self-realizations, that this total educational experience can be a forceful and dynamic one. While the accumulation of knowledge and the development of skills are vital aspects of the learning process, these must be considered within the totality of the learning experience. When we think of learning in this way, we recognize its very personal and individual nature.

The School, the Teacher, and the Self-Concept

Thomas Hopkins stresses the importance of the environment in the early life of the child.[21] His description of the self-concept development of a child at six years of age shows how the child is beginning to form concepts of himself—concepts that identify him as a six-year-old now but, even more important, concepts that accumulate gradually in all these and other areas to blend later in the individual's self-identity.

[21] Thomas Hopkins, "Who Am I?" *Childhood Education* 39:416–419, May 1963.

Obviously, as we noted earlier, the home is responsible for the initial perceptions that form the basis for the evolution of the self-concept. Members of the family are significant influencers, remaining significant but sharing significance with the teacher and classroom peers when the child enters school. Although the importance of the home and early interactions with family members as the foundation of a child's attitudes and behaviors is sufficiently obvious, the years of schooling represent a period when these can be modified and changed. This emphasizes the very important role of the school in self-concept development.

H. G. Morgan, illustrating the importance of the home and school in building self-esteem, suggests a number of directions for the school in self concept development.[22] Citing the teacher as a most significant person, he indicates several possible directions whereby the doctrine of individual differences can be translated to classroom action, leading to the fuller development of human potential. He very clearly challenges current classroom grouping practices, classroom organization, the availability of teachers for conferences with pupils, and pupil appraisal practices.

J. W. Staines,[23] in investigating the influence of the teacher in self-concept formation, observed the classrooms of two pairs of teachers who were rated comparable in experience and proficiency. Teacher self-referents were categorized (performance, status, physique, values, traits, wants, etc.) and coded for probable effect (positive, negative, neutral, and ambivalent— in that they could affect a child either way). Staines concluded that teachers differ widely in their self-references, noting that comments on performance and status were most frequent.

Interviews with children to ascertain the effect of these teacher-pupil interactions, while difficult to quantify, indicated that the students were sensitive to the comments and influenced by them. In a follow-up experiment using pre- and post-self-ratings, two classes were compared. In the experimental group the teacher attempted to provide for various aspects of the child's self-concept. Staines found that the experimental teacher was

. . . able to make his pupils more sure of what they are like and more accepting of what they are, more able to differentiate themselves and to see themselves with moderation as well as with certainty, more certain of what they want to be like, and more aware of what judgments they think others make of them.[24]

---

[22] H. Gerthon Morgan, "Building Self-Esteem at Home and School," *Childhood Education* 38:278–280, February 1962.

[23] J. W. Staines, "The Self-Picture As a Factor in the Classroom." In *The Self in Growth, Teaching, and Learning,* Don E. Hamachek (Ed.) (Englewood Cliffs, N.J.: Prentice-Hall, 1965), pp. 404–423.

[24] *Ibid.,* p. 421.

Davidson and Lang[25] conducted a study to investigate the relation between children's perceptions of their teacher's feelings toward them and their self perception, school achievement and behavior. Using boys and girls in the intermediate grades, they found that the children who perceived their teacher as feeling positive toward them tended to see themselves positively. Children who had a positive perception of their teacher's feelings achieved better and displayed more desirable classroom behavior. The study also indicated that, in general, girls perceived the feelings of their teachers toward them more positively than did boys.

William Morse,[26] in a study of 600 children (alternate grades from three to eleven), used a self-report inventory to assess the self, social, home, and school self-concepts. He reported that student's self-regard decreased with each higher grade level. The school self-concept also decreased with each succeeding grade. Morse concluded:

While the number of negative responses in both the self-picture and the school self-esteem is unpleasant to contemplate, the school self appears to grow gradually less positive with time. Whatever else we have done, we have communicated a sense of personal failure to many of our pupils. In general, the longer we have them the less favorable things seem to be.[27]

Obviously, the classroom is going to have the most influence on the self-concept development of an individual. The school counselor will have little opportunity, if any, to be involved directly with self-concept formation or change. He can, through the counseling function, help youth in clarifying and integrating their concepts of self. Being able to show school staff members where they can help students and their development is just as important.

The school counselor, through his consulting function, can help teachers to become more aware of the self-concept development of students. He can help them to understand how they can (1) contribute to the development of the self-concept in their day-to-day contacts, (2) plan experiences that will help children to use and expand their self-concept, (3) observe behaviors that indicate or exhibit the nature and direction of an individual's self-concept development, and (4) work directly with individual students who might need special attention or specific experiences.

[25] Helen Davidson and Gerhard Lang, "Children's Perceptions of Their Teachers' Feelings Toward Them Related to Self-Perception, School Achievement and Behavior," *Journal of Experimental Education* 29:107–118, December 1960.

[26] William C. Morse, "Self Concept in the School Setting," *Childhood Education* 41:195–198, December 1964.

[27] *Ibid.,* p. 198.

He can work to develop the necessary teacher understandings that undergird this kind of teacher concern and involvement. Among the understandings he would hope to develop are the following:

(1) Teachers are influential agents in the development of the self-concept.
(2) Teacher interaction with a student usually involves some aspect of a student's self-concept.
(3) Teachers have feelings and needs that are often in conflict with those of a student.
(4) Teachers can identify an individual's concept of self and over a period of time can identify a constellation of these, indicating the general tendency of the self-concept.
(5) Teachers should expect the student to display behaviors indicating concepts of self that appear contradictory, vague, or unclear.
(6) Teachers can secure self-concept information in formal and informal ways including observations of student behavior, student statements directly expressed, and self-reporting devices.

The School and the Self-Concept of the Disadvantaged

In working with those adolescents who come from disadvantaged populations, the self-concept is often a base from which the school can offer relevant and vital experiences. While there are many characteristics attributed to disadvantaged youth, a negative view of self or inadequate feelings of self-worth—in general, a low level of self-esteem—are commonly identified. Couple this distorted image of one's worth with various authority hang-ups, underlying feelings of anger and hostility, and value orientation conflicts, and you have no small problem indeed.

In many ways the counselor can help these adolescents through individual counseling. On the other hand, the classroom is the central source of self-concept change and the counselor can use his special knowledge and skills in helping teachers to make necessary classroom adjustments and manipulations that can foster positive attitudes toward self and others. The developmental counselor, by means of his consulting relationship with the classroom teachers, can suggest approaches to the teaching-learning process which are appropriate to the needs of disadvantaged youth. Large segments of disadvantaged youth in our secondary schools are being exposed to an educative process that presupposes middle class goals, middle class needs for achievement, and middle class values. Even more importantly, it assumes the more typical middle class self-concept.

In emphasizing the important role of the classroom teacher, it is thus necessary to provide means whereby teachers can become more fully aware of their feelings about the disadvantaged—that they engage in some assessment of their own attitudes on racial and ethnic issues and their feelings of anger or attitudes of prejudice. The developmental counselor can help them to identify and deal with their own hang-ups concerning the disadvantaged and their own behaviors in reacting to the disadvantaged adolescents in their classrooms. This will probably occur through individual counseling sessions with teachers as an ultimate extension of the consulting function (third level).

It is not my intention here to discuss all the elements of the self-concept of the disadvantaged and the manner whereby these could (and often do) differ from that of their middle class counterparts. However, some of these characteristics associated with the self-concept are worthy of examination and further study:

(1) ambivalent identifications of masculinity-femininity
(2) feelings of guilt and tension resulting from repeated failures, discipline, etc.
(3) attitudes of suspicion, fear and a general lack of trust of others
(4) defensiveness
(5) aggressiveness
(6) feelings of rejection
(7) attitudes of hostility
(8) group loyalty.

The Self-Concept and School Marks

It can be said that schools have emphasized grades to the detriment of the self. Grades and all they entail in the school life of a child have become the symbol of the learning process—the earmark of school success. Students, eager to excel, under pressure to achieve, or in fear of survival, have become immersed in what Steven Raiken dubbed "grade-grubbing" in his address to the faculty at the beginning of this chapter.

Grades, and those who determine them, represent the power complex of the student world. Learning, as we would envision it, loses its meaning when students select a course with an eye for the grade as opposed to its value for them. The scholarly pursuit of grades, which can begin as early as kindergarten, diminishes learning and subjects the self of a student to the whim of his evaluator—the teacher who grades his work. If he succeeds, he may feel positive; if he fails (or in many cases fails to excel), he may feel negative about school and—more important—about himself. The compilation of these experiences year after year after year takes its toll on human potential.

The realization and the utilization of self become mere concepts about human development and to talk about these as a product of the teaching-learning process is futile. Using courses as a means of exploring an interest, learning a skill, or testing oneself in a world of new experiences is far less likely to occur. A student feels he can't afford to fail; he can't dare to risk the unknown.

Such an environment is not conducive to the process of learning-maturation. This condition is characterized by many of the human feelings that are better known for inhibiting learning when excessively applied—fear, guilt, anxiety, and pressure. The essence of pupil involvement in the tasks of learning are soon lost; study and homework assume far too much significance. What could be creative, happy days becomes years of tests and tension. The individual, as a matter of fact, either digs in and performs and conforms or he soon falls back. In many instances he drops out of school, usually in disgust—an "also ran."

I don't feel that I have overdrawn the influence of present-day marking practices and pressures. We shall soon have to reevaluate the measure of marks—and their toll—on the youth of our land. If we are to highlight self-concept development and if we mean to do more than mock those efforts designed to help young people toward realization and utilization of self, we must examine very closely what exists—as opposed to what could be.

Although I would personally prefer to have our present system of evaluating students discontinued, I would encourage and endorse any procedures which emphasize the involvement of a student in assessing his progress and behavior in relation to any aspect of his school life. I would hope for evaluation which would encourage a student to say, "I don't know but I'd like to find out." I would hope for a system that fosters curiosity, that rewards originality, that allows an individual to risk an idea or an opinion, that encourages him to explore and to move into the unknown, and, above all, that challenges the depth of his inner resources that these may be realized and utilized rather than left untapped, stagnant, unknown, underdeveloped.

I believe a marking system which can create excitement in learning will prove more beneficial to the individual—and ultimately to our society—than one that is stultifying and deadly. I believe we need a system that speaks for the individual not to him. In this way he can learn to say "This is where I am, this is what I am; this is where I hope to go, this is what I hope to be." As it is, our system says to him, "This is what *we* think you are."

The Self-Concept and School Achievement

There is sufficient evidence to indicate that the self-concept of boys and girls is significant in their feelings about school and in their approach to learning. However, research on the relationship between self-concept and school achievement is conflicting, making it difficult to establish any distinct course of action.

The school has valued school achievement and it has expended time and money to measure individual student achievement each year. In fact, teachers get quite involved emotionally in interpreting individual and class achievement test profiles. The measure of a successful year of learning is often determined by the amount of student growth evidenced in these kinds of tests.

One cannot dispute the school's concern for the intellectual growth of the individual. But one should dispute the almost complete concern for achievement that is represented by the mastery of subject matter content which relies almost exclusively on the mental processes of memory and recall. Even allowing for good objective-type tests that necessitate using other mental processes in arriving at "the answer," there are other ways of viewing intellectual achievement and other avenues of student growth that should be considered. We need more research based on a perspective of school achievement that extends beyond mastery of subject matter content and skills.

The Self-Concept and Interpersonal Communication

We read and hear more and more about the importance of interpersonal relations in human communication each year. We experience the problems that occur when people fail to communicate adequately among themselves. Many of the institutional difficulties that erupt in demonstrations, sit-ins and other forms of protest are in part attributable to breakdown in the lines and forms of human communication.

This is happening in the giant corporations where efforts for some time have been directed toward helping the individual recognize his worth within the total institutional structure. This has taken many forms but chief among them have been practices designed to develop a sense of loyalty to the corporation and a personal identification with it. As our institutional structures become bigger and bigger—regardless of whether they are business, school, municipal government, or whatever—and as our population continues to swell, people will strive even harder to achieve a sense of personal identity. Assuming that the trends of the past decade will continue, and accelerate, people will need to be able to communicate more freely and openly with one another. This means helping people to use effectively all means of communication—verbal and nonverbal. This is predicted on feelings of personal worth that are associated with self-understanding and self-identity.

Even as adults we shudder at the mere mention of the words confrontation or encounter. Somehow they connote trouble. Clark Moustakas has defined the confrontation as ". . . a private, intimate conflict between persons which happens, often spontaneously and unexpectedly, when a crisis arises in a relationship and the persons must either reach a new level of life together or face the consequences of a broken relationship."[28] He goes on to say,

> In the classroom confrontation, the child must have the right to be in dis-agreement with his teacher. Paradoxical as this seems, when persons can openly disagree, it is possible for them to establish genuine bonds. When the teacher forces the child to submit through repetitious phrases and commands, through conditioning, belittling, group pressures, brainwashing devices, or intimida-tion, the child soon realizes that the only acceptable way is the path of con-formity. Increasingly, the child becomes insensitive to his own self and un-responsive to his own experience.[29]

Unfortunately, the student does not always "have the right" to differ with his teacher. Some children are raised with the notion that the teacher is always "right." Those who are not conditioned to this belief soon learn that it does not pay to disagree with the teacher. We must find better ways of dealing with these levels of interpersonal communication.

At one time it was common for children to be seen and not heard. And at one time it was common to hitch the horse to the buggy to go to town. The society that we sketched so briefly here and in other chapters must have people who are active, alive, and real—who are free to speak out. If the self that we are developing leads to passivity and conformity, then our educational goals are a sham. This doesn't seem to be the case with all of our youth. There are young adults who dare to confront openly the society they experience. There are also those who do not.

A confrontation need not carry the connotation of rebellion and vio-lence, of irresponsibility, or of anarchy. People can confront one another and move to new and higher levels of understanding and relating. To live in that world of tomorrow, today's youth must be forthright and bold rather than subdued, fearful and defensive. How can we really help create a flexi-ble, adaptable man if he has not been free to experience himself as a per-son? This should be an integral part of his education. This should be a part of his search for personal and social balance. This should be a significant aspect of his finding commitment.

Moustakas has defined the encounter as ". . . a direct meeting between two persons who happen to come together."[30]

[28] From *Creativity and Conformity* by Clark Moustakas, p. 45. Copyright © 1967, by Clark E. Moustakas, by permission of Van Nostrand Reinhold Company.
[29] *Ibid.,* p. 46.
[30] *Ibid.,* p. 56.

The human encounter is not a superficial experience but rather one in which two people engage each other at deeper, more intense levels of interaction. There is concern for one another, yet neither is restricted by the social conformities which so often prevent genuine expressions that communicate feeling and involvement with each other. This would seem to characterize more accurately the type of teacher-pupil interaction demanded in these times.

How much better teacher-student relations might be if students were able to encounter their teachers under these conditions. Many disagree, indicating that such encounters would encourage disrespect and disobedience leading to unmanageable or chaotic conditions. This is always a possibility under any conditions. I presume the best measure we have of our ability to deal with interpersonal matters of communication in the school lies in an analysis of teacher talk in the faculty lounge or of student talk at home or among themselves. Some would contend, and I would join them, that both teacher and student would grow if they were free to communicate more openly with one another. Not only would both feel better, but chances are good that both would come to better understand and know the other.

Human learning as an inner process calls upon an individual to draw from the wells of all his resources, to use himself in all the creative and imaginative ways he can. In this way, with each new experience, he emerges with new and different perspectives. He learns to use his inner resources not only for his own growth but for the welfare of others. His contacts with people take on meaning and significance. Instead of abandoning learning, he seeks more. He is motivated and challenged.

We are always moving *toward* self-realization and self-utilization. It really never ends, nor do we ever achieve full awareness of the potential that lies deep within us. We learn as long as we live. We learn to use what we have and most of us learn to use it effectively. While it is safe to use only those parts of ourselves of which we are sure, when we are free to move away from the known toward the unknown, when we are willing to risk and to accept new challenges, only then do we really test our potential and the limits of it. Then have we moved *toward* the fuller utilization of our self.

The Body and the Self-Concept

As we noted in discussing the physical maturation of the adolescent in Chapter Ten, schools have emphasized physical growth and health. Very few schools have attempted to deal with body experiences leading to more acute body awareness. Sidney Jourard speaks of the importance of body contact, stating, "Touching another person is the last stage in reducing distance between people. Each person lives as if with an invisible fence around his body,

a fence that keeps others at that distance which one feels most safe and comfortable."[31] Although our society has developed an unwritten code for body
contact (the "touch taboo"), if the body is as important to the self-concept
as some of the research suggests, we need to take another look at our approach to human communication through physical contact.

Jourard reports research with 168 males and 140 female unmarried
college students in which he attempted to ascertain the willingness of an
individual to be seen (visual) or touched (tactual) by another person and
to identify the body regions of such contact.[32] As we might expect, more
visual than tactual contact was reported. Except for relationships with an
opposite sex friend, most body regions were untouched. Body contacts between father and son were restricted to fewer body regions than between
father and daughter. Subjects who saw themselves as attractive reported
more body contact than those who saw themselves as unattractive.

If we believe that physical contact can remove barriers between people,
making them more available for human interaction, then it is possible that
body contact can enhance one's ability to relate with his fellow man and to
use himself more fully with others. At the same time, he may find himself
a more desirable person.

If the studies of body awareness and accessibility have any implication
for secondary education (and I believe they have) and for the development
of the self-concept, we should begin to incorporate into the regular program
of the school more activities designed to provide students with a greater
number and a wider variety of body experiences.

In beginning to implement such a program a few basic explanations
may help. First, we must recognize the existing "touch taboo" that characterizes the social code for interpersonal tactual behaviors. Although we do
not have data of a normative nature on touching and touching patterns for
our society, we can begin with the assumption that human communication
and interpersonal relations can be enhanced—that we can reduce the distance between two people—if we can encourage people to include touching
as a mode of relating. If we can accept this assumption, this would constitute
an important step forward. Second, while I am inclined to caution and conformity, I am also willing to risk. Some schools and many teachers will not
be ready to allow youth this experience. The element of risk in any community must be considered, for there will be community members who will not
understand the nature and purpose of body contact experiences. Third, most
adults have been conditioned not to touch another person. We are carefully

[31] Sidney M. Jourard, *Disclosing Man to Himself* (Princeton: Van Nostrand,
1968), pp. 136–137.
[32] *Ibid.,* pp. 136–151.

trained to "excuse ourselves" even if we accidentally brush an arm or a leg against another's body. We must recognize the effects of social conditioning and we should observe the parent prerogative to inculcate these same behaviors in their children.

IMPLICATIONS FOR SECONDARY SCHOOL GUIDANCE

Guidance has long purported to deal with the self of the individual, yet there is reason to wonder if the development of the self-concept has really been a focus of the school counselor's concern. At best, efforts have been directed toward the adjustment of the individual—toward helping the individual fit into the socialized system of the school. Such attention must be considered in relation to its remedial rather than its developmental focus. Further, it tends to be restricted to those students who evidence patterns of deviant learning. In looking to the future role of the developmental counselor, those secondary school programs that will truly take on a developmental character will exhibit a concern for all students. These programs will attempt to facilitate self-concept development within the variant learning patterns which all students display. The individuality of each learner will be recognized.

The developmental counselor is in a position to help teachers employ the doctrine of individual differences more fully in the teaching-learning process and to examine the learning outcomes with reference to the development of each individual's self concept. This, then, represents a shift from working primarily with selected students who have problems to working primarily with classroom teachers who are in a position to contribute to the day-to-day development of adolescents, giving the program more of a *preventive* emphasis.

Such a shift is not readily nor easily implemented. It depends on a certain commitment that must permeate the system. It necessitates helping teachers to view the individual and his learning in ways to which they are not accustomed. The school counselor needs to be aware of these factors in deliberating with members of the school staff on ways of approaching self-concept development.

The school and its personnel are most likely to move toward objectives and activities that are subject to measurement and appraisal. The school is organized and the curriculum is sequenced to accommodate periodic appraisals of student progress. It is only recently that we have altered the traditional progression of student progress from grade level to grade level to allow for ungraded classes and more individualized instruction. Teaching personnel may incorrectly expect individual movement toward self-identity to progress precisely and logically. They may need help in understanding the very unique and often amorphous aspects of self-maturation.

In many ways, the growth of the self is the antithesis of the usual school expectancies. It is difficult to measure, to authenticate, or to corroborate. It is resistant to the quantifiable outcomes of the teaching-learning process. School counselors need to be prepared to counteract the conventional arguments which can be used to thwart the inauguration of self-concept activities in the school. The introduction of practices which are designed to enhance self-concept development is not an either-or proposition. It is more a matter of integration of these concerns with those others which the school has equally accepted as its objectives.

While we can characterize the concept of self-identity and employ practices that hopefully, help an individual to become aware of himself, we need to recognize the limitations of the secondary school experience. For many adolescents—in fact for most perhaps—the secondary school provides only the base upon which the self-identity process will continue after he leaves the school.

The continuing complexities of American society may well extend the duration of the "psychological moratorium" of which Erikson has spoken. Even though this period may extend beyond the high school years, the role of the secondary school remains vital. It can help young people to recognize more fully what they are experiencing and it can contribute to their ability to deal with their own self-realization. To *expect* self-identity upon the completion of high school would be as ridiculous as another frequent expectation—readiness to choose a career. It seems more reasonable to assume that self-maturation, while life-long, is a predominant aspect of one's learning that may extend well into the twenties, and for some individuals into the early thirties.

There is another more immediate implication for the collection of information about the student and the maintenance of pupil personnel records. Records that characterize a student as others see him may have very limited value. We still rely heavily on these records in preparing student evaluations for potential employers and in writing recommendations for college. The school will probably be involved in these activities for some time to come since there is little evidence at this time to indicate radically different demands. Nevertheless, we need to reexamine our entire pupil appraisal and evaluation practices, which presently rely on reports of student development *as viewed by school personnel solely.* There is little in our student records to indicate how the student views himself or his world. This has been a serious shortcoming. It has caused school counselors considerable distress at times. In cases where counselors have known the student well they have attested to his potential in the face of record data which would evoke a contrary opinion.

I suspect that we shall always need counselors who have faith in their counselees and who are capable of predictive judgments. But we also need to invite students to participate more frequently in reporting their perceptions of their *own* growth and progress. We need to incorporate *their* judgments far more often than we presently do.

Our involvement of the student in reporting his own progress and in reviewing his own successes or failures should begin very early in school life. It is not something to be delayed until the last year of school. The student who is invited early and often to participate in his own evaluation is far more able to engage in it than one who has learned to depend solely on the evaluation of others.

Here again we square off with the conventional standards of evaluation in our schools and our society. Some schools that have attempted to discard the standard reporting practices, particularly the traditional report card, have been opposed by parents who want a professional judgment of their child's progress, preferably in the form of a grade which they can understand and evaluate. We need to recognize these parental needs and demands and to help them learn other ways of evaluating the learning-maturation of their children.

This is a large order for the school and one that will test the professional creativity of school personnel. If we view self-concept development within the framework of "self" and "other" evaluations, we can then proceed to implement these procedures within our classrooms and in our reporting to parents as conditions allow. This means an active program whereby school personnel can communicate these goals, as well as those involving content achievement, to the community.

Implementation within the classroom is the first step. Teacher-student or small-group communication can provide the teacher and the student with feedback that can be used to foster self-growth. A teacher is not always "right" in his or her judgments about every student. Communication between the teacher and the student can reduce the differences that may exist; at least it can afford an opportunity for them to discuss their differences. And how often these differences do exist! For example, a student may feel his short story was most creative whereas his teacher did not. The possibilities that can emanate from discussing their differing judgments are endless. The teacher may gain insights that will help her to know the student better and perhaps to provide more appropriately for his growth. The student should gain in his own self-understanding and may come to understand his teacher more fully.

While we must recognize the limitations of time that impose on the number of such opportunities, we must also acknowledge that we have but scratched the surface in availing ourselves of those that we do have. It is time we committed ourselves to these goals. It is toward establishing these commitments that developmental guidance holds promise.

The Counseling Functions

(1) Helping individuals or groups of individuals to clarify and understand their normal fears, guilts, anxieties, and resultant behaviors which inhibit their self-concept development and interfere with the nature and direction of their learning-maturation.

(2) Helping individuals or groups of individuals to consider both their positive and negative concepts of self, to clarify concepts of self as they are integrated in the constellation of self-perceptions that form their general or overall view of self, and to plan and engage in experiences that may help them to clarify less known aspects of self, or help them in changing negative expectancies and evaluations to more positive ones.

(3) Helping adolescents achieve a fuller measure of self-identity by assisting them in their examination of their needs, attitudes, capacities, and feelings.

(4) Helping individual students whose view of self is inhibiting their ability to learn or to deal with the tasks of learning.

The Consulting Functions

(1) Helping teachers to discover ways whereby they can influence the development of the self-concept in positive directions (through an evaluation of school and classroom practices such as grouping, grading, classroom communications, and reporting procedures).

(2) Helping school personnel interpret societal trends, the social significance of these trends, and their meaning for the development of the self-concept and student growth toward self-identity.

(3) Helping school personnel to understand better the development of the self-concept and the importance of the school in contributing to and influencing its development in each individual.

(4) Helping teachers to identify, develop and use methods and materials that will help youth to examine their own self-concept and facets of it.

(5) Working with parents, either individually or in small groups, to help them identify ways in which they can enhance the self-concept development of their child.

The Coordinating Functions

(1) Planning and conducting research activities that will assist teachers in evaluating their efforts to enhance self-concept development.

(2) Conducting seminars for parents to help them understand better the development of the self-concept and the influence of the home, the school, and the community on its development.

(3) Evaluating current procedures for collecting and appraising information about the student, relating such practices to ideas about the development of the self-concept and self-maturation.

SUGGESTED READING

COMBS, ARTHUR W. and SNYGG, DONALD, *Individual Behavior* (New York: Harper and Row, 1959), revised edition.
JOURARD, SIDNEY, *The Transparent Self* (Princeton: Van Nostrand, 1964).
MOUSTAKAS, CLARK, *Creativity and Conformity* (Princeton: Van Nostrand, 1967).
MOUSTAKAS, CLARK, *Individuality and Encounter* (Cambridge, Mass.: Howard A. Doyle, 1968).

FOURTEEN

VOCATIONAL MATURATION:

LEARNING TO MAKE DECISIONS

Among the many pressures on our youth none are more constant than those which continually remind him of his need to plan for the future, to make choices and decisions about his educational plans and occupational life. From the time he is old enough to understand the meaning of "What are you going to be when you grow up?" he is continually faced with this matter of choice. This simple question, when asked independently by a dozen or more different people, is a puzzling and confusing one to the adolescent who must respond to this same inquiry week after week and month after month. This is most emphatically compounded when we realize that the individual adolescent is immersed in finding his own identity.

We have always conceived of occupational commitment as a choice which an individual makes at some point in time, usually in the last year of high school or in the few years thereafter. When we talk with young people about their future, we usually imply that at some future time a choice will be made about the kind of work they will do. We encourage adolescents to think about this choice simply by asking questions about their future plans. They very quickly grasp the importance adults attach to occupational planning and the singleness or finality of choice as it is inferred in "Oh well, you have a few years before you must decide," or "You'll make up your mind one of these days." We view occupational selection as *the* choice. We act as if this were fact and we communicate this to youth. It is little wonder that some adolescents become quite anxious and tackle the career planning task with all the fervor they can muster, while others become so distressed they avoid it like the plague.

Many young people have all they can do to handle the day-to-day affairs of "growing up." They reserve career planning for that "time" when such considerations seem more appropriate and necessary. It is more natural to the human learning-maturation process to delay life-long commitments until one has achieved a better understanding of himself and his society. The individual seems to defend himself from commitments until he has had an opportunity to think about some of the more philosophical aspects of living.

Work is an actuality, a necessity of existence for most people in this society. Other than establishing the fact that one must work to earn a living, little has been done to help young people consider the necessity for and the meaning of work in the life of man. At one time, and even today to a large degree, it was considered that man, and particularly the male, made two primary decisions—his work and his mate. Females became these mates and settled into roles of wife and mother. For girls, then, the pressure of career choice has been one they could avoid if the right man came along. While this may seem like an oversimplification of career evolvement, there is a substantial basis for this way of thinking. The importance of a man's work and its pervasive influence was aptly stated by Alba M. Edwards. He commented:

The most nearly dominant single influence in a man's life is probably his occupation. More than anything else, perhaps, a man's occupation determines his course and his contribution in life. . . . Indeed, there is no other single characteristic that tells so much about a man and his status—social, intellectual, and economic—as does his occupation. A man's occupation not only tells, for each workday, what he does during one-half of his waking hours, but it indicates, with some degree of accuracy, his manner of life during the other half —the kind of associates he will have, the kind of clothes he will wear, the kind of house he will live in, and even, to some extent, the kind of food he will eat. And, usually, it indicates, in some degree, the cultural level of his family.[1]

Much of what Edwards has said remains current. Certainly work is an important part of a man's life. It is becoming an important part of a girl's life, too. Females no longer can rely on housewifery as a life-long occupation.

Today's world is different, and work, while remaining significant, may not offer all the personal satisfactions nor meet all of a man's needs as it once did. Those changes and trends in our society which were dis-

---

[1] Alba M. Edwards, *Comparative Occupation Statistics for the United States: 1870–1940*, Sixteenth Census of the United States, 1940 (Washington, D.C.: Government Printing Office, 1943), p. xi.

cussed in Chapter Two, for example, will influence greatly the meaning and significance of work in the life of man. Not only is it necessary to learn more about the changing meaning of work, it is essential that we learn more about the processes of evolving a career. We have made some important gains in understanding the processes of career development. And we are faced with the problems of changing some of our current stereotypes to accommodate these newer ideas. It is about these understandings and their importance in vocational maturation that this chapter is concerned.

The Changing Meaning of Work

While work in the past has encompassed a major portion of man's waking hours, over the past three or four decades a reduced working week and extended vacation and holiday time have provided man with a great deal more time away from his job. The implications of this change alone should cause us to reexamine our stereotyped ideas about the importance of work in the everyday life of an individual. However, there are other changes occurring every year that magnify our need to get on with the task as quickly as possible.

The labor market and manpower trends in our country have added greatly to the changing nature of work. Many of these changes are in progress; they are the actualities of scientific and technological advances. Machines have changed the work life and patterns of man most drastically with the automated advances of recent years. Yet the mind of man has not been able to grasp and assimilate the significance of these changes in terms of the differences they may incur in his life. Historically, we understand the technological changes leading to mass production and work specialization that have resulted, over a period of time, in some work role displacement. But our current advances portend changes that will reach many more workers.

Seymour Wolfbein cites "change" as the most significant force in the world of work in this century, identifying what he terms "the seven faces of change": (1) the changing length of working life; (2) the changing composition of the work force; (3) the changing industrial structure; (4) the changing occupational standings; (5) the changing geography of American industry; (6) the changing productivity of the American worker; and (7) the changing educational and training prerequisites for employment.[2] These are the changes, major ones, which have already

[2] Seymour L. Wolfbein, "Labor Trends, Manpower, and Automation." In *Man in a World at Work,* Henry Borow (Ed.) (Boston: Houghton Mifflin, 1964), pp. 155–166.

taken place. These alone stagger our imagination and challenge many of our existing beliefs and attitudes about the world of work and man's involvement in it. We become especially concerned when we realize that these changes, as well as others to follow, are the realities of the world of work which the young people now in our schools will experience. We wonder to what extent the educative process has been geared to help them meet these new challenges and demands.

It has been projected that man may find it necessary to change his occupation a number of times in the course of his work life. This has been talked about for years. For example, nearly a decade ago, Harold Reed, in dealing with the implications of technological advancement, noted, "It is anticipated that the average entry worker today will have to make not less than three major job adjustments during the course of his work life."[3] New occupations are being created at a rapid pace. The latest *Dictionary of Occupational Titles, Volume I, Definitions of Titles,* a standard source of occupational opportunities in our society, defines 6,432 new job titles out of a total of 35,550 listed.[4] This provides another indication of the changing structure of the American labor force. We can anticipate even more in the years immediately ahead. Wolfbein, in looking to the future impact of all these changes, suggests a direction to be considered:

We are only beginning to understand the nature of work and jobs under conditions of automation and technological change. The little evidence available points up the need, not for narrowly specialized individuals, but for those with the kind of learning experience that enables them to be as maneuverable, adaptable, and responsive as possible to emerging needs, many of which cannot be foretold under current conditions.[5]

C. G. Wrenn, in discussing occupational identity as an index of personhood, indicates that work increasingly fails to meet man's need for meaning and significance in life. Less opportunities for human expression and creativeness in work roles result in less personal satisfaction and pride in work productivity.

This is a part, and perhaps a significant part, of the depersonalization or dehumanization that is occurring in our society. Wrenn believes ". . . that a sense of personal significance, a sense of contribution to the world,

---

[3] Harold J. Reed, "Certain Aspects of Vocational Guidance in a Technological Age," *Vocational Guidance Quarterly* 10:90, Winter 1962.

[4] Bureau of Employment Security, United States Department of Labor, *Dictionary of Occupational Titles, Volume I, Definitions of Titles* (Washington, D.C.: Government Printing Office, 1965).

[5] Wolfbein, *op. cit.,* pp. 171–172.

is a basic human need—or at least it is a need for the American with his particular heritage of work as a moral value and occupation as 'meaning something.' "[6] He then goes on to observe, "The *nature of employed work in our society has changed, and its power to give satisfaction to the worker has diminished;* the sooner we accept this fact, the sooner we can develop a comprehensive set of solutions."[7] Wrenn further suggests that with increasing amounts of time available away from one's work (what he terms non-employed time), we should begin to think about helping individuals to strive toward self-fulfillment and self-actualization through the more effective personal utilization of both employed and nonemployed time. In considering both of these as a means of achieving a sense of worth and personal significance, he proposes that the concept of work be extended to include the use of an individual's nonemployed time. Thus he envisions, "The key to this concept is that 'work' not be restricted to employed activities. One may work in an occupation and he may work out of the occupation. If work in an occupation is not personally satisfying and lacks the capacity to make one feel significant, then let work 'out of the occupation' fill the need."[8] In this way, according to Wrenn, on the job and off the job activity need not be considered "as a polarity but as a fusion."[9] Here again, the implications for all facets of human maturation are many but, for vocational development in particular, broader, more encompassing concerns are suggested.

Schools have been sufficiently alerted to the educational needs of youth in two areas. First, with regard to the external considerations of the occupational structure, we have ample evidence to show that work roles and work life will be different. These differences will reflect an ever-changing society moving with its continual scientific advances. The implications for helping young people assess work possibilities—career exploration—are many. Even more importantly, is the need to help them view the social and self-manifestations of work in the life of man. Second, we have been advised as to the nature of the individual—the kind of person —that society will need.

It appears that the kind of individual who will best survive in the years ahead is the one that can respond and adapt to change. This speaks not solely to vocational maturation but to human maturation and the development of a person who is flexible and adaptable—one who can adjust to changing ways and ideologies. This not only has implications for voca-

[6] C. Gilbert Wrenn, "Human Values and Work in American Life." In *Man in a World at Work*, Henry Borow (Ed.) (Boston: Houghton Mifflin, 1964), p. 34.
[7] *Ibid.,* p. 35.
[8] *Ibid.,* p. 37.
[9] *Ibid.,* p. 37.

tional development but for the entire educative process. It is a challenge that cannot be ignored.

To do something about these two areas for the many adolescents now in high school may be too late because many of these changes are already actualities and the personal dimensions required to cope with them are needed immediately. These times demand action and it behooves education to get on with the task of preparing to serve better the vocational development of youth.

CONCEPTS OF VOCATIONAL DEVELOPMENT

During the past two decades vocational psychologists and others have provided us with a number of partial theories and some research findings, causing us to reexamine the constellation of factors in career determination and especially the way in which an individual chooses an occupation. Already we have enough evidence to explode some of the myths and the stereotypes about "picking a career." We also know that some of our expectations for the adolescent in career development are quite unrealistic.

Many researchers caution repeatedly regarding the limitations of their findings and the tentative nature of theoretical views. This has kept us from adapting ideas in a helter-skelter way, but, on the other hand, it has exacted a reserve in using the information and postulations that afford a base from which vocational development can be further tested and examined. From the many studies that have been reported, there is a growing set of consistent findings that should enable the school to approach the vocational maturation of the adolescent with more assurance than has been previously possible. In the most recent years there has been sufficient agreement on these views to allow the school counselor to apply these findings with some confidence.

Some Notions About Vocational Development

Donald Super is one of the more significant and prolific contributors to the formulation of a theory of vocational development. His research has provided valuable insights from which a number of new ideas and concepts about vocational development have emerged. His work has encouraged others to pursue related investigations. Since the notion of vocational development springs primarily from the work of Super, his approach is significant to our understanding of it.

Vocational development is conceived of as one aspect of individual development. Like social development, emotional development, and intellectual development, it has both distinctive characteristics which make focusing on it worth while and common characteristics which reveal it as one way in which the general development of the individual manifests itself.[10]

Thinking of vocational development as a distinct aspect of human maturation is a relatively new concept. Few textbooks have isolated vocational maturation. In fact some texts make little mention of it, indicating that the selection of an occupation is a task that most adolescents must face. Super has caused us to reflect on it as an important dimension of development and he has attempted to determine some of the features that distinguish it. Other research efforts, such as those studies carried on by Tiedeman at Harvard (the Harvard Studies in Career Development) have contributed greatly to supporting and expanding the concept of vocational development.

The following five concepts about vocational development represent those which appear to be most common in various theoretical views and are supported rather consistently by a number of studies of occupations and occupational life.[11]

(1) Vocational development is a process extending over a long period of time—perhaps a lifetime.
(2) Vocational development is concerned with those physiological, psychological, sociological, and economic forces impinging on the decisions of an individual making both internal (personal) and external (environmental) considerations necessary and significant.
(3) Vocational development consists of a series of decisions which eventuate, over a period of time, in occupational involvement.
(4) Vocational development is experiential in nature, necessitating trial-exploratory behavior of a real and simulated nature allowing one to explore further his self and self-in-vocation.
(5) Vocational development is the progressive and compromising process of achieving self-identity in work roles.

These five concepts may seem too few and too relative to other areas of human maturation to justify a focus as a discrete aspect of human development. Yet as we shall see, the component elements of each concept are quite complex. We shall need to learn more about these. In the meantime, there are more reasons to promote vocational development than to reject it.

[10] Donald E. Super, *The Psychology of Careers* (New York: Harper, 1957), p. 185.
[11] I should like to acknowledge my indebtedness to the many research contributions from which these concepts were distilled.

The following sections will expand on these five concepts of vocational development serving to provide a base for the further understanding and implementation of each one in the secondary school.

Vocational Development as Process

Vocational development is a process. This point is crucial. Earlier in this chapter we spoke of the current view of occupational choice as a decision which an individual makes at a given point in time. This belief about *a* choice has been given further support in the three-step process of Parsonian guidance. You may recall the matching of talents and tasks and the fit that could hopefully evolve through reasoning. Super speaks to our stereotyped belief about occupational choice saying,

The term *vocational choice,* . . . conveys a misleading notion of neatness and precision in time, of singleness and uniqueness in the life of the individual. . . . Drawings showing a fork in a road, each branch leading to a different occupation, with a young man standing at the crossroads, epitomize this notion of the neatness and precision of the event in time.
    Choice is, in fact, a process rather than an event.[12]

As a process, then, when does it begin and end? There are some who would doubt the process of vocational choice. Caplow attributes occupational choice to the accident of birth. Ascribing to a view in which there may be little choice, Caplow holds that ". . . error and accident often play a larger part than the subject himself is willing to concede."[13] For example, Caplow refers to occupational inheritance indicating that some youth are destined to carry on a family business or an occupational tradition. Certainly, any approach to vocational development needs to account for such possibilities in the choice process. The accident of birth seems no more a factor than any other sociological consideration. There are those who contend that labor market opportunities determine occupational choice. And in some instances, they do.

While these ideas have interest, they seem to be sociological and economic influences in the process that can alter choice at different times. They could be determining factors in short term choices that are reconsidered later in another phase of the process. The son of a doctor may start his preparation in medicine to continue the family tradition of an M.D. but he may never complete the program. We have too much evi-

[12] Super, *op. cit.,* p. 184.
[13] Theodore Caplow, *The Sociology of Work* (Minneapolis: University of Minnesota Press, 1954), p. 214.

dence in studies of careers and career evolvement to rely on the "picking" of an occupation and the exigencies that go with the shorter term nature of that approach.

Super, capitalizing on earlier studies defining work periods, characterizes the life stages of the vocational development process.[14] These are summarized as follows:

(1) *Growth* stage (from birth–14 years). It includes three substages: *fantasy* (4–10); *interest* (11–12); *capacity* (13–14). This stage is characterized by the development of the self-concept.

(2) *Exploratory* stage (age 15–24). It includes three substages: *tentative* (15–17); *transition* (18–21); *trial* (22–24). This is a period of tentativeness and transition characterized by self-assessment in trial-exploratory situations.

(3) *Establishment* stage (age 25–44). It includes two substages: *trial* (25–30); *stabilization* (31–44). This is a period of further trial and career building with real effort to stabilize and secure the work role.

(4) *Maintenance* stage (age 45–64). This stage is characterized by permanency and status quo.

(5) *Decline* stage (age 65+). It includes two substages: *deceleration* (65–70); *retirement* (71+). A period of slowdown, decline, and eventual ceasing of work.

These life stages make it easier to think about vocational development in its life-long dimensions. They provide a framework for looking at career development as an evolving process rather than a one-shot or haphazard affair. They help to explain the gradual and continual nature of an individual's finding himself, rather than a niche, in the world of work. They offer some substantive guidelines to the process though they are intended to be flexible and suggestive rather than rigid and prescriptive.

Super is utilizing the life stages in his current twenty year study of vocational development. Initiated in the early 1950s as the Career Pattern Study, Super and his associates are examining the career evolvement of individuals (all males) from early high school until a period when their occupational life may be more stabilized. Thus this study should provide many insights into career evolution particularly during the very important exploratory and establishment stages.

Encompassed in the life stages construct as delineated by Super are the findings of an earlier study by Ginzberg et al.[15] The study was designed

[14] Donald E. Super, *et al., Vocational Development: A Framework for Research* (New York: Bureau of Publications, Teachers College, Columbia University, 1957), pp. 40–41.

[15] Eli Ginzberg, Sol Ginsburg, Sidney Axelrad, and John Herma, *Occupational Choice* (New York: Columbia University Press, 1951).

primarily to ascertain the relative importance of subjective (needs, interests, values) and objective factors (work opportunities, job requirements) in occupational choice. They identified three periods in the occupational choice process: fantasy (6–11+ years); tentative (12–16 years); realistic (18+). They concluded (1) that occupational choice is a developmental process involving a number of decisions made over a period of time; (2) that occupational choice involves the element of compromise between the internal and the external; and (3) that the process of occupational choice is actually a series of decisions in which each decision influences succeeding ones. This study supports several of the concepts discussed here. However, it was one of the earliest studies to suggest the process aspects of vocational maturation.

Thinking of vocational choice as a process is a quite different experience for most individuals. The concept of an occupational choice has not represented very adequately the work history of man for some years. It is the less common (and perhaps more fortunate) man who knows what he wants to do—and does it! Many men have grappled with themselves and their loved ones as they struggled through the trial and error of occupational exploration. I have encountered many young men and women who have had feelings of inferiority, guilt, and uselessness simply because they couldn't "find themselves" in the world of work.

Many have felt pressure from relatives and friends who couldn't understand why they were unable to decide about a job or to stick with one regardless of their feelings about it. Employers are likely to regard applicants who appear to be "job hoppers" with disfavor. Work histories are replete with such experiences. Yet, the idea of one choice persists. One of our primary tasks, then, is to communicate the more appropriate notion of process and to supplement it with behaviors and practices that will reinforce it.

The Internal-External Considerations of Vocational Development

Figure 14.1 depicts the internal-external considerations of vocational development highlighting the integrative nature of the personal and the environmental. The individual, as he deals with the vocational development process, must become aware of both the internal and external aspects of four major societal (or environmental) forces: physiological, sociological, psychological, and economic. Individual considerations of an internal nature are shown in the inner circle and the external factors are revealed in the outer circle. The interaction of these is represented by the arrows indicating the flow between and among the internal and the external considerations.

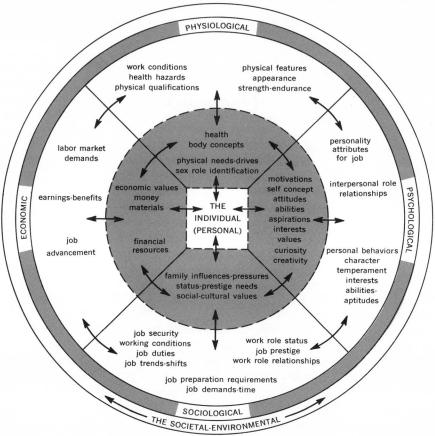

Figure 14.1. The internal-external considerations in vocational development.

Actually, we have been aware of these considerations for a long time. But we have done very little with the internal field perhaps because of its highly subjective nature. Certainly the "facts" of the external domain are easier to pin down and to assess. Recently we have started to broaden the scope of career exploration to include many of the internal aspects that were heretofore frequently overlooked. There is also evidence that we are becoming more involved with some of the external sociological and psychological components that were seldom explored before.

Figure 14.1 details some of many aspects that an individual should consider in the career development process. In the past, as the result of the availability of standardized tests, an emphasis has been placed on the assessment of interests and scholastic abilities and aptitudes. Quite frequently (more often than we care to admit), these assessments are restricted to a discussion of standardized test results and their occupational implications. Even considering the limited number of considerations that could be incorporated in Figure 14.1, it is immediately obvious to the observer that career exploration and planning consists of many more considerations than those usually marked for discussion.

To engage the individual as fully as possible in all the assessments and experiences, both internal and external, that can be helpful, should be an integral part of his day-to-day learning-maturation. While the career unit, the field trip, the program planning interview (a yearly matter in some school guidance programs), and other activities designed to contribute to vocational development are desirable, they must be planned in relation to the total learning experiences of an individual.

We have been more adept in exposing youth to the external dimensions of career exploration. We have encouraged youth to learn about the expansiveness of the world of work and have facilitated job exploration by alerting them to the many considerations which are pertinent to studying and assessing an occupation. Through their many exposures to job opportunities, youth have become oriented to studying work opportunities with reference to the nature of the work, job duties, work conditions, places of employment, employment trends and prospects, job qualifications and requirements, opportunities for advancement, and earnings. Most school guidance programs can point with pride to their means for providing occupational information—a vital dimension of the external field. In the area of the internal considerations, however, we are just beginning to probe the possibilities for helping youth and to blend the internal with the external in the vocational maturation process.

There is a good deal of evidence accumulating to support helping students examine their values and to relate them to career planning. Anderson and Dipboye studied the values of 1,181 high school students in grades nine and twelve. They concluded that these students were more interested in obtaining intrinsically satisfying and stable jobs than they were in attaining ones in which they would have opportunities to work on their own or in which they could advance rapidly. Security and interesting work, they contend, are important ingredients in career planning, being considered more important than work independence or job advancement.[16] Obviously, security and interesting work are individual variables of an internal kind while opportunities for advancement and work role conditions are more characteristic of work situations.

[16] W. J. Dipboye and W. F. Anderson, "The Ordering of Occupational Values by High School Freshmen and Seniors," *Personnel and Guidance Journal* 38:121–124, October 1959.

Robert Hoppock, whose life has been devoted to the study of occupations and occupational life and who is considered an expert on occupational information, emphasizes the importance of needs in an individual's decisions about occupations. In a series of ten speculative statements, he has developed a composite theory which he finds helpful in explaining how people make vocational plans and decisions. His theory consists of the following speculations:

1. Occupations are chosen to meet needs.
2. The occupation that we choose is the one that we believe will best meet the needs that most concern us.
3. Needs may be intellectually perceived, or they may be only vaguely felt as attractions which draw us in certain directions. In either case, they may influence choices.
4. Vocational development begins when we first become aware that an occupation can help meet our needs.
5. Vocational development progress and occupational choice improves as we become better able to anticipate how well a prospective occupation will meet our needs. Our capacity thus to anticipate depends upon our knowledge of ourselves, our knowledge of occupations, and our ability to think clearly.
6. Information about ourselves affects occupational choice by helping us to recognize what we want and by helping us to anticipate whether or not we will be successful in collecting what the contemplated occupation offers to us.
7. Information about occupations affects occupational choice by helping us to discover the occupations that may meet our needs and by helping us to anticipate how well satisfied we may hope to be in one occupation as compared with another.
8. Job satisfaction depends upon the extent to which the job that we hold meets the needs that we feel it should meet. The degree of satisfaction is determined by the ratio between what we have and what we want.
9. Satisfaction can result from a job which meets our needs today or from a job which promises to meet them in the future.
10. Occupational choice is always subject to change when we believe that a change will better meet our needs.[17]

Although the reader will grasp immediately the many significant dimensions of Hoppock's beliefs, Hoppock's emphasis on the individual and his needs is pervasive. Needs are an important internal consideration and

[17] Robert Hoppock, *Occupational Information* (New York: McGraw-Hill, 1967), third edition, pp. 111–112.

the educative process can assist an individual in identifying and clarifying his needs. This, too, is a longer term aspect of the maturation process and is better accomplished on a day-to-day basis.

Super relates vocational development and the self concept, stating:

. . . holding and adjusting to a job is for the typical beginning worker a process of finding out, first, whether that job permits him to play the kind of role he wants to play; secondly, whether the role the job makes him play is compatible with his self-concept—whether the unforeseen elements in it can be assimilated into the self or modified to suit the self; and, finally, it is a process of testing his self-concept against reality, of finding out whether he can actually live up to his picture of himself.[18]

This, then, assumes a good deal of self-exploration emphasizing the importance of helping youth move toward social and self-identity.

The importance of internalization and self-awareness were established in the two previous chapters. However, the interrelationships between self, social, and vocational maturation are located within the internal dimension.

Galinsky and Fast emphasize the importance of self-identity in vocational choice, indicating that problems in achieving a social or self-identity are often surfaced when one lacks the internal wherewithal to come to grips with occupational choice. They assert that many identity problems, in varying degrees, can be associated with the manner in which an individual approaches the evolution of his career. Self-doubt or uncertainty, fear of failure, dissatisfaction with aspects of one's self, and perceived necessity to change one's self to accommodate the personal requirements of an occupation are common identity distortions which they feel inhibit the career development process.[19] The behavioral results of such self-uncertainties or dissatisfactions can be noted in adolescents who delay career exploration, who avoid making choices or decisions with career implications, or who exhibit extreme anxiety through a need to make *a* choice.

Further relationships between the external and internal aspects of vocational development are suggested in a conceptual scheme for the systematic research of occupational choice developed by Blau et al.[20] They emphasize the dual aspects of choice originating from the physical conditions (external) and the biological conditions (internal). The internal dimension considers personality development and sociopsychological at-

---

[18] Super, *The Psychology of Careers, op. cit.*, p. 191.

[19] M. David Galinsky and Irene Fast, "Vocational Choice As a Focus of the Identity Search," *Journal of Counseling Psychology* 13:89–92, Spring 1966.

[20] Peter M. Blau, John W. Gustad, Richard Jessor, Herbert S. Parnes, and Richard C. Wilcock, "Occupational Choice: A Conceptual Framework," *Industrial Labor Relations Review* 9:531–543, July 1956.

tributes as basic to job entry. The external dimension emphasizes historical change and socioeconomic organization. The social structure is depicted in their schema as a variable affecting both the development of the individual and the external opportunities available. Their conception of the process provides a framework for integrating the economic, the sociological, and the psychological factors that must be accounted for in the process of evolving a career. While their schema has not been elaborated in practice, it is helpful to the school counselor in understanding how the many factors of an internal and external nature can be interrelated. Readers may wish to examine their schema and to relate it to that which is presented in Figure 14.1.

Joseph Samler refers to the relation between the internal and external aspects of job exploration, expressing a concern that the dynamics of these be examined with specific reference to work roles and functions. He indicates that he and co-workers have looked ". . . in vain for a dynamic appreciation of work in terms of the individual's role, his self-concept or identity, the exercise of his attitudes and fulfillment of his values, status consideration, and other related factors."[21] Samler makes the point that occupational information is restricted primarily to the traditional portrayal of external data—such as job requirements, duties, hazards, employment outlook. While he cautions against an overemphasis on personality considerations to the exclusion of work role relationships, he advocates developing that elusive blend toward which we have long been working. He emphasizes the need to get at the psychological and the sociological aspects that cause an individual to consider

. . . the worker's role, his ability to work at a task that is congruent with his identity, the exercise of his values and attitudes, considerations of status, ways of meeting anxiety, patterns of interaction with others, out-of-work style of life, and totally, the way in which his personality needs will be met.[22]

He pleads for more research and more material to help the counselor in this task. Now, nearly a decade later, we can reaffirm this need though some progress is being made.

The on-going aspects of "self" development and appraisal obviously harmonize with vocational maturation. The interrelationships among all facets of an individual's learning-maturation serve to support one's preparation for his involvement in the world of work. Although the school counselor will likely be charged with a responsibility for work role infor-

---

[21] Joseph Samler, "Psycho-social Aspects of Work: A Critique of Occupational Information," *Personnel and Guidance Journal* 39:459, February 1961.
[22] *Ibid.,* p. 460.

mation, the important contributions of the classroom teacher, both as a source of information and as a person who can abet vocational maturation with timely interpretations and associations, should not be overlooked. The relevancy of the school program to significant considerations of a psychological and sociological nature, as well as the economic considerations, can be achieved, in many instances, through subject matter references and inferences right in the classroom.

Vocational Development as Decision Making

Vocational development involves decision making processes. This concept is one of the most deceiving. We readily understand the meaning and significance of decision making. But the nature of the decision making process is very complex and we have need of far more research to help us understand how it evolves in human thinking and learning.

Ginzberg et al., whose research findings were summarized earlier, reported that the process of occupational choice was irreversible. They stated,

This is a result of the fact that each decision made during the process is dependent on the chronological age and development of the individual. Time cannot be relived; basic education and other exposures can only be experienced once. Of course, the individual can shift even after he has tentatively committed himself to a particular choice. But the entire process of decision-making cannot be repeated and later decisions are limited by previous decisions.[23]

The postulate concerning "irreversibility" has triggered much interest. It has raised a number of concerns regarding the nature of some decisions which are required of the secondary school student particularly those involved in high school course selection. And school counselors, because of their responsibilities with these matters, have long recognized the critical choices which students are forced to make in early adolescence. For example, in many schools students are forced to make course selections as early as eighth grade. Despite guidance program attempts to provide necessary information that will aid the student in making these choices, the "in-process" state of their identity formation precludes choices which they might not later wish to change. The very fact that adolescents must choose from among several programs of study (college entrance, vocational, accelerated) and elect certain courses (especially in the area of mathematics) initiates the career decision making process very early (around age 13 or 14).

[23] Ginzberg et al., *op. cit.,* p. 185.

Many school schedules and courses of study have been so constructed that once a student is "tracked" his opportunities to change programs diminish. While schools are relaxing those policies which jeopardize the student who changes his mind, these conditions highlight the manner in which school organization and practice figure in vocational development. More importantly, it is another manifestation of the need to engage individuals in all kinds of decision making activity early and often.

David Tiedeman,[24] as part of the Harvard Studies in Career Development, proposes a paradigm of the process of decision in vocational development:

The analysis of vocational development is oriented by each of several *decisions* with regard to school, work, and life which a person makes as he matures. With regard to *each* decision, the problem of deciding may be profitably divided into two *periods* or aspects, a period of anticipation and a period of implementation or adjustment.[25]

The *period of anticipation,* as he conceives it, consists of four stages: (1) exploration (the consideration and "measure" of alternatives), (2) crystallization (the clarification and order of relevant "measures"), (3) choice (the act of choice with varying degrees of commitment), and (4) specification (final elaboration of position and readiness to act on choice). The *period of implementation and adjustment* consists of three stages: (1) induction (beginnings of action on choice with responsiveness behavior and assimilation of choice and goal), (2) transition (modification of group and self goal, assertiveness behavior), and (3) maintenance (equilibrium and maintenance of status quo).[26]

Tiedeman explains vocational development within the context of many decisions indicating that ". . . events of relevance to decision may be unfolding with regard to *several* decisions simultaneously. . . ."[27] A career evolves, he maintains, as one makes choices (anticipation period) and acts on these (implementation) over a period of time. "Each decision potentially consists of seven distinct phases. Each decision is also to be considered in relation with a wider context of past and future decisions leading to the presentation of career before the world in pride and in confidence."[28]

Although Tiedeman pleads for the tentativeness of his model urging

---

[24] David V. Tiedeman, "Decision and Vocational Development: A Paradigm and Its Implications," *Personnel and Guidance Journal* 40:15–21, September 1961.
[25] *Ibid.,* p. 15.
[26] *Ibid.,* pp. 15–18.
[27] *Ibid.,* p. 18.
[28] *Ibid.,* p. 19.

more study and research, it has utility in helping school personnel consider the nature of choice, the process of decision, the complexity of the process in vocational development, and the interrelationship of decisions in effecting all aspects of an individual's development. While we have been conceptually aware of decision as a single and discrete act and of its exponential effect, our efforts, beyond individual counseling, have been minimal. We caution and advise individuals (in whatever stage of the anticipation period), but few attempts have been made to help them understand the decision making process. We should help children to examine the process of decision making just as we should help them with valuing or socializing or any other aspect of their development.

Decision making is closely allied with the development of the thinking processes and the mental growth of the individual. It can be considered in relation to many facets of the school program. What is basically important at this point, with the knowledge that we do have available, is our willingness to proceed to facilitate the individual's internalization of school learnings and the integration of these learnings in whatever ways seem helpful to him. As difficult as this may seem, students can be readily involved in examining the decision making process and their own involvement in it. They are able to differentiate among the types of decisions they make and the factors that influence their choices. In the past, we have been overly concerned with the nature and rationality of these choices labeling them as "wise," "sound," "fanciful" or "unrealistic." Our approach to decision making has been essentially problem-oriented employing the process of reasoning to arrive at rational decisions. In assisting young people to resolve problems we help them look at the alternatives and the possible implications of each. We expect them to make the choices and often all help stops there.

In all aspects of their learning-maturation, we have many opportunities to help them examine their choices over a period of time. We have innumerable chances to explore not only the outcomes or results of a choice but the actual process and its constituent factors. By helping young people to learn how to make and examine their own choices, they should be better able to apply choice and decision making understandings and skills to career planning situations and demands. Also, some of the reluctance to become involved in career planning would possibly dissipate as adolescents become more secure in their own ability to handle choice situations.

In our school guidance programs, we tend to settle mainly for periodic status reviews. That is, we ascertain at given points in time how an individual sees himself and we try to determine insofar as possible the general direction in which an individual is headed. We review past hurdles and crystal gaze about those ahead—both real and anticipated. This tends to hit at the tangible aspects of the process in terms of succeeding versus fail-ing or for meeting future expectations and deadlines. There is little reason why the adolescent cannot be aided in his vocational maturation if we are willing to begin with his readiness to engage in the process.

Using Tiedeman's paradigm, the high school years represent the period of implementation in the sense that the individual is implementing choices about his program of study. He moves through the various stages of this period as he proceeds through school. At the same time he is ex-periencing the period of anticipation with regard to his post-high school plans. School guidance programs, as presently organized, cater to the ex-ploration stage. This seems quite in accord with the maturational level of the adolescent. However, the paradox lies in the expectation that by high school graduation he will have miraculously progressed through the stages of crystallization to those of choice and specification. Even acknowledging that upon graduation he must make *a* choice, we need to help him under-stand the nature of this choice within the whole decision making process. Earlier choices to be reexamined and assessed, as well as others that may be faced in the future, should be considered more relevant to vocational development during these years.

Vocational Development as Experiential

Vocational development is dependent on trial-exploratory experiences which allow an individual to test who he is and to explore ways in which his self can be expressed in the world of work. This exploring begins very early in life. It consists of many exposures and the development of many concepts and ideas. These experiences need not be actual work experiences. Any exposure which helps the individual to find out more about what he can do or how he responds—almost any activity that allows the individual to grasp more fully a feeling for himself and an awareness of who he is can be considered a valuable exploratory experience.

The more closely some of these exposures can be tied to work roles and work ways the better. There was a time when young people had more opportunities to experience the world of work. They could watch, from an early age, their fathers and others at work and later they were able to help them. Today these opportunities are more limited than they were even twenty years ago. Most fathers and mothers work away from the home or community and it is the exceptional child who gets to see his father at work in any regular way. Many elementary school children are unable to identify either their father's or mother's work.

Adolescents do not fare much better though they can usually associate their parent(s) with a company or an employer. "He's a (name of company) man" or "Mom works at (name of company)" are illustrative of the frequent responses to an inquiry about a parent's occupation. Boys and girls probably learn more about occupations from attending the movies or watching television than any other source. This kind of learning has value but it doesn't replace on-the-job observations or experiences where one has an opportunity to try his skills, to test work role and interpersonal relationships, or to contend with on-the-job conditions, noises, and odors.

Labor legislation and the union movement, among other forces in the labor market, have combined to restrict the work opportunities for adolescents. At one time a young person could be considered for almost any kind of work. Today, and for urban youth in particular, many of these opportunities are restricted by law or closed to nonunion workers. Youth now find themselves greatly limited in the variety of work opportunities until they reach 18 years of age. Until then, there are limited job possibilities for girls (such as babysitter or store clerk) and for boys (such as gas station attendant or stock boy). Part-time or summer jobs offer very little variety and they seldom provide more than random experiences to really test oneself.

More than specific work learnings, these jobs offer an individual the chance to develop attitudes toward work and to test his interpersonal relations in an on-the-job setting. These are fairly well tested in two or three weeks and after that, young people report, they find staying with the job a test of endurance more than anything else. After they reach the age when they are no longer restricted by labor legislation, usually a year or so after high school graduation, they can more readily locate employment which can offer more job exploratory possibilities.

On the other hand, adolescents today have more opportunity to explore themselves in more varied nonemployed settings. Many recreational and leisure time outlets offer them possibilities for further self-exploration. Through hobbies, sports and travel—all of which are available in growing numbers—young people can ferret out unknown facets of their own being, pursue interests in greater depth, and find new and different challenges. While these nonemployed experiences may only provide clues to actual vocational possibilities, they add to the background of an individual's experiences helping him to formulate some ideas about his preferred way of life. Further, as C. Gilbert Wrenn suggests, students may find through these outlets, other sources and ways of attaining personal significance and satisfaction.

He can be encouraged to try new experiences which afford him an opportunity to explore some of the lesser known regions of his being or which cause him to have to venture into areas of endeavor of which he is less sure. Opportunities to travel, to speak before a group, to serve in a community activity or to work with a group of children are examples of experiences which an individual might find new or different for him, yet helpful.

Sometimes students in testing a choice fail. However, it helps to fail gracefully and with support and understanding, as opposed to failure with the aftermath of "I told you so," or "You were warned not to try that." As adults, whether parent, teacher, or counselor, we sometimes become overly protective in trying to prevent what is commonly perceived as the humiliation of failure. Failure can be a rewarding learning experience and adults who are caring and empathic can help to keep the hurt and sadness minimal.

Vocational Development as Compromising

Compromising can be viewed as a part of the internalization process and as such is a higher order activity in the more complex levels of the affective domain. It involves exploratory and decision making behaviors over a period of time. It describes the combination of thinking and experiencing whereby an individual considers his self and the occupational possibilities available to him, and progressively blends these in ways which the individual perceives he will find personally satisfying and situationally successful. It entails discovering distortions in his view of self and the occupational opportunities available to him, examining discrepancies between the way he believes he performs and the way others report he does perform, and differentiating between what he would like to do and what he can do. It requires that the individual accept, assimilate, and use these awarenesses in reestablishing or redirecting his vocational aspirations and plans.

To understand the compromising aspects of vocational development one must first divorce himself from the vestiges of an outdated concept—that which views an individual as "picking an occupation." Further, it requires that one recognize that labels and opinions are often attached to people while they are maturing vocationally. For example, adults are prone to label vocational aspirations with adjectives that reflect their judgment and valuing of an individual's particular choice ("wise," "unrealistic," "sound"). Or they might react to a student's decision to seek a skilled trade by saying, "He could do better than that." These judgments and reactions are, at best, opinions and, if stated at all, should be prefaced as such. They represent a lack of understanding of the process of vocational development and of compromising as a part of the process.

Super prefers the term "synthesizing" to describe the progressive modifications or compromises in the series of decisions that result in one's achieving self-identity in work roles.[29] He feels that "compromise" fails to describe the longer term and interactive nature of the process, implying an action that occurs later in the vocational development of an individual, probably closer to the time when reality testing in work roles actually begins. Synthesizing, he feels, more adequately portrays the interactive process. He states:

Before attempting to describe the synthesizing process which is interaction, it may help to remind ourselves of what is being synthesized. It is, on the one hand, the personal needs and resources of the individual, and on the other the economic and social demands and resources of the culture. . . . [synthesizing] . . . is a *learning process,* and as such often takes place without verbalization, without full awareness on the part of the individual of what is taking place within himself or between himself and his environment.[30]

Super is actually suggesting synthesis as the learning about self as this takes place in internalization and as the individual learns to use this self in ways which are satisfying and self-fulfilling to him. In synthesizing, the individual is ever compromising as he learns what he can and cannot do, what is meaningful to him or not meaningful, or how he feels in different situations. As these become clearer to him, he is able to make the necessary modifications (compromises) that help him to maintain "balance." In this sense, he is able to translate these to his occupational ambitions and plans.

Obviously, some of these compromises must occur in reality testing. Occupationally, this can occur in all the life stages but one compromises more frequently in the exploratory and establishment stages. While some compromising may occur without self-awareness, it is quite questionable if any learning has occurred. And without some self-learning, it is doubtful if the situation can be considered a part of one's vocational maturation.

It is important that we recognize the learning aspect of compromising as it takes place over a long period of time. An individual's ability to deal with distortion, discrepancy, and differentiation are dependent on what he has learned from his life experiences. His future compromises will stem from what he has been able to internalize as a result of his experiences and their resultant learnings. The synthesizing of which Super speaks more aptly refers to the way in which the individual brings these learnings to-

---

[29] Donald E. Super, "Vocational Development: The Process of Compromise or Synthesis," *Journal of Counseling Psychology* 3:249–253, Winter 1956.
[30] *Ibid.,* p. 251.

gether and the meanings which he is able to deduce as a result of his synthesis.

What occurs as the individual synthesizes is the same as that which was described in the higher levels of the internalization process. The learning, an outcome of this synthesizing, is used in making future decisions and choices. As these are reflected in future decisions, the individual can be said to be compromising. Thus compromising is an outgrowth of learning, yet an integral part of maturation.

The fear of failure is often involved in an individual's compromising behaviors. To the extent that an individual is compromising on the grounds that he is afraid to fail is an example where synthesizing may have incorporated learnings which do not necessarily apply but which have been more heavily weighted. For example, it may be best for an individual to try an experience (a course of study, a part time job, a trip), yet he is afraid to become involved for fear that he will not be successful. In such instances (and this occurs frequently) the decision rests on learnings that are often irrelevant but significant. The compromises that an individual displays, therefore, do not always appear rational or logical to another person. This only serves to emphasize the importance of all facets of an individual's learning-maturation.

As the educative process attends to matters of social and self-maturation, it contributes to the adolescent's vocational development. There is little reason in the normal course of learning-maturation to differentiate among these. While the adolescent is concerned with his social self (social identity), and his feelings about himself (self-identity), we can help him to relate these self and social learnings to the development of his vocational goals.

Thus while social, self, and vocational development may be considered as synonymous, they are, more appropriately, simultaneous. Much of the compromising that occurs in the adolescent and early adult years is among these areas of development. Vocational ambitions and goals, as well as personal aspirations and motivations, are a part of the balance the individual continually seeks for himself. The very progressive nature of one's integration and internalization is represented by the compromise he forges between himself and his social world. This is the major task of the adolescent and an important one for later testing in the world of work.

Some Program Emphases Suggested

There is much about vocational development still untapped and a great deal more to be discovered. We have some guidelines which can be used in charting new directions for vocational development in the secondary school.

A few program emphases to be considered in the modern focus on career development are suggested below.

(1) We need to establish the concepts of vocational development more firmly in the base of secondary school guidance emphasizing the process of vocational maturation rather than the choice of an occupation.

(2) We need to help young people examine the meaning of work and the evolving nature of occupational identification.

(3) Work satisfactions, in an occupational sense, may not have the same significance they have had in the past. Many work opportunities, as they have been traditionally characterized and portrayed, cannot be sufficiently patterned in the future to have relevance in the usual "planning" tradition. Programs should incorporate activities that can help individuals to explore ways of finding personal significance and meaning in life through the use of nonemployed time.

(4) Programs should contribute to helping the individual understand the decision making process emphasizing assistance in examining the network of choices, past and future, that characterize decision making responsibilities in career development. The adolescent should be assisted in examining the process of career evolvement and helped to understand that, contrary to popular notions and behaviors, choices and decisions about his life and his work role in life may continue well into his middle years.

(5) Programs should emphasize both the internal and the external dimensions of career development. It is time for secondary school guidance programs to begin to incorporate activities that serve the internal considerations of career development by examining current practices and moving immediately to implement and extend those that are limited to the external domain.

THE CONCEPT OF VOCATIONAL MATURITY

Our progress in understanding vocational maturity has been slow. One line of reasoning to account for this stems from the complex interrelation of vocational maturation with other developmental variables making it a most difficult concept for researchers to grapple with. The progress in making clearer the dynamics of vocational development has helped in coming to grips with the concept of vocational maturity.

Super was among the early psychologists to employ the term vocational maturity using it ". . . to denote the degree of development, the place reached on the continuum of vocational development from exploration to decline."[31] Recognizing a need to specify it more definitively, he

---

[31] Super, *The Psychology of Careers, op. cit.,* p. 186.

postulated five dimensions of vocational behavior that could serve as indices to an individual's vocational maturity in the adolescent years. These five dimensions include the following:

(1) Orientation to vocational choice (awareness of need to make occupational choice and concern with this need)

(2) Information and planning about preferred occupations (specificity of occupational interests and the extent of information about these occupations)

(3) Consistency of vocational preferences (consistency of preferences over time and the relatedness of these preferences by occupational field or level if several preferences are held)

(4) Crystallization of traits (extent to which an individual has achieved some identity of self and related this self to occupational possibilities-preferences)

(5) Wisdom of vocational choice (agreement between individual choice and reality demands).[32]

John O. Crites, in commenting on these dimensions, stated,

It is clear from the definitions of these dimensions that the concept of vocational maturity is more comprehensive than vocational choice, including not only the selection of an occupation but also attitudes toward decision making, comprehension and understanding of job requirements, planning activity and ability, and development of vocational capabilities.[33]

Crites holds that vocational maturity can be viewed with reference to its *degree* (how far an individual has progressed—that is, the life stage of his development) and its *rate* (how an individual's behavior compares with his peers). Obviously, most adolescents will be in the exploratory stage, making the maturational rate the more important consideration. Thus, the dimensions add specificity to the maturational process, helping us to assess the rate of development.

We are learning a little more each year about the normative qualities of vocational maturity in adolescents. For the developmental counselor, this information can be extremely valuable for it helps to identify those

---

[32] Super, *Vocational Development: A Framework for Research, op. cit.,* pp. 60–63.

[33] John O. Crites, "Measurement of Vocational Maturity in Adolescence: 1. Attitude Test of Vocational Development Inventory," *Psychological Monographs: General and Applied,* Volume 70, No. 2 (Washington, D.C.: American Psychological Association, 1965), p. 4. Copyright © 1965 by the American Psychological Association, and reproduced by permission.

maturational expectations we might anticipate for the average adolescent. Here again Crites offers some help. Combining three of Super's dimensions (orientation, information/planning, and crystallization), Crites proposes what he calls "choice competencies" and "choice attitudes." He describes these two factors in this way:

Conceived of primarily as cognitive or ego functions, choice competencies involve such mental processes as assimilating information about self and reality, resolving conflicts between alternative courses of action, establishing future goals, and relating means to ends through planning. In contrast, choice attitudes are more conative in nature and refer to involvement in the choice process, orientation toward work, independence in decision making, preference for choice factors, and conceptions of the choice process. Together with the "consistency of vocational choice" and "wisdom of vocational choice" dimensions, these choice competencies and attitudes can be thought of as comprising the construct of vocational maturity. . . .[34]

He has developed an attitudes test for the measurement of vocational attitudes in adolescence as a part of a *Vocational Development Inventory.* Data from early standardization studies corroborate, in part, the process aspects of vocational maturity supporting the notion that the vocational behaviors of individuals mature with increasing age.[35]

Super, in the Career Pattern Study, found some support for two of his dimensions: (1) orientation to vocational choice, and (2) information and planning about preferred occupations in the vocational maturity of ninth grade boys.[36] Super and Overstreet report that ninth grade boys in the study were concerned with immediate and intermediate choices indicating some awareness of the need to make choices. Their concern, however, was short term, seeming to indicate that while a degree of readiness to tackle career planning can be expected, ninth grade boys are concerned with choices more immediate to their planning.

They also report that these boys had more information about the requirements for preferred occupations than about the nature of the occupation itself. For this age level the dimensions concerned with the consistency and wisdom of vocational preferences were not supported and do not appear to be adequate indices to vocational maturity. It seems safe to assume, however, that *readiness* for choice (awareness and concern) and *responsi-*

---

[34] *Ibid.,* pp. 4–5.

[35] *Ibid.,* p. 27.

[36] Donald E. Super and Phoebe L. Overstreet, *The Vocational Maturity of Ninth Grade Boys* (New York: Bureau of Publications, Teachers College, Columbia University, 1960), Chapter VII.

bility for planning are two important aspects of vocational maturity with which the developmental counselor can be working.

Vocational Readiness

In the past, counselors may have assumed that all adolescents were ready to engage in career planning. Much of the guidance effort in the early years of high school (grades 8 and 9 in particular), through group guidance and career units, has been directed at occupational exploration. Much of the effort in the final years of high school has been focused on the choice of an occupation or on narrowing the choices to facilitate post-high school planning. These past efforts cannot be considered inappropriate though much of their value seems to lie in their purpose and intent. School counselors need to reconsider present practices in relation to adolescent readiness for involvement in career development.

Efforts directed toward enhancing the individual's readiness to engage in occupational planning and to accept responsibility for the choices and decisions attendant to such planning appear to be more valid objectives for career planning in the secondary school years. Super speaks directly to this point: "This early adolescent stage is one, not of making and implementing a vocational choice, but rather of developing planfulness, of preparing to make a series of educational and occupational decisions."[37] Thus, "planfulness" implies helping an individual to become aware of his need to make choices and to help develop the attitudes that will promote his ability to accept responsibility for his own planning.

Readiness to engage in occupational planning, both in terms of immediate and longer range choices, is closely allied to the individual's developing self-concept. The adolescent needs time to test all facets of himself and until he can feel comfortable and somewhat secure in his own appraisal of his interests, abilities, attitudes, and values, he very wisely defends himself against efforts which cause him to specify his future plans. In this sense, then, the readiness and responsibility components of vocational maturation are dependent on other areas of his learning-maturation.

Readiness for vocational planning can be facilitated by all those experiences which contribute to an individual's understanding of himself. More specifically, experiences that provide a clearer perspective of work realities and opportunities can be helpful, although these are more meaningful after the individual has developed an awareness of the kinds of information that are useful in career planning and of the factors that are uniquely significant to his own plans.

[37] *Ibid.,* p. 152.

Gribbons and Lohnes, in a seven-year longitudinal study of the career development of 111 students (57 males, 54 females) from grade 8 until two years after high school, suggest that perhaps there are differential career processes, that perhaps we have relied too heavily on one normative model of career evolvement. They suggest four patterns:

1. Constant Maturity: Consistent, persistent, realistic pursuit of the first stated goal.
2. Emerging Maturity: Passage through the stages and tasks of Super's developmental model.
3. Degeneration: Progressive deterioration of aspirations and achievement, accompanied by frustration and loss of status.
4. Constant Immaturity: Persistent fixation on fantastic, unrealistic goals, with no advances in achieved level.[38]

Many of their findings suggest that school counselors can expect or can develop a vocational readiness in the early years of high school. Specifically, they suggest that counselors expend more effort in helping students with valuing and value awareness activity and with programs that will help to expand an individual's awareness of career possibilities. Contrary to a very popular notion that adolescents are forced to make high school program choices too early, Gribbons and Lohnes, in finding many eighth grade students evidencing more "readiness" than some in tenth grade, raise this possibility: ". . . that delay in forced curriculum choice is not so much the answer as would be *early* identification of those with low RVP [Readiness for Vocational Planning]."[39]

Research is increasingly suggesting that we redirect our efforts to focus more clearly on matters of individual vocational readiness and responsibility. This is not to suggest that we immediately dump the several activities that can extend an individual's information about the world of work. Rather it is to suggest that we heed these findings and begin to test the many directions they can follow. We have little to lose and much to gain.

THE SCHOOL AND CAREER EVOLVEMENT

There are a number of ways that school guidance programs can begin to incorporate these newer concepts and to implement the new directions sug-

---

[38] Warren D. Gribbons and Paul R. Lohnes, *Emerging Careers* (New York: Teachers College Press, Teachers College, Columbia University, 1968), p. 104.
[39] *Ibid.*, p. 108.

gested. In the following sections we shall examine some of the ideas and methods that pertain to teaching and counseling.

A focus on the vocational development of youth, to be even minimally effective, will have to extend well beyond the one or two yearly, hurried interviews commonly allocated students now. Some students may need little or no help, others may need more. The framework for handling matters of a vocational nature should be no different than those for any other dimension of the secondary school guidance effort. As a matter of fact, when a student is in regular counseling, it is more than likely that self, social, intellectual and physical maturation concerns will be the subject of discussion as often as those of a vocational nature. Since all of these are interactive and since all are related ingredients of vocational maturation, there is little need to differentiate among the topics discussed in counseling except as students themselves find it necessary to do so for their own clarification and growth.

Although students do differ greatly, we might speculate about what a counselor might anticipate with counselees from the seventh grade forward. In junior high, students may evidence more informational needs though these are likely to be random and sporadic. Student exposures here can be multidimensional; however, it is important that students grasp particularly the process aspect of career planning at this point. Here is an opportunity to counteract the single choice concept with which they may be thoroughly imbued, unless similar efforts in the elementary school have counteracted the usual trend. Career information programs should be exploratory, ranging as widely across the occupational spectrum as the time and energies of all school personnel will allow.

These exposures would allow for as much actual life experience as time and conditions will permit. Some of the newer approaches, such as simulation, offer opportunities for lifelike situations in which students can engage in problem solving and decision making. Through gaming techniques and role playing, students can be provided with all sorts of experiences in which they will have to think and act much as they would in *real* situations. While simulation offers the opportunity to contribute to social, self and mental maturation, experiences associated with the world of work also allow for these to occur naturally within the context of vocational exploration and planning. Simulation techniques provide for the interacting and synthesizing elements that lead to compromising and decision making —vital components of vocational maturation.

Simulation offers many possibilities for working with the disadvantaged. It can reveal work situations, decision making activities—almost any work-life situation "as it is" providing as real a backdrop as can be constructed. Disadvantaged youth, in the safe environment of the simulated experience, can expose themselves and their values more freely. They can examine and talk about the attitudinal and behavioral differences between the value system of the disadvantaged and the broader society. In the simulated experience the motivational aspects of work can be explored and problems of employment can be actually tested and discussed.

Opportunities for the most success in these experiential ventures will occur in subject matter classrooms where teachers can relate course content to matters concerning vocational maturity in live, demonstrable ways. Less effective and more remote are experiences such as group guidance classes or occupational information classes, taught by counselors. The classroom, as the pivotal point of readiness activities, can be the source of experiences that contribute to the planfulness of which Super and others speak.

In the classroom, the student can cope on a day-to-day basis with those components that are deemed vital to his development. This planfulness is associated with two major aspects, among others, of vocational development. First, readiness involves helping students to grasp the process aspects of career evolvement (a point we have stressed earlier). Second, it entails exposing them to the process of decision making in which they are already well immersed even though they may be unaware of it, or unaware of its relation to their own career evolvement.

Our purpose is to help them to become more aware of the interdependency between thought and action—that is, between what they are exploring and thinking about and what they are actually experiencing or testing. Adolescents proceed through high school having both anticipatory and implementational experiences (as theorized by Tiedeman in the "period of anticipation" and the "period of implementation"). Vocational development rests on helping them to become aware of these and to relate these to their present accomplishments and future plans.

There is one fundamental point here that must be kept firmly in mind —this approach is premised on a long term, evolving, developmental concept of occupational choice. The choice of a career—even the specification of post-high school plans—is *not* the prime concern (and need not be until the student reaches a point where such a decision needs to be made in order to continue in the career evolvement process).

The focus is to help adolescents as they progress from year to year to examine their own choices and decisions and to relate these as they find it necessary to their accomplishments and plans. We do not teach them the process of decision making as we would teach a scientific principle or a rule of grammar. We expose them to principles and we help them with the process. Teachers and counselors can help young people to explore, to crystallize, to clarify, and to specify—all aspects of choosing. As adolescents proceed through high school, they are better able to deal with the decision making process and, hopefully, they are better able to assume responsibility for their own choices and decisions, including those that are more long term involving career and life plans.

Three principles may help to guide the role of the counselor in this regard: First, vocational readiness is an emerging concept that is associated with the development and maturation of the individual. Unlike aspects of physical and mental maturation, it will not necessarily occur in the natural course of an individual's development. It must be cultivated and nourished and the individual must be helped to examine this facet of his maturation in relation to other dimensions of his growth toward maturity. Second, responsibility for choices and decisions grows out of an individual's readiness to deal with the tasks of decision making and this, too, emerges in the vocational maturation of the child as he progresses through the secondary school years. Third, the combination of these helps to determine the capability of the individual to deal with the actual choices he must make at the more critical point of high school graduation.

In part this is dependent on how much attention has been focused on his vocational development during the high school years with the focus not on post-high school plans but on those decisions and choices he is making day after day, year after year in the secondary school situation. Some will leave high school undecided. Many will have made decisions, even if they are last-minute ones, toward more specific goals involving higher education or work. How well they continue in the process of career evolvement and how well they handle these post-high school choices and decisions will depend in large measure on how we have helped them to deal with the process.

Getting at this type of information necessitates a different type of student follow-up from that which seeks evaluative data about the school curriculum and about changes in the occupational or educational plans of graduates. Such studies might easily incorporate techniques that will help the school to assess how adequately it has prepared its graduates to cope with the decisions and choices faced in the after school years of career development.

The need for occupational information is clearly evident. Wide exposure to work opportunities is a correlative to the readiness and process factors which have been delineated. Most authorities on the informational services describe three kinds of informational needs—educational, occupational, and social (or personal-social). All three of these areas are important to vocational development. Such materials should be readily available and easily accessible to students, although teachers and counselors should be prepared to meet uniquely individual requests.

Our increasing technologies are making, or propose to make, radical changes in the sources and use of informational materials. The constantly improving resource materials offer possibilities, but unless youth can use them in ways that enable them to internalize the learnings they provide, we shall continue to miss our target.

One of the more challenging problems in the collection and use of occupational information lies in the types of materials and techniques to be employed in working with disadvantaged youth. Our present materials and approaches are hardly sufficient for the middle class adolescent, and they are most inappropriate for the disadvantaged minorities. Surely we need more materials which can bring the world of work close to the world of the disadvantaged boy or girl. Probably, above all, he needs to learn that there is opportunity for him and he needs to see these opportunities and, even more importantly, he needs to see his kind working in these jobs. He needs to feel there is a place for him. We have little knowledge or research to draw on. Our progress with this dimension of occupational information will require the most creative abilities of the developmental counselors who will need to move in these directions.

Many career experts have expressed concern for the limited occupational preferences indicated by high school students. In fact they have been even more concerned with the restriction of these preferences to professional level occupations such as engineering and medicine. The fact that students reveal very limited and mostly professional occupational preferences can have very little to do with the actual extent of the occupational information to which they have been exposed. What it tends to indicate is that the exposure didn't take!

This does not necessarily reflect on the school or the guidance program. Learning media such as television, the movies, and teenage magazines, are potent forces with which to contend. So are parents who want the best for their children. If we wish to have adolescents really grasp the range of possibilities available, we are going to have to approach the informational function with more dynamic materials and technologies. To insure learning, we must apply means which allow students to internalize information helping them to find meaning and significance in it.

One obvious way is to provide for more individual or small group counseling designed to provide adolescents with an opportunity to help one another with the integrating and the synthesizing aspects of learning. Wherever these opportunities have been afforded young people, more enthusiasm and interest has been displayed. Here again, the classroom can be a source for learning about occupations—another old saw but still a potent one.

I have long advocated that self and vocational matters, of an informational type are logically a province of the classroom teacher particularly as these matters relate directly to the subject matter concerns of a teacher. In other publications I have referred to the vital guidance function of teachers indicating their responsibility for helping boys and girls adjust to the everyday problems of school life and to formulate plans and goals for the future.

The secondary school teacher has many opportunities for guidance. He meets boys and girls in the classroom—the center of learning activities—and he is most strategically placed for helping them.[40] There are many opportunities for the classroom teacher to not only provide information but to help the individual in his internalization of it. The following suggest several classroom areas of opportunity:

(1) Self-appraisal, involving an appraisal of one's interest, ability, and progress in the subject

(2) The contributions of the subject in helping the individual to work toward life goals

(3) The value of the subject, in relation to its general purposes and objectives, the development of hobbies, the activities of the community, and the extracurricular activities of the school

(4) The study of subjects at succeeding grade levels

(5) Career exploration, particularly with regard to the occupational implications of the subject.

All of these serve vocational maturation in a number of important ways. In these ways teachers and counselors complement each other, further insuring that the vocational maturation needs of youth are attended, not ignored.

The senior year of high school has traditionally been the year of decision—the crucial point, the fork in the road. Of all the secondary school years, this is the year that youth experience that one last, final fling. At one time this was dubbed "senioritis" and I presume that teachers and counselors have equally curious terms today for the same condition. If our new directions in vocational development have taken hold, we may reduce the choice anxiety though I doubt if we can ever change entirely how young people view that last year of high school.

To remove choice anxiety would be a great step forward, though we must remember the magnitude of this task as we consider the many other significant influences impinging on youth. Counselors who are busily engaged in coordinating college application procedures and job interviews

[40] Harold L. Munson, *Guidance Activities For Secondary School Teachers of* (*English*), (*Social Studies*), (*Mathematics*), (*Science*), *and* (*Foreign Languages*) (Chicago: Science Research Associates, 1965). Five booklets.

(or handling these matters personally) are far too occupied to be available on any extended basis for counseling. Many hundreds of counselors find themselves in this dilemma.

Their preoccupation with these matters only emphasizes the importance attached to *the choice* that characterizes the transition from high school to the next year of life. Much so-called vocational and educational guidance is supposedly crammed into this year. Young people are indeed "processed" out of high school. Beyond that I fear too little is accomplished. I am certain that hits do occur, that young people are processed in facilitating directions. But, too, we all know of cases that were misses. While we shall always have a share of both, we can move to improve our batting average. Viewing departure from high school from a developmental point of view would allow everyone to consider this year of transition and choice more calmly and, perhaps, more assuredly.

If we could begin to attend to vocational readiness earlier and more frequently, we might alleviate much of the choice stress and choice avoidance which so many adolescents exhibit. We have allowed the exigencies of the senior year to run students, counselors, parents, and even teachers ragged. They dominate program efforts, preventing school personnel from taking advantage of other opportunities to assist young people in their career planning.

Guidance in the secondary school has run afoul of developmental principles. It has gone overboard in one direction, rationalizing its restricted emphasis on the basis of necessity and urgency. It has permitted itself to be maneuvered so far off course that it has almost lost its bearings. It has only one possibility and little time—it must about-ship or founder.

THE FUNCTIONS OF SECONDARY SCHOOL GUIDANCE

The functions of the secondary school counselor enumerated in the following sections may seem very much like those in which counselors have always been involved. In many instances this may be the case. However, it is hoped that school counselors will consider (or reconsider) these functions, keeping in mind the concepts of vocational development as they have been discussed in this chapter.

The Counseling Functions

Counseling for vocational development is construed to encompass more than a discussion of occupational and educational requirements and plans. It involves more than a matching of talents and tasks. It is uniquely individual in that it draws on, and frequently focuses on, other areas and aspects of an individual's development. Readers who have not read the earlier sections of this chapter are encouraged to do so in order that they might understand better the bases upon which these counseling functions are projected.

(1) Counseling with individual students to assist in career development including, as appropriate, readiness to become involved in career planning, responsibilities in the process of evolving career plans, needs for information and exploration, and the formulation of tentative career plans.

(2) Counseling with individual students who exhibit unusual problems or developmental difficulties in dealing with the regular aspects of the career planning process (such as pressure to make *a* choice, anxiety over inability to make a tentative career commitment, self-doubt, or fear of failure).

The Consulting Functions

(1) Helping teachers and parents to assess their present attitudes toward career development and to establish, as necessary, the meaning and significance of vocational development as an important dimension of the school's contribution to an individual's learning-maturation.

(2) Helping teachers, within the content of their instructional responsibilities, to create learning exposures that will contribute to the vocational maturation of adolescents.

(3) Helping teachers, parents, and other school personnel to become more aware of the decision making process and of ways in which the educative process can contribute to the development of an individual's understanding of the process and his ability to participate in it.

The Coordinating Functions

(1) Helping to plan and conduct liaison activities designed to facilitate the transition and placement of students from the high school to higher education, the military, or work situations.

(2) Providing informational materials and resources of an educational, occupational, and social nature for students, teachers, and parents.

(3) Conducting workshops and seminars designed to help dispel old stereotypes of vocational choice by providing experiences and exposures which will expose participants to newer concepts of vocational development.

(4) Planning and conducting research and evaluation activities that will aid school personnel in understanding better the meaning and significance of vocational development and the nature of vocational maturation in the adolescent years.

SUGGESTED READING

BOROW, HENRY (Ed.), *Man in a World at Work* (Boston: Houghton Mifflin, 1964).

GRIBBONS, WARREN D. and LOHNES, PAUL R., *Emerging Careers* (New York: Teachers College Press, Teachers College, Columbia University, 1968).

HOLLIS, JOSEPH W. and HOLLIS, LUCILE U., *Personalizing Information Processes* (New York: Macmillan, 1969).

HOPPOCK, ROBERT, *Occupational Information* (New York: McGraw-Hill, 1967), third edition.

PETERS, HERMAN J. and HANSEN, JAMES C. (Eds.), *Vocational Guidance and Career Development* (New York: Macmillan, 1966).

SUPER, DONALD E., *The Psychology of Careers* (New York: Harper, 1957).

SUPER, DONALD E.; CRITES, JOHN O.; HUMMEL, RAYMOND C.; MOSER, HELEN P.; OVERSTREET, PHOEBE L. and WARNATH, CHARLES F., *Vocational Development: A Framework for Research* (New York: Bureau of Publications, Teachers College, Columbia University, 1957).

SUPER, DONALD E. and OVERSTREET, PHOEBE L., *The Vocational Maturity of Ninth Grade Boys* (New York: Bureau of Publications, Teachers College, Columbia University, 1960).

TIEDEMAN, DAVID V. and O'HARA, ROBERT P., *Career Development: Choice and Adjustment* (New York: College Entrance Examination Board, 1963).

BIBLIOGRAPHY

ACES–ASCA COMMITTEE, *Expectations and Commitments* (Washington, D.C.: American Personnel and Guidance Association, 1969).

ALLEN, JAMES E., JR., "Good Guidance—And Enough of It." (Albany: The State Education Department, December 2, 1957).

ALLPORT, GORDON W., "Psychological Models for Guidance," *Harvard Educational Review* 32:373–381, Fall 1962.

American School Counselor Association, *Statement of Policy for Secondary School Counselors* (Washington, D.C.: American Personnel and Guidance Association, 1964).

APOSTAL, ROBERT A., and MILLER, JOHN G., *A Manual For The Use of a Set of Diagnostic Categories* (Columbia, Mo.: University of Missouri Testing and Counseling Service, 1959), Mimeograph.

ASCH, SOLOMON E., *Social Psychology* (Englewood Cliffs, N.J.: Prentice-Hall, 1952).

AUSUBEL, DAVID P., "Creativity, General Creative Abilities, and the Creative Individual," *Psychology in the Schools* 1:344–347, October 1964.

BALDWIN, ALFRED L., *Theories of Child Development* (New York: John Wiley, 1967).

BECK, CARLTON E., *Philosophical Foundations of Guidance.* (Englewood Cliffs, N.J.: Prentice-Hall, 1965).

BENNIS, WARREN G.; BENNE, KENNETH; and CHIN, ROBERT (Eds.), *The Planning of Change* (New York: Holt, Rinehart and Winston, 1969), second edition.

353

BENTLEY, JOSEPH C., *The Counselor's Role, Commentary and Readings* (Boston: Houghton Mifflin, 1968).

BLAU, PETER M.; GUSTAD, JOHN W.; JESSOR, RICHARD; PARNES, HERBERT S.; and WILCOCK, RICHARD C., "Occupational Choice: A Conceptual Framework," *Industrial Labor Relations Review* 9:531–546, July 1956.

BLOCHER, DONALD H., *Developmental Counseling* (New York: Ronald Press, 1966).

BLOOM, BENJAMIN S. (Ed.), *Taxonomy of Educational Objectives, Handbook I: Cognitive Domain* (New York: David McKay, 1956).

BORDIN, EDWARD S., "Diagnosis in Counseling and Psychotherapy," *Educational and Psychological Measurement* 6:169–184, Summer 1946.

BOROW, HENRY (Ed.), *Man in a World At Work* (Boston: Houghton Mifflin, 1964).

BREWER, JOHN M., *History of Vocational Guidance* (New York: Harper and Brothers, 1942).

BRUCE, PAUL, "Three Forces in Psychology and Their Ethical and Educational Implications," *The Educational Forum* 30:277–285, March 1966.

BRUNER, JEROME S., "The Course of Cognitive Growth," *American Psychologist* 19:1–15, January 1964.

BRUNER, JEROME S., *The Process of Education* (New York: Vintage Books, 1960).

BUCHHEIMER, ARNOLD, and BALOGH, SARA C., *The Counseling Relationship* (Chicago: Science Research Associates, 1961).

Bureau of Employment Security, United States Department of Labor, *Estimates of Worker Traits for 4,000 Jobs* (Washington, D.C.: U.S. Government Printing Office, 1957).

CAPLAN, GERALD, *Concepts of Mental Health and Consultation* (Washington, D.C.: Children's Bureau, U.S. Department of Health, Education, and Welfare, 1959).

CAPLOW, THEODORE, *The Sociology of Work* (Minneapolis: University of Minnesota Press, 1954).

CARKHUFF, ROBERT R., and BERENSON, BERNARD G., *Beyond Counseling and Therapy* (New York: Holt, Rinehart and Winston, 1967).

CARTWRIGHT, DORWIN, (Ed.), *Studies in Social Power* (Ann Arbor: University of Michigan, 1959).

Children's Bureau, *The Nation's Youth* (Washington, D.C.: U.S. Department of Health, Education and Welfare, 1968).

COLE, LUELLA, and HALL, IRMA N., *Psychology of Adolescence* (New York: Holt, Rinehart and Winston, 1964), sixth edition.

COLEMAN, JAMES S., *The Adolescent Society* (Glencoe, Ill.: Free Press, 1961).

COMBS, ARTHUR W., and SOPER, DANIEL W., "The Self, Its Derivate Terms, and Research," *Journal of Individual Psychology* 13:134–145, November 1957.

COMBS, ARTHUR W., and SNYGG, DONALD, *Individual Behavior* (New York: Harper and Row, 1959), revised edition.

COTTLE, WILLIAM C., and DOWNIE, N. M., *Procedures and Preparation for Counseling* (Englewood Cliffs, N.J.: Prentice-Hall, 1960).

CRITES, JOHN O., "Measurement of Vocational Maturity in Adolescence: 1. Attitude Test of Vocational Development Inventory" *Psychological Monographs: General and Applied,* Volume 70, No. 2 (Washington, D.C.: American Psychological Association, 1965).

DAVIDSON, HELEN, and LANG, GERHARD, "Children's Perceptions of Their Teachers' Feelings Toward Them Related to Self-Perception, School Achievement and Behavior," *Journal of Experimental Education* 29:107–118, December 1960.

DAVIS, HOWARD V., *Frank Parsons: Prophet, Innovator, Counselor* (Carbondale and Edwardsville, Ill.: Southern Illinois University Press, 1969).

DAVIS, JESSE B., *Vocational and Moral Guidance* (Boston: Ginn and Company, 1914).

DIPBOYE, W. J., and ANDERSON, W. F., "The Ordering of Occupational Values by High School Freshmen and Seniors," *Personnel and Guidance Journal* 38:121–124, October 1959.

DUBIN, ROBERT (Ed.), *Human Relations in Administration* (Englewood Cliffs, N.J.: Prentice-Hall, 1961), second edition.

ELKIN, FREDERICK, *The Child and Society* (New York: Random House, 1960).

ENGLISH, HORACE B., and ENGLISH, AVA, *A Comprehensive Dictionary of Psychological and Psychoanalytical Terms* (New York: David McKay, 1958).

ERIKSON, ERIK H., *Childhood and Society* (New York: W. W. Norton, 1963), second edition.

ERIKSON, ERIK H., *Identity: Youth and Crisis* (New York: W. W. Norton, 1968).

ERIKSON, ERIK H., *Youth: Change and Challenge* (New York: Basic Books, 1963).

Ethics Committee (APGA), "Ethical Standards," *Personnel and Guidance Journal* 40:204–209, October 1961.

"Facing the Facts of Life," *Life* 67:35–41, September 19, 1969.

FISHER, SEYMOUR, "Sex Differences in Body Perception," *Psychological Monographs: General and Applied,* Volume 78, No. 14 (Washington, D.C.: American Psychological Association, 1964).

FISHER, SEYMOUR, and CLEVELAND, SIDNEY E., *Body Image and Personality* (Princeton: Van Nostrand, 1958).

FLANDERS, NED A., *Teacher Influence, Pupil Attitudes, and Achievement* (Washington, D.C.: U.S. Department of Health, Education and Welfare, 1965).

FLAVELL, JOHN H., *The Developmental Psychology of Jean Piaget* (Princeton: Van Nostrand, 1963).

FRENCH, JOHN R. P., JR., and RAVEN, BERTRAM, "The Bases of Social Power." In *Studies in Social Power,* Dorwin Cartwright (Ed.) (Ann Arbor: University of Michigan, 1959), pp. 150–167.

FRIEDENBERG, EDGAR Z., *The Vanishing Adolescent* (New York: Dell, 1959).

GALE, RAYMOND F., *Developmental Behavior* (New York: The Macmillan Company, 1969).

GALINSKY, M. DAVID, and FAST, IRENE, "Vocational Choice As a Focus of the Identity Search," *Journal of Counseling Psychology* 13:89–92, Spring 1966.

GESELL, A. F.; ILG, FRANCES; AMES, LOUISE B., *Youth: The Years from Ten to Sixteen* (New York: Harper and Row, 1956).

GETZELS, JACOB W., and THELEN, HERBERT A., "The Classroom Group as a Unique Social System." In *The Dynamics of Instructional Groups,* Nelson B. Henry (Ed.). The fifty-ninth Yearbook of the National Society for the Study of Education, Part II (Chicago: University of Chicago Press, 1960), Ch. IV.

GETZELS, J. W., and GUBA, E. G., "Social Behavior and the Administrative Process," *The School Review* 65:423–441, Winter 1957.

GINZBERG, ELI; GINSBURG, SOL; AXELRAD, SIDNEY; and HERMA, JOHN, *Occupational Choice* (New York: Columbia University Press, 1951).

GLADSTEIN, GERALD A., *Classification of Non-Verbal Leads.* College of Education, University of Rochester (Rochester, N.Y.), Mimeograph.

GLANZ, EDWARD C., and HAYES, ROBERT W., *Groups in Guidance* (Boston: Allyn and Bacon, 1967), second edition.

GOLDHAMER, HERBERT, and SHILS, EDWARD A., "Types of Power and Status," *American Journal of Sociology* 45:171–182, September 1939.

GOSLIN, DAVID A., *The School in Contemporary Society* (Chicago: Scott Foresman, 1965).

GOULD, JULIUS, and KOLB, WILLIAM (Eds.), *A Dictionary of the Social Sciences* (Toronto: Collier-Macmillan, 1964).

GOWIN, D. B., "Prospects for Philosophic Inquiry in Guidance," *School Review* 69:191–205, Summer 1961.

GRIBBONS, WARREN D., and LOHNES, PAUL R., *Emerging Careers* (New York: Teachers College Press, Teachers College, Columbia University, 1968).

GROSS, NEAL; MASON, WARD; and MCEACHERN, ALEXANDER, *Explorations in Role Analysis* (New York: John Wiley, 1958).

GUILFORD, J. P., *The Nature of Human Intelligence* (New York: McGraw-Hill, 1967).

HALPIN, ANDREW W., *Theory and Research in Administration* (New York: Macmillan, 1966).

HEISS, JEROLD (Ed.), *Family Roles and Interaction* (Chicago: Rand McNally, 1968).

HILGARD, ERNEST R. (Ed.), *Theories of Learning and Instruction.* The Sixty-third Yearbook of the National Society for the Study of Education, Part I (Chicago: University of Chicago Press, 1964).

HITT, WILLIAM D., "Two Models of Man," *American Psychologist* 24:651–658, July 1969.

HOLLAND, JOHN, *The Psychology of Vocational Choice* (Waltham, Mass.: Blaisdell, 1966).

HOLLIS, JOSEPH W., and HOLLIS, LUCILE U., *Personalizing Information Processes* (New York: Macmillan, 1969).

HOLT, JOHN, *How Children Fail* (New York: Dell Publishing Company, 1965).

HOPKINS, THOMAS, "Who Am I?," *Childhood Education* 39:416–419, May 1963.

HOPPOCK, ROBERT, *Occupational Information* (New York: McGraw-Hill, 1967), third edition.

JOURARD, SIDNEY M., *Disclosing Man to Himself* (Princeton: Van Nostrand, 1968).

JOURARD, SIDNEY M., *The Transparent Self* (Princeton: Van Nostrand, 1964).

JOURARD, S. M., and SECORD, P. F., "Body-Cathexis and the Ideal Female Figure," *Journal of Abnormal and Social Psychology* 50:243–246, March 1955.

JOURARD, S. M., and SECORD, P. F., "Body-Cathexis and Personality," *British Journal of Psychology* 46:130–138, May 1955.

JOURARD, S. M., and SECORD, P. F., "Body Size and Body-Cathexis," *Journal of Consulting Psychology* 18:184, June 1954.

KAHN, ROBERT; WOLFE, DONALD; QUINN, ROBERT; SNOEK, J. DIEDRICK; and ROSENTHAL, ROBERT, *Organizational Stress: Studies in Role Conflict and Ambiguity* (New York: John Wiley, 1964).

KARIER, CLARENCE J., *Man, Society and Education* (Glenview, Ill.: Scott, Foresman, 1967).

KRATHWOHL, DAVID R.; BLOOM, BENJAMIN S.; and MASIA, BERTRAM B., *Taxonomy of Educational Objectives, Handbook II: Affective Domain* (New York: David McKay, 1964).

LECKY, PRESCOTT, *Self-Consistency* (New York: Island Press, 1951), second edition.

LEONARD, GEORGE, *Education and Ecstasy* (New York: Delacorte Press, 1968).

LIFTON, ROBERT JAY, "Protean Man," *Partisan Review* 35:13–27, Winter 1968.

LINTON, RALPH, *The Study of Man* (New York: Appleton-Century, 1936).

LIPPITT, RONALD, "Dimensions of the Consultant's Job," *Journal of Social Issues* 15:5–12, 1959.

LIPPITT, RONALD; WATSON, JEANNE; and WESTLEY, BRUCE, *The Dynamics of Planned Change* (New York: Harcourt, Brace and World, 1958).

LLOYD-JONES, ESTHER M., and ROSENAU, NORAH (Eds.), *Social and Cultural Foundations of Guidance* (New York: Holt, Rinehart and Winston, 1968).

MAIER, HENRY W., *Three Theories of Child Development* (New York: Harper and Row, 1965).

MALLERY, DAVID, *High School Students Speak Out* (New York: Harper and Row, 1962).

MASLOW, A. H., *Motivation and Personality* (New York: Harper and Row, 1954).

McCANDLESS, BOYD R., *Children: Behavior and Development* (New York: Holt, Rinehart and Winston, 1967).

McCULLY, C. HAROLD, "The Counselor—Instrument of Change," *Teachers College Record* 66:405–412, February 1965.

MORGAN, H. GERTHON, "Building Self-Esteem at Home and School," *Childhood Education* 38:278–280, February 1962.

MORSE, WILLIAM C., "Self Concept in the School Setting," *Childhood Education* 41:195–198, December 1964.

MOUSTAKAS, CLARK, *Creativity and Conformity* (Princeton: Van Nostrand, 1967).

MOUSTAKAS, CLARK, *Individuality and Encounter* (Cambridge, Mass.: Howard A. Doyle, 1968).

MUNSON, HAROLD L., *Elementary School Guidance: Concepts, Dimensions and Practice* (Boston: Allyn and Bacon, 1970).

MUNSON, HAROLD L., *Guidance Activities for Teachers of English (Social Studies), (Mathematics), (Science), (Foreign Languages)* (Chicago: Science Research Associates, 1965).

MUNSON, HAROLD L., "Guidance and Instruction: A Rapprochement." In *Guidance for Education in Revolution,* David R. Cook (Ed.) (Boston: Allyn and Bacon, 1971).

MUUSS, ROLF E., *Theories of Adolescence* (New York: Random House, 1962).

OHLSEN, MERLE M., *Group Counseling* (New York: Holt, Rinehart and Winston, 1970).

PARSONS, FRANK, *Choosing a Vocation* (New York: Agathon Press, 1967), reprint of original 1909 edition.

PATTERSON, C. H., *Theories of Counseling and Psychotherapy* (New York: Harper and Row, 1966).

PECK, ROBERT F., and HAVIGHURST, ROBERT J., *The Psychology of Character Development* (New York: John Wiley, 1960).

PETERS, HERMAN J., and FARWELL, GAIL F., *Guidance: A Developmental Approach* (Chicago: Rand McNally, 1967), second edition.

PETERS, HERMAN J., and HANSEN, JAMES C. (Eds.), *Vocational Guidance and Career Development* (New York: Macmillan, 1966).

RATHS, LOUIS E.; JONAS, ARTHUR; ROTHSTEIN, ARNOLD; and WASSERMAN, SELMA, *Teaching for Thinking: Theory and Application* (Columbus, Ohio: Charles E. Merrill, 1967).

RATHS, LOUIS; HARMIN, MERRILL; and SIMON, SIDNEY, *Values and Teaching* (Columbus, Ohio: Charles E. Merrill, 1966).

REED, HAROLD J., "Certain Aspects of Vocational Guidance in a Technological Age," *Vocational Guidance Quarterly* 10:90–93, Winter 1962.

Report of the *Commissioner's Conference on the Views of Youth* (Albany: The New York State Education Department, 1967).

ROBINSON, FRANCIS P., *Principles and Procedures in Student Counseling* (New York: Harper, 1950).

ROEBER, EDWARD C.; WALZ, GARRY R.; and SMITH, GLENN E., *A Strategy for Guidance* (Toronto: Collier-Macmillan, 1969).

ROGERS, CARL R., *On Becoming a Person* (Boston: Houghton Mifflin, 1961).

ROGERS, CARL R., "Toward a Science of the Person." In *Behaviorism and Phenomenology,* T. W. Wann (Ed.) (Chicago: University of Chicago Press, 1964: Phoenix edition, 1965).

SAMLER, JOSEPH, "Psycho-social Aspects of Work: A Critique of Occupational

Information," *Personnel and Guidance Journal* 39:458–465, February 1961.

SCHEFFLER, ISRAEL, "Philosophical Models of Teaching," *Harvard Educational Review* 35:131–143, Spring 1965.

SCHILDER, PAUL, *The Image and Appearance of the Human Body* (London: Kegan Paul, Trench, Trubner, 1935).

SCHUTZ, WILLIAM C., *The Interpersonal Underworld* (Palo Alto, Calif.: Science and Behavior Books, 1966).

SECORD, P. F., and JOURARD, S. M., "The Appraisal of Body-Cathexis: Body-Cathexis and the Self," *Journal of Consulting Psychology* 17:343–347, October 1953.

SEXTON, PATRICIA C., *The Feminized Male* (New York: Random House, 1969).

SHERTZER, BRUCE, and STONE, SHELLEY C., *Fundamentals of Counseling* (Boston: Houghton Mifflin, 1968).

SHONTZ, FRANKLIN C., *Perceptual and Cognitive Aspects of Body Experience* (New York: Academic Press, 1969).

SILBERMAN, CHARLES E., *Crisis in the Classroom* (New York: Random House, 1970).

SNYGG, DONALD, and COMBS, ARTHUR W., *Individual Behavior: A Perceptual Approach to Behavior* (New York: Harper, 1949).

The Staff of the Division on Child Development and Teacher Personnel, *Helping Teachers Understand Children* (Washington, D.C.: American Council on Education, 1945).

STAINES, J. W., "The Self-Picture As a Factor in the Classroom." In *The Self in Growth, Teaching, and Learning,* Don E. Hamachek (Ed.) (Englewood Cliffs, N.J.: Prentice-Hall, 1965), pp. 404–423.

STEFFLRE, BUFORD (Ed.), *Theories of Counseling* (New York: McGraw-Hill, 1965).

STEWART, LAWRENCE H., and WARNATH, CHARLES F., *The Counselor and Society* (Boston: Houghton Mifflin, 1965).

SUPER, DONALD E., *The Psychology of Careers* (New York: Harper, 1957).

SUPER, DONALD E., "Vocational Development: The Process of Compromise or Synthesis," *Journal of Counseling Psychology* 3:249–253, Winter 1956.

SUPER, DONALD E.; CRITES, JOHN; HUMMEL, RAYMOND; MOSER, HELEN; OVERSTREET, PHOEBE; and WARNATH, CHARLES; *Vocational Development: A Framework for Research* (New York: Bureau of Publications, Teachers College, Columbia University, 1957).

SUPER, DONALD E., and OVERSTREET, PHOEBE L., *The Vocational Maturity of Ninth Grade Boys* (New York: Bureau of Publications, Teachers College, Columbia University, 1960).

TIEDEMAN, DAVID V., "Decision and Vocational Development: A Paradigm and Its Implications," *Personnel and Guidance Journal* 40:15–21, September 1961.

TIEDEMAN, DAVID V., and O'HARA, ROBERT P., *Career Development: Choice and Adjustment* (New York: College Entrance Examination Board, 1963).

TOLBERT, E. L., *Introduction to Counseling* (New York: McGraw-Hill, 1959).

TORRANCE, E. PAUL, *Guiding Creative Talent* (Englewood Cliffs, N.J.: Prentice-Hall, 1962).

TYLER, LEONA E., *The Work of the Counselor* (New York: Appleton-Century-Crofts, 1969), third edition.

WALLACH, MICHAEL, and KOGAN, NATHAN, *Modes of Thinking in Young Children* (New York: Holt, Rinehart and Winston, 1965).

WEINBERG, CARL, *Social Foundations of Educational Guidance* (New York: The Free Press, 1969).

WEITZ, HENRY, "Counseling As a Function of the Counselor's Personality," *Personnel and Guidance Journal* 35:276–280, January 1957.

WILLIAMS, WARREN S., "Classroom Climate," *Research and the Classroom Teacher,* May 1965. (A publication of the Genesee Valley School Development Association, Rochester, N.Y.)

WILLIAMSON, E. G., *How to Counsel Students* (New York: McGraw-Hill, 1939).

WILLIAMSON, E. G., *Vocational Counseling: Some Historical Philosophical, and Theoretical Perspectives* (New York: McGraw-Hill, 1965).

WILSON, L. CRAIG; BYAR, T. MADISON; SHAPIRO, ARTHUR S.; and SCHELL, SIDNEY H., *Sociology of Supervision* (Boston: Allyn and Bacon, 1969).

WOLFBEIN, SEYMOUR L., "Labor Trends, Manpower, and Automation." In *Man in a World at Work,* Henry Borow (Ed.) (Boston: Houghton Mifflin, 1964), pp. 155–166.

WRENN, C. GILBERT, "Human Values and Work in American Life." In *Man in a World at Work,* Henry Borow (Ed.) (Boston: Houghton Mifflin, 1964).

WRENN, C. GILBERT (interview), "International Guidance: A Conversation with C. Gilbert Wrenn," *Caps Capsule* 3:3, Fall 1969.

WRENN, C. GILBERT, "Philosophical and Psychological Bases of Personnel Services in Education." In *Personnel Services in Education,* Nelson B. Henry (Ed.). The Fifty-eighth Yearbook of the National Society for the Study of Education, Part II (Chicago: University of Chicago Press, 1959).

AUTHOR INDEX

SUBJECT INDEX

A

Abilities in counseling, 127-128
Acceptance:
  in consulting, 158-159
  in counseling, 120
Accommodation, 60-61, 232, 264-266
Acculturation, 57
ACES-ASCA Committee, *Expectations and Commitments*, 87, 353
Adaptation, 60-61
Adolescence, 56-61
  defined, 56-57
  and maturation, 57-58
  and mental growth, 59-61
  and physical maturation, 202-221
  and self identity, 58-59, 293-294, 298-300
  social identity in, 260-266
  and vocational maturation, 316-318
Affective domain, 67
Affluence, 26-27
ASCA Statement of Policy For Secondary School Counselors, 13, 15, 101, 150, 153, 155, 173, 184, 194, 198, 353
Assimilation, 60-61, 232
Attitudes in counseling, 125-126

B

Beliefs in counseling, 123-124

Body image, 206-210
  attitudes toward body and self, 206-210, 214
  body cathexis, 207
  body size, 207
  and self concept, 309-311
Bureau of Employment Security (U.S. Department of Labor), 319, 354

C

Career development program, 339
Career evolvement, 343-349
Caring, 117-118
Case conferences, 183-184
Children's Bureau (U.S. Department of Health, Education and Welfare), 36, 354
Civil Rights Act of 1964, 31
Classroom climate, 266-269
Cognitive domain:
  cognitive growth, 233-236, 240-241
  defined, 67
Communication:
  with the disadvantaged, 35
  interpersonal, 307-309
  non-verbal leads in, 131-132
  with parents, 42-44
  touching as a means of, 310
  verbal leads in, 130-131